Distributed .NET
Programming in C#

TOM BARNABY

Distributed .NET Programming in C#
Copyright ©2002 by Tom Barnaby

ISBN (pbk): 1-59059-039-2

Printed and bound in the United States of America 12345678910

Technical Reviewer: Gordon Wilmot

Editorial Directors: Dan Appleman, Peter Blackburn, Gary Cornell, Jason Gilmore, Karen Watterson, John Zukowski

Managing Editor: Grace Wong

Project Manager: Alexa Stuart

Copy Editor: Ami Knox

Production Editor: Kari Brooks

Compositor: Susan Glinert Stevens

Artist: Cara Brunk, Blue Mud Productions

Indexer: Valerie Robbins

Cover Designer: Kurt Krames

Manufacturing Manager: Tom Debolski

Marketing Manager: Stephanie Rodriguez

Distributed to the book trade in the United States by Springer-Verlag New York, Inc., 175 Fifth Avenue, New York, NY, 10010 and outside the United States by Springer-Verlag GmbH & Co. KG, Tiergartenstr. 17, 69112 Heidelberg, Germany.

In the United States, phone 1-800-SPRINGER, email orders@springer-ny.com, or visit http://www.springer-ny.com.

Outside the United States, fax +49 6221 345229, email orders@springer.de, or visit http://www.springer.de.

For information on translations, please contact Apress directly at 2560 9th Street, Suite 219, Berkeley, CA 94710.

Phone 510-549-5930, fax: 510-549-5939, email info@apress.com, or visit http://www.apress.com.

The information in this book is distributed on an "as is" basis, without warranty. Although every precaution has been taken in the preparation of this work, neither the author nor Apress shall have any liability to any person or entity with respect to any loss or damage caused or alleged to be caused directly or indirectly by the information contained in this work.

The source code for this book is available to readers at http://www.apress.com in the Downloads section.

To my Mom and Dad,
who had no idea what they were starting
when they bought me a
TI-99/4A computer almost 20 years ago.
Or did they?

Contents at a Glance

Foreword .... *xv*

About the Author .... *xvii*

About the Technical Reviewer .... *xix*

Acknowledgments .... *xxi*

Introduction and AFAQ
(Anticipated Frequently Asked Questions) .... *xxiii*

Chapter 1   The Evolution of Distributed Programming *1*

Chapter 2   This Is .NET *27*

Chapter 3   Introduction to .NET Remoting *91*

Chapter 4   Distributed Programming with .NET Remoting *119*

Chapter 5   Additional Remoting Techniques *175*

Chapter 6   Understanding XML Web Services *237*

Chapter 7   Understanding COM Interop *273*

Chapter 8   Leveraging Component Services *289*

Chapter 9   .NET Message Queuing *357*

Appendix   Data Access with ADO.NET *395*

Index *469*

Contents

Foreword .... *xv*

About the Author .... *xvii*

About the Technical Reviewer .... *xix*

Acknowledgments .... *xxi*

Introduction and AFAQ
(Anticipated Frequently Asked Questions) .... *xxiii*

Who Is This Book For? .... *xix*
What Do I Need to Run the Examples? .... *xx*
Why Isn't There Any Real-World Code? .... *xx*
How Come You Don't Have Tables Listing All the
    Options/Methods/Parameters of Each Tool/Class/Method? .... *xx*
Why Do I Keep Getting "File Not Found" Exceptions
    When I Run the Example Code? .... *xxi*
What's Up with the Spinal Tap Quotes? .... *xxi*

Chapter 1   The Evolution
                of Distributed Programming *1*

Overview of Distributed Programming *1*
    Layering an Application *2*
    The Five Principles of Distributed Design *3*
    Defining Scalability *11*
A Short History of Distributed Programming *13*
    Centralized Computing *13*
    Two-tier Client/Server Architecture *14*
    Three-tier and N-tier Client/Server Architecture *15*
    The Web Architecture *17*

Microsoft and Distributed Computing *18*
    The Era of PC Dominance *19*
    The Age of Enlightenment *19*
    The Days of Disillusionment *21*
    The Present: .NET *23*

Summary *24*

Chapter 2   This Is .NET *27*

Understanding the .NET Infrastructure *27*
    The Importance of Type *28*
    The Three Cs of .NET: CTS, CLS, and CLR *28*
    Using Namespaces *30*
    Assemblies and Manifests *32*
    Intermediate Language *32*

Building and Configuring .NET Assemblies *33*
    Building a Private Assembly *33*
    Building a Shared Assembly *44*

Understanding .NET Versioning *54*
    Setting an Assembly's Version Information *54*
    Revisiting the Application Configuration File *57*
    Setting Machine-wide Version Policies *58*
    Using the .NET Framework Configuration Tool *58*
    Configuring Publisher Policy *61*
    Policy Precedence *64*
    Using the <codeBase> Element *64*
    Viewing the Assembly Binding Log *66*
    Summary of the Binding Process *68*

Understanding Attributes and Reflection *68*
    Using CLR Attributes *69*
    Implementing Custom Attributes *71*
    Reflecting upon Reflection *72*
    Attributes and Reflection in Perspective *75*

Understanding Garbage Collection *75*
    Reference Counting vs. Garbage Collection *76*
    Garbage Collection Internals *78*
    Implementing the Finalize Method *79*
    Implementing the IDisposable Interface *81*
    Garbage Collection in Perspective *84*

Serialization 84
   Using the Serializable Attribute 85
   ISerializable and Formatters 87

Summary 89

Chapter 3   Introduction to .NET Remoting 91

What Is Remoting? 91

Understanding Application Domains 92
   Programming with Application Domains 93
   Understanding Context 95

Marshaling Objects 105
   Marshal By Value Objects 105
   Marshal By Reference Objects 106
   Static Methods and Other Remoting Details 107
   Summarizing Marshaling and Context Agility 108

Examining the .NET Remoting Framework 109
   Looking at the Big Picture 109
   Well-Known vs. Client-Activated Objects 110
   Understanding Proxies 111
   Understanding Channels and Formatters 114

Summary 117

Chapter 4   Distributed Programming
             with .NET Remoting 119

Implementing Well-Known Objects 119
   Building the Server 119
   Building the Client 123
   Singleton Mode vs. SingleCall Mode 127
   Looking (Briefly) at Some Remoting Issues 130
   Remoting Configuration 130

Implementing Client-Activated Objects 138
   Building the Server 140
   Building the Client 142
   Understanding Lease-based Lifetimes 144

Building Remoting Hosts 159
   Hosting Remotable Objects in a Windows Service 159
   Hosting Remotable Objects in ASP.NET 167

Summary 172

Chapter 5   Additional Remoting Techniques 175

Solving the Metadata Deployment Issue 175
Deploying Metadata Assemblies 176
Deploying Interface Assemblies 186
Using the Soapsuds Utility 193
Summary of Deployment Issues 200

Calling Remote Objects Asynchronously 201
Understanding Delegates 201
Using Delegates for Local Asynchronous Calls 206
Using Delegates for Remote Asynchronous Calls 214
Summarizing Asynchronous Remoting 227

Understanding Call Context 228
Call Context vs. Thread Local Storage 229
Using Call Context with Remoting 230
Using Call Context with Asynchronous Calls 233
Using Call Context Headers 235

Summary 236

Chapter 6   Understanding XML Web Services 237

Web Services Overview 237
Why Web Services? 238
Web Service Composition 239
The World Wide Web Consortium 247

Building and Consuming Web Services in .NET 248
The IIS to ASP.NET to Web Service Relationship 248
Using Code-Behind 249
Building Web Services with Visual Studio .NET 251
Consuming the Web Service 255
Calling Web Services Asynchronously 258
Returning Custom Types from the Web Service 259
Using the ASP.NET Session Object 268

Remoting vs. Web Services 270

Summary 271

Chapter 7   Understanding COM Interop 273

The Need for COM Interop 273
Managed to Unmanaged Interop 274
   Understanding the Runtime Callable Wrapper 274
   Building an Interop Assembly 275

Unmanaged to Managed Interop 276
   Understanding the COM Callable Wrapper 277
   Registering an Assembly for COM Interop 278
   Writing Managed Code for COM Interop 279
   Managed Code and COM Versioning 285

Summary 288

Chapter 8   Leveraging Component Services 289

Component Services Overview 289
   Component Services Motivation 290
   Revisiting Context 290
   Survey of Component Services 291
   Survey of COM+ Configuration Settings 292

Building Serviced Components in Managed Code 295
   Populating the COM+ Catalog 296
   Experimenting with a Simple Serviced Component 299
   Examining COM+ and .NET Interaction 317
   Just-In-Time Activation 319
   Understanding Object Pooling 329
   Using Object Construction 334

Automatic Transactions 335
   The Distributed Transaction Coordinator 336
   Enabling Transactions 338
   Determining the Transaction's Outcome 339

Consuming Serviced Components 346
   Exposing Objects with DCOM 346
   Exposing Objects with .NET Remoting 348

Investigating New Features in COM+ 1.5 351
   Application Recycling and Pooling 351
   Configurable Transaction Isolation Levels 353
   SOAP Services 354

Summary 355

Chapter 9   .NET Message Queuing 357

Message Queuing Overview 357
Why Message Queuing? 358
Message Queuing Architecture 359
Message Queuing vs. Remoting vs. Web Services 360

Installing and Administering MSMQ 360
MSMQ Installation Options 360
Creating and Managing Queues 363

Using .NET Message Queuing 365
Building the Sender 365
Building the Receiver 370
Sending Custom Types in Messages 376

Writing Queued Components in Managed Code 384
The Queued Component Architecture 385
Implementing a Queued Component 387
Handling Queued Component Exceptions 388

Summary 391

Appendix   Data Access with ADO.NET 395

The Need for ADO.NET 395
ADO.NET: The Big Picture 396

Understanding ADO.NET Namespaces 397

The Types of System.Data 398

Examining the DataColumn Type 399
Building a DataColumn 401
Adding a DataColumn to a DataTable............................ 403
Configuring a DataColumn to Function as a Primary Key 403
Enabling Autoincrementing Fields 404
Configuring a Column's XML Representation 406

Examining the DataRow Type 407
Understanding the DataRow.RowState Property................... 407
The ItemArray Property 410

Details of the DataTable 411

Building a Complete DataTable 413

   Manipulating a DataTable: Deleting Rows 416

   Manipulating a DataTable: Applying Filters and Sort Orders 417

   Manipulating a DataTable: Updating Rows 420

Understanding the DataView Type 422

Understanding the Role of the DataSet 425

   Members of the DataSet 427

   Building an In-Memory DataSet 427

Expressing Relations Using the DataRelation Type 432

   Navigating Between Related Tables 433

Reading and Writing XML-Based DataSets 437

Building a Simple Test Database 438

ADO.NET Managed Providers 440

Working with the OleDb Managed Provider 441

   Establishing a Connection Using the OleDbConnection Type 442

   Building a SQL Command 444

   Working with the OleDbDataReader 445

   Connecting to an Access Database 447

   Executing a Stored Procedure 448

The Role of the OleDbDataAdapter Type 451

   Filling a DataSet Using the OleDbDataAdapter Type 452

Working with the SQL Managed Provider 455

   The System.Data.SqlTypes Namespace 456

   Inserting New Records Using the SqlDataAdapter 456

   Updating Existing Records Using the SqlDataAdapter 459

Autogenerated SQL Commands 461

Filling a Multitabled DataSet (and Adding DataRelations) 464

Summary 467

Index 469

Foreword

COM ON A WIRE, also known as DCOM, was a great boon to the distributed programmer. Under the model of DCOM, a client was able to interact with COM objects located literally anywhere, without requiring a change of code base. Using the indirection provided by AppIDs, stubs, proxies, and channels, our distributed endeavors involved little more than the use of declarative tools such as dcomcnfg.exe and the Component Services snap-in. However, all was not well in the world of DCOM (or COM for that matter). Although the clicking of check boxes made COM-based remoting appear quite simple on the surface, we suffered through numerous registry conflicts, a lifetime of passing interface pointers by reference, and the dreaded prospect of crossing firewalls.

Just as ADO.NET has nothing to do with classic ADO, the .NET Remoting story has nothing to do with classic DCOM. The most obvious case in point is the fact that .NET assemblies are not registered with the system registry. Given this, we have no AppID. Without an AppID, we have no RemoteServerName value, which means no reference to oleaut32.dll and thus no more COM-based stub and proxies. In short, everything we knew about interacting with types across the wire has changed *dramatically*.

Under .NET, we are provided with dozens of new remoting constructs. Not only do we need to contend with numerous TLAs (three-letter acronyms) such as WKO, CAO, and the like, but we are also required to be content with new spins on existing ideas (for example, the distinction between "real" versus "transparent" proxies) as well as the role of XML configuration files.

Many programmers who are faced with the task of learning the story of .NET distributed programming turn to MSDN. Here, they are confronted with numerous code examples, partial white papers, and diagrams that require a 21-inch monitor to view in their entirety. This approach is bound to lead to frustration and a disjointed knowledge base. What is sorely needed is a practical, approachable, and in-depth treatment of how all of these new technologies fit together in the context of an Enterprise application.

Tom's latest book (the one currently in your grasp) provides such a treatment. Here, you will find logical and clear explanations that (surprise, surprise) actually provide insight to the richness of the .NET Remoting layer. Not only does Tom pound out the gory details of this suite of new TLAs, but he also rounds out your understanding by providing coverage of numerous related Enterprise-centric technologies such as building configured components (a.k.a. COM+), .NET messaging, Web services, and interoperability with classic COM types.

For a number of years now, Tom and I have worked together here at Intertech, Inc. (`http://www.intertech-inc.com`). I have witnessed him teach numerous courses on the topics of classic COM and .NET (including his Expert Distributed .NET class). I have also had the pleasure to work with him on numerous development efforts. I can speak from the heart when I say you are in good hands.

Enjoy!

Andrew Troelsen
Partner and Trainer, Intertech, Inc.
Minneapolis, MN

About the Author

TOM BARNABY is an instructor and software architect at Intertech, Inc., a company dedicated to teaching top programmers how to develop enterprise-level software. As an instructor, he is in constant contact with developers from around the world and knows the problems they must solve and the questions they have. As a software architect, he advises companies on the design and implementation of their IT systems. Before becoming a teacher, Tom developed a variety of applications ranging from a proprietary 4GL/Database system on Unix to a fully distributed ERP application on Windows. In his spare time, Tom enjoys playing with his son Max, watching movies, and playing power chords on his electric guitar with the amp volume turned to 11.

About the Technical Reviewer

GORDON WILMOT is a director of ICEnetware Ltd., a company specializing in Internet and network management and monitoring software. He has held positions ranging from software engineer to systems architect and has been developing software using Microsoft products and architectures for over 20 years. Over this time he has designed and developed many products and systems for various industries such as finance, manufacturing, and telecommunications. All his spare time is eaten up by making cakes (badly) for his three-year-old twins, Charlotte and Georgina, and being beaten continuously by his seven-year-old son, Andrew, on the PS2. When he grows up he'd still like to be an astronaut.

Acknowledgments

WRITING A BOOK is by far the hardest thing I have ever done. Yet it would have been completely impossible if I didn't have the help and support of the following folks:

Thanks to *everyone* at Apress. Gary Cornell, for taking a chance on me, a complete unknown wishing to write about a hot topic. Ami "Damn Yer Good" Knox, for being even more analytical than I in regards to writing. Grace Wong and Kari Brooks for keeping the great wheels of book production churning even if I was burning (out). And a huge thanks to Alexa Stuart, who somehow kept this project running smoothly in spite of me. Finally thanks to Peter Blackburn.

Thanks to my technical editor, Gordon Wilmot, who not only provided great feedback, but also a tremendous amount of encouragement.

Thanks to Kelly Kari for proofreading several chapters. But more importantly, thanks for actually laughing at my attempts at humor scattered throughout.

Thanks to *everyone* at Intertech. I feel privileged to work for a company filled with such talented and dedicated individuals. Thanks to all my cohorts, Steve Close (Java is toast), Gina Accawi (XML is just a big string), and Andrew "Gunnar" Sondgeroth (see Steve Close) for providing a challenging, fun, and invigorating work environment. Special thanks to Andrew Troelsen for contributing an appendix, and whose, um, unique brand of encouragement ultimately lead to this book. Finally, thanks to Tom Salonek, founder of Intertech, for somehow tolerating the bizarre antics of us admitted prima donnas.

Thanks to Rabi, my cat, for keeping my shoulders warm while I worked. Finally, and most important of all, many, many thanks to my wife Tammy and son Max. Nobody sacrificed more for the sake of this book. I will be forever grateful.

Introduction and AFAQ (Anticipated Frequently Asked Questions)

THE SUBJECT OF DISTRIBUTED PROGRAMMING is vast. To implement distributed applications properly, you must understand everything from low-level networking details to high-level architectural issues. .NET is a brand new platform deserving of several thousand pages of documentation. So the challenge I faced when writing this book was this: how do I combine these two immense subjects into a single, digestible volume?

My answer: I don't. In other words, I had to make assumptions regarding the level of experience of the reader, which is tough given that .NET is such a new technology. Even harder, though, I had to make difficult decisions about what the book would and would not be. On a few issues I was resolute. The book would not be a regurgitation of documentation. The book would not be a thousand-page boat anchor covering dozens of subjects and none of them well.

Rather than list other things this book is not, however, I want to discuss what this book is. I think of it as a guided tour through the fundamental technologies you use to build distributed applications with .NET, such as .NET Remoting, Web services, serialization, COM+, and MSMQ. These technologies are the tools we developers use to craft distributed applications. And they are complex enough in themselves to warrant in-depth examination. The focus, then, is on the use of each technology and the role it plays in a distributed application. Think of it as pulling each tool out of the box, examining it, and experimenting with it to get a sense of the problems it can solve. Like any craft, distributed programming is best learned by doing, but wherever possible I discuss the pros and cons of using one tool over another.

In an attempt to set the proper expectations (and to head off some angry e-mails), I've compiled the following list of anticipated questions.

Who Is This Book For?

Since you pulled this book off the shelf, I assume you are a programmer who is interested in using .NET technologies to build distributed applications. I also assume you have a grounding in C# and object-oriented programming. An understanding of .NET basics is also very helpful, but Chapter 2 covers a few of the fundamentals. Most importantly, I assume you are willing to invest some time downloading (or typing in) and running the examples, looking up details in MSDN, and sometimes reading over a paragraph a couple times to internalize the concepts presented. These assumptions have helped to keep this book down to a manageable number of pages.

What Do I Need to Run the Examples?

You can download almost all the code presented in the book from the Apress Web site (http://www.apress.com). At a minimum, to run the code you will need the final release version of the .NET Framework, which you can download for free from Microsoft (http://msdn.microsoft.com/netframework). Many examples in the book can be implemented and tested using nothing more than the compilers and tools provided in the .NET Framework and a text editor such as Notepad. However, I assume Visual Studio .NET is the preferred development tool, and the online code includes Visual Studio .NET solution files.

For later chapters you will need other software to run the examples, including COM+, IIS, and MSMQ. The examples were developed using Windows XP Professional, but I believe they will also run on Windows 2000.

Why Isn't There Any Real-World Code?

Actually, this book is bursting with real-world code. That is, code that helps you solve everyday problems you will experience while building distributed applications in .NET. But I know what you mean—I have not provided a pizza delivery service, or a contacts service, or a working e-commerce site. It is my opinion that these types of examples are overrated, especially when there are so many new fundamental concepts to impart. Too much time and too many trees would be spent mired in the details of an e-commerce system, rather than discussing (and learning) the truly essential concepts. Therefore, the code examples in this book are short, sweet, and to the point.

How Come You Don't Have Tables Listing All the Options/Methods/Parameters of Each Tool/Class/Method?

This is a tutorial book first, a how-to book second, and a reference book last. The definitive .NET reference has already been written; it is called MSDN. I see no reason to repeat the fine work Microsoft has done to document every option of every tool, every method of every class, every parameter of every method, and so on. I do, however, see the need for a book that leads the reader through a logical progression of topics while clarifying complex concepts. I also wanted to produce a book that was beach-bag friendly—that is, a book you could carry around in your briefcase, backpack, laptop case, or beach bag without breaking your back. Hopefully, this book meets these goals.

Why Do I Keep Getting "File Not Found" Exceptions When I Run the Example Code?

Some example projects in this book are fairly complex, requiring several custom dependent assemblies. These assemblies have to be in particular locations for the project to run. You *must* read and internalize the assembly binding process documented in Chapter 2. In particular, note the Assembly Binding Log Viewer tool explained in "Viewing the Assembly Binding Log," and the assembly binding flowchart in "Summary of the Binding Process." These two sections provide the information you need to diagnose the problem.

What's Up with the Spinal Tap Quotes?

In my opinion, Spinal Tap is the greatest rock and roll band ever. But due to poor management, interfering girlfriends, and numerous drummers mysteriously dying, the band slowly sunk into oblivion in the early '80s. The whole sad affair is documented in the movie *This Is Spinal Tap*, where the band members offer many pearls of wisdom that are surprisingly applicable to the world of software development. I wanted to share their profound insights with all my readers.

So, assuming you haven't placed this book back on the shelf, let's get started!

CHAPTER 1

The Evolution of Distributed Programming

"It's like, how much more black can this be?
and the answer is none. None more black."

—Nigel Tufnel (*This Is Spinal Tap*)
speaking on the state of software development.

TODAY, BUZZWORDS LIKE enterprise programming, distributed programming, n-tier, and scalability are floated in nearly every product announcement. So before tackling the nuances of distributed development in .NET, this chapter attempts to de-marketize such terms by applying real meaning and context to these ubiquitous words. Also, while this book is primarily a nuts-and-bolts "how to" guide, it is important to have a clear understanding of why you should distribute applications and how to design a distributed application. To this end, this chapter offers five principles to help guide your distributed development in .NET or any other platform.

Finally, in order to drive home the principles of distributed programming, this chapter takes a lighthearted look at past distributed development models and the reasons they were replaced by new models. As you will see, this goes a long way towards explaining why Microsoft created a new development platform called .NET to replace COM.

Overview of Distributed Programming

What is distributed programming? Now, there is a question few dare to ask. The term is so common today that some may be embarrassed to question its meaning. Rest assured there is no need to be. I routinely ask my students to define it, and rarely do I get the same answer.

Distributed programming is characterized by several distinct physical components working together as a single system. Here, "distinct physical components" could mean multiple CPUs or, more commonly, multiple computers on a network. You can apply distributed programming to a wide variety of problems, from predicting the weather to purchasing a book. At its heart, the premise of distributed programming is this: if one computer can complete a task in 5 seconds, then five computers working together in parallel should complete the task in 1 second.

Of course, it is never quite that easy. The problem is the phrase "working together in parallel." It is difficult to get five computers on a network to cooperate efficiently. In fact, the application software must be specifically designed for this to be effective. As an analogy, consider a single horse pulling a carriage. A horse is a powerful animal, but, in terms of power-to-weight ratios, an ant is many times stronger (we will just assume ten times stronger). So, if I gather and harness enough ants to equal the mass of the horse, I can move ten times the amount of material in the carriage. A perfect example of distributing the workload, right? The calculations are reasonable, but hopefully you are chuckling at the ludicrous vision of millions of ants with tiny harnesses pulling together.

Layering an Application

As demonstrated with the horse-vs.-ant analogy, distributed computing raises the issue of coordinating the work of several computers. There is also the issue of decomposing the application into tasks that can be distributed. Luckily, here you can draw on the lessons learned from earlier applications. Over the years, it has become clear that most business applications consist of three primary sets of logic: presentation, business, and data source.

- **Presentation logic**. This is the part of the application that the end users use to enter orders, look up customer information, and view business reports. To the user, this *is* the application.

- **Business logic**. This is the heart of the application and where developers spend most of their time and effort. It contains the business rules that define the way the business is run. For example, business rules specify when customers receive discounts, how shipping costs are calculated, and what information is required on an order.

- **Data source logic**. This is where orders, customer information, and other facts are saved for future reference. Luckily, database products such as SQL Server and Oracle take care of most of the work. But you still have to design the data layout and the queries you will use to retrieve the data.

The first design point of any nontrivial business application should be to partition these sets of logic into distinct layers. In other words, you should not mix business logic code with the presentation logic code. Do not take this to mean, however, that each layer must run on a separate machine, or in separate process. Instead, code from one layer should only interact with that in another layer through a well-defined interface. Typically, the layers are physically implemented within separate code libraries (DLLs).

The Five Principles of Distributed Design

Layering allows you to change the implementation of one layer, without affecting another layer. It also provides the flexibility to physically separate the layers in the future. However, as the upcoming sections show, the decision to execute each layer in a separate process or machine should not be made lightly. If you do decide to distribute the layer, you must design it specifically for distribution. Confusing the issue even more is the fact that some of these design tactics contradict classical object-oriented principles. To help clarify the issues, this section describes several principles you can use to effectively distribute an application and why you should use them.

Principle 1: Distribute Sparingly

This may seem like a surprising principle for a book about distributed programming. However, this principle is based on a simple, undeniable fact of computing: invoking a method on an object in a different process is hundreds of times slower than doing the same on an in-process object. Move the object to another machine on a network, and the method call can be another ten times slower.

So when should you distribute? The trite answer is only when you have to. But you are probably looking for a little more detail, so let's consider a few examples, starting with the database layer. Typically an application's database runs on a separate, dedicated server—in other words, it is distributed relative to the other layers. There are several good reasons for this:

- Database software is complicated, expensive, and typically requires high-powered hardware. Therefore, it isn't cost effective to distribute many copies of the database software.

- A database can contain and relate data shared by many applications. This is only possible, however, if each application server is accessing a single database server, rather than their own local copy.

- Databases are designed to run as a separate physical layer. They expose the ultimate "chunky" interface: the Structured Query Language (SQL). (See Principle 3 for details on chunky interfaces.)

Therefore, the decision to distribute the data source logic is typically made the moment you decide to use a database. However, the decision to distribute the presentation logic is a little more complex. First of all, unless all the application users walk up to a common terminal (like an ATM), then some aspect of the presentation layer must be distributed to each user. The question is how much. The trend lately, of course, is to execute the bulk of the logic on the server and send simple HTML to client Web browsers. This is actually in keeping with the principle to distribute sparingly. However, it also requires each user interaction to travel to the server so that it can generate the appropriate response.

Before the proliferation of the Web, it was more common to execute the entire presentation logic on each client machine (in keeping with Principle 2). This provides faster interaction with the user since it minimizes round trips to the server, but also requires user interface updates to be deployed throughout the user base. In the end, the choice of which client you use has little to do with distributed design principles, and everything to do with the desired user experience and deployment issues.

So the data logic almost always executes on a separate computer, and the presentation layer frequently does. That leaves us with the business layer, and the most complex set of issues. Sometimes, the business layer is deployed to each client. Other times it is kept on the server. In many cases, the business layer itself is decomposed into two or more components. Those components related to user interface interaction are deployed to the client, and those related to data access are retained on the server. This holds to the next principle, which is to localize related concerns.

As you can see, you have many distribution options. When, why, and how you distribute is driven by a variety of factors—many of which compete. So the next few principles offer further guidelines.

Principle 2: Localize Related Concerns

If you decide or are forced to distribute all or part of the business-logic layer, then you should ensure that those components that frequently interact are kept close together. In other words, you should localize related concerns. For example, consider the e-commerce application shown in Figure 1-1. This application separates Customer, Product, and ShoppingCart components onto dedicated servers, ostensibly to allow parallel execution. However, these components need to interact many times while adding a product to the shopping cart. And each interaction incurs the overhead of a cross-network method call. Therefore, this cross-network activity will easily eclipse any parallel processing gains. Multiply this by a few thousands users, and you have a scenario that can devastate performance. Relating this to the earlier horse and carriage analogy, this is the equivalent of harnessing each leg of the horse rather than the entire horse.

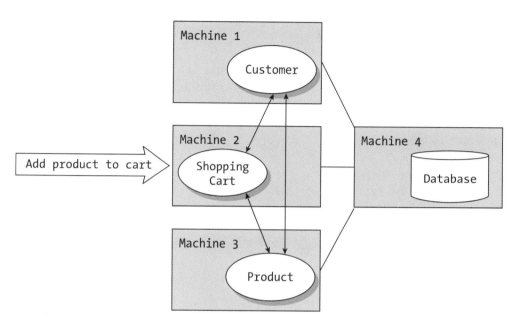

Figure 1-1. How NOT to design a distributed application

So how can you leverage the power of distributed programming, namely parallel processing, while still localizing related concerns? Buy another horse. That is, duplicate the entire application and run it on another dedicated server. You can use load balancing to route each client request to a particular server. This architecture is shown in Figure 1-2. Web-based applications often use this model by hosting the identical Web site on several Web servers, a setup sometimes referred to as a *Web farm*.

Duplicating and load balancing application servers is a great way to increase the capacity, or scale, of an application. You do need to very conscious, however, of how you manage state. For more details, see Principle 4.

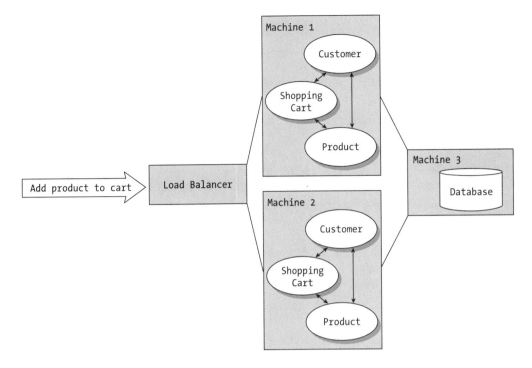

Figure 1-2. How to distribute an application

Principle 3: Use Chunky Instead of Chatty Interfaces

One of the philosophies of object-oriented programming is to create objects with many small methods, each focused on a particular behavior. Consider the following Customer class.

```
class Customer
{
    public string FirstName()
    { get; set;}
    public string LastName()
    { get; set;}
    public string Email()
    { get; set;}
    // etc. for Street, State, City, Zip, Phone ...

    public void Create();
    public void Save();
}
```

This implementation would garner nods of approval from most object-oriented experts. My first reaction, however, is to question where this object will run relative to the calling code. If this `Customer` class is accessed strictly in process, then the design is fine—correct, even, by most standards. However, if it is called by code executing in another process or on another machine, now or in the future, then this is a dreadful design. To see why, consider the following code and imagine it running on a client in New York while the `Customer` object runs on a server in London.

```
static void ClientCode()
{
    Customer cust = new Customer();
    cust.Create();
    cust.FirstName = "Nigel";
    cust.LastName = "Tufnel";
    cust.Email = "ntufnel@spinaltap.com";
    // etc. for Street, State, City, Zip, Phone ...

    cust.Save();
}
```

Again, if the `Customer` object were in the client's process, this example would pose no problems. But imagine each property and method call traveling over the Atlantic Ocean, and you can see serious performance issues.

This `Customer` class is a classic example of a class with a *chatty interface*, or, in more highbrowed terminology, a *fine-grained interface*. In contrast, objects that are accessed even occasionally by out-of-process code should be designed with *chunky interfaces*, or *course-grained interfaces*. Here is a chunky version of the Customer class.

```
class Customer
{
    public void Create(string FirstName, string LastName, string Email,
                    // etc for Street, State, City, Zip, Phone ...
                    );
    public void Save(string FirstName, string LastName, string Email,
                    // etc for Street, State, City, Zip, Phone ...
                    );
}
```

Granted, this is not nearly as elegant as the first `Customer` class. But while the former earns you object-oriented accolades, the latter protects your job when your employer's Web site suddenly becomes the next Amazon.com and needs to scale to support the influx of new customers.

As a slight tangent, I should mention that it is possible to simplify the chunky `Customer` class interface. Instead of passing each piece of customer data as a separate parameter, you can encapsulate the data into a custom class and pass it instead. Here is an example.

```
[Serializable] // <-- Explained in Chapter 2!
class CustomerData
{
    public string FirstName()
    { get; set;}
    public string LastName()
    { get; set;}
    public string Email()
    { get; set;}
    // etc for Street, State, City, Zip, Phone ...
}

class Customer
{
    public void Create(CustomerData data);
    public void Save(CustomerData data);
}
```

At first glance, this example simply moves that chatty interface from the `Customer` to the `CustomerData` class. So what is gained? The key lies in the `Serializable` attribute just above the `CustomerData` class definition. This tells the .NET runtime to copy the entire object whenever it is passed across a process boundary. Therefore, when the client code calls the `CustomerData` properties, it is actually accessing a local object. I will discuss serialization and serializable objects further in Chapter 2 and Chapter 3.

Principle 4: Prefer Stateless Over Stateful Objects

If the last principle simply annoys object-oriented purists, this principle infuriates them. Measuring against strict object-oriented definitions, the term *stateless object* is an oxymoron. However, if you want to take advantage of the load-balanced architecture shown previously in Figure 1-2, you need to either manage state very carefully in your distributed objects or not have state at all. Keep in mind that this principle, like the previous one, only applies to those objects that are on a distributed boundary. In-process objects can live happy, state-filled lives without jeopardizing the application's scalability.

The term *stateless object* seems to cause a lot of confusion among developers. So allow me to define it as succinctly as possible: a stateless object is one that can be safely created and destroyed between method calls. This is a simple definition, but it has many implications. First, note the word "can." It is not necessary for an application to destroy an object after a method call for it to be stateless. But if the application chooses to, it can destroy the object without affecting any clients. This characteristic does not occur for free. You have to specifically implement your class such that it does not rely on instance fields lasting beyond the invocation of a publicly exposed method. Because there is no reliance upon instance fields, stateless objects are predisposed to chunky interfaces.

Stateful objects negatively affect scalability for two reasons. First, a stateful object typically exists on the server for an extended period of time. During its lifetime, it can accumulate and consume server resources. Thus it prevents other objects from using the resources even if it is idling and waiting for another user request. Although some have pointed to memory as the key resource in contention, this is really a relatively minor consideration. As Figure 1-3 shows, a stateful object that consumes scarce resources such as database connections are the true culprits.

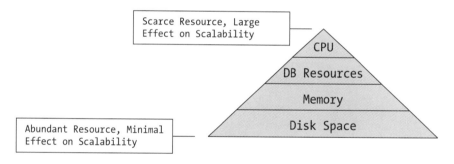

Figure 1-3. The relative quantity of computer resources

The second reason stateful objects negatively impact scalability is that they minimize the effectiveness of duplicating and load balancing an application across several servers. Consider the scenario in Figure 1-4.

Think of Figure 1-4 as a snapshot of the application at a certain point in time. At some point prior to this snapshot the system was under a heavy load. However, several clients have since disconnected, leaving only three. Unfortunately, this application uses stateful objects, and all three objects were created on Server A during the period of heavy load. Now, even though Server B is completely idle, requests from the existing clients must be routed to the heavily taxed Server A because it contains the client state. If this application used stateless objects, however, the load balancer could direct each client request to the server with the lightest load, regardless of which server was used before.

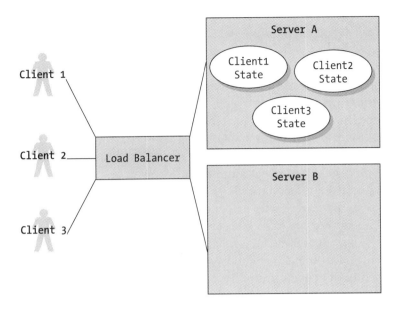

Figure 1-4. Stateful objects don't work well in load-balanced scenarios.

With some clever caching, session management, and load balancing, you can avoid or at least minimize the issues that come with using stateful objects. This is why Principle 4 states that stateless objects are preferred, not required. I also want to reiterate that this principle applies only to objects exposed to code executing in another process or on another machine.

Principle 5: Program to an Interface, Not an Implementation

Since the previous two principles directly contradict typical object-oriented practices, it may seem as though object-oriented programming has no place in distributed programming. I'm not trying to suggest that at all. Rather, I am suggesting that certain object-oriented principles, namely chatty interfaces and stateful objects, should not be applied to objects living on the distributed boundaries of an application.

Other object-oriented principles translate extremely well into the distributed world. In particular, the principle of programming to an interface rather than an implementation resonates within the universe of distributed programming. The issues this solves do not relate to performance or scalability. Instead, interfaces provide easier versioning and thus less frequent and less problematic deployment.

Given that COM was purely interfaced based, the move to .NET has caused some speculation that interface-based programming is also falling out of favor. This is not true. Although .NET allows direct object references, it also fully supports interface-based programming. And, as you will learn in Chapter 5, interfaces provide a convenient way to deploy type information to a client.

Defining Scalability

Throughout this section, I have been using the term *scale* or *scalability.* Since this is yet another nebulous term used far too often in product announcements, it may be helpful to study exactly what this means.

First, although scalability is related to performance, they are not the same thing. Performance is a measure of how fast the current system is. Scalability is a measure of how much performance improves when you add resources, such as CPUs, memory, or computers (see Figure 1-5).

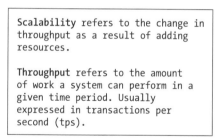

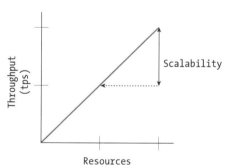

Figure 1-5. Scalability is related to performance.

There are two types of scaling:

- **Vertical scaling (scaling up)** occurs when you remove slower hardware and replace it with new, faster hardware. For example, moving from a Pentium 500 to a Pentium 1G is scaling up. For poorly designed applications, this is often the only way to scale. However, it is typically more expensive and exposes a single point of failure.

- **Horizontal scaling (scaling out)** occurs when you add an additional, load-balanced server to the existing application. This protects your current hardware investments and provides a failover if the other server goes down. While this is far cheaper in terms of hardware, the application must support the five principles discussed earlier in order to scale horizontally.

Some techniques that optimize performance in the short run diminish scalability in the long run. As an example, take a look at Figure 1-6, which compares two applications. The first optimizes performance at the expense of scalability. The second optimizes scalability. At first, the performance-optimized application performs well, because it squeezes every ounce of throughput from the current hardware. However, as additional hardware is added, the inflexibility necessitated in this first application starts to take its toll. Soon it plateaus, while the scalable application continues to rise in throughput.

One classic example of a performance maximizing, but scalability limiting technique is the use of the ASP Session object to cache per-user information. For a Web site with just a single server, this technique increases application performance since it minimizes the number of times the application must call the database. However, if the popularity of the Web site outgrows the capacity of the single server, the typical reaction is to add another Web server. Unfortunately, using the ASP Session object violates the principle to prefer stateless objects. Therefore, it cannot scale out.

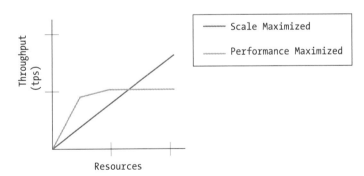

Figure 1-6. A performance vs. scalability optimized application

A Short History of Distributed Programming

The five principles of distributed programming did not come easily. These were established through years of pioneering work, ever-changing technologies, and thousands of failed projects. To better appreciate these principles and to define some other common distributed programming terms, let's review some of the history of distributed computing.

Centralized Computing

In the beginning, applications were built around a central mainframe computer. By their nature, mainframes are large, expensive, and proprietary. The mainframe manages and controls all aspects of the application including business processing, data management, and screen presentation. Typically, a user interacts with the mainframe application using a *dumb terminal*, which consists of just a screen, a keyboard, and a wire to the mainframe. Because the terminal has no processing power, it relies on the mainframe for everything, including presentation. The user interfaces are simple character-based screens that in many cases require weeks of training for users to become proficient.

Centralized computing is the antithesis to distributed computing. Yet many recent trends mimic some of the concepts. For example, the dumb terminal is really the ultimate *thin client*. And it was only a few years ago that some computer vendors were promoting the use of cheap computers called *Web appliances* that had limited hardware and a full-time Internet connection. These trends highlight the primary benefit of centralized computing: low deployment costs. Because the entire application, including presentation logic, is contained within one machine, applying updates and installing new versions is quick and easy. Furthermore, as soon as the update is applied, all users can immediately use the new, improved application.

In spite of the deployment advantage, centralized computing suffers from many problems, including these:

- The entire processing burden, including data access, business logic, and presentation logic, is placed on one computer.

- Monolithic applications are extremely difficult to maintain because of their sheer size.

- Their proprietary nature makes integration with other applications on other platforms difficult.

Eventually, many companies replaced mainframes with cheaper minicomputers, which often ran a version of the Unix operating system instead of a proprietary operating system. The applications, however, were still centralized because it was still too expensive to outfit users with hardware other than dumb terminals. The availability of relatively low-cost minicomputers, however, did portend the coming of the client/server paradigm and the beginning of distributed programming.

Two-tier Client/Server Architecture

As hardware became cheaper, it became feasible to provide users with personal computers, which were far more powerful than dumb terminals. In fact, early PCs had enough power to handle all or at least significant portions of the processing load. Most importantly, these PCs could provide users with graphical user interfaces that were more intuitive than the text-based interfaces of dumb terminals. The client/server model, in all its forms, tries to leverage the computing power of the PC. In other words, part of the load is distributed to the PC. This frees up processing cycles on the mainframe while providing the user with a more aesthetic and intuitive interface, which can drastically reduce user training costs.

Early client/server systems were two-tiered. In this architecture, the processing is spread across two machines: a client and a server. The client machine typically executes both the presentation and business logic, while the server machine provides access to the data. The server machine is usually a dedicated server running a relational database management system (RDMS), such as Oracle or SQL Server. On the client side, tools like Visual Basic opened the world of Windows user-interface development to mere mortals, making it possible for businesses to create custom applications for their employees. Indeed, tools like Visual Basic were so effective in increasing developer productivity that a new development philosophy was created, termed *rapid application development* (RAD).

In the late '80s through the early '90s, companies rushed to adopt the two-tier architecture. It was cheap, applications could be built quickly, and users were happy with the flashy new interfaces. It wasn't too long, however, before the industry started to discover the disadvantages of this architecture:

- Two-tier tools and culture promote RAD techniques. However, its propensity to intermix business and presentation logic on the client creates maintenance nightmares as the system evolves.

- On a related note, updates to business and presentation logic must be deployed throughout the user base, which may include thousands of employee computers. In addition to deploying application updates, you must also consider updates to database drivers, network stacks, and other third-party components. In general, deployment is a huge time- (and money-) consuming effort.

- If the application accesses data from several data sources, then specialized client-side logic is required. This even further complicates the previous issues.

- It is impossible for clients to share scarce resources such as database connections. Because it can take several seconds to establish a database connection, two-tier clients typically open connections early and hold them for the duration of a session. So a database licensed for 20 concurrent connections can only serve 20 client applications, even if many of them are idling.

In spite of these disadvantages, two-tier client/server systems perform fine for small applications with few concurrent users. However, an application and its user base tends to grow over time, so if you decide on a two-tier architecture for the current project iteration, make sure the implementation does not prevent an easy transition to a three-tier architecture. The best practice, in this case, is to logically separate the business layer from the presentation and data layers.

Three-tier and N-tier Client/Server Architecture

A popular adage in computer science is that any problem can be solved with another level of indirection. In the '90s, this philosophy was applied to two-tiered architecture to solve its, by now, well-known issues. Due to the additional level of indirection, this new architecture was dubbed *three-tier architecture*.

In two-tier architectures, the business layer is rarely implemented as a separate logical entity. Instead, it is mixed within the presentation logic or within the database as stored procedures. In three-tier computing, the business logic becomes a first-class citizen. At a minimum it is logically separated from the presentation and data layers, and most times it is physically separated and hosted on a dedicated server called an *application server*. If an application server hosts the business logic, then many clients can connect to the server and share the business logic.

There is some disagreement over the exact definition of n-tier computing. Some say that adding any additional tier to the three-tier model, such as a Web-server tier, constitutes n-tier development. Others equate it to the partitioning of the business logic across many application servers. Sometimes each application server is dedicated to a particular aspect of the business process—for example, a dedicated customer management server or a dedicated order entry server. Complicating issues even more are those who contend that any logical layer constitutes a tier. It is pointless to argue all the semantics. So, in the end, it is best to think of n-tier architecture as any distributed design consisting of three or more tiers.

An n-tier architecture provides the following benefits:

- Clients are thinner because they do not contain business logic. This makes deployment and maintenance far easier, because updates to the business logic need only be applied to the application server. This is especially note-worthy given that the business-logic layer tends to be the most dynamic layer.

- Clients are isolated from database details. The application server can coordinate several different data sources and expose a single point of access for clients.

- N-tier programming promotes disciplined partitioning of the application layers and communication between layers through well-defined interfaces. In the long term, this provides easier maintenance since you can update a layer's implementation without changing its interface.

- N-tier applications can scale horizontally. That is, if designed correctly, the business logic can be duplicated and distributed to several load-balanced application servers. You can add more servers as user demands increase.

- The application server can pool scarce enterprise resources and share them among many clients.

The last point in this list deserves a little more explanation, since I feel it is the most important benefit of n-tier programming. The canonical example of a scarce resource is a database connection. Using the earlier scenario where you have a database license for only 20 concurrent connections, an application server can open all 20 connections and use them to fulfill incoming client requests. Since client applications have a large amount of "think time" between requests, the application server can effectively handle hundreds of clients with the same 20 connections. While one client is processing the results from its last request (that is, "thinking"), the application server can use the open database connection to serve another client's request.

Although these advantages are significant, n-tier applications have a key disadvantage: they are extremely difficult to implement. Furthermore, bad design decisions at critical points can cripple an n-tier application, making it perform and scale no better than the two-tier application it replaced. Many of the issues surrounding n-tier development, however, are shared across all n-tier implementations. These include database connection management, thread pooling, security, and transaction monitoring. So it wasn't long before software vendors were shipping products that simplified these tasks, allowing developers to focus on the business problem rather than the infrastructure. Microsoft in particular has been very active in this marketplace, providing technologies such as COM, DCOM, MTS, COM+, and finally .NET. These technologies are explained more in the next section.

The Web Architecture

Obviously, the Web has played a key role in distributed programming since the mid '90s. Ironically, the Web began very modestly with Web servers transmitting static HTML to browsers. Everything about the Web was designed to be simple. The network protocol, HTTP, is a simplification of TCP/IP. HTML is a simple implementation of SGML. Web browsers (at least the early ones) simply render text-based HTML graphically. And Web servers (at least the early ones) simply listen on port 80 for incoming HTTP requests and send back the requested HTML document. The success of the Web, however, lies in this original state of simplicity. Because of the simplicity of HTTP, HTML, and browser software, Web browsers were soon ubiquitous. This allowed information contained in static HTML documents to be delivered and aesthetically displayed to users regardless of their chosen hardware or operating system.

My how things change. Today's Web browsers are anything but simple. In addition to rendering HTML, they can interpret and execute embedded script code that responds to user action on the page. They expose complicated object models and can host binary components via plug-ins or ActiveX technology. Not all browsers support the more advanced technologies, but even the least-common-denominator level of support is significantly more complex than that of the original browsers.

Web servers have also increased in complexity, to the point where the Web server has become the application server. Today's Web servers can host server-side business logic, access databases, validate security credentials, and integrate with transaction monitors such as COM+. Unlike the application server in the n-tier model, however, a Web server does more than host the business logic; it also builds the user interface by generating a mixture of HTML and embedded client-side script and sending it to the browser.

Interestingly, in this architecture the presentation, business, and data logic are all server side. In this respect, it is similar to the centralized model, so I have been known to call Web browsers "glorified dumb terminals." This does not endear me to my Web programming coworkers, however, who point out how much more inter-active and pleasing browser-based interfaces are over dumb terminals. Furthermore, if you have updates to any part of the application, including the user interface, you need only make the update on the server side. Therefore, Web architec-tures enjoy all the benefits of the n-tier model, plus the ease of client deployment enjoyed by the centralized model.

However, the Web model not only suffers from the same issues as n-tier appli-cations, it tends to exacerbate them. In a traditional (that is, non–Web-based) n-tier application, you typically know how large the target user base is and how many concurrent users to expect. However, the ease of deployment and omnipresent browsers makes it feasible to expose a Web application to users across the entire organization, nation, or world. Therefore, the load on a Web application is unpredictable; it may serve anywhere from a few to thousands of concurrent users. This makes scalability a much higher priority in Web applications designed for public consumption. This level of scalability can only be achieved with careful design.

The other issue with Web architectures is the reliance on the browser as the client. Today's advanced browsers allow a browser-based user interface to be *almost* as rich and interactive as the traditional fat client. However, when implementing a sophisticated browser-based user interface, you must contend with the following issues:

- Although browsers make it easy to create simple user interfaces, it is difficult to create really sophisticated presentations. User interface idioms that are easy to implement in Visual Basic, for example, can be extremely difficult using DHTML and JavaScript.

- Creating a sophisticated user interface often requires techniques that are browser dependent. For example, only Internet Explorer can host ActiveX controls. This minimizes one of the key advantages of Web architectures: its ability to reach users regardless of platform or browser.

- Even if only a simple interface were required, it takes time for fat client developers to become accustomed to the statelessness of the Web and how data must be passed from page to page.

In spite of these challenges, many IT departments have implemented the Web architecture for internal, or intranet, applications used by company employees. Though some of this was due to hype and mindless marches to "Web enable" applications, it also demonstrates how serious the issue of deployment is. IT groups are willing to tackle the difficulties of browser-based interface development because it saves deployment costs and its myriad headaches.

Microsoft and Distributed Computing

Given that Microsoft was the primary software vendor for PC applications, it follows that the company also played a major role in client/server computing. Initially, Microsoft tools and technologies were focused on the client tier, including Visual Basic, Access, and FoxPro. With the release of Windows NT, however, Microsoft turned its attention to the server side, providing various technologies that ease n-tier application development.

Throughout the last decade, COM was the foundation for nearly all of Microsoft's technologies. .NET, however, completely replaces COM and therefore marks a radical departure for the company and the millions of developers (like you and me) who use its tools. Still, it is instructive to look back through the lineage that begat Microsoft's current .NET technology.

The Era of PC Dominance

Since Microsoft was a pioneer in early PC software and development tools, the company was quick to promote the benefits of two-tier client/server development. It was during this era that the Windows operating system attained dominance in the PC market. Furthermore, Visual Basic made it easy for almost anyone to develop a Windows user interface and interact with an RDMS like Oracle or SQL Server.

At the same time, Microsoft was refining its Dynamic Data Exchange (DDE) technology, looking for more flexible ways to share data between applications, in particular between applications in its Office suite. Out of this work came Object Linking and Embedding (OLE), a technology that is long dead but whose legacy (and acronym) continues to survive. OLE is worth mentioning here because Microsoft soon realized that the problems it solves transcend spreadsheets and word processors, and could be used as the foundation for a new style of programming called *component-based programming*. Which brings us into the next era.

The Age of Enlightenment

Two major shifts occurred to mark what I call the "age of enlightenment." First, there was the move to component-based programming, where monolithic applications were decomposed into smaller cooperating binary components. This philosophy fit naturally into the world of distributed three- and n-tier applications and built upon accepted object-oriented principles. To be effective, however, the component model required technologies that made it easy for separate components to interoperate, that is, to call methods on and share data with objects residing within another component. When you boil it down, this is exactly what OLE did. Therefore, Microsoft refined OLE to create the Component Object Model (COM), which soon became the primary technological enabler in the Microsoft world for the rest of the decade.

COM is partly a specification. Developers can write COM components using any language that can create binary images matching the COM specification. In theory, COM components built in different languages can interoperate. In practice, however, C++ COM developers must take care to only expose types that can be consumed by less powerful languages such as JavaScript or VBScript. Visual Basic was reengineered between versions 3 and 4 in an attempt to make COM development more accessible to the average programmer—and was a huge success.

When Microsoft pushed into the server-side market, it extended COM to create Distributed COM (DCOM). DCOM provides the infrastructure necessary for COM components to interoperate over a network as if they were on the same machine. With DCOM, you can take the COM business objects that were deployed to each client machine and move them to a central server without changing the client layer or the business layer's code. Unfortunately, this describes exactly what companies did in many cases—but that story will have to wait until the next section.

The second monumental shift in the age of enlightenment was the emergence of the Web. Unlike component technology, Microsoft was relatively slow to embrace Web technology. It wasn't until the Web was clearly here to stay that the company starting searching for a way to enter the market with a bang. It didn't have to look far. Microsoft took what was then a little-known, low-level technology with a boring name and repackaged it with a sexy new name: ActiveX. Of course, the little-known technology I'm referring to is COM. Regardless, Microsoft hit the Web running with a volley of "Active" technologies: ActiveX Controls, ActiveX Documents, Active Server Pages (ASP), and Active Data Objects (ADO). All of these were built from or relied upon COM in one way or another.

Microsoft also provided Web browser and server implementation in the form of Internet Explore (IE) and Internet Information Server (IIS), respectively. IE was unique among browsers in that it could host ActiveX Controls and ActiveX Documents. Ironically, although IE came to dominate the browser market, these client-side ActiveX technologies never gained much traction.

IIS, on the other hand, had to fight for every bit of its modest Web server market share. Yet ASP, a server-side scripting engine exclusively available with IIS, gained broad acceptance with IIS users. Before IIS, Web servers interacted with applications through the Common Gateway Interface (CGI) or through proprietary Web server APIs. In both cases, the Web server forwards an incoming HTTP request to some application that generates a dynamic response. Typically, the response is static HTML mixed with a small amount of dynamic HTML. This requires a language that allows quick-and-easy text manipulation. Therefore, CGI popularized the use of scripting languages, like Perl, that provide powerful string and regular expression utilities.

As with other Web servers, IIS exposes an API. The IIS API is called ISAPI, and any application that uses this API is called an ISAPI extension. Soon after its introduction, IIS shipped with a useful ISAPI extension called ASP. With this, Web page developers do not have to use CGI or understand ISAPI to write dynamic content. Instead, you can write static HTML as normal, and insert some script code where dynamic HTML generation is necessary. When IIS processes the page, the ASP ISAPI extension interprets any embedded script code and inserts the generated HTML from the script into the stream of HTML flowing back to the browser. Thus, from the browser's perspective, all of the HTML comes from a simple static page.

ASP effectively turned dynamic Web page development upside down. Whereas CGI forces programmatic code with a lot of HTML embedded within, ASP pages contain static HTML with some programmatic code (VBScript or JavaScript) embedded within. This proved to be a far more productive way to build dynamic Web content. However, the interpreted nature of ASP slows down complex calculations, and the mixture of script and HTML within one page tends to get overly complex and difficult to maintain. Enter COM, again. ASP script code can create COM objects and invoke their methods. Therefore, you can compile complex business rules and data access logic into COM components and access them from ASP. This minimizes the scripting code in the ASP page and keeps it focused on a single task: the dynamic creation of HTML.

Thanks to (D)COM, some creative thinking, and endless marketing, Microsoft appeared ready to dominate on the server side. But things did not quite work out that way, as explained in the next section. Before moving on to the next section, it is important to point out again that, during this era, COM technology was woven into the entire Microsoft architecture, and this practice continued into the next period, which I call . . .

The Days of Disillusionment

It was only a matter of time before Microsoft and its customers learned what mainframe and other Online Transaction Processing (OLTP) vendors always knew. The problems associated with an OLTP application, that is an application allowing a large number of remote clients to read and modify a central data store, are very different from the problems associated with a desktop application. Nothing bore this out more than the early practice of moving "chatty" COM objects from the client to an application server without redesign. While this did result in a three-tier architecture, it also resulted in poor performance as the user interface layer made multiple calls over the network to communicate with the COM object. Worse, those who held fast to object-oriented principles when building their business objects were hit the hardest when they tried to distribute the objects to the middle tier. Confusion reigned as developers struggled to correlate object-oriented dogma to the world of distributed programming.

When Microsoft introduced Visual Basic 4, it immediately created millions of new COM programmers. But during this period, developers were learning that COM development in Visual Basic had its downfalls. Compared to Visual C++, Visual Basic COM development is far simpler. However, some of the design decisions that made Visual Basic COM development easier hindered its use in the middle tier. For example, all Visual Basic COM objects are apartment threaded. This causes serious scalability problems when storing Visual Basic objects in the ASP Session object and prohibits them from participating in object pooling. To be fair, in many business scenarios, these issues could be avoided or had minimal impact on the application. But the limitations were enough for many to decide they would rather tackle the complexity of COM development in Visual C++.

This period also saw COM itself coming under fire. A few of the major complaints follow:

- COM component versioning and registration is complex and poorly understood, contributing to the malaise known as DLL hell, in which installations of one product break another.

- COM objects developed for ASP script consumption require special consideration because interfaces—a key part of COM programming—cannot be consumed by ASP scripts.

- In DCOM, remote COM objects are marshaled by reference by default. This means a client's method calls must travel over the network to the COM object. It is decidedly nontrivial to implement a by value marshaling scheme whereby a custom COM object is copied from one application to another, thus allowing the client to call methods on the local copy.

In spite of my sobering title for this period, I should note that some of Microsoft's most impressive work came out of this era. One example is Microsoft Transaction Server (MTS). This product bridged the gap between the realities of programming OLTP applications and the idealism of object-oriented programming by associating the lifetime of a transaction with that of an object. Microsoft refined MTS into what is now known as COM+. Microsoft also started promoting the Distributed interNet Architecture (DNA), an umbrella term for its n-tier services and technologies such as COM+, IIS, ASP, and SQL Server. More importantly, DNA included architecture advice and recommendations so that others could avoid the mistakes made by the early n-tier adopters. Finally, Microsoft delivered Windows 2000, which proved that Microsoft could build a stable, feature-rich operating system for server-side computing.

Armed with these technologies and a new awareness of the perils of distributed programming, developers delivered many high-quality applications using DNA. But in spite of these and other strong products, Microsoft's server market share plateaued and even started to shrink. Strong competition from Java's J2EE technology and open source Linux started to take its toll. When faced with such a challenge from the Web, Microsoft turned to COM for the solution. Now, they realized, COM was the problem. Advertised as the glue that connected the pieces of DNA together, COM development was too complex in C++, and too restrictive in Visual Basic. Furthermore, Microsoft found that server-side applications often involved hardware and operating system platforms from a variety of vendors. COM, however, was designed from the start as a Windows technology, and attempts to port COM to other operating systems were dismal failures.

In the end, it was clear that after a nine-year reign as the foundation of all that was Microsoft, COM needed to be replaced. This, of course, brings us to the present, .NET, and the purpose of this book.

The Present: .NET

After nine years of touting the benefits of COM, it is understandable why Microsoft refers to .NET as an evolution rather than a revolution. And honestly, looking at it from a goal-oriented point of view, this description is accurate. Both COM and .NET share the same goals. .NET just does it better.

- **Language Independence.** You can build .NET applications in any language that supports the Common Language Specification. Currently, you can choose from about 20 different languages.

- **Component interoperability.** .NET components share a common type system, therefore, .NET achieves nearly seamless interoperability between components regardless of the implementation language. In fact, you can derive a VB .NET class from a C# class.

- **Location Transparency.** Code accessing a local (in-proc) object is identical to the code accessing a remote (out-of-proc) object. Details are handled through configuration.

- **Robust Versioning.** .NET provides and enforces a flexible and robust versioning scheme. DLL hell is solved.

In Chapter 2, you will see more detail regarding these items. For now, understand that while the goals of COM and .NET may be similar, the underlying technology is completely different. For example, IUnknown, IDispatch, and the other standard COM interfaces are not part of .NET. .NET components are not registered in the system registry. And object lifetime is determined through garbage collection instead of reference counting.

Distributed applications share the same set of problems regardless of development platform. So many of the new .NET technologies simply replace the functionality of existing COM-based technologies. Table 1-1 shows the relationship between COM and .NET technologies in the context of distributed programming.

Table 1-1. Comparing COM Technologies to .NET Technologies

Distributed Problem	COM Solution	.NET Solution
How does the application interact with the database?	ADO	ADO.NET
How does an application access the services of another application?	DCOM	DCOM, Remoting, or Web services
How does data get passed from one application to another? `IMarshal` or brute force serialization.	CLR Serialization	
What provides distributed transactions, Just-In-Time activation, and other services required by an application server?	COM+	COM+
What provides asynchronous messaging with guaranteed delivery?	MSMQ	MSMQ

Of course, these technologies are the focus of the rest of the book. And as you will see, .NET provides a productive, powerful, and extensible framework for developing distributed applications.

Summary

Designing and implementing distributed applications is hard. The available options and their inevitable tradeoffs can be overwhelming. This chapter discussed several topics that hopefully have brought some clarity to what is inherently a difficult subject:

- You have learned five key distributed design principles and how they affect the application.

- You have seen how the distributed programming has evolved and what mistakes were made in the past.

- You have learned why Microsoft created .NET to replace COM.

In the next chapter, you will learn the basics of .NET. In particular, the chapter focuses on the fundamental .NET technologies that have the largest impact on distributed programming.

This Is .NET

"Certainly, in the topsy-turvy world of heavy rock, having a good solid piece of wood in your hand is often useful."

—Ian Faith (*This is Spinal Tap*) speaking on the
importance of a dependable set of tools.

.NET IS A BRAND NEW TECHNOLOGY, so it would be naïve for me to assume that my readers are all expert .NET programmers. On the other hand, if I bloviated on all the .NET details, this book would easily eclipse 1000 pages. Therefore, in this chapter, I will only cover a few of the most critical concepts.

To begin, I will do a brief overview of the technologies and concepts that comprise the foundation of .NET. Then, I will discuss several items in more detail, namely assemblies, garbage collection, attributes, reflection, and serialization. This will lay the groundwork required for understanding the more advanced topics in the upcoming chapters.

Understanding the .NET Infrastructure

.NET is a whole new world for Windows programmers. The Win32 API is less important. COM is relegated to just another legacy technology. Even the names we give to compiled components are different. The purpose of this section is to give a quick overview of the key concepts and terms you will need to understand in order to write .NET applications.

 NOTE *If you want to learn more about any of the topics discussed in this section, look no further than Andrew Troelsen's book,* C# and the .NET Runtime, *also from Apress.*

The Importance of Type

Quick! What's this?

```
0000 0000 0000 0000 0000 0000 0100 1101
```

And the answer "a bunch of ones and zeros" does not count. If you answered "77," you are correct. If you answered "M," you are also correct. If you answered "1.079e-403," then you took this exercise way too seriously, but you are also correct. How can all of these different interpretations be correct?

The secret is "type." If you apply a 32-bit integer type to this sequence of bits, the result is 77. If you apply a character type to it, the result is the character M. Finally, if you apply a float type, the result is 1.079e-403. The bottom line is that the data in itself is not sufficient information. A running application needs the data and the type to correctly interpret the data.

The issue of type is the bane of language and platform interoperability. Languages and platforms often differ in their support and implementation of data types. Therefore, cross-language and/or cross-platform interoperability is problematic at best. Until .NET, there were two competing solutions: the Java way and the COM way.

The Java solution is amazingly effective. It involves standardizing on one language (Java) and one platform (Java), effectively nullifying the issue. Furthermore, the Java platform has been ported to many different operating systems, providing the "write once, run anywhere" capability so dearly loved by Java advocates. The downside, however, is that you must be willing and able to write all of your components in Java.

The COM solution is more ambitious. COM defines a binary standard; supporting languages ensure that their compiled binary executables adhere to this standard. COM executables can communicate through interfaces defined in terms of variant-compliant types—a "least common denominator" set of primitive types. With COM, components can interoperate even if they were implemented in different languages. However, the only practical operating systems for COM development are the Windows family of operating systems. Also, the COM infrastructure is extremely complex and fragile.

The Three Cs of .NET: CTS, CLS, and CLR

The .NET approach to interoperability takes the best of both the Java and COM solutions. Whereas COM defines a standard binary format, .NET defines a type standard called the *Common Type System* (CTS). This type system is far more inclusive than the COM variant-compliant types, plus it defines how you can extend the types by creating your own custom types. Any language that targets the .NET platform must map its types to those in the CTS. Since all .NET languages share this type system, they interoperate seamlessly. This scheme also provides cross-language inheritance. For example, you can derive a class written in VB .NET from a class written in C#.

Obviously, programming languages differ in other ways than just type. For example, some but not all languages support multiple inheritance. Some but not all languages support unsigned types. Some but not all languages support operator overloading. You get the idea. .NET restrains the interoperability issues that these differences may cause by defining the *Common Language Specification* (CLS). The CLS codifies the minimal features that a language must support if it wishes to target the .NET platform and the complete features required if it wishes to interoperate with other .NET languages. It is important to recognize that the features in question transcend simple syntactical differences between languages. For example, the CLS does not care what keywords a language uses to implement inheritance, it just cares that the language supports inheritance.

The CLS is a subset of the CTS. This means that a language feature may be fine by CTS standards, but outside the realm of the CLS. For example, C# supports unsigned numerical types, a feature that passes the CTS tests. However, the CLS recognizes only signed numerical types. Therefore, if you use C#'s unsigned type capability in a component, it *may* not be able to interoperate with another .NET component built in a language that does not have unsigned types (like VB .NET). I wrote "*may* not" instead of "*will* not" because it really depends on the visibility of the non–CLS-compliant item. In fact, the CLS rules apply only to types or parts of types that a component exposes to other components. In effect, you can safely implement items that are private to the component using the full capabilities of your chosen .NET language and without regard to CLS compliance. On the other hand, if you require .NET language interoperability, then your component's *publicly* exposed items must be in full CLS compliance. Consider the following C# code:

```
public class Foo
{
    // The uint (unsigned integer) type is non-CLS compliant.
    // But since this item is private, the CLS rules do not apply.
    private uint A = 4;

    // Since this uint member is public, we have a CLS
    // compliance issue.
    public uint B = 5;

    // The long type is CLS compliant.
    public long GetA()
```

```
    {
        return A;
    }
}
```

The last of the Cs we need to cover is the *common language runtime* (CLR). Succinctly put, the CLR is an implementation of the CTS. In other words, the CLR is an application execution engine and a full-featured class library built to the stringent specifications of the CTS. As an application execution engine, the CLR is responsible for loading and running your application code safely, that is with garbage collection of unused objects and security checks. Code that runs under the watchful eye of the CLR is called *managed code.* As a class library, the CLR provides hundreds of useful types that you can use as is or extend through inheritance. Types exist for file I/O, creating dialog boxes, starting threads—basically anything you would otherwise use the Windows API to do.

Let's put these Cs in their proper perspective. Developers building custom distributed applications should devote the majority of their mind space to learning the intricacies of the CLR rather than the CTS or CLS, because the CLR is what you will be programming directly against. Typically, only language and tool vendors wishing to target the .NET platform need to understand the CTS and CLS in detail. That said, since interoperating components is the hallmark of distributed applications, it is important to have an understanding of how .NET achieves this through the definition of common types.

Using Namespaces

Historically, Windows programmers had to build applications using the Windows API. This behemoth consists of thousands of global functions with no logical organization. The result is a library with an immense learning curve. Technologies such as Microsoft Foundation Classes (MFC) and Visual Basic mitigated this to some degree, but even with these you often had to resort to API calls to accomplish a task. In the case of Visual Basic, this was especially problematic, given that the API is written primarily in C with types that are very different from those in Visual Basic (there's that type issue again!).

The CLR provides a type library that, among other things, neatly wraps the vast majority of functionality historically provided by the Windows API. This in itself would simply transfer the complexity from thousands of global functions to thousands of global class types. So, the CLR uses namespaces to logically organize and categorize related types, making them far easier to find and use.

For example, the CLR implements a `Console` class that provides console window I/O. This class is defined in the `System` namespace. To access the class, you must provide both the namespace name and the class name as shown in the following code:

```
class HelloWorld
{
    static void Main(string[] args)
    {
        // Access Console class in the System namespace.
        System.Console.WriteLine("Hello World");
    }
}
```

This example shows the `Console` class accessed via its fully qualified name. Since typing in namespaces can quickly become tedious, many .NET languages provide a shortcut mechanism to use the types in a namespace without specifying the namespace. In C#, this shortcut is the "using" directive. The following code demonstrates this.

```
using System; // Types in the System namespace can now be accessed
              // without qualifying the namespace.

class HelloWorld
{
    static void Main(string[] args)
    {
        // Use Console class in the System namespace.
        Console.WriteLine("Hello World");
    }
}
```

You can use namespaces to organize your own custom types. For example, the following code defines `Foo` and `Bar` classes within the `MyCustomStuff` namespace:

```
namespace MyCustomStuff
{
    public class Foo
    { ... }

    public class Bar
    { ... }
} // End MyCustomStuff namespace
```

Everything in .NET resides in some namespace. So throughout this book, you will be introduced to the types and functionality available in several namespaces.

Assemblies and Manifests

Historically, when you compile a Windows C++ or Visual Basic application, the result is either a file with an .ext or .dll extension. This has *not* changed in .NET, although these files do get a new name: assemblies. The differences do not end there. In .NET, the internal format of these files is very different. Before .NET, DLLs and EXEs contained platform-specific code. In contrast, all .NET assemblies contain platform-agnostic code called the *Common Intermediate Language.*

Typically, an assembly will consist of exactly one DLL or exactly one EXE. However, assemblies can be composed of many DLLs or EXEs. Clients that use the types defined in the assembly are blissfully unaware of its actual physical composition. Therefore, from a logical perspective, you can think of an assembly as simply a collection of types: classes, structures, enumerations, and so on. Assemblies pull this trick off by providing a manifest.

The assembly manifest contains vital information about the assembly. For example, in the case of a multifile assembly, the manifest will list all the DLLs or EXEs that compose the assembly. It also lists version, culture, and type reference information. If an assembly depends on other assemblies, the manifest also lists these dependencies. In generic terms, the manifest information is called *metadata,* since it describes the assembly. The manifest is not the only place where metadata is stored. Within the heart of the assembly, each implemented type also has metadata associated with it. The bottom line is that an assembly is completely self-describing.

Assemblies come in two flavors: private and shared. A private assembly can only be used by a single application, while a shared assembly can be used by many applications. COM components have more in common with shared assemblies; there are enough differences, however, to make managing multiple shared assemblies orders of magnitude easier than managing multiple COM components. Even so, the default assembly type is private; you must take explicit steps to turn a private assembly into a shared assembly. Later in this chapter, you will see a more detailed explanation of private and shared assemblies.

For distributed programmers, understanding assemblies is critical. Assemblies are the unit of deployment in .NET and thus define a versioning and security scope. In other words, assemblies are components. Later in this chapter, you will see more details about building assemblies.

Intermediate Language

All .NET language compilers emit platform-neutral code called Common Intermediate Language (CIL or simply IL). In concept, this is very similar to what Java calls bytecode. Unlike Java bytecode, however, Microsoft designed IL to be created easily by compilers from any language.

As mentioned earlier, assemblies contain IL instead of native code. At runtime, when a method is called for the first time, a Just-In-Time (JIT) compiler converts the method's IL code into native (that is, platform-specific) code for faster execution. The .NET runtime only compiles a section of IL when it is needed at runtime. However, it does cache the resulting native code so that subsequent calls will go directly to the native code.

Considered together with the CTS and CLR, IL provides the *potential* for .NET to be ported to other operating systems beyond Windows. If that happens, you could develop platform-independent applications in *any* language. Of course, the key word here is "potential," because currently .NET runs only on Windows operating systems.

Building and Configuring .NET Assemblies

Any .NET application is composed of assemblies. When you compile your application, the compiler will create assemblies. When you deploy a .NET application, you will be deploying assemblies. When you version your .NET application, you will be assigning your version numbers to each assembly in the application. When you use a component from another vendor, you will be referencing an assembly provided by that vendor.

The point is this: the assembly concept permeates all aspects of .NET programming, distributed or otherwise. With a solid understanding of assemblies, you will be able to quickly track down deployment errors, manage versioning issues with your own components or with third-party components, and correctly decide when to use a shared assembly vs. a private one. Therefore, this section describes, in sometimes excruciating detail, how to build and use assemblies.

To help manage some of the detail involved, we begin by walking through the creation of two simple assemblies. One is a DLL named MathLibrary, which contains a `SimpleMath` class. This is consumed by an EXE assembly named MathClient. These two assemblies will be used to demonstrate many different concepts, so I encourage you to build them yourself so that you can experiment with some of the procedures outlined in the chapter.

Building a Private Assembly

We will start by creating a private assembly using the C# Class Library project type. Recall that a private assembly can only be used by a single application.

To begin, we open a new project in Visual Studio and select a C# Class Library project type (Figure 2-1).

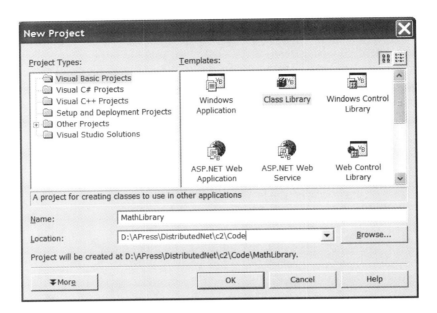

Figure 2-1. Creating a class library assembly

Then we enter the following code in a file called SimpleMath.cs:

```
// In SimpleMath.cs
namespace MathLibrary
{
   public class SimpleMath
   {
      public static int Add(int n1, int n2)
      {
         return n1 + n2;
      }
```

```
        public static int Subtract(int n1, int n2)
        {
            return n1 - n2;:
        }
    }
}
```

This code has no main function, since the only purpose of this assembly is to provide a SimpleMath class that other client assemblies can consume.

When we build this project, it generates the MathLibrary.dll file. But remember, this is not just any old DLL; it's a .NET assembly. Therefore, it contains IL code, and all that lovely metadata described in the previous section.

Consuming the Assembly Types

Now let's build another assembly to consume this SimpleMath class. This time we start by selecting a C# Console Application project and enter the following code:

```
using System;
namespace MathClient
{
    class MathClient
    {
        static void Main(string[] args)
        {
            Console.WriteLine(" 5 + 3 = {0}", MathLibrary.SimpleMath.Add(5,3));

            Console.WriteLine(" 5 - 3 = {0}",
                MathLibrary.SimpleMath.Subtract(5,3));

            Console.ReadLine();
        }
    }
}
```

When we attempt to build this project, however, we get a number of compiler errors. This is because we have not yet referenced the MathLibrary assembly in our client project. Therefore, the compiler is unable to recognize the SimpleMath class type.

We can correct this error by opening the Add Reference dialog box (Project | Add Reference). By clicking the Browse button, we can navigate to the directory containing the MathLibrary.dll file and select the file (see Figure 2-2).

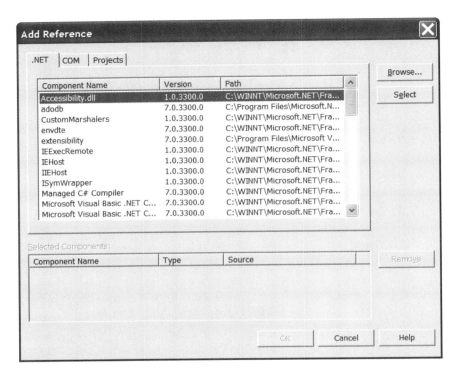

Figure 2-2. Adding an assembly reference

Visual Basic 6.0 programmers will likely recognize this process because it mimics the process for adding a reference to a COM DLL. The critical difference is that in VS .NET, the IDE *copies* the assembly from its current location to the target build directory of your project.

After referencing the MathLibrary assembly, we can successfully build the client project. Figure 2-3 shows how the target build directory looks after we build the project. Currently, MathLibrary is a private assembly. As such, a client application can only use it if it resides in the same directory as the client executable. Later, we will see how a private assembly can also reside in a subdirectory of the application directory.

Investigating the Assembly Manifest

Let's take a moment now to investigate the contents of the MathClient assembly. Earlier, I said the assembly manifest lists all the other assemblies that it requires. We can test this claim by viewing the assembly in ILDasm. This extremely useful tool ships with the .NET Framework SDK and is designed to browse .NET assemblies. Figure 2-4 shows the ILDasm tool after loading the MathClient assembly.

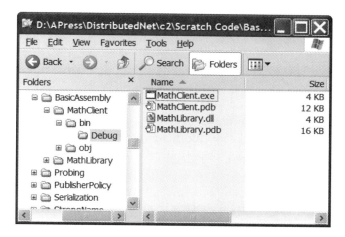

Figure 2-3. The MathClient target build directory

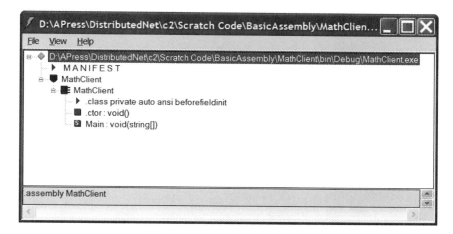

Figure 2-4. Viewing the MathClient assembly in ILDasm

When we double-click the Manifest node, ILDasm displays the contents of the manifest. At the top of the manifest, you see the following entries:

```
.assembly extern mscorlib
{
  .publickeytoken = (B7 7A 5C 56 19 34 E0 89 )
  .ver 1:0:2411:0
}
.assembly extern MathLibrary
{
  .ver 0:0:0:0
}
```

The purpose of the [.assembly extern] items is to enumerate the assemblies that this assembly depends on. As you can see, the MathClient assembly depends on the mscorlib and MathLibrary assemblies. The mscorlib assembly is the core library for the CLR and contains many useful types. For example, it implements the System.Console class used by MathClient.

When a client assembly needs a type defined in any external assembly, it passes an *assembly request* to the CLR assembly loader service. The assembly request consists of the assembly name and all the information in the corresponding [.assembly extern] block. The assembly loader uses this information to find and load the requested assembly through a process called *assembly binding*. While assembly binding is conceptually similar to the workings of the COM Service Control Manager (affectionately known as SCuM), know that the process *never* checks the system registry. The binding mechanism is (thankfully) completely different.

The information recorded for our current MathLibrary assembly is rather sparse. The following excerpt shows an assembly reference with all available information specified. Table 2-1 describes each item.

```
.assembly extern SomeLibrary
{
  .publickeytoken = (99 CB 5A D9 7D 10 88 C5 )
  .ver 1:0:552:41586
  .locale = (65 00 6E 00 00 00 )


}
```

Table 2-1. Assembly Request Details

Assembly Request Item	Description
.assembly extern SomeLibrary	Indicates the friendly name of the external assembly.
.publickeytoken = (…)	An eight-byte hash that uniquely represents the publisher of the external assembly. See "Building a Shared Assembly" for more details.
.ver=1:0:552:41586	Indicates the version number of the external assembly. The format is *major:minor:build:revision*.
.locale =(…)	Indicates the culture of the external assembly, for example, English, German. Used exclusively for assemblies that provide only resources (strings, bitmaps, and so on). The default culture is "neutral".

If you look at the information recorded for each referenced assembly, you might notice an important piece missing: the location of the assembly. How does the loader find it? The answer, at least in this case, is that the loader finds the MathLibrary assembly because it resides in the same directory as the MathClient assembly. However, keep in mind that searching the current application directory is just one step of many that the loader takes to find external assembly references. In fact, there is a well-defined process for this called *probing*, which is part of the assembly binding process.

 Source Code *The code for this example is in Chapter2\BasicAssembly.*

Creating Application Configuration Files

The first step in the probing process is to search for a specially formatted file called the *application configuration file*. This file must always reside in the application directory and must have the same name as the application plus an additional .config extension. For example, the configuration file for the MathClient.exe assembly is named MathClient.exe.config. By authoring a configuration file, you can direct the loader to search for the specified assembly in any direct or indirect subdirectory of the application directory.

For example, to clean up the application's directory structure, you may wish to move all libraries, including MathLibrary, to a subdirectory called libs. However, if you do this and run the MathClient application, it will fail with the exception shown in Figure 2-5.

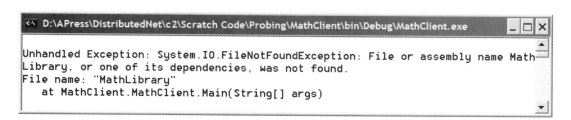

Figure 2-5. Moving a referenced assembly out of the application directory causes an exception.

To solve this problem, you can create an application configuration file. Visual Studio .NET provides a handy mechanism for creating and maintaining application configuration files. First, go to Project | Add New Item, select the Text File icon, and enter the name "app.config" (see Figure 2-6). Then click Open.

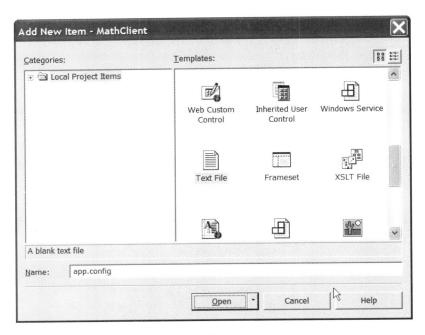

Figure 2-6. Adding the app.config file

This creates a file named app.config in the same directory as your source and project files. But remember, it must also be saved in the same directory where the application EXE resides with the name mathclient.exe.config. In fact, Visual Studio .NET automatically does this each time you build the project. It will even change the name of the target application configuration file appropriately to accommodate a change in the target executable name. Figure 2-7 shows what the project and bin\debug directories should look like after adding this file to the project and compiling.

Now enter the following in the configuration file.

```
<configuration>
    <runtime>
        <assemblyBinding xmlns="urn:schemas-microsoft-com:asm.v1">
            <probing privatePath="libs" />
        </assemblyBinding>
    </runtime>
</configuration>
```

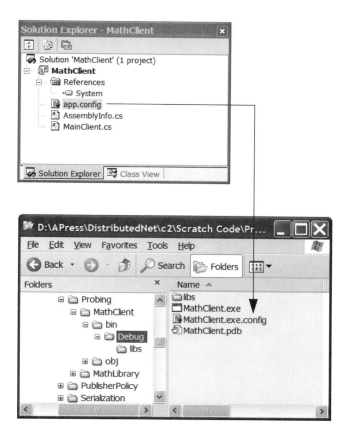

Figure 2-7. The app.config file is converted to mathclient.exe.config at compile time.

As you can probably tell, the configuration file format is XML. By definition, the configuration file must begin with the root element <configuration>. Our ultimate goal is to specify the probing privatePath attribute, but to get there we must first specify the <runtime> and <assemblyBinding> elements. If needed, you can also specify multiple subdirectories to search as shown here:

```
<probing privatePath="libs;libs/moreLibs;yetMoreLibs" />
```

Now if you start the MathClient application, it runs without error.

 Source Code *The code for this example is in Chapter2\Probing.*

Probing the Probing Process

Probing actually entails much more than simply searching the current application directory and specified subdirectories. For example, if the assembly request provides a culture, the runtime checks for a subdirectory with the culture name and searches it for the assembly.

As is the case with many complicated processes, the entire probing heuristic is best described using pseudocode. So if we were to imagine a function called ProbeForAssembly, written in an imaginary language called Db (pronounced "D-flat"), it would look something like the following. When stepping through this code, assume that the function will immediately exit if any search succeeds.

```
function ProbeForAssembly( AsmName, AppBase, Culture, PrivatePath)
   // AsmName = The friendly name of the assembly, e.g., MathLibrary
   // AppBase = Path where the requesting application resides
   // Culture = The assembly reference culture, e.g., "En"
   // PrivatePath = The list of search paths specified in the app config file

   // Search first for DLL extension then EXE extension.
   for each Ext in {"dll", "exe"}
      Search( AppBase\AsmName.Ext )

      if Culture == "neutral" Then
         Search( AppBase\AsmName\AsmName.Ext )
      else
         Search( AppBase\Culture\AsmName.Ext )
         Search( AppBase\Culture\AsmName\AsmName.Ext )
      end if

      // Search in all the paths specified in the app config file
      for each Path in PrivatePath
         if Culture == "neutral" Then
            Search( AppBase\Path\AsmName.Ext )
            Search( AppBase\Path\AsmName\AsmName.Ext )
         else
            Search( AppBase\Path\Culture\AsmName.Ext )
            Search( AppBase\Path\Culture\AsmName\AsmName.Ext )
         end if
      next Path
   next Ext
end function
```

Just in case you are not up on Db syntax, allow me to explain a few of the main points.

- The probing process takes four critical pieces of information as input: the friendly name of the requested assembly, the path of the requesting assembly, the culture of the requested assembly, and the `privatePath` setting as found in the application configuration file.

- The probing process has two main cycles. On the first pass, it searches for an assembly with a DLL extension. On the second pass, it searches for an assembly with an EXE extension.

- The probing process always searches the application directory first, regardless of the `privatePath` or culture information.

- The probing process determines if a subdirectory with the assembly name exists. If so, it searches this subdirectory for the assembly.

- If the culture is something other than "neutral", the probing process determines if a subdirectory exists with the culture name. If so, it searches this subdirectory for the assembly.

- When enumerating the subdirectories specified in the `privatePath`, the probing process also checks for subdirectories with the assembly or culture name (if provided).

The Benefits of Private Assemblies and Probing

Now let's take a moment to consider the implications of the .NET probing mechanism to bind assembly references. To put this in perspective, let's pretend that MathLibrary is a COM DLL consumed by MathClient. To deploy the application, your installation routine must copy and register MathLibrary.dll. Once deployed, if you changed the location MathLibrary.dll you would also need to re-register it. Furthermore, if you wish to deploy a new version of MathLibrary.dll without breaking the client, you have to carefully follow a number of steps to ensure the new build is compatible with the old. Finally, consider what the issues would be if you created a newer version of the entire MathClient application, including newer versions of all the supporting COM DLLs, but wanted to run the old and the new versions on the same machine.

Okay, you can remove yourself from this dystopian world of make-believe, because the .NET assembly probing mechanism greatly simplifies the situation. To deploy the application, all you need to do is copy the entire application directory and any subdirectories containing supporting assemblies. You can accomplish this with a simple call to the XCOPY command. No registration required. Furthermore, you can change the location of the MathLibrary assembly to any subdirectory of the application directory. In this case, all you need to do is update the configuration file to direct the assembly loader to the appropriate directory. You can even deploy a new version of MathLibrary by copying the new version over the old because the runtime does not verify versioning on private assemblies (more details on assembly versioning are coming up shortly). Finally, if you wish to run a new version of the entire MathClient application side-by-side with the old, you need only deploy the new version to a different directory than the one containing the old version.

By now, you should be convinced that private assemblies are a good thing, provided you have no need to share the assembly with other applications. Should that requirement arise, you must take some extra steps to turn the private assembly into a shared assembly.

Building a Shared Assembly

No matter how hard you may try to avoid it, there will come a time when you need to share an assembly across many applications. Shared assemblies differ from private assemblies on two major points: location and identification.

Whereas private assemblies must be located in the application directory or subdirectory, you typically install shared assemblies into a special machine-wide global cache called the *Global Assembly Cache* (GAC). On Windows machines, the GAC resides in a directory called Assembly under the Windows installation directory (for example, C:\WinNT\Assembly).

Although the friendly name of a shared assembly is the same as a private assembly, the .NET runtime identifies shared assemblies by a *strong name* (also called a *shared name*). A strong name is a combination of the friendly name (such as MathLibrary), culture information (for example, English), a version number (such as 1.2.0.0), a public key, and a digital signature. This strict level of identification provided by the strong name is required because

- You want assemblies created by your company to have unique names that no other company can duplicate.

- You may wish to share numerous versions of an assembly that differ in implementation or by culture.

- You want to ensure that a hacker's "Trojan horse" assembly cannot impersonate your assembly and wreak havoc on the machine using the client's access rights.

To demonstrate these points further, we will be converting our MathLibrary assembly into a shared assembly.

Applying a Strong Name to an Assembly

The first thing we must do to transform MathLibrary into a shared assembly is to generate a strong name. As noted earlier, the strong name is really a number of assembly informational items joined together. Currently, if we look into the MathLibrary manifest, we see the following entry:

```
.assembly MathLibrary
{
  // Note, some lines cut for clarity ...
  .hash algorithm 0x00008004
  .ver 0:0:0:0
}
```

NOTE *If you have been following along by building these assemblies and wish to see the manifest exactly as shown in the preceding example, comment out all the lines in the AssemblyInfo.cs file. Visual Studio automatically adds this file when you create a new project.*

The [.assembly] tag without the "extern" adornment indicates that this block of information applies to the current assembly. The items in bold are the friendly name (MathLibrary) and the version (0:0:0:0). Therefore, we are still missing a couple pieces of information to correctly build a strong name.

It may seem as though we are missing the required culture information. Actually, the culture of this assembly is considered "neutral" by virtue of not specifying a culture. Culture applies only if we are building an assembly that contains resources, such as strings, bitmaps, and so on, that need to be customized for several spoken languages. This type of assembly is called a *satellite assembly* and by definition cannot contain any code. Since MathLibrary does contain code, we will not be applying a specific culture.

Asymmetric Cryptography and Strong Names

The last pieces of the strong name puzzle involve the application of asymmetric (or public-key) cryptography techniques. Understand that the purpose of this cryptography is not to encrypt the contents of the assembly. Rather, it provides the ability to ensure the following:

- No one has tampered with the contents of the assembly since it was built or installed.

- No two publishers can create assemblies with identical strong names.

- All versions of the assembly originate from the same publisher.

Here is how it works. Asymmetric cryptography involves the use of two keys, the public key and the private key. These keys are mathematically related such that only the public key can decrypt data encrypted by the private key. When you build a shared assembly, you also supply the compiler with this public/private key pair (you will see how to do this in the next section). The compiler uses the private key to "digitally sign" the contents of the assembly. The signing process entails hashing the entire contents of the assembly down to a few hundred bytes, which are then encrypted using the private key. This yields the assembly's digital signature. The assembly stores the public key in its manifest and embeds the digital signature in a location accessible to the CLR.

The assembly is now fit to be installed in the GAC. At install time, the GAC retrieves the assembly's digital signature and decrypts it using the public key stored in the assembly manifest. This provides the hash value of the assembly contents that the compiler generated at build time. The GAC then hashes the contents of the assembly again using the same hashing algorithm used in the build process. If this hash value matches the hash value found in the digital signature, then the assembly contents have not been altered (perhaps maliciously) since it was built.

Now let's say we need to reference this shared assembly from another. When the compiler builds the consuming assembly, it retrieves the public key from the shared assembly's manifest and hashes it down to an eight-byte value called the *public key token*. The only purpose for this hash process is to compress the public key into a smaller chunk of data. Public keys are rather large, and any given assembly may need to store the public keys for multiple referenced shared assemblies. So, the consuming assembly stores only the public key token in its manifest. However, even in this compressed form, public key tokens are statistically unique enough to identify the publisher of the required assembly.

NOTE *Early beta versions of .NET called the public key token the originator. Keep this in mind if reading older documentation.*

Finally, we can discuss the process that occurs at runtime when the consuming assembly needs to load the types in the shared assembly. First, when the runtime loads the shared assembly, it reads its public key and generates a public key token. It then compares this against the public key token stored in the consumer's manifest. If they match, then the runtime has successfully verified that the shared assembly originated from the publisher the consumer was expecting. If they do not match, then the runtime raises an exception.

After verifying the public key token, the runtime hashes the contents of the shared assembly and compares the resulting value against the value stored in the shared assembly's digital signature. In essence, it is mimicking the process that the GAC performs when you install the shared assembly. However, this runtime check ensures that no one has maliciously tampered with the assembly since it was installed in the GAC.

Unless you are familiar with asymmetric key cryptography, this section may have your head spinning. Take heart. In the next section, you will see all of this applied to our MathLibrary assembly. Before we continue, I must admit that the previous description was simplified somewhat because I assumed the assembly was of the single file variety. Multifile assemblies complicate the process somewhat, but ultimately the results are the same.

Generating a Public/Private Key Pair

Recall that the compiler requires a public/private key pair in order to sign a shared assembly. You generate these keys using the Strong Name command line utility (sn.exe). This utility has a number of options, but most of the time all you need is the -k option. This instructs the tool to create a brand new public/private key pair and save it to the specified file (see Figure 2-8).

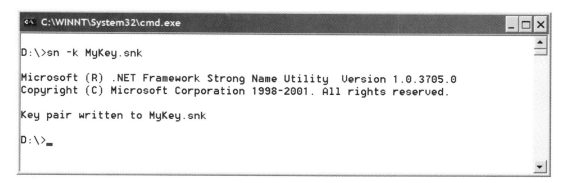

```
C:\WINNT\System32\cmd.exe

D:\>sn -k MyKey.snk

Microsoft (R) .NET Framework Strong Name Utility  Version 1.0.3705.0
Copyright (C) Microsoft Corporation 1998-2001. All rights reserved.

Key pair written to MyKey.snk

D:\>_
```

Figure 2-8. Using the Strong Name utility (sn.exe)

As mentioned earlier, the compiler uses these keys to sign the assembly, but you must tell it where the keys are located. You can accomplish this programmatically by specifying the key file path using an assembly attribute called the `AssemblyKeyFile` attribute. The following code shows how:

```
// The AssemblyKeyFile attribute lives in this namespace
using System.Reflection;
[assembly: AssemblyKeyFile(@"D:\MyKey.snk")]
```

You can place this code in any of your project's code files provided the assembly attribute appears before any namespace or class declarations. However, the conventional location is the AssemblyInfo.cs file. When you create a new C# project, Visual Studio automatically includes this file in the project.

Now when we build the MathLibrary assembly, the compiler uses the key pair to sign the assembly. We can confirm the results by investigating the assembly manifest in ILDasm, which is shown in Figure 2-9.

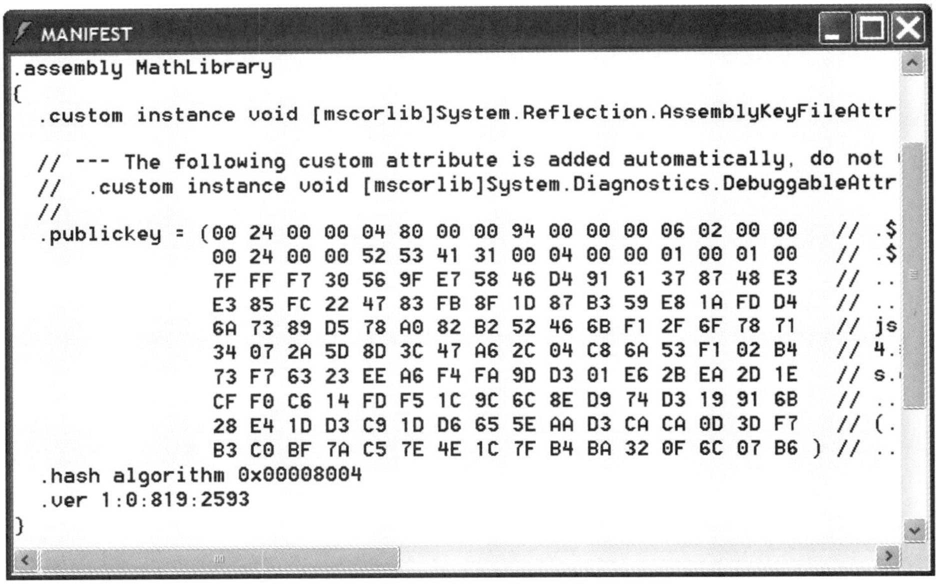

Figure 2-9. Viewing the public key in the MathLibrary manifest using ILDasm

Note the new [.publickey] entry in the identity block. As you might expect, this is the public key. The MathLibrary assembly is now ready to be installed in the GAC.

If you are a component vendor, it is extremely important that you keep the public/private key pair information in a safe and private place. It is your identity. Do not lose it. Do not let any one else have it. If you lose it and create another, clients built against your previous assemblies will not be able to bind to subsequent assembly versions without being recompiled. If a hacker gets your key pair, he or she can distribute a malicious version of the assembly using your identity, and redirect clients to his or her version by simply updating the machine configuration file.

> **WARNING** *It is extremely important that you keep the key pair information in a safe and private place.*

Rebuilding the MathClient Assembly

Before we install the MathLibrary assembly into the GAC, let's build the MathClient assembly again to see what effect these changes to MathLibrary has on it. First let's view the MathClient's manifest to see how it is currently referencing the MathLibrary assembly. This is shown in Figure 2-10.

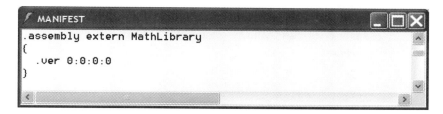

Figure 2-10. The MathClient's manifest before building against the strong named MathLibrary

Figure 2-11 shows the reference after building the MathClient against our new strong-named version of the MathLibrary assembly. Note the additional [.publickeytoken] entry in the assembly reference information.

> **TIP** *You should remove the MathLibrary reference from the MathClient project and add it back in order for Visual Studio to recognize that the assembly now has a strong name. You can tell that Visual Studio recognizes the strong name by highlighting the MathLibrary reference in the Solution Explorer window and examining the Strong Name property in the Property window.*

Figure 2-11. The MathClient's manifest after building against the strong-named MathLibrary

If you execute the MathClient program, it will run exactly as before, demonstrating that even though MathLibrary has a strong name, you can still use it as a private assembly. In the next section, we will install the MathLibrary in the GAC and use it as a shared assembly.

Installing the Assembly in the GAC

.NET ships with a special shell extension (shfusion.dll) that allows you to view the GAC by navigating to it in Windows Explorer (Figure 2-12). The easiest way to install the MathLibrary assembly in the GAC is to open it in Windows Explorer and "drag-and-drop" MathLibrary.dll just as if you were copying the file to another directory.

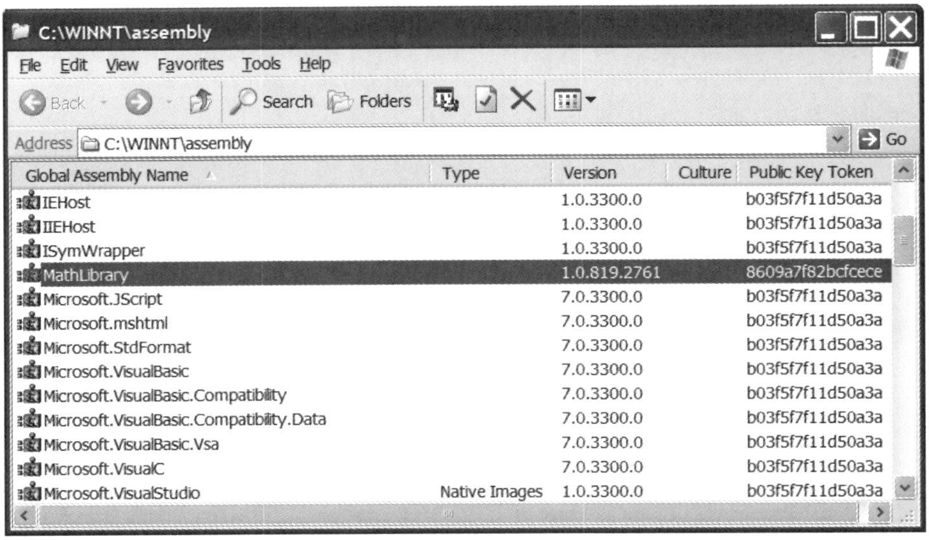

Figure 2-12. Viewing the MathLibrary assembly in the GAC

Batch files and installation programs can use the gacutil.exe command line utility to install shared assemblies. The /i option installs the specified assembly in the GAC.

```
gacutil /i MathLibrary.dll
```

 NOTE *You must have administrator privileges on the computer to install assemblies in the GAC.*

Regardless of the mechanism, once you have installed MathLibrary in the GAC, any assembly on the machine may use it. To test this, remove MathClient's application configuration file (MathClient.exe.config) and any local copies of MathLibrary.dll. Then run MathClient.exe. Since the loader can now find the MathLibrary assembly in the GAC, the application should run fine.

Recall that when we added a reference to the private MathLibrary assembly from the MathClient project, Visual Studio automatically copied the assembly to the application directory. However, now that MathLibrary has a strong name and is installed in the GAC, if you reference this assembly again, Visual Studio will *not* make a copy. You can see if Visual Studio is copying an assembly at every build by viewing its Copy Local property in the Property window (Figure 2-13).

Figure 2-13. The MathLibrary reference's Copy Local property in Visual Studio

On a final note, you may be wondering what would happen if you also copied the MathLibrary assembly into the client's application directory. Which copy would be loaded, the one in the GAC or the one in the application directory? The answer lies in how the assembly is referenced in the MathClient manifest. If the MathClient manifest has a public key token recorded for the MathLibrary assembly, the runtime will check the GAC first. If the assembly is not found in the GAC, then the runtime will begin probing. On the other hand, if the MathLibrary's public key token is not recorded in the MathClient manifest, then the runtime begins probing and does not check the GAC. As it turns out, this latter case is doomed to fail, because the assembly reference, which has a public key token value of null, does not match the found assembly, which has a public key token of 8609A7F82BCFCECE. However, since compilers automatically create the public key token when referencing an assembly with a strong name, the latter case should almost never happen.

These and other "what if" scenarios are covered in a later section of this chapter "Summarizing the Binding Process."

Using Delayed Signing

Given the sensitive nature of the public/private key pair used to sign strong-named assemblies, an organization may wish to avoid distributing the key pair even to its developers. On the other hand, for testing purposes, developers need to re-create the actual deployment environment as closely as possible. Meaning that if an assembly is intended to be shared, it is best developed and tested in that manner early in the development process. This is impossible to do without generating a strong name for the assembly.

The solution to this dilemma is to use delayed signing. In this process, only the public key is provided to developers. As is normally the case, this public key is embedded within the assembly manifest, and any client assembly built against the assembly stores the corresponding public key token within its manifest. However, since there is no private key, the assembly is not digitally signed. When the application is ready for deployment, then all assemblies can be handed off to those responsible for maintaining the organization's private key and signed.

The first step in delayed signing is to retrieve only the public key from the key pair. The strong name tool (sn.exe) provides the -p option for this purpose. The following command retrieves the public key from the MyKey.snk file and stores it in the MyPublicKey.snk file.

```
sn -p MyKey.snk MyPublicKey.snk
```

This public key file can now be freely distributed to all developers for delayed signing.

Armed with the public key, you now need to specify that the assembly uses delayed signing. This can be done using the assembly attribute `AssemblyDelaySign`. For example:

```
// Specify the use of delayed signing
[assembly: AssemblyDelaySign(true)]

// Specify the location of the public key
[assembly: AssemblyKeyFile(@"D:\MyPublicKey.snk")]
```

Note that the `AssemblyKeyFile` attribute no longer specifies the file containing the full key pair. Instead, it specifies the location of the public key file created in the previous step.

When this assembly is built, the compiler places the public key in the manifest and reserves space for the digital signature. However, since there is no digital signature, you must turn off the signature verification that takes place whenever the assembly is installed in the GAC or loaded by a client at runtime. Again, the strong name utility can be used to accomplish this using the -Vr option, as shown in the following example:

```
sn -Vr mathlibrary.dll
```

Now, whenever a client requests this assembly, the verification process is skipped. Furthermore, you can install this assembly in the GAC and develop clients against it just as if it had a full strong name. Finally, since the correct public key is in the assembly's manifest, client assemblies built against the assembly contain the correct public key token and do not need to be rebuilt when the assembly is signed with the private key. Keep in mind that the previous command does not alter the assembly itself. Instead, it simply registers the assembly for verification skipping on the current machine only. To reenable verification for the assembly, use the -Vu option.

Of course, once the application is complete the delay sign assemblies must be signed with the private key before they are deployed. As you can probably guess, the Strong Name utility also provides an option for this: -R. For example, the following command signs the MathLibrary assembly with the private key found in the MyKey.snk file:

```
sn -R mathlibrary.dll d:\mykey.snk
```

Sorting Out Some Terminology: Strong-named vs. Shared

To be honest, I am not particularly fond of the private/shared assembly terminology, because it describes how the assembly is used rather than the internal structure of the assembly. For example, you can use a strong-named assembly as a private assembly or a shared assembly, depending on whether or not it has been installed in the GAC. Unfortunately, the term *shared* is often used incorrectly when *strong-named* is really meant.

So, from this point on I will use the *shared* terminology only to describe a strong-named assembly that is also installed in the GAC, and the term *regular assembly* to describe one that does not have a strong name. I will use the term *private assembly* when this usage of the assembly rather than its internal structure is important. If needed, I will fully qualify a reference to an assembly, for example "strong-named private assembly" or "regular private assembly."

Understanding .NET Versioning

Many COM developers have violent negative reactions at the mere mention of the word *versioning*. Although the COM versioning rules are simple, the implementation of them is not. Furthermore, Windows development tools like Visual Basic and Visual C++ vary drastically in their automation of versioning. Visual Basic 6.0 hides too much of the ugly versioning details behind a simple dialog box that offers little assistance when faced with a versioning error. Visual C++ 6.0 places the grunt work of versioning entirely on the developer. The .NET versioning solution is much more elegant. However, keep in mind that versioning is inherently a complicated matter and requires diligence on the part of all members of a development team.

Setting an Assembly's Version Information

An assembly's version is described by a four-part version number stored in the manifest. The parts are usually delimited with either a period (.) or a colon (:).

```
<Major version>.<Minor version>.<Build number>.<Revision>
```

You can set an assembly's version number using the AssemblyVersion attribute. Like the AssemblyKeyFile attribute, the conventional location for this is in the AssemblyInfo.cs file:

```
// Format: <Major version>.<Minor version>.<Build number>.<Revision>
[assembly: AssemblyVersion("1.0.*")]
```

In the preceding example, the major version is 1 and the minor version is 0. The asterisk tells the compiler to automatically generate the build and revision values. The compiler then stores the resulting version number in the manifest. Let's try this out on the MathLibrary assembly. Figure 2-14 shows the manifest after building the project.

```
 MANIFEST
.assembly MathLibrary
{
  .custom instance void [mscorlib]System.Reflection.AssemblyKeyFileAttri
  // --- The following custom attribute is added automatically, do not u
  //   .custom instance void [mscorlib]System.Diagnostics.DebuggableAttri
  //
  .publickey = (00 24 00 00 04 80 00 00 94 00 00 00 06 02 00 00   // .$.
               00 24 00 00 52 53 41 31 00 04 00 00 01 00 01 00   // .$.
               7F FF F7 30 56 9F E7 58 46 D4 91 61 37 87 48 E3   // ...
               E3 85 FC 22 47 83 FB 8F 1D 87 B3 59 E8 1A FD D4   // ...
               6A 73 89 D5 78 A0 82 B2 52 46 6B F1 2F 6F 78 71   // js.
               34 07 2A 5D 8D 3C 47 A6 2C 04 C8 6A 53 F1 02 B4   // 4.x
               73 F7 63 23 EE A6 F4 FA 9D D3 01 E6 2B EA 2D 1E   // s.c
               CF F0 C6 14 FD F5 1C 9C 6C 8E D9 74 D3 19 91 6B   // ...
               28 E4 1D D3 C9 1D D6 65 5E AA D3 CA CA 0D 3D F7   // (..
               B3 C0 BF 7A C5 7E 4E 1C 7F B4 BA 32 0F 6C 07 B6 ) // ...
  .hash algorithm 0x00008004
  .ver 1:0:550:39732
}
.module MathLibrary.dll
```

Figure 2-14. MathLibrary's version as recorded in the manifest

If you wish, you can explicitly set your own build and revision numbers, as shown in this example:

```
// Format: <Major version>.<Minor version>.<Build number>.<Revision>
[assembly: AssemblyVersion("1.0.5.121")]
```

Whenever you build a project that references other assemblies, the compiler will store the version numbers of all its referenced assemblies in the manifest. Let's try this out by rebuilding the MathClient assembly. Figure 2-15 shows how the client manifest records the version information.

Recall that the CLR uses the information in these assembly references to bind to the correct assembly at runtime. And without any further input, the CLR will *only* bind to an assembly with these characteristics. The bottom line is our MathClient application will successfully run only if the runtime can find the MathLibrary assembly version 1.0.550.39732. Understand, however, that this policy only applies to strong-named assemblies. While a regular assembly can have an associated version, the runtime will completely ignore it.

```
 MANIFEST                                             _ □ ✕
.assembly extern MathLibrary
{
  .publickeytoken = (86 09 A7 F8 2B CF CE CE )
  .ver 1:0:819:20734
}
```

Figure 2-15. MathLibrary's version as recorded in MathClient's manifest

 NOTE   *Early beta versions of .NET had a concept called Quick Fix Engineering (QFE), also known as the default versioning policy. This allowed the runtime to load an assembly if only its revision or build numbers differed from the requested version. In practice, this policy proved too lenient, and was replaced by a more explicit form of binding called publisher policy (discussed later). Keep this in mind if you run across the term in older documentation.*

This strict versioning policy is fine until you need to update the referenced assembly. For example, assume we found a bug in the MathLibrary assembly after deploying the application. How can we build and deploy a bug-free assembly? We have a couple options.

- **Update and deploy the entire application.** We can fix the MathLibrary assembly and rebuild the entire application in our development environment. This will update the reference version in the MathClient manifest. Then we can deploy the whole application as a unit. In this particular example, this may be a reasonable approach. But if this were a large application with many assemblies, it would be impractical.

- **Update and deploy the MathLibrary assembly.** Obviously, this is the preferred method. But how do we get the previously deployed MathClient application to correctly bind to the updated version of the MathLibrary assembly? We could freeze the version number so that the updated assembly's version does not change, but that defeats the whole purpose of a version number. The solution to our dilemma lies in the application configuration file.

Revisiting the Application Configuration File

Earlier we used the application configuration file to list subdirectories that the runtime could probe for referenced assemblies. You can also use this file to redirect a request for a particular assembly version to another version using the <bindingRedirect> element. The beauty of this solution is that you do not need to recompile the application in order to bind to updated assemblies

For example, assume we have fixed and rebuilt our MathLibrary assembly and its new version number is 1.0.550.41003. We must redirect our MathClient assembly to load this instead of version 1.0.550.39732 as listed in its manifest. The following configuration file accomplishes this:

```
<configuration>
    <runtime>
        <assemblyBinding xmlns="urn:schemas-microsoft-com:asm.v1">
            <probing   privatePath="libs" />
            <dependentAssembly>
                <assemblyIdentity name="MathLibrary"
                                  publicKeyToken="99cb5ad97d1088c5" />
                <bindingRedirect oldVersion="1.0.550.39732"
                                 newVersion="1.0.550.41003" />
            </dependentAssembly>
        </assemblyBinding>
    </runtime>
</configuration>
```

In this example, we use the `oldVersion` attribute of the <bindingRedirect> element to specify the version request we wish to redirect. We set the `newVersion` attribute to the version we wish to use instead. The `oldVersion` attribute can also accept a range, in case we wish to redirect multiple versions to a single version.

```
<bindingRedirect oldVersion="1.0.0.0 - 1.0.550.39732"
                 newVersion="1.0.550.41003" />
```

The <bindingRedirect> element is actually a child element of <dependentAssembly>. Each <dependentAssembly> element encapsulates binding information for the assembly identified in the <assemblyIdentity> element. <assemblyIdentity> provides `name` and `publicKeyToken` attributes that we can use to specify the exact assembly we wish to redirect. This means the configuration file can have several <dependentAssembly> elements, each redirecting a referenced assembly to a new version. For example:

```
<assemblyBinding xmlns="urn:schemas-microsoft-com:asm.v1">
   <probing  privatePath="libs" />
   <dependentAssembly>
      <assemblyIdentity name="MathLibrary"
                        publicKeyToken="99cb5ad97d1088c5" />
      <bindingRedirect oldVersion="1.0.550.39732"
                       newVersion="1.0.550.41003" />
   </dependentAssembly>
   <dependentAssembly>
      <assemblyIdentity name="AnotherLibrary"
                        publicKeyToken="99cb5ad97d1088c5" />
      <bindingRedirect oldVersion="1.0.337.67001"
                       newVersion="2.0.622.12345" />
   </dependentAssembly>
</assemblyBinding>
```

Setting Machine-wide Version Policies

As cool as the application configuration file is, its one limitation is that it can only affect a single application. What if you wish to redirect all the references from one assembly version to another version regardless of the application? For this, you can use the *machine configuration file*. The path to this file is <.NET Install Path>\Config\Machine.config.

The machine and application configuration files share a similar format, but the former has more elements for configuring machine-wide systems like ASP.NET. The pattern for redirecting version requests, however, is exactly the same. In the case of conflicting settings, the application configuration file overrides the machine configuration file.

Using the .NET Framework Configuration Tool

The .NET Framework encourages the use of simple text editor tools like Notepad to edit application configuration files. That is one of the benefits of using XML. However, XML is (by design) very unforgiving of poorly formed documents. Consider what would happen if you edited the machine configuration file and misplaced a > character. I did that (once) and every .NET-based application on my machine displayed the message shown in Figure 2-16.

Because of this, I recommend using the .NET Framework Configuration tool (mscorcfg.msc) to edit the machine configuration file. The .msc extension indicates that this tool is actually a Microsoft Management Console (MMC) snap-in. MMC snap-ins provide a common user interface for managing a variety of services. If you have ever configured an MTS or COM+ application, or created an SQL Server database or a virtual directory in IIS, then you are already familiar with MMC idioms because all of these activities are facilitated through various MMC snap-ins.

Figure 2-16. An invalid machine configuration file causes this error message.

You can start the tool using the following command (assuming your Windows installation is on the C: drive):

```
mmc c:\winnt\Microsoft.NET\Framework\<Version Number>\mscorcfg.msc
```

Figure 2-17 shows the tool's initial screen. Like all snap-ins, it has a tree control on the left-hand side that lets you drill down to exactly what you need to see. The panel on the right shows various views based on the node you have selected in the tree control. Right-clicking any node displays a context-sensitive menu of additional activities that can be performed on that node.

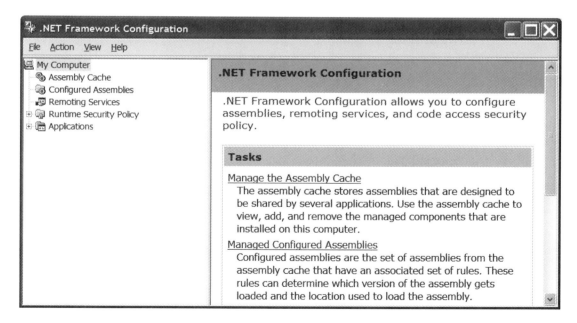

Figure 2-17. The .NET Framework Configuration tool

Let's use this tool to set a machine versioning policy for the MathLibrary assembly. First, right-click the Configured Assemblies node and choose Add. The resulting dialog box allows you to select an assembly from the GAC or enter an assembly manually. After selecting the MathLibrary from the GAC, the tool then displays a dialog box that allows you to enter the version redirections under the Binding Policy tab (see Figure 2-18).

Figure 2-18. Using the .NET Framework Configuration tool to set machine-scoped binding policies

Once you click OK, the tool writes the following to the machine configuration file:

```
<runtime>
  <assemblyBinding xmlns="urn:schemas-microsoft-com:asm.v1">
    <dependentAssembly>
      <assemblyIdentity name="MathLibrary" publicKeyToken="99cb5ad97d1088c5" />
      <bindingRedirect oldVersion="1.0.550.39732" newVersion="1.0.550.41003" />
    </dependentAssembly>
  </assemblyBinding>
</runtime>
```

As you can see, the tool is simply generating the XML you would otherwise have to write manually.

You can also edit application configuration files using the snap-in. First, right-click the Applications node and select Add from the context menu. Then browse for the application you wish to configure. Once the application is added, you can view all the assemblies it depends on and configure version bindings much like we did with the machine configuration file. However, instead of updating the machine configuration file, the tool will update the application's configuration file.

This handy tool can do much more, but I do not want to bore you with all the details now. The interface is intuitive, especially if you have used an MMC snap-in before. Throughout the remainder of this book, I will focus on the manual forms of configuration because I believe this gives you the best understanding of what is really happening. However, I will refer back to the configuration tool if you can use it to accomplish the same task.

Configuring Publisher Policy

Let's do a quick review. You can configure version binding at the application level using the application configuration file. You can also configure version binding at the machine level using the machine configuration file. Now imagine you were a component vendor sheepishly distributing a fix for a bug-ridden assembly. Do you really want to instruct the already perturbed client to edit these configuration files? Would it not be better if the client could just install the new (and hopefully bug-free) assembly version in the GAC, and all applications referencing the assembly would automatically bind to the new version? Of course it would be. Therefore, .NET also supports the notion of a publisher policy.

A *publisher policy* allows you, as an assembly vendor, to redirect applications to a newer version of an assembly. You distribute a publisher policy file along with the new assembly and install it in the GAC. Unlike the application and machine configuration files, which were simple text, publisher policy files are actually assemblies themselves.

Building the Publisher Policy Assembly

For the runtime to recognize an assembly as a publisher policy, you must name it using the following convention:

```
policy.<major>.<minor>.<assemblyname>
```

where <major> is the major version number, <minor> is the minor version number, and <assemblyname> is the name of the assembly to which you are applying the policy. For example, the publisher policy file for our MathLibrary assembly would be named policy.1.0.MathLibrary.dll.

Unfortunately, as of this writing the Visual Studio IDE does not provide a project template for building a publisher policy assembly. However, there is a command line tool called the *Assembly Linker* (al.exe) that can do the job. First, you need to create an XML file with the appropriate version redirects. This XML file format is exactly the same as the application configuration file. The following example demonstrates how to redirect a request for MathLibrary version 1.0.1.1 to version 1.0.1.2.

```
<configuration>
   <runtime>
      <assemblyBinding xmlns="urn:schemas-microsoft-com:asm.v1">
         <dependentAssembly>
            <assemblyIdentity name="MathLibrary"
                              publicKeyToken="99cb5ad97d1088c5" />
            <bindingRedirect oldVersion="1.0.1.1"
                             newVersion="1.0.1.2" />
         </dependentAssembly>
      </assemblyBinding>
   </runtime>
</configuration>
```

Assume this XML was stored in a file named PublisherPolicy.xml. To wrap this in an assembly, you use the following Assembly Linker command:

```
al /link:publisherpolicy.xml /out:policy.1.0.MathLbrary.dll /keyf:d:\mykey.snk
/v:1.0.0.0.
```

This "compiles" the XML file into an assembly named policy.1.0.MathLibrary.dll. It also assigns a strong name to the assembly using the public/private key file created earlier. Finally, it sets the version number of the publisher policy assembly to 1.0.0.0. Note that this version has nothing to do with the version of MathLibrary we are attempting to redirect. The version applies to the publisher policy assembly only.

Once the publisher policy assembly is built, simply install it in the GAC (see Figure 2-19). With this publisher policy file in place, all requests for MathLibrary version 1.0.1.1 are redirected to MathLibrary version 1.0.1.2. In fact, due to the naming convention used, the runtime reads this policy file for any 1.0.* version request. This should lead you to conclude (correctly) that publisher policy files can only be used to redirect requests for a given major and minor number.

Although Visual Studio .NET does not have a publisher policy project template, you could build a policy file using a class library project. Just delete the default class it creates and add the PublisherPolicy.xml file to the project. Set the key file and version using the `AssemblyKeyFile` and `AssemblyVersion` attributes in the AssemblyInfo.cs file.

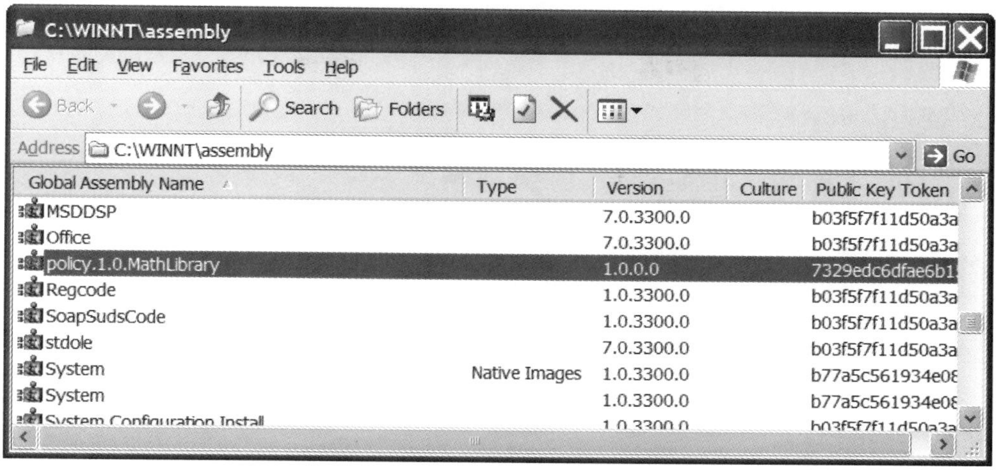

Figure 2-19. Viewing the MathLibrary publisher policy file in the GAC

Forcing Publisher Policy Off

Before distributing a publisher binding policy with a new assembly version, you should make sure the new version is completely backwards compatible. Typically, this means that you have not changed any existing public interfaces, and have not changed implementation in a way that would negatively affect client application behavior. Adding assembly items such as new types, methods, and properties to an assembly or fixing bugs does not make the new assembly incompatible.

If you mistakenly redirect applications to an incompatible version of the assembly, the (now *really* perturbed) client has a couple of options. First, the client can set the correct version redirects in the application configuration file since that overrides the publisher policy. Second, the client can add a <publisherPolicy> element to the application configuration file to turn off any applicable publisher policies. This is called *safe mode*.

Depending on where the <publisherPolicy> element is placed within the application configuration file, it can affect the entire application or just specific assembly requests. If it is a child of the <assemblyBinding> element, then it applies to the entire application.

```
<configuration>
   <runtime>
      <assemblyBinding xmlns="urn:schemas-microsoft-com:asm.v1">
         <publisherPolicy apply="no" />
      </assemblyBinding>
   </runtime>
</configuration>
```

On the other hand, if it is a child of a <dependentAssembly> element, then it only applies to that assembly.

```
<configuration>
   <runtime>
      <assemblyBinding xmlns="urn:schemas-microsoft-com:asm.v1">
         <dependentAssembly>
            <assemblyIdentity name="MathLibrary"
                              publicKeyToken="99cb5ad97d1088c5" />
            <publisherPolicy apply="no"/>
         </dependentAssembly>
      </assemblyBinding>
   </runtime>
</configuration>
```

Policy Precedence

You have now seen the third and final way of specifying a binding policy. You can combine these in many different ways to affect the outcome of the bind. To help you understand the possible outcomes, keep the following points in mind:

- The runtime processes the application configuration file, then the publisher file, and then the machine configuration file.

- If there are multiple policies specified in the configuration files, the application policy takes precedent, followed by the publisher policy, and then the machine policy.

- You cannot chain the policies. For example, imagine an application requests version 1.0.0.0. The application policy redirects version 1.0.0.0 to 1.0.0.1. The publisher policy redirects version 1.0.0.1 to 1.0.0.2. Will the runtime bind to version 1.0.0.2? No. The runtime honors only one redirect. In this case, it binds to the 1.0.0.1 version because the application policy has the highest precedence.

Using the <codeBase> Element

So far, we have seen that assemblies can reside in two places: the GAC, or some direct or indirect subdirectory of the application directory. The other place the runtime will look to bind an assembly is far more inclusive: any directory on your machine or network, or any Web site. Of course, this requires that you specify the exact location of the assembly, which you can achieve using the <codeBase> element. The following configuration example shows how:

```
<configuration>
   <runtime>
      <assemblyBinding xmlns="urn:schemas-microsoft-com:asm.v1">
         <probing privatePath="libs" />
         <dependentAssembly>
            <assemblyIdentity name="MathLibrary"
                              publicKeyToken="99cb5ad97d1088c5" />
            <bindingRedirect oldVersion="1.0.550.39732"
                             newVersion="1.0.550.41003" />
            <codeBase version="1.0.550.41003"
                      href="file://d:/MathLibrary.dll" />
         </dependentAssembly>
      </assemblyBinding>
   </runtime>
</configuration>
```

Like the <bindingRedirect> element, <codeBase> is also a child of <dependentAssembly>. We set the href attribute to direct the runtime to find the assembly at the given URL. We set the version attribute to indicate what version requests should be routed to the URL. Note that the runtime always examines the <codeBase> element after the version binding redirect. So, in this case, even though our client requests version 1.0.550.39732, the <bindingRedirect> element redirects the version request to 1.0.550.41003. Now the version request matches that in the <codeBase> element, so the runtime fetches the assembly from the given URL.

In this example, the URL points to a location in the file system. Of course, you can also specify a Web site:

```
<codeBase version="1.0.552.41586"
          href="http://www.mywebsite.com/MyAssemblies/MathLibrary.dll" />
```

In the previous examples, the <codeBase> element referred to a strong-named assembly. You can also use it to look up a regular assembly. However, the runtime will only allow a regular assembly to bind if it is located in a direct or indirect sub-directory of the application directory. So, a regular assembly downloaded from a Web site will not bind. In addition, for regular assemblies the runtime ignores the version attribute. In fact, you do not have to specify the <codeBase> version attribute for a regular assembly. The following configuration shows <codeBase> being used to look up a regular assembly:

```
<configuration>
   <runtime>
      <assemblyBinding xmlns="urn:schemas-microsoft-com:asm.v1">
         <dependentAssembly>
            <assemblyIdentity name="MathLibrary" />
            <codeBase
              href="file://D:\MathClient\bin\Debug\libs\MathLibrary.dll" />
         </dependentAssembly>
      </assemblyBinding>
   </runtime>
</configuration>
```

Viewing the Assembly Binding Log

Obviously, the assembly binding process is complex. If an assembly fails to load, there could be several causes. You could have mistyped the public key token or version in the configuration file. The configuration file could be missing a key XML token. The assembly may not be installed in the GAC. If using <codeBase> to download an assembly from a Web site, the Web site might be down. To help you diagnose the source of the problem, .NET provides the Assembly Binding Log Viewer (fuslogvw.exe).

When an assembly bind fails, two things occur. First, the runtime raises an exception, typically TypeLoadException. Second, the runtime logs a descriptive entry to the Assembly Binding Log. While the exception does give some indication of what went wrong, it does not always display enough information. The log entries, on the other hand, are very detailed, allowing you to quickly see the source of the problem.

Figure 2-20 shows the main window of the log viewer. You can select any item in the list and click the View Log button to see the entire log entry. Figure 2-21 shows an example of a log entry.

By default, the runtime only logs entries if there was a binding error. However, you may wish to see details of all binds, even the successful ones. To activate this, simply set the system registry entry HKLM\Software\Microsoft\Fusion\ForceLog as shown in Figure 2-22. This proved very useful as I was writing this chapter. But beyond writing books, the log can help you confirm that the runtime is binding to the intended assembly, for example, to the assembly in the application directory instead of the one in the GAC.

TIP *The .NET install does not add the ForceLog item to the registry, but you can manually add it. Just remember to choose the DWORD value type.*

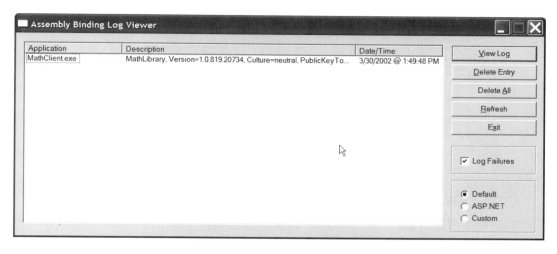

Figure 2-20. The main window of the Assembly Binding Log Viewer tool

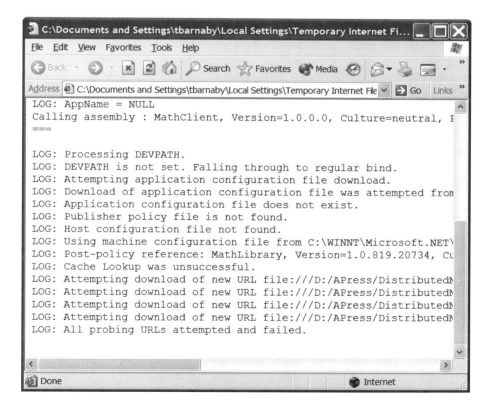

Figure 2-21. Viewing an assembly binding log entry

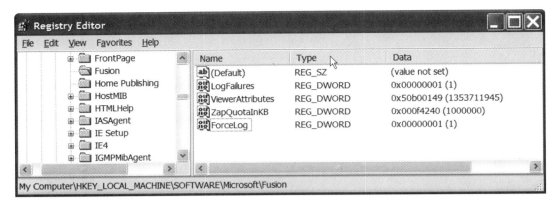

Figure 2-22. Setting the ForceLog registry entry to force logging of all assembly binds

Summary of the Binding Process

As you can see, the process the runtime uses to locate and bind to assemblies is very flexible, but also complex. In reading through this section, it is natural for you to think of a number of "what if" scenarios. What if a private assembly is in the application directory, but the configuration file points to a subdirectory to load assemblies? What if the runtime finds the assembly in the GAC and in a specified <codeBase>? The number of possibilities is overwhelming. Since I cannot possibly foretell all "what ifs," I have provided a flowchart to help clarify the binding process (Figure 2-23). Used together with the pseudocode implementation of the probing process shown earlier, you can unambiguously determine exactly how an assembly request will bind regardless of the scenario.

Keep in mind that this flowchart only documents how the runtime finds the requested assembly. Once the assembly is found, the runtime verifies it against the assembly request. In the case of a strong-named assembly, this means that the identity of the located assembly must *exactly* match the assembly request. The same is true for a regular assembly, except that the runtime ignores version information.

Understanding Attributes and Reflection

You can't get very deep into the .NET runtime without stumbling upon attributes. They are everywhere. In fact, you have already seen a couple attributes put to use: `AssemblyKeyFile` and `AssemblyVersion`. These attributes provide additional information about the assembly. Like these two examples, all attributes provide a way to assign more information to some item. In addition to assemblies, you can apply attributes to classes, structures, interfaces, fields, methods, properties, return values, and more.

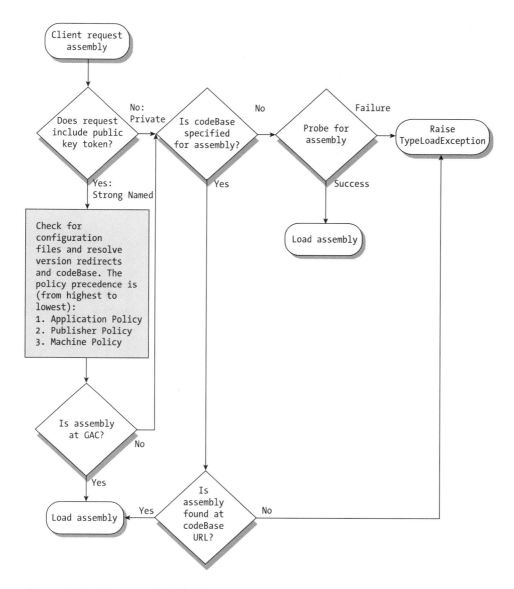

Figure 2-23. The assembly binding process

Using CLR Attributes

The CLR defines hundreds of attributes. When applied to an item in code, these attributes direct the runtime or compiler to take some special action with the item. One easy example is the Serializable attribute. You can apply this attribute to a class to allow the runtime to serialize the instances of the class when needed, as shown here:

```
[Serializable]
public class Car
{
   // Class implementation
}
```

If you have worked with IDL before, this syntax probably looks familiar. The attribute is defined within square brackets preceding the item it describes. If you have multiple attributes to apply, you delimit each with a comma. For example:

```
[Serializable, Obsolete(@"No one uses horse and buggies anymore. Use the
Car class instead", false)]
public class HorseAndBuggy
{
   // Class implementation
}
```

The compiler recognizes the Obsolete attribute and issues the provided warning message whenever another programmer attempts to use the HorseAndBuggy class (see Figure 2-24).

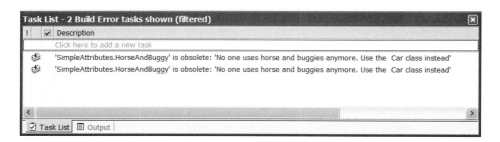

Figure 2-24. Results from the Obsolete *attribute*

The example also demonstrates that attributes can take parameters, in this case a warning message and a boolean indicating whether this should be a compiler error or just a warning. In fact, attributes are nothing more than a class derived from a special CLR-based class called Attribute. Given this, you can recognize that the attribute code shown in the previous example is calling the default constructor for the Serializable attribute, and a constructor that takes a string and a boolean for the Obsolete attribute.

NOTE   *By convention, the actual class name of any attribute is the attribute name appended with "Attribute". Thus, the* Serializable *attribute is actually a class named* SerializableAttribute. *As a shortcut, C# and VB .NET allow you to leave off the Attribute suffix when applying the attribute.*

Implementing Custom Attributes

In addition to the many attributes declared by the CLR, you can create your own custom attributes as well. To write a custom attribute, start by deriving a class from the CLR's Attribute class:

```
[AttributeUsage(AttributeTargets.Class | AttributeTargets.Method)]
public class MyCustomAttribute : Attribute
{
    private string mDescription;

    public MyCustomAttribute(string Description)
    {
        mDescription = Description;
    }

    public string Description
    {
        get {return mDescription;}
    }
}
```

As you can see, this looks like any other class definition, except for the fact that there is an AttributeUsage attribute applied to our custom attribute class! AttributeUsage allows you to specify the items your custom attribute can be applied to. The CLR defines the AttributeTargets enumeration that lists all the possible items. The example also uses the bitwise "or" operator (|) to combine the Class and Field targets (this only works because the AttributeTargets enumeration is decorated with the Flags attribute—I told you attributes were everywhere). Therefore, MyCustomAttribute is only applicable to class and method items.

The following code example shows this custom attribute in action.

```
[MyCustom("This is yet another car class")]
public class Car
{
    // Uncomment line below to get compile error.
    //[MyCustom("Can't apply to a field")]
    private string mColor;

    [MyCustom("Apply to a method")]
    public int Accelerate()
    { ... }
}
```

Reflecting upon Reflection

Now you may be wondering what the point is. After all, the built-in attributes affect runtime and compiler behavior. The value of that is obvious. But what do custom attributes accomplish? To answer that question, we need take a bit of a philosophical turn and cover another .NET concept called *reflection*. Let's take a moment to define this term, but if you are patient, I will tie it back to the question on the utility of custom attributes.

As Descartes said, "I think, therefore I am," .NET assemblies say, "I have metadata, therefore I am." Recall that assemblies fully describe themselves, down to each class, each method, and each private field declared within. ILDasm presents this metadata in a graphical way that is easy to digest and navigate for humans. Wouldn't it be nice if you could access this type information from one of your own running programs? In fact, you can, and this process is called reflection. Through reflection, you can discover all the types defined within an assembly at runtime. Given any one of those types, you can list all of the properties, fields, and methods it defines. Given any method, you can list each of the method parameters. Given any parameter … well, you get the idea.

The key class in reflection is System.Type. This is your window into the assembly metadata. It is an abstract class, so you will never directly create an instance with new. Instead, C# provides a typeof operator that constructs the appropriate Type object given a type name. You can also grab a Type object by calling an object's GetType method (inherited from System.Object), or you can invoke the static GetType method on the Type class itself. The following code demonstrates all of these techniques.

```
// The many ways of getting a Type object ...
Type t;

// Use the typeof operator
t = typeof(SimpleMath);

// Use the GetType method inherited from Object
t = new SimpleMath().GetType();

// Use the static Type.GetType method.
// String format: "<namespace>.<classname>, <assemblyname>"
t = Type.GetType("MathLibrary.SimpleMath, MathLibrary");
```

Once you have a Type object, you can use it to invoke the GetMethods method, which retrieves an array of MethodInfo objects. Each MethodInfo object contains metadata for a method in the class. The following code demonstrates how to reflect over the methods of a type. Figure 2-25 shows the output.

```
t = typeof(SimpleMath);

foreach (MethodInfo mi in t.GetMethods())
{
    Console.WriteLine(mi.ToString());
}
```

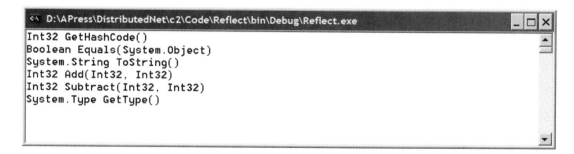

Figure 2-25. *Reflecting over the* SimpleMath *class*

You have likely already guessed that the Type class also implements methods such as GetProperties, GetFields, GetConstructors, and so on, that work exactly like GetMethods.

The Type class also implements a GetCustomAttributes method, which brings us back to the question that prompted this discussion about reflection—what do custom attributes accomplish? The answer: almost anything you can imagine. The catch is that custom attributes are useful only to the extent that a client reflects over the type and takes special action based on the presence and settings of any custom attributes. For example, the following code reflects over the Car class as defined in the earlier attribute discussion and searches for the MyCustomAttribute attribute.

```
class MyCustomAttributeDriver
{
    static void Main(string[] args)
    {
        // Process the attributes applied to the class. Although the function
        // takes a MemberInfo arg, this still works because Type derives from
        /// the MemberInfo class.
        ProcessCustomAttributes(typeof(Car));

        // Process the attributes applied to all members in the Car class
        foreach (MemberInfo mi in typeof(Car).GetMembers())
        {
            ProcessCustomAttributes(mi);
        }

        Console.ReadLine();
    }

    // Process all the custom attributes on any given member.
    private static void ProcessCustomAttributes(MemberInfo info)
    {
        MyCustomAttribute myAttr;
        foreach (Attribute a in info.GetCustomAttributes(false))
        {
            // Is the attribute of type MyCustomAttribute?
            if ((myAttr = a as MyCustomAttribute) != null)
            {
                Console.WriteLine(myAttr.Description);
            }
        }
    }
} // MyCustomAttributeDriver
```

In the preceding example, the ProcessCustomAttributes function contains the important logic. Given a MemberInfo instance, the function enumerates all of the attributes applied to the member. For each attribute, it determines if it is of type

MyCustomAttribute. If so, then it writes the Description property to the console window.

Looking within the Main function, you might be surprised at this line:

```
ProcessCustomAttributes(typeof(Car));
```

The typeof operator returns a Type object, but the ProcessCustomAttributes function takes a MemberInfo parameter. How does this compile? Actually, Type derives from MemberInfo, therefore you can pass a Type instance into a MemberInfo parameter.

Attributes and Reflection in Perspective

Granted, the simple example given earlier probably does little to convince you that attributes are the "next big thing." Unfortunately, in an overview chapter, I cannot possibly do justice to the power of attributes and reflection. However, imagine that your application checks for a custom Persistence attribute and, if found, saves the object to a database. This Persistence attribute may even define the table name. Or imagine a custom error logging routine that checks for a DeveloperInfo attribute and displays the name and phone number of the programmer responsible for maintaining the class that caused the error. The possibilities are endless.

If you are still not convinced, understand that throughout the rest of the book you will see many CLR attributes and a few custom attributes applied to various types, demonstrating more concrete examples of attribute usage. For now, just imagine. As John Lennon said, "It's easy if you try."

Understanding Garbage Collection

The problem of how to efficiently manage resources has plagued computer programmers from the beginning. Once a program allocates a resource (memory, file handle, transaction lock, etc.), how can the system ensure that the program also deallocates the resource in a timely fashion for other programs to use?

Different languages have different philosophies in regards to resource management. C++, for example, puts the entire burden on the programmer, who must explicitly call the delete operator to free an object. While this is very efficient, any small programming mistake can easily cause a memory leak. These types of bugs are extremely difficult to find. Visual Basic leverages COM for its memory management. COM uses reference counting to track object usage, and automatically frees objects when their reference count goes to zero.

One of the most fundamental, yet controversial, shifts in .NET is the implementation of garbage collection for resource management. This replaces the reference counting mechanism employed in COM. In most of your day-to-day programming tasks, garbage collection will work transparently, cleaning up unused objects whenever necessary. However, there are a few situations where the mechanics of garbage collection need to be clearly understood.

Reference Counting vs. Garbage Collection

COM developers are familiar with the concept of reference counting for resource management. With reference counting, each object is responsible for maintaining a count of all references to the object. When a new reference is directed to the object, it increments the reference count. When a reference is dropped, the object decrements the reference count. The object actually destroys itself when the reference count goes to zero.

Depending on the development tool, the previous process can be automatic or manual. For example, in Visual Basic all reference counting is completely transparent. However, in C++, clients that reference a COM object have to explicitly call the Release method of the IUnknown interface to decrement the reference count.

Reference Counting Advantages

Reference counting provides three key benefits:

- **Deterministic Finalization.** When an object's reference count goes to zero, the next action on that thread of execution is to destroy the object and any consumed resources. This is called deterministic finalization because you can predict exactly when the object will be destroyed (that is, finalized).

- **Resource Sharing.** References to objects can be safely passed to other parts of the program. The reference counting contract simply requires that a client call the object's Release method when it is finished using the object. In Visual Basic (prior to .NET), this happens automatically when an object reference variable goes out of scope. This resource sharing benefit actually derives from the one described next.

- **Lifetime Encapsulation.** The object itself is responsible for maintaining the object reference count. When the last client has released the object, it will destroy itself. This way, any given client does not need to be concerned about whether it holds the final reference to the object, or just one of many references.

Reference Counting Disadvantages

So far, reference counting seems like a good solution. Then why does .NET use garbage collection instead? The answer lies in reference counting's disadvantages.

- **Circular References.** The situation might arise where object A contains a reference to object B, and object B contains a reference to object A. Without some outside interference, this circular reference cannot be broken, and these objects, along with their allocated resources, will persist for the lifetime of the application.

- **Thread Safety.** The reference counting mechanism sounds very straight-forward until you consider what happens if multiple threads are sharing an object. To handle this, the object must wrap the reference count increment and decrement operations with special Windows API calls to ensure each operation and corresponding test proceed atomically. Otherwise, due to unpredictable context switches, the reference count could get out of synch. The need for safely incrementing and decrementing reference counts in the face of multiple threads adds considerable overhead to the extremely common task of assigning two object references.

Taken together, these two disadvantages make reference counting a poor choice as a general solution for resource management. For example, prior to .NET, Visual Basic used reference counting for all objects. However, to avoid the overhead of thread safe reference counting, a Visual Basic object had to live in a single threaded context, which bound an object to the thread where it was created. In other words, Visual Basic objects exhibited thread affinity. Therefore, a Visual Basic object could not participate in COM+ object pooling, nor could it be stored in any machine-wide cache (like the ASP Session object) without causing significant scalability issues.

In a typical C++ program, only a few objects at the application boundaries are COM objects and therefore reference counted. The rest of the objects require manual resource management. Therefore, the overhead of thread safe reference counting is isolated to a small portion of the application. However, manual resource management, although efficient, is highly prone to programmer error, which usually results in the dreaded memory leak.

Why Garbage Collection?

Garbage collection provides automatic resource management without suffering the reference counting disadvantages listed earlier. The .NET garbage collector can detect circular references and clean up the objects correctly. Furthermore, since reference counting is not used, garbage collected objects perform fine in multithreaded applications. However, garbage collection cannot provide deterministic finalization. In addition, to provide lifetime encapsulation and resource sharing, you have to implement your own custom reference counting.

For C++ developers moving to C#, garbage collection is a huge win. Manual memory management, and all its associated bugs and memory leaks, fades away like a bad dream. Those who exclusively worked with, or developed, COM components can also benefit. .NET object clients no longer need to call `Release` when finished using an object, and developers no longer need to keep watch for circular references.

For VB developers moving to VB .NET or C#, the picture is not as rosy. Since all VB objects were reference counted and VB automatically called `Release` when needed, garbage collection provides few apparent benefits. And some have argued that, due to its nondeterministic behavior, garbage collection is inferior to VB's reference counting. Ultimately, a VB developer's opinion is typically influenced by how critical he or she feels multithreading and object pooling is, and how many times he or she has been burned by a circular-reference bug.

Garbage Collection Internals

For the most part, you do not need to be concerned about how garbage collection works. But like me, you probably have a hard time accepting that you can just allocate an object and not have to worry about deallocating it when finished. And, like me, you might have concerns about how garbage collection impacts performance. Understanding how it really works can help ease your troubled mind.

First off, the garbage collector only runs when it has to. The runtime makes this determination based on a variety of factors, the primary one being how full the managed heap is. It also considers current thread activity to ensure it is safe to stop the threads in order to run the garbage collector. Yes, you read that correctly. When the garbage collector executes, the runtime pauses all threads in the application. The reason will become clear in a moment.

Once the garbage collector starts, it locates the application "root" references. These are object references that are global, static, or allocated on the thread stack (that is, a local variable reference). The garbage collector then investigates each root object, searching for reference data members. Next, it investigates each of these member objects, searching for more reference members, and so on. As it performs this process, the garbage collector records each object it visits in a graph. Therefore, it can tell if it has already visited a referred object and will not attempt to again. If this were not true, a circular reference would put the garbage collector into an infinite loop!

When finished, the resulting graph represents the "reachable" objects in the application. Armed with this information, the garbage collector can compare this graph against the objects actually allocated on the managed heap. When it discovers an object on the manage heap that has not been graphed (that is, it is unreachable), one of two things occur. If the object does not implement a `Finalize` method, the garbage collector immediately destroys the object and reclaims the memory. If the object implements `Finalize`, then the runtime places a reference to the object in an internal structure called the *freachable* queue. We will get to that scenario in a moment.

After the garbage collector finishes clearing out the unused objects, the managed heap will have gaps between surviving objects where each unreachable object was. To promote faster heap allocation, the garbage collector compacts the entire managed heap, thus removing all the empty gaps. Of course, this means that it must move surviving objects within the heap and update all references in the application to reflect their new location. This is the reason why the runtime must pause all the threads in the application while the garbage collector runs.

As mentioned earlier, the garbage collector handles objects that implement `Finalize` much differently. When it determines that such an object is unreachable, the garbage collector adds a reference to the object in the freachable queue. In essence, this makes a previously unreachable object reachable again. In other words, the object is resurrected, but its afterlife serves a limited purpose. After the garbage collector finishes cleaning up the unreachable objects, it starts another thread that calls `Finalize` on each of the references in the freachable queue, and then clears the queue. Finally, on the *next* garbage collection, the finalized objects are removed from the manage heap.

Implementing the Finalize Method

As you can see, if an object implements the `Finalize` method, it causes far more garbage collection overhead. These objects also take longer to allocate, because when the runtime allocates a finalizable object, it places a pointer to the object in an internal data structure called the finalization queue. For these reasons, you should try to create objects that do not require finalization.

Of course, that is not always possible, but it might be far more frequent than you think. The whole point of a finalizer is to allow the object to clean up resources it has allocated during its lifetime. For example, it may have created other objects, or opened files, or grabbed a database connection, and so on. Just as garbage collection relieves you from explicitly freeing the resources you allocate, it relieves objects of the same. As long as an object only contains managed (that is, garbage-collected) resources, there is no reason for it to implement `Finalize`. It is only when you venture into the realm of allocating unmanaged resources that `Finalize` becomes mandatory. Typically, these will consist of OS resources you accessed by circumventing the CLR and calling a Windows API function directly. Remember, the CLR wraps a large part of the Windows API with managed classes, so there should be few cases where this is required.

The following example shows the C# syntax for a finalizer.

```
class SimpleMath
{
    ~SimpleMath()
    {
        // Finalization code here
    }
}
```

This syntax should look very familiar to C++ programmers, because C++ uses the same syntax to declare destructors. In fact, C# documentation refers to this as a destructor. I think that is unfortunate, because a C++ destructor and a finalizer are very different. First, C++ programmers routinely implement destructors on nearly every class they write. In C#, this practice can devastate garbage collection performance for the reasons given earlier. Second, in C++ destructors run deterministically: either when a stack-allocated object falls out of scope, or when you explicitly free a heap-allocated object via the delete operator. On the other hand, C# destructors run nondeterministically; you never know when the garbage collector will actually run the destructor. So while the C# destructor may look exactly like a C++ destructor, it really is best to think of them as completely different. In fact, the C# destructor actually resolves to the IL equivalent of the following:

```
protected override void Finalize()
{
    try
    {
        // Finalization code here
    }
    finally
    {
        base.Finalize();
    }
}
```

However, do try to write this C# code yourself instead of using the destructor syntax. If you do, the C# compiler issues an error, telling you to use destructor syntax instead.

In spite of the potential confusion it may cause C++ developers, I will use the destructor terminology to describe the C# finalize mechanism to remain consistent with Microsoft C# documentation. When in Rome …

Implementing the IDisposable Interface

Unlike reference counting, garbage collection only guarantees that it will finalize an unused object at some future time. What is the impact of this nondeterministic finalization behavior? Imagine that you write an object that allocates scarce resources during its lifetime. By "scarce resources," I mean resources such as files opened for exclusive access, handles to window objects, and database connections. As a good programmer, you would implement the object's destructor to free all acquired resources. However, the garbage collector only runs periodically. Therefore, the object could sit unused for a long period before the garbage collector executes its destructor and destroys the object. In the meantime, all those scarce resources are also idle.

Therefore, when an object must allocate scarce resources during its lifetime, then it should expose a public teardown method that the client can explicitly call to release the object as soon as possible. Microsoft recommends that you call this method Dispose. In fact, to help formalize this pattern, the CLR contains an interface called IDisposable:

```
public interface IDisposable
{
   void Dispose();
}
```

Even if a class implements IDisposable, it is still a good idea in most cases to provide a destructor. This acts as a safety net just in case the client fails to call Dispose to tear down the object (and this *will* happen). The ResourceWrapper class shown in the following example demonstrates the implementation pattern.

```
public class ResourceWrapper : IDisposable
{
   public void Dispose()
   {
      // 1. Call Dispose on contained disposable objects
      // 2. Free any contained unmanaged resources
      // 3. Suppress finalization as shown below:
      GC.SuppressFinalize(this);
   }
   ~ResourceWrapper()
   {
      // 1. Free any contained unmanaged resources
      // 2. Do NOT call Dispose on contained managed objects
   }
}
```

Here is a detailed description of each Dispose step:

1. **Call Dispose on any contained managed object.** If the object allocates other disposable objects, then it should call Dispose on each one.

2. **Free any contained unmanaged resources.** If the object allocates resources that are not garbage collected, then it should free those resources using the appropriate mechanism.

3. **Suppress finalization.** Once Dispose runs, the garbage collector no longer needs to finalize the object. To improve garbage collection performance and to ensure that the object does not attempt to free a resource twice, you should call the GC.SuppressFinalize method as shown earlier. This will prevent the garbage collector from executing the provided destructor.

You might be wondering about step 2 in the destructor. Why wouldn't you call Dispose on contained managed resources? The answer, once again, lies in the non-deterministic nature of garbage collection. Not only is the time of garbage collection unpredictable, so is the order of garbage collection. In other words, it is very likely that the contained managed objects have already been garbage collected by the time this destructor runs, and trying to invoke a method on a destroyed object rightly causes an exception. For this reason, it is critical that you never touch contained managed objects from within a destructor; they may no longer exist.

Using Disposable Objects

At first glance, using a disposable object seems straightforward. First, you create it, then you use it, and when finished you call Dispose. For example:

```
// How NOT to use a disposable object.
public void SomeFunction()
{
    ResourceWrapper rw = new ResourceWrapper();

    // Use the resource wrapper object.
    // What if an exception happened?

    // When finished, dispose of the object
    rw.Dispose();
}
```

The problem with the preceding code is that it does not consider the effect of an exception. If an exception occurs while using the object, execution is passed to the nearest try block, skipping the call to Dispose and all the timely resource freeing logic implemented within. The solution, then, is to place the Dispose call within the finally portion of a try block. For example, here is the correct way to use the disposable object:

```
public void SomeFunction()
{
   ResourceWrapper rw = new ResourceWrapper();
   try
   {
      // use the resource wrapper object
   }
   finally
   {
      // Now dispose is called, guaranteed.
      rw.Dispose();
   }
}
```

Using Using (Again)

Placing the call to Dispose within the finally block ensures the method is called even in the event of an exception. However, writing exception handling code just to use a disposable object can quickly become unwieldy, so C# offers a shortcut: the using keyword. The following example shows how the preceding code can be rewritten with the using keyword:

```
public void SomeFunction()
{
   using (ResourceWrapper rw = new ResourceWrapper())
   {
      // Use the resource wrapper object
   } // Dispose is called on resource wrapper object
}
```

Unfortunately, C# is following its C++ ancestry here in overloading the meaning of a keyword. In one context, using provides a shortcut for specifying namespaces, and in another it provides a special scope for a specified disposable object. When execution leaves this scope, whether normally or by exception, the object's Dispose method will be called. Guaranteed.

> **NOTE** *The expression after the* using *keyword must return an object that implements the* IDisposable *interface.*

Garbage Collection in Perspective

If you are a veteran distributed COM(+) developer you might be panicking after reading this section. One of the key tenets of programming scalable systems states that you should return scarce resources to the available pool as quickly as possible. Although the Dispose pattern accomplishes this, it places the burden of calling Dispose on the client. And seasoned distributed developers know that clients cannot be trusted to release resources.

Before getting too worried, consider the next couple of points. First, understand that in the distributed world, many of the resource-intensive objects you create are stateless, meaning that an object only lives for the duration of a method call. Therefore, it can only allocate and consume resources for the duration of the method call. Second, client-activated remote objects have another object lifetime model built on top of garbage collection called *leased-based* object lifetime. I will describe this mechanism in more detail in the next chapter. Suffice to say for now that it proves to be a far more effective solution for distributed resource management than the reference counting schemes of yore.

Serialization

The term *serialization* refers to the process of converting the current state of an object into a stream of bytes. The term *deserialization* refers to the reverse process, converting a stream of bytes into an object. While this may not sound too interesting at first, there are many important reasons to use serialization. Once you serialize an object, those bytes can be stored in a file, in a database, in memory—almost anywhere. When you wish to retrieve the object, you simply deserialize it from its storage location. This form of object persistence is critical in stateless Web applications because it allows important state information to persist across user requests.

Serialization also allows objects to cross application boundaries. You can pass the stream of bytes representing the object state over a network and deserialize it into a matching object on the other side. In essence, serialization allows an object to be passed "by value" to another application. The .NET Remoting Framework (discussed in Chapter 3) uses serialization extensively to marshal object data across processes.

Serialization is not a new concept introduced in .NET. Windows programmers have been working with various forms of serialization: the archive mechanism in MFC, the `PropertyBag` in Visual Basic, and the `IPersistStream` interface in COM. What makes .NET serialization different from all of these? In a word, simplicity. Before .NET, serialization was a manual proposition. It was up to you, the class designer, to implement the serialization for the class, and while it was not necessarily a difficult thing to implement, it was a dull, time consuming task. In .NET, the process is completely automatic. All you have to do is mark a class as serializable using—what else—the `Serializable` attribute. The runtime does the rest.

How does .NET runtime pull off this great trick? With mirrors, of course. Or more precisely, with *reflection*. Recall that an assembly is chock full of self-describing data known as metadata. The assembly metadata fully describes each type in the assembly, including information regarding every private field contained within the type. Through the process of reflection, the runtime can investigate this metadata and use it to determine how a class must be serialized.

Using the Serializable Attribute

As mentioned, if you want to allow the runtime to serialize your object, you must mark the class using the `Serializable` attribute. The following code defines two classes marked with the `Serializable` attribute.

```
[Serializable]
public class Car
{
    private string mColor;
    private int mTopSpeed;

    // Reference to another object
    private Radio mRadio;

    [NonSerialized]  // Runtime will not serialize this field
    private string mNickName;

    public Car(string nickName, int topSpeed, string color)
    {
        mNickName = nickName;
        mTopSpeed = topSpeed;
        mColor = color;
        mRadio = new Radio();
    }
}
```

```
[Serializable]
public class Radio
{
    private int mVolume = 5;
}
```

As you can see, the Car class' mNickName field is marked with the NonSerialized attribute. This directs the runtime to skip the item when serializing. All other instance fields, however, participate in the serialization. Also, note that the mRadio field is a reference to another object, which means the runtime must serialize it too. In fact, when told to serialize an object, the runtime builds an object graph (like the garbage collector) using the given object as the root. All objects in the graph must also be serializable or the runtime will raise an exception.

The following code demonstrates how to serialize a Car object into a file.

```
static void Main(string[] args)
{
    Car myCar =  new Car("Christine", 150, "Red");
    FileStream mySoapFile = File.Create("Car.txt");

    // Use a SOAP formatter object to serialize the object.
    new SoapFormatter().Serialize(mySoapFile, myCar);

    mySoapFile.Close();
}
```

The runtime does not control the actual format of the serialized data. Instead, a special formatter object is responsible for formatting the serialized output. The .NET Framework comes with two formatters built in: a SOAP formatter and a binary formatter. In the preceding code, the SoapFormatter object serializes the object into a SOAP message and sends it to the specified stream. Figure 2-26 shows the contents of the Car.txt file after this code executes.

If you look closely at Figure 2-26, you can easily see the how SOAP represents each object and its data members. This readability comes at a cost though—size. The binary formatter uses a far more compact schema. This may be important to you if you need to send objects across the network and are more concerned with conserving network bandwidth than with readability.

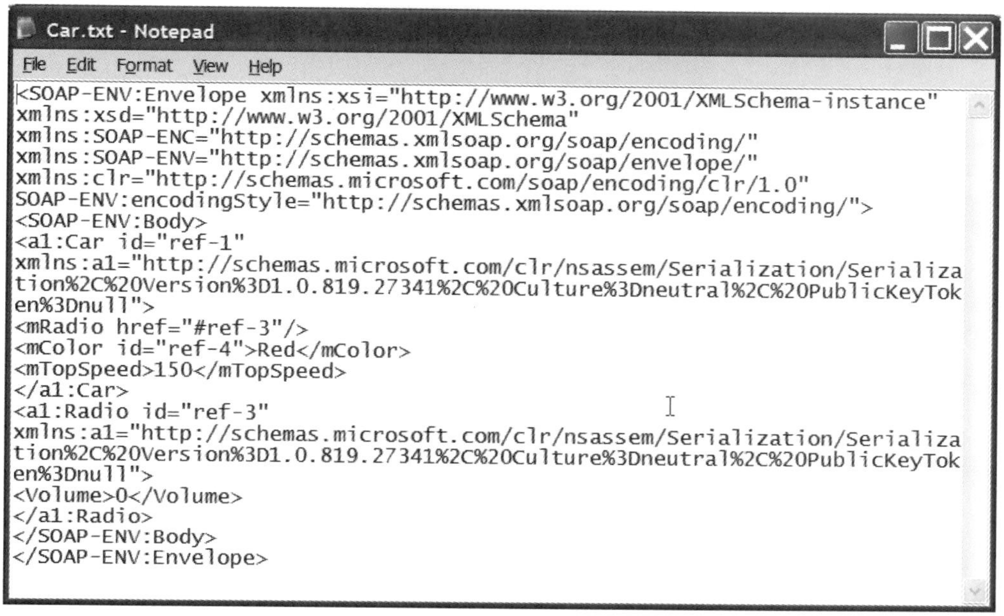


```
<SOAP-ENV:Envelope xmlns:xsi="http://www.w3.org/2001/XMLSchema-instance"
xmlns:xsd="http://www.w3.org/2001/XMLSchema"
xmlns:SOAP-ENC="http://schemas.xmlsoap.org/soap/encoding/"
xmlns:SOAP-ENV="http://schemas.xmlsoap.org/soap/envelope/"
xmlns:clr="http://schemas.microsoft.com/soap/encoding/clr/1.0"
SOAP-ENV:encodingStyle="http://schemas.xmlsoap.org/soap/encoding/">
<SOAP-ENV:Body>
<a1:Car id="ref-1"
xmlns:a1="http://schemas.microsoft.com/clr/nsassem/Serialization/Serializa
tion%2C%20Version%3D1.0.819.27341%2C%20Culture%3Dneutral%2C%20PublicKeyTok
en%3Dnull">
<mRadio href="#ref-3"/>
<mColor id="ref-4">Red</mColor>
<mTopSpeed>150</mTopSpeed>
</a1:Car>
<a1:Radio id="ref-3"
xmlns:a1="http://schemas.microsoft.com/clr/nsassem/Serialization/Serializa
tion%2C%20Version%3D1.0.819.27341%2C%20Culture%3Dneutral%2C%20PublicKeyTok
en%3Dnull">
<Volume>0</Volume>
</a1:Radio>
</SOAP-ENV:Body>
</SOAP-ENV:Envelope>
```


Figure 2-26. The Car object serialized using the SOAP formatter

To read this object back into memory, you simply call the `SoapFormatter.Deserialize` method:

```
static void Rehydrate()
{
   FileStream mySoapFile = File.Open("Car.txt", FileMode.Open);

   Car myCar = (Car) new SoapFormatter().Deserialize(mySoapFile);

   mySoapFile.Close();
}
```

ISerializable and Formatters

In the rare case where you need more functionality than that provided by the default serialization mechanism, you can implement the `ISerializable` interface. This provides a much finer grain of control over exactly what data will be serialized. However, it does not provide any control over the format of the data. For this, you need to extend the `Formatter` class.

The following code demonstrates how to implement the ISerializable interface.

```
[Serializable]
public class Car : ISerializable
{
    private string mColor;
    static private int mTopSpeed;
    private Radio mRadio;

    [NonSerialized]
    private string mNickName;

    // Required by the ISerializable interface
    public void GetObjectData(SerializationInfo info, StreamingContext context)
    {
        info.AddValue("mColor", mColor);
        info.AddValue("mTopSpeed", mTopSpeed);
        info.AddValue("mRadio", mRadio);
    }

    // This contructor is required to deserialize the object
    private Car(SerializationInfo info, StreamingContext context)
    {
        mTopSpeed = info.GetInt32("mTopSpeed");
        mColor = info.GetString("mColor");
        mRadio = (Radio) info.GetValue("mRadio", typeof(Radio));
    }
. . .
}
```

When the runtime serializes the object, it will call the ISerializable.GetObjectData method and pass in a SerializationInfo object and a StreamingContext structure. The SerializationInfo object provides an AddValue method, which allows you to store a value in the object with an associated name. VB 6.0 programmers may recognize the SerializationInfo object as another incarnation of the PropertyBag. However, unlike the PropertyBag, which only stored variants, the SerializationInfo object can store strongly typed data. AddValue is overloaded several times to allow adding any of the primitive CLR types. You can investigate the contents of the incoming StreamingContext structure to determine exactly what the catalyst of this serialization process was. For example, you may wish to serialize the object differently if it is being passed to another process as the following code demonstrates:

```
public void GetObjectData(SerializationInfo info, StreamingContext context)
{
    // If serializing across process, then skip the radio object
    if (context.State != StreamingContextStates.CrossProcess)
    {
        mRadio = (Radio) info.GetValue("mRadio", typeof(Radio));
    }
    info.AddValue("mColor", mColor);
    info.AddValue("mTopSpeed", mTopSpeed);
}
```

This example investigates the State field of the incoming StreamingContext structure. This enumeration specifies the source or destination of the serialized object. If it is equal to StreamingContextStates.CrossProcess, the destination is another process on the same machine. In that case, the code does not serialize the contained Radio object.

Implementing the ISerializable interface allows you to control *what* is serialized. To control *how* the object is serialized, you must extend the Formatter class. This requires that you implement several methods, including Serialize, Deserialize, WriteBoolean, WriteByte, WriteArray, and much more. This is a bit more in-depth than we need to go, so I'll leave it as an exercise for the curious reader.

Summary

The goal of this chapter was to discuss the fundamental .NET concepts that are critical to distributed programming. These include the following:

- .NET achieves language and platform interoperability by establishing the Common Type System (CTS) and the Common Language Specification (CLS).

- The common language runtime (CLR) represents an implementation of the CTS. It is an object-oriented wrapper around the Windows operating system and a runtime environment for .NET programs.

- A .NET assembly represents a versionable unit of deployment. It provides a container for all the types defined within. Strong-named assemblies can be used by a single application (a private assembly) or you can install them in the Global Assembly Cache to be used by many applications (a shared assembly).

- Attributes allow you to provide additional information about a code item. Some attributes are recognized by the compiler and runtime and direct them to take special action with the code item. Custom attributes are attributes you create and are useful only if they are detected and acted upon through reflection.

- .NET uses garbage collection for resource management, replacing the notion of reference counting used in COM. Garbage collection does not suffer from circular reference issues or performance issues in multithreaded environments. However, unlike reference counting, it cannot provide deterministic finalization.

- Through reflection, .NET provides automatic type serialization. The only requirement is that you apply the `Serializable` attribute to the types that you wish to be serialized by the runtime. You can take control over the serialization process by implementing the `ISerializable` interface.

Of course, the .NET universe is much too large to cover in a single chapter, but I hope that this chapter has given you the knowledge required to tackle the rest of the book.

CHAPTER 3

Introduction to .NET Remoting

"It's such a fine line between stupid and clever."

—David St. Hubbins (*This is Spinal Tap*)
speaking on the importance of application boundaries.

HONESTLY, I REALLY TRIED to avoid writing this chapter. Here you are three chapters into the book and all of it so far has been "overview." You may be wondering if we are ever going to see a "detail" chapter and I don't blame you. Unfortunately, there is no practically way to dive into the details of implementing distributed applications using .NET Remoting without first describing some key terms and concepts from thirty thousand feet. Luckily, this technology is exciting and cool even in overview form. And in the next chapter we will shake hands with the devil (in the details).

What Is Remoting?

Most modern operating systems, including the various versions of Windows, isolate running applications within the confines of a process. This keeps a misbehaving application, whether by accident or by design, from tampering with the data and code in other applications. Furthermore, if an application crashes, the process prevents the crash from affecting any other applications. A process achieves this isolation by placing a protective boundary around its memory and resources. Other processes cannot see or use these resources unless they are exposed programmatically via Interprocess Communication (IPC) channels such as named pipes or sockets.

Process isolation is both a boon and a bane for distributed programmers. On one hand, it keeps important parts of the distributed application running even while others have failed. On the other hand, it adds significant overhead and complexity to the task of sharing information and services between applications—a key part of distributed programming. Regarding the issue of overhead, nothing can make a cross-process action perform as well as an in-process action. We simply have to pay the price for isolation and safety. Over the years, however, a few technologies have evolved that abstract away many (but by no means all) of the complexities involved when using IPC to share data and resources across processes. In its most general sense, the term *remoting* refers to the use of these technologies to invoke methods on and share data with objects running in another process.

COM is one of these technologies. A key feature of COM is its notion of *location transparency*, which means that the code you write to activate and use an object in the current process (that is, a local object) is the same code used to activate and use an object in a different process (that is, a remote object). Distributed COM (DCOM) extended this notion to include objects running in a different process on a different machine. COM uses various registry settings to resolve the location of a requested object. Therefore, connecting to a remote object is an issue of configuration, rather than an issue of code.

The .NET Remoting model builds on these and other ideas borrowed from COM. The underlying implementation, however, is completely different. For example, remote object information can reside in the application configuration file rather than the system registry. .NET Remoting also provides several points of extensibility, allowing .NET programmers from any language to take full control over the details of remoting, from object serialization to the use of network protocols. Finally, .NET introduces another application boundary, called *application domains*, which run within a process.

The existence of application domains changes the general definition of remoting, at least as it applies to the .NET universe. In .NET, the primary application boundary is not a process but an application domain. Therefore, .NET Remoting refers to the use of runtime services to invoke methods on and share data between objects running in separate application domains.

Understanding Application Domains

Processes are effective in isolating applications, but they suffer from a few shortcomings. First, a process is a very low-level operating system construct; the exact behavior of a process is determined by the operating system. Thus, a Windows 2000 process is very different from a Unix process. Second, creating and managing processes are expensive tasks in terms of computer resources. Finally, there are times when the isolation provided by a process is required, but not at the cost of the extra overhead associated with IPC mechanisms.

.NET addresses these problems by introducing the application domain. An application domain is the .NET runtime's representation of a *logical* process. Any physical operating system process can contain multiple application domains. Application domains provide the following benefits:

- Application domains hide the operating system details of a process. This allows .NET to be ported to a variety of operating systems.

- Application domains provide isolation. Applications running in separate domains cannot directly share global data, static data, objects, or other resources even though they may be running in the same process. Therefore, if one application domain fails, it does not affect the others in the same process.

- Application domains allow the .NET runtime to optimize communication between applications running in the same process where expensive IPC mechanisms are not required.

Since application domains are isolated, all .NET objects are bound within the application domain where they were created. When an object reference is passed across an application domain boundary, the object is said to be remoted.

Programming with Application Domains

The CLR's AppDomain class allows programs to interface with the application domain at runtime. The following code demonstrates a few things you can do with the AppDomain class.

```
static void Main(string[] args)
{
    // Grab a reference to the current domain
    AppDomain myDomain = AppDomain.CurrentDomain;

    // Show some info about our current app domain
    Console.WriteLine("Info about our current app domain ...");
    Console.WriteLine("  Hash Code = {0}", myDomain.GetHashCode());
    Console.WriteLine("  Friendly Name = {0}", myDomain.FriendlyName);
    Console.WriteLine("  App Base = {0}", myDomain.BaseDirectory);
    Console.WriteLine("  Probing paths = {0}", myDomain.RelativeSearchPath);

    // Create a new domain and assign the name "MathClient"
    AppDomain mathDomain = AppDomain.CreateDomain("MathClient");

    // Tell the domain to execute the MathClient assembly. This assumes
    // the assembly is in the same folder as the current applicaiton.
    mathDomain.ExecuteAssembly("MathClient.exe");
}
```

After displaying some general information about the current application domain, this code example creates a new application domain and assigns it the friendly name of "MathClient". It then calls ExecuteAssembly, passing in the name of the assembly to execute in the new domain. Before executing this code, let's make a few changes to the MathClient assembly so that it too displays information about the current application domain.

```
public class MathClient
{
    static void Main(string[] args)
    {
        Console.WriteLine();

        // Grab a reference to the current domain
        AppDomain myDomain = AppDomain.CurrentDomain;

        // Show some info about the math client app domain
        Console.WriteLine("Info about the math client app domain ...");
        Console.WriteLine("  Hash Code = {0}", myDomain.GetHashCode());
        Console.WriteLine("  Friendly Name = {0}", myDomain.FriendlyName);
        Console.WriteLine("  App Base = {0}", myDomain.BaseDirectory);
        Console.WriteLine();

        Console.WriteLine(" 5 + 3 = {0}",
        SimpleMath.Add(5,3));

        Console.WriteLine(" 5 - 3 = {0}",
        SimpleMath.Subtract(5,3));

        Console.ReadLine();
    }
}
```

Figure 3-1 shows the output when this code is executed. The fact that two different hash codes are displayed proves that the assemblies are running in separate application domains.

For the most part, only developers creating .NET runtime hosts, such as Internet Explorer or Internet Information Server, will need to work directly with application domains. However, keep in mind that application domains are the primary application boundary in .NET.

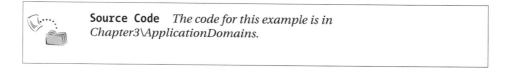

```
file:///D:/APress/DistributedNet/c3/Code/ApplicationDomains/bin/Debug/MathClient.EXE    _ □ ×

Info about our current app domain ...
  Hash Code = 1
  Friendly Name = ApplicationDomains.exe
  App Base = D:\APress\DistributedNet\c3\Code\ApplicationDomains\bin\Debug\

Info about the math client app domain ...
  Hash Code = 16
  Friendly Name = MathClient
  App Base = D:\APress\DistributedNet\c3\Code\ApplicationDomains\bin\Debug\

  5 + 3 = 8
  5 - 3 = 2
```

Figure 3-1. Loading and running an assembly in a separate application domain

> **Source Code**   *The code for this example is in
> Chapter3\ApplicationDomains.*

Understanding Context

In addition to application domains, .NET provides another type of application
boundary called a *context*. An application domain can contain many contexts, but
must have at least one called the *default context*. Contexts provide the following:

- An environment consisting of a set of properties shared by all objects
  residing within the context

- An interception boundary, such that the runtime can apply pre- and post-
  processing to all method calls from outside the context

- A home for objects with similar runtime requirements such as synchronization, thread affinity, or just-in-time activation

Figure 3-2 shows the relationships between processes, application domains,
and contexts.

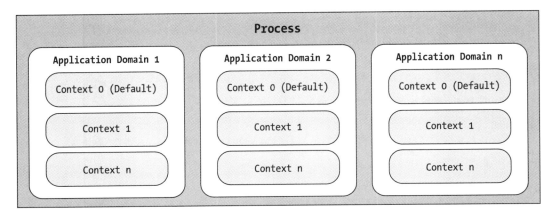

Figure 3-2. The process-to-application domain-to-context relationship

When the runtime creates an object, it investigates the object's context requirements and places it within a compatible context. If a compatible context does not exist, then the runtime creates one. Most objects have no specific context requirements, and therefore are created within the default context. These objects are called *context agile* because they can be accessed directly from anywhere within the application domain. Objects that do have context requirements are called *context bound* objects and must derive from the ContextBoundObject class.

Code executing outside of a context never holds a direct reference to the contained context bound objects. Instead, cross-context access to a context bound object is provided by a runtime-generated proxy that mimics the actual object. The proxy allows the runtime to intercept cross-context calls and apply any required pre- or post-processing. It also means that access to any context bound object incurs some overhead, so they should be used only when needed.

A Context Example: Synchronization

You define a type's context requirements by applying a special type of attribute known as a *context attribute*. One example of a context attribute is the SynchronizationAttribute class. When you apply this attribute to a class, the runtime ensures that only one thread at a time can access any instance of the class. To enforce this behavior, the runtime must create the object in a special context and intercept any incoming calls from outside the context. If a thread is currently executing within the context, the runtime forces all calls from other threads to wait until the thread exits. Consider the following code:

```
namespace SimpleContext
{
    using System.Runtime.Remoting.Contexts; // Synchronization attribute

    // A context bound class
    [Synchronization]
    public class MyContextBoundClass : ContextBoundObject
    { }

    // This is a context agile class
    public class MyAgileClass
    { }
}
```

This code example defines two classes. The first, called MyContextBoundClass, is context bound because it derives from ContextBoundObject. Also note that the class is adorned with the Synchronization attribute. Therefore, when the runtime creates an instance of this type, it will place the object within a synchronized context. The second class, called MyAgileClass, is context agile by virtue of the fact that it does not derive, either directly or indirectly, from ContextBoundObject.

The following example tests the behavior of these two new classes.

```
namespace SimpleContext
{
    using System;
    using System.Runtime.Remoting;          // RemotingServices class

    class SimpleContextMain
    {
        static void Main(string[] args)
        {
            MyContextBoundClass myBound = new MyContextBoundClass();
            MyAgileClass myAgile = new MyAgileClass();

            // Are they in or out of context?
            Console.WriteLine("\nIs myBound out of context? {0}",
                RemotingServices.IsObjectOutOfContext(myBound));

            Console.WriteLine("Is myAgile out of context? {0}",
                RemotingServices.IsObjectOutOfContext(myAgile));
```

```
        // Direct reference or proxy?
        Console.WriteLine("\nIs myBound a proxy? {0}",
            RemotingServices.IsTransparentProxy(myBound));

        Console.WriteLine("Is myAgile a proxy? {0}",
            RemotingServices.IsTransparentProxy(myAgile));

        Console.ReadLine();
    }
  }
} // namespace SimpleContext
```

In this example, the Main routine starts out by creating the context bound and the context agile objects. It continues by displaying whether each object is out of the current context and whether each object reference is a direct reference or a proxy. This is accomplished using a couple handy static methods provided by the RemotingServices class. The IsOutOfContext method returns true if the given object resides in a different context. The IsTransparentProxy method returns true if the given object reference is a proxy rather than a direct reference.

Figure 3-3 shows a graphical snapshot of the application at runtime. Note that the SimpleContextMain class holds a direct reference to the agile object, but only holds a reference to a proxy to the context bound object. This fact is reinforced by the application output shown in Figure 3-4.

 Source Code   *The code for this example is in Chapter3\SimpleContext.*

Application Domain
Context 0 (Default)
Context 1 (Synchronization)
myAgile
SimpleContextMain
Proxy to myBound
myBound

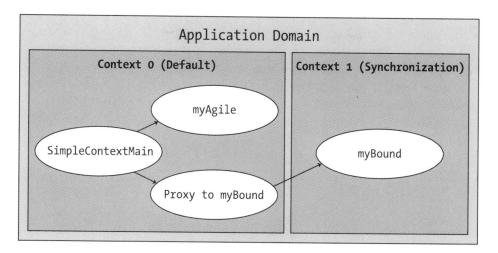

Figure 3-3. Snapshot of the SimpleContext application at runtime

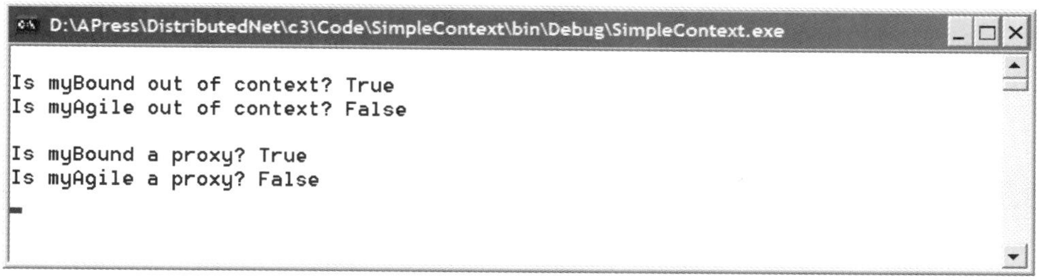

D:\APress\DistributedNet\c3\Code\SimpleContext\bin\Debug\SimpleContext.exe
Is myBound out of context? True
Is myAgile out of context? False
Is myBound a proxy? True
Is myAgile a proxy? False

Figure 3-4. The output from the SimpleContext application

Retrieving Context Information

You can grab a reference to the current executing context using the static
`Thread.CurrentContext` method. This returns a `Context` object, which you can use to
find various bits of information regarding the context. For example, the following
`DisplayContextInfo` function lists all the properties of the current context.

```
public class Diagnostics
{
   // Displays the context id and properties for the given context.
   public static void DisplayContextInfo()
   {
      Context ctx = Thread.CurrentContext;
      Console.WriteLine("   Properties for context id: {0}", ctx.ContextID);
      foreach(IContextProperty ctxProp in ctx.ContextProperties)
      {
         Console.WriteLine("      {0}", ctxProp.Name);
      }
   }
}
```

This example uses the `Context.ContextProperties` property to retrieve a collection
of all the properties applied to the context. Context properties have diverse implementations, but at the very least each must implement the `IContextProperty`
interface. This interface provides a `Name` property that is used to display the name
of the context property.

The following code example tests the `DisplayContextInfo` method by calling it
from two different contexts.

```
using System;
using System.Runtime.Remoting.Contexts; // Synchronization attribute
using System.Runtime.Remoting;          // RemotingServices class
using System.Threading;                 // Thread class

namespace DisplayContextInfo
{
   class DisplayContextInfoMain
   {
      static void Main(string[] args)
      {
         // Display the default context info
         Console.WriteLine("\n*** In Main *** ");
         Diagnostics.DisplayContextInfo();
```

```
        // Constructor displays synchronized context info
        MyContextBoundClass myBound = new MyContextBoundClass();

        Console.ReadLine();
    }
}

// A context bound class
[Synchronization]
public class MyContextBoundClass : ContextBoundObject
{
    public MyContextBoundClass()
    {
        Console.WriteLine("\n*** In MyContextBoundClass Constructor ***");
        Diagnostics.DisplayContextInfo();
    }
}
}
```

This example calls the `Diagnostic.DisplayContextInfo` method from within `Main` and a `MyContextBoundClass` constructor. Given that this constructor runs in a synchronized context, we would expect the output to list the synchronization context property. As Figure 3-5 shows, this is exactly what happens. The output also demonstrates that the `MyContextBoundClass` object lives within context 1, which defines two properties including a `Synchronization` property. However, the `Main` method executes with context 0, the default context.

 Source Code   *The code for this example is in Chapter3\DisplayContextInfo.*

```
D:\APress\DistributedNet\c3\Code\DisplayContextInfo\bin\Debug\DisplayContextInfo.exe

*** In Main ***
   Properties for context id: 0
      LeaseLifeTimeServiceProperty

*** In MyContextBoundClass Constructor ***
   Properties for context id: 1
      LeaseLifeTimeServiceProperty
      Synchronization
```

Figure 3-5. Discovering context properties at runtime

Context Agile Objects

A context agile class is exactly that—agile. Its members always execute within the caller's context. We can demonstrate this by adding a `DisplayContextInfo` method to `MyAgileClass` and invoking it from two different contexts. Here is the new `MyAgileClass` definition:

```
// This is a context agile class
public class MyAgileClass
{
    public void DisplayContextInfo()
    {
        Console.WriteLine("\n*** MyAgileClass.DisplayContextInfo() ***");
        Diagnostics.DisplayContextInfo();
    }
}
```

Next, we add a constructor to the `MyContextBoundClass` that invokes the `DisplayContextInfo` method on a given agile object. Here is the new MyContext-BoundClass definition:

```
// A context bound class
[Synchronization]
public class MyContextBoundClass : ContextBoundObject
{
    public MyContextBoundClass()
    {
        Console.WriteLine("\n*** MyContextBoundClass Constructor ***");
        Diagnostics.DisplayContextInfo();
    }

    // The " : this()" at the end calls the default constructor
    // before executing the code in this constructor.
    public MyContextBoundClass(MyAgileClass myAgile) : this()
    {
        // Display the given object's context info. Since this is an agile
        // object, it should be in the context bound object's context.
        myAgile.DisplayContextInfo();
    }
}
```

Finally, the `Main` method directly invokes the `MyAgileClass.DisplayContextInfo` method and then creates a `MyContextBoundClass` object using the new constructor. Here is the code:

```
class ContextAgileMain
{
    static void Main(string[] args)
    {
        MyAgileClass myAgile = new MyAgileClass();

        // Display myAgile's context info. Since this is an agile object,
        // it should be in the default context.
        myAgile.DisplayContextInfo();

        // Send myAgile into the context bound object.
        MyContextBoundClass myBound = new MyContextBoundClass(myAgile);

        Console.ReadLine();
    }
    // snip ...
}
```

In this example, the `Main` method, executing in context 0, invokes the `Display-ContextInfo` method on the `MyAgileClass` object. It also passes the agile object into a `MyContextBoundClass` constructor. The constructor, executing in context 1, invokes the `DisplayContextInfo` method on the agile object. The output (Figure 3-6) proves that the `MyAgileClass` object freely moves between the two contexts. Note that when called from `Main`, the output shows the agile object is executing within context 0. But when called from the context bound object, the output shows the object is executing within context 1. Figure 3-7 shows the logical layout of the application.

 Source Code   *The code for this example is in Chapter3\ContextAgile.*

The previous code examples are meant to demonstrate the behavior of the .NET context—not how you would use them in reality. For the most part, contexts work transparently, providing the runtime with an interception point necessary to apply special runtime services such as synchronization. From an academic viewpoint, contexts serve as a microcosm of what happens in a true remoting scenario in which calls are passed across application domains. In this case, calls are facilitated by a proxy object much like cross-context calls.

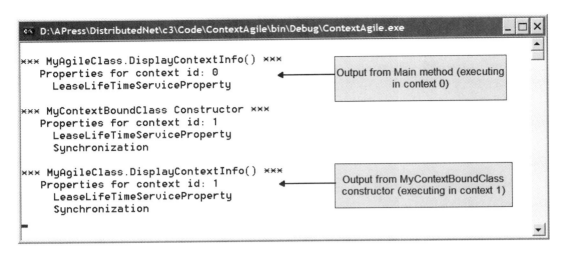

Figure 3-6. Calling a context agile object from two different contexts

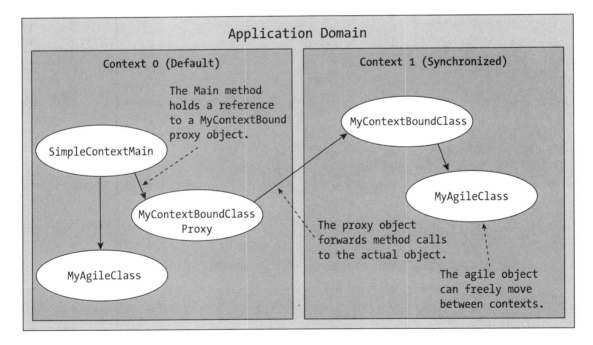

Figure 3-7. Agile objects execute within the caller's context.

Marshaling Objects

Now that you have seen what application boundaries exist in the .NET universe, it is time to address the different ways the runtime marshals objects—in other words, how it passes objects across the aforementioned application boundaries.

At a high level, .NET marshals objects in two different ways: marshal by value (MBV) and marshal by reference (MBR). Conceptually, these marshaling techniques are similar to the notion of passing a parameter by value vs. by reference, where a by value parameter is a copy of the original, and a by reference parameter is pointer to the original.

For example, without getting into too many remoting details (yet), let's say you were able to invoke the following method on an object running in a separate application domain:

```
public SomeClass GetAnObject()
{
    return new SomeClass();
}
```

If SomeClass were defined as a MBV type, then the method call returns a copy of the object to the caller. On the other hand, if SomeClass were defined as a MBR type, then the method call returns a "pointer" to the object, otherwise known as a proxy. Each technique is valid. Which one you choose depends on the intended use of the object.

Marshal By Value Objects

When marshaling by value, the runtime creates a copy of the remote object in the client's application domain by serializing the remote object and deserializing it on the client side. Of course, the runtime uses the same serialization mechanism described in the previous chapter. Therefore, the runtime will only marshal an object by value if you mark its class with the Serializable attribute as shown here:

```
[Serializable()]
public class MyMBVClass
{
    // Class implementation
}
```

MBV objects are extremely useful if an object primarily encapsulates data, for example, a customer object that contains first name, last name, e-mail address, and so on. This allows all the customer data to be copied to the client application domain, where it can be accessed and modified as a local object.

Marshal By Reference Objects

In many remoting scenarios, you will use objects that are marshaled by reference (MBR). MBR objects remain in the application domain where they were created. Clients invoke methods on MBR objects through a proxy that forwards the calls through the .NET Remoting plumbing to the remote object. By definition, MBR objects must derive either directly or indirectly from the `MarshalByRefObject` class as shown here:

```
public class MyMBRClass : MarshalByRefObject
{
    // Class implementation
}
```

Recall that context bound types also require a proxy for all out-of-context method calls. In fact, all such types derive from `ContextBoundObject`, which in turn derives from `MarshalByRefObject`. Therefore, all context bound types are MBR types.

The use of a MBR type is appropriate when its methods need to execute within a different application domain, process, or machine. In other words, MBR types allow you to distribute the processing. Continuing with the previous customer example, imagine a MBR `CustomerService` class that encapsulates standard customer data operations and business logic. The class could expose a `GetCustomerByEmail` method that returns a MBV customer data object. The following code demonstrates this idea:

```
// A MBV type that encapsulates the customer data.
[Serializable]
public class CustomerData
{
    private string mFirstName;
    private string mLastName;
    private string mEmail;
    // Etc.
}
```

```
// A MBR type that encapsulates customer data access
public class CustomerService : MarshalByRefObject
{
    public CustomerData GetCustomerByEmail(string email)
    {
        CustomerData custData = new CustomerData();
        // Lookup customer in DB and fill in CustomerData then return
        // it (by value) back to the caller.
        return custData;
    }
}
```

The following code demonstrates how a client might use these types.

```
class ClientMain
{
    static void Main(string[] args)
    {
        // Since CustomerService is MBR, this returns a proxy to the
        // remote object. Note: this is oversimplified. Later we will see the
        // exact mechanics for connecting to a remote MBR object.
        CustomerService custService = new CustomerService();

        // CustomerData is MBV, so this call returns a copy of the
        // remote object.
        CustomerData custData =
            custService.GetCustomerByEmail("hsimpson@atomic.com");

        // Use CustomerData ...
    }
}
```

Static Methods and Other Remoting Details

In most cases, the methods of an MBR object execute within the remote application domain. However, be aware of the following exceptions.

- **Static members.** Static methods always execute in the caller's application domain. Public static fields are always accessed via direct memory (not through property methods) and therefore cannot be accessed directly from outside the original application domain. Static fields can be accessed by instance methods since they do execute in the remote application domain.

- **Instance fields.** If the MBR object exposes public instance fields, then the runtime-generated proxy automatically defines property methods (that is, getters and setters) for field access on the remote object. In general, you should avoid exposing public instance fields because it violates the object oriented principle of encapsulation.

- `System.Object` **methods.** To improve performance, calls to methods inherited from `System.Object` are executed in the caller's application domain. However, if the MBR type overrides `Equals` (the instance version) or `ToString`, then these will be executed in the remote object's application domain. On the other hand, `GetHashCode`, the static version of `Equals`, and `MemberwiseClone` always execute in the caller's application domain.

Summarizing Marshaling and Context Agility

Already, we have discussed several ways to define a type that impacts how it is marshaled out of an application domain or context. So Table 3-1 provides a summary of your options and how they affect the runtime's marshaling behavior.

Table 3-1. Summary of Marshaling and Agility Options

Type	Base Class and Attributes	Description
Not Remotable	Not derived from `MarshalByRefObject`. Not decorated with `Serializable`.	This type cannot be marshaled out of an application domain. It is agile within a domain, so code in another context holds a direct reference. Use for types that must never be accessed from another domain.
Marshal By Value	Not derived from `MarshalByRefObject`. `Serializable`.	When this type is marshaled out of an application domain, it is serialized, transported across the domain boundary, and deserialized in the client domain. However, it is agile within a domain, so code in another context holds a direct reference. Use for types that primarily encapsulate data and have no methods that need to execute within the server domain.

Table 3-1. Summary of Marshaling and Agility Options (Continued)

Type	Base Class and Attributes	Description
Marshal By Reference	`MarshalByRefObject`. No specific attribute requirements.	When this type is marshaled out of an application domain, the client domain builds a proxy to the remote object. It is agile within the domain, so code in another context holds a direct reference. Use for types that must execute within the application domain where they were created.
Context Bound	`ContextBoundObject`. Decorate with any context attribute.	When this type is marshaled out of an application domain or a context, the client code builds a proxy to the object. Use for types that require special runtime services such as synchronization.

Examining the .NET Remoting Framework

So far, we have discussed what remoting is and what constitutes an application boundary. We have seen that how you define your class affects the way .NET marshals the instances across application boundaries. Now we can turn to the actual remoting design and infrastructure. In other words, we can discuss how this all works. Keep in mind that the .NET Remoting service is a vast infrastructure with several points of extensibility. Therefore, you can extend base classes and implement standard interfaces to refine the architecture to suit your needs. However, the .NET Remoting architecture also provides fully implemented types that can (and likely will) be used "as is" by the majority of developers.

In this section, we will take a high-level look at the remoting framework. However, many of the terms and concepts are discussed in greater detail later in the next chapter.

Looking at the Big Picture

In the broadest sense, the remoting infrastructure consists of proxies, channels, and messages. Proxies are local objects that impersonate the remote object. That is, they expose the exact same methods and properties as the remote object. However, the proxy implementation of a given method typically passes the call on to the channel object. The channel object represents a connection to the remote application. Each channel object contains a formatter object that converts the method call into a message with a known format. The message is then sent to the server where a mirror image of the client-side channel object is listening for incoming requests. This channel object also contains a formatter object that deserializes the message and sends it to an internal object called the *StackBuilder*. This converts the incoming message back into a method call and invokes the method on the remote object. Figure 3-8 summarizes this architecture.

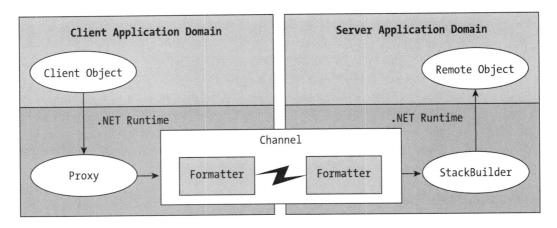

Figure 3-8. A high-level view of the .NET Remoting architecture

Well-Known vs. Client-Activated Objects

An application domain can expose MBR types as either *well-known* objects or *client-activated* objects. Each will be detailed in Chapter 4, but a quick introduction is needed now to grasp upcoming topics.

The differences between well-known and client-activated objects boil down to how each is created and, once created, how the runtime manages the object's lifetime. With well-known objects, you assign a unique and commonly known name that clients pass to the runtime in order to connect to the remote object. In response, the server instantiates the object using the default constructor. In regards to lifetime, a well-known object can either be shared by all clients and persist between client requests (called *Singleton mode*), or it can live and die in the span of a single method call (called *SingleCall mode*).

> **NOTE** *It is common to see well-known objects referred to as server-activated objects. For example, the .NET documentation seems to prefer the server-activated terminology. However, as you will see, the methods and configuration elements that work with these types use the well-known terminology, and therefore I will use it as well.*

Unlike a well-known object, a client-activated object allows the client to activate it using any constructor, not just the default constructor. Furthermore, the lifetime of a client-activated object is dictated by the Leasing Distributed Garbage Collector, which assigns each client-activated object a specific lease. When that lease time expires, the runtime orphans the remote object, thereby exposing it to the next garbage collection.

Understanding Proxies

Proxies are a common pattern in the distributed programming world. In the general sense, a proxy creates the illusion that a remote object is actually in the same process as the client. It does this by implementing the same methods and properties as the remote object. This is true for .NET Remoting proxies as well. However, the .NET runtime actually uses two types of proxies in conjunction: transparent proxies and real proxies.

When client program uses runtime API calls such as `Activator.GetObject` to connect to a remote object, the runtime actually returns a *transparent proxy* to the client. This proxy provides a client-side interception layer for the runtime, allowing it to verify that the method call has the correct number and type of parameters. It also enables the runtime to determine whether the object is running locally or remotely. If local, then the runtime can directly invoke the method without going through the entire remoting plumbing and the associated overhead. Lastly, the transparent proxy packages the method call and all arguments into an `IMessage` object and passes it to the `RealProxy` (described next) via its `Invoke` method. The transparent proxy is dynamically created by the runtime and cannot be extended to create custom types.

The transparent proxy is contained within a *real proxy*. Like the transparent proxy, the runtime generates the real proxy dynamically. However, unlike the transparent proxy, you can extend and customize the real proxy. In fact, the real proxy provides an interception point for a developer to insert custom behavior during the processing of a remote call. Recall that the transparent proxy calls the `Invoke` method of the real proxy object. The default implementation of `Invoke` simply passes the `IMessage` object to the channel object (which is described later).

Dynamic Proxy Generation

As noted in the previous section, proxy objects (both kinds) are created dynamically by the runtime. Just how does this happen? Well, the magic lies in a mixture of runtime reflection and the CLR's `ObjRef` class. To understand how this works, let's look at a couple of remoting scenarios.

First consider the following remotable types:

```
public class Customer : MarshalByRefObject
{ // Implementation ...
}

public class CustomerService : MarshalByRefObject
{
   public Customer CreateCustomer()
   {
      return new Customer();
   }
}
```

Here we have two MBR objects. The `CustomerService` class exposes a factory method that creates and returns a `Customer` object. Assuming that the server application exposes the `CustomerService` type as a well-known object, the following client code can be used to create a proxy to the remote object:

```
// Note: This CLR call will be explained in Chapter 4
CustomerService custSvc = (CustomerService) Activator.GetObject( ... );
```

For the sake of clarity, the preceding code does not include the arguments passed to the `Activator.GetObject` method. This is described in detail in Chapter 4. For now, simply understand that this method accepts arguments that specify the type and location of the remote object. Given this information, the client-side runtime reflects over the remote object's type information to discover each public method and its signature to create the transparent proxy. Where does the client-side runtime find the remote object's type information? This is the question that gets to the heart of much of the complexity in remoting. However, the answer in many cases is simple: the assembly containing the remote type is distributed to the client. Since this assembly contains all the remote object's type information in its metadata, the client-side runtime can reflect over this assembly to generate the proxy. In fact, given that the client code refers to the `CustomerService` class directly, this code will not even compile unless the client references the assembly implementing `CustomerService`.

In many situations, distributing the remote type's assembly to the client may not be desirable. For example, the implementation details may contain sensitive information or proprietary code. Chapter 5 examines a variety of ways to distribute the remote type metadata without distributing the entire assembly.

It is also important to note that this call to `Activator.GetObject` does not cause any network activity. Its task is to build and return a proxy, all of which can be done without involving the server application domain. In fact, no message is sent to the server until the client code invokes a method on the transparent proxy.

Proxy Generation and ObjRef

Speaking of invoking a method, consider the following client-side code:

```
Customer cust = custService.CreateCustomer();
```

When this line is executed, the runtime serializes the method call, sends it through the remoting plumbing, and invokes the method on the server-side object. It gets interesting here because the `CreateCustomer` method returns a reference to a `Customer` object that is also marshal by reference. Therefore, the client-side runtime must still generate a proxy representing the remote `Customer` object, but without the benefit of a call to the `Activator.GetObject` method. How does the runtime generate a proxy in this case?

As it turns out, the client runtime gets a little help from the server. In fact, the server-side runtime does not return a `Customer` reference at all. Instead, it returns an `ObjRef`. An `ObjRef` is a CLR object that contains information regarding the remote type including:

- The fully qualified type name of the remote object, including assembly information

- The type names of all the remote object's base classes

- The type names of all the interfaces implemented by the remote object

- The object URI and information regarding the channels registered on the server

The `ObjRef` is a marshal by value type. Therefore, the `ObjRef` is serialized and returned back to the client-side runtime in lieu of the actual `Customer` object. The client-side runtime uses the information contained within the `ObjRef` object to generate the proxy. In fact, as you will see later, this information is exactly the same information you would otherwise have to manually provide in the call to `Activator.GetObject`.

An `objRef` is created and serialized whenever a MBR object is passed into a remote method or returned from a remote method either as a return value or as an out parameter. For example, consider the following code executing within the `CustomerService` object:

```
// Somewhere in the CustomerService class
Customer cust = new Customer();
remoteObject.SomeMethod(cust);
```

Assuming that `remoteObject` is another remote object, the `SomeMethod` call sends a `Customer` object into the remote object. Since `Customer` is an MBR type, an `ObjRef` is created, serialized, and sent to the remote application domain where it is used to generate a proxy.

The `Customer` object used in the previous examples represents a third category of remoted type, as it is neither well-known nor client-activated. Both "well-known" and "client-activated" describe objects that clients can use as entry points into a server application domain. Therefore, clients can activate them directly. The Customer object, on the other hand, is not activated directly by the client. Instead it is activated and marshaled into the client application domain via a method call on a well-known object. Since I have seen no formal term to describe this category of remoted object, I will suggest my own: *marshaled object*. Other than the activation issue, a marshaled object behaves like a client-activated object; it is stateful and is released when its lease expires.

Understanding Channels and Formatters

Channels are a remoting framework abstraction that hides the complexities of the underlying wire protocol used to communicate between the client and the server application. The channel object is ultimately responsible for transporting each method call from the client to the server, and transporting the return value, if any, back to the client.

Each channel contains a *formatter* object that serializes the method call into a payload appropriate for the underlying network protocol. The CLR provides base classes and interfaces that can be used to develop custom channels and formatters. Formatter and channel objects are "pluggable," meaning that you can associate any type of channel object with any type of formatter object.

HTTP Channel vs. TCP Channel

While you are certainly able to implement your own channels and formatters, the CLR provides two complete implementations that will suit most developer's needs: the HTTP channel and the TCP channel.

The TCP channel (represented by the `TcpChannel` class) provides connectivity using the TCP/IP network protocol. By default, this channel uses the `BinaryFormatter` to convert method calls into a proprietary binary format. The size of the binary payload is relatively small, making the TCP channel perform better than the HTTP channel. However, the TCP channel requires that you establish unique network ports on server machines. This, along with its proprietary binary format, makes it difficult to pass method calls through a firewall. Still, for high performance connectivity in a closed network environment (that is, behind a firewall), the TCP channel is the best choice.

The HTTP channel (represented by the `HttpChannel` class) provides connectivity using the HTTP network protocol, the same protocol used between Web servers and Web browsers. By default, this channel uses the `SoapFormatter` to convert method calls into SOAP format. Since SOAP is based on XML, it results in a much larger transfer payload. Therefore, the HTTP channel is slower than the TCP channel. On the other hand, it is far more flexible. For example, IIS can serve as a host for remote objects and expose them over the HTTP channel. Since IIS is listening at port 80 (the default port number for all Web servers), you do not have to open a new port to provide access to the remote objects. Furthermore, firewalls are typically configured to allow requests over port 80. Therefore, the HTTP channel is much more firewall friendly. This is an important characteristic for businesses that have many departments hosting their own intranets.

For an effective compromise between the raw speed of the TCP channel and the flexibility of the HTTP channel, you can use the HTTP channel with the binary formatter. This still provides the flexibility to host the remote object with IIS and to pass easily through firewalls, while using the more compact and efficient binary payload. However, the TCP channel in itself is more efficient than the HTTP channel; therefore, the TCP channel/binary formatter combination is still faster than the HTTP channel/binary formatter combination.

Registering Channels

Both servers and clients must choose a channel implementation and register it with the runtime. You can accomplish this programmatically using methods on the CLR-provided `ChannelServices` class (details coming later).

Registering a channel accomplishes two important things. First it establishes an endpoint. An *endpoint* describes the location of the application within a network. It typically consists of the host machine's network IP address and the port number. Second, registering a channel in a server application causes the runtime to establish a "listener" thread executing in the same application domain. The purpose of this thread is to listen at the established endpoint for remote method calls and forward them to the remoted object.

The runtime allows only one channel of a given type to be registered per application domain. Therefore, in one application domain you can register an HTTP channel and a TCP channel. However, you cannot register two HTTP channels in the same application domain.

The Channel Sink Chain

As noted before, the .NET Remoting Framework provides several points of extensibility, allowing you to refine the behavior of the system to suit your needs. One interesting example of this is the concept of the channel sink chain. When a method is invoked on a remote object, the two proxies convert the method call into an IMessage object and pass it to the channel. At this point, the message must pass through a series of objects, each of which processes the message and passes it on to the next object. These objects are called *channel sinks,* and they are chained together to create the channel sink chain.

By implementing your own channel sinks and inserting them into the chain, you can intercept the message and perform any required task. For example, you can insert an encryption sink to secure the messages across the wire. Or you can insert a logging sink to track all remote calls.

The channel sink chain exists in both the client and the server application domains. On the client side, the first sink in the chain is typically the channel formatter, namely either the binary or soap formatter. As you can see, the formatter is actually just a type of channel sink. Once the formatter is finished converting the message into the proper serialized format, it passes the converted message on to the next channel sink in the chain. The last sink in the client-side chain is the transport sink. The transport sink is responsible for transmitting the final message to the remote application domain.

The server-side channel sink chain is a mirror image of the client-side chain. Therefore, the first sink in the server chain is the transport sink and the last sink is the formatter sink. In this case, the formatter sink deserializes the message back into a method call so that the runtime can invoke the method on the object.

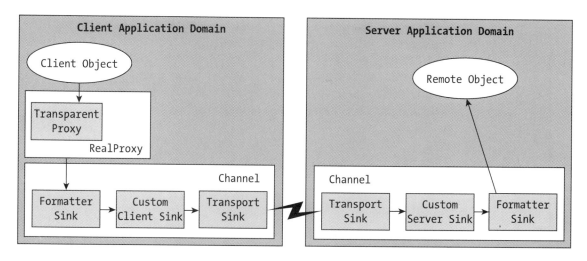

Figure 3-9. The channel sink chain in the client and server application domains

Summary

In this chapter, we examined the .NET Remoting Framework from a high level and defined a number of critical terms. Here is a quick summary:

- In general, the term *remoting* refers to the ability to invoke methods on and share data with objects across application boundaries.

- The primary application boundary in .NET is the application domain. Objects called from another application domain are said to be remoted.

- An application domain can contain many contexts. A context provides a home for objects with similar runtime requirements, and an interception layer that allows the runtime to meet those requirements. Types deriving from ContextBoundObject are said to be context bound. All others are context agile.

- An object can be marshaled out of an application domain in one of two ways: marshal by reference or marshal by value. These are semantically similar to the notion of passing a method argument by reference or by value.

- The runtime facilitates access to remote marshal by reference types by a dynamically generated proxy. The client-side runtime creates the proxy by reflecting over the metadata contained within a local copy of the type's assembly.

- The CLR provides two channel implementations: HTTP and TCP. The TCP channel is appropriate when you require a high-performance connection within a closed network environment. The HTTP channel is slower, but provides firewall-friendly remoting.

In the next chapter, we will continue the exploration of the .NET Remoting Framework by implementing both well-known and client-activated objects.

CHAPTER 4

Distributed Programming with .NET Remoting

"These go to eleven."

—Nigel Tufnel (*This is Spinal Tap*)
commenting on the power of .NET Remoting.

NOW THAT YOU HAVE seen the big picture in regard to the .NET Remoting Framework and learned some of the core terminology, we can finally dive into the details. In this chapter, you see how to implement the concepts introduced in the previous chapter, including how to build well-known objects and client-activated objects, how to influence the runtime's Leasing Distributed Garbage Collector, and how to create sponsor objects. You also learn how to build several different types of server applications for hosting remotable objects, including Window services and ASP.NET.

Implementing Well-Known Objects

Having established an understanding of the fundamental remoting concepts in the previous chapter, it is finally time to look at some real remoting code. We will start by implementing a server application that exposes a well-known object (WKO) for client consumption. But before we start, keep in mind that there are a number of ways to accomplish similar remoting tasks. For the purpose of demonstration, we first look at the most verbose and least transparent technique, and work towards techniques that require less code and are more transparent.

Building the Server

Our first foray into .NET Remoting will be to create a server that activates and exposes a well-known object. Recall that well-known objects are identified by a commonly known and unique name, that is, a well-known name. Thankfully, the naming mechanism is no longer a meaningless GUID as in DCOM. Instead, the more familiar URL format is used. In other words, well-known objects are distinguished by a URL just like Web sites. The .NET Remoting service provides methods that allow you to register a type as a well-known object and assign it a URL that clients can use to access the type.

Here are the steps to build the server:

1. Add a reference to the System.Runtime.Remoting.dll assembly.

2. Implement a class that derives from `MarshalByRefObject`.

3. Choose one of the provided channel implementations (TCP or HTTP), and register it using the `ChannelServices.RegisterChannel` method.

4. Register the class as a well-known object using the `RemotingConfiguration.RegisterWellKnownServiceType` method.

5. Keep the server alive waiting for client requests.

For our remoted class, we will create a `SimpleMath` class much like the one from Chapter 2 and compile into a MathLibrary assembly. This time though, the class will derive from `MarshalByRefObject` and each method will write a simple trace message to the console. The trace messages will help us confirm that the object is running in the server's application domain rather than the client's.

```
namespace MathLibrary
{
    public class SimpleMath : MarshalByRefObject
    {
        public SimpleMath()
        {
            Console.WriteLine("SimpleMath ctor called");
        }

        public int Add(int n1, int n2)
        {
            Console.WriteLine("SimpleMath.Add({0}, {1})", n1, n2);
            return n1 + n2;
        }
```

```
      public int Subtract(int n1, int n2)
      {
         Console.WriteLine("SimpleMath.Subtract({0}, {1})", n1, n2);
         return n1 - n2;
      }
   }
}
```

Next, we create a console application called MathServer and register the SimpleMath class as a well-known object. Here is the code:

```
using System;
using System.Runtime.Remoting; // General remoting stuff
using System.Runtime.Remoting.Channels; // Channel Services
using System.Runtime.Remoting.Channels.Http; // HTTP Channel

namespace MathServer
{
   class ServerMain
   {
      static void Main(string[] args)
      {
         // Create a channel specifying the port #
         HttpChannel channel = new HttpChannel(13101);
         // Register the channel with the runtime remoting services
         ChannelServices.RegisterChannel(channel);

         // Register a type as a well-known type
         RemotingConfiguration.RegisterWellKnownServiceType(
            typeof(MathLibrary.SimpleMath), // The type to register
            "MyURI.soap",                   // The well-known name
            WellKnownObjectMode.Singleton   // SingleCall or Singleton
         );

         // Keep the server alive until Enter is pressed.
         Console.WriteLine("Server started. Press Enter to end");
         Console.ReadLine();
      }
   }
}
```

In this example, the first lines within the Main function create a channel and register it with the remoting service. In this case, we are creating an HttpChannel object and telling it to listen at port number 13101. Recall that the HTTP channel uses the HTTP protocol and serializes data using the SOAP formatter. When the channel object is instantiated, it starts a thread that listens at the specified port number for incoming client requests.

NOTE *Port numbers identify applications listening for incoming network requests. For example, Web servers use port 80; FTP uses ports 20 and 21. You can choose any port number you like, provided it isn't being used by another application on the same machine. Port numbers below 1024 are reserved for well-known protocols such as FTP.*

The call to the RemotingConfiguration.RegisterWellKnownServiceType method is where the real work is done. With this method call, we are registering SimpleMath as a type that can be remoted by the .NET Remoting service. We also assign it an object URI, "MyURI.soap", which becomes part of the well-known name that clients use to refer to the object. Finally, we specify that the runtime should activate the object in Singleton mode. In this mode, one instance of the remote object serves every client request. Contrast this to SingleCall mode, where each client request is served by a new instance that is released when the requested method returns. Singleton and SingleCall modes are discussed in more detail later in the section "Singleton Mode vs. SingleCall Mode."

NOTE *The server code refers directly to the SimpleMath type. Therefore, the MathServer project must reference the MathLibrary assembly.*

Because a separate thread is listening for client requests, all we need to do in the main function after registering the well-known type is to keep the primary thread alive. In this case, it is kept alive until the user presses the Enter key.

Figure 4-1 shows the output, what little there is, when we run this application. Since the purpose of this server is only to expose the SimpleMath type to remote clients, there is little for it to do until a client connects. Note that the server has not yet even constructed a SimpleMath object. If it had, we would see the trace message in the console output.

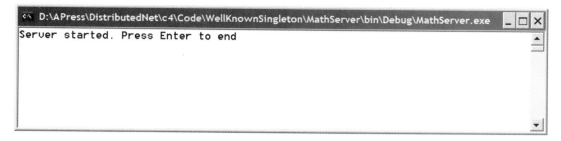

Figure 4-1. The minimal output from our server

Building the Client

The next step, of course, is to build a client application that uses the remote `SimpleMath` type. Before doing so, we need to know four pieces of information regarding the remote server, which are listed here:

- The name of the machine that is hosting the server application

- The type of channel the server is using to expose the object

- The port number where the server is listening for incoming requests

- The remote object's assigned URI

You combine all of this information into a URL that uniquely identifies the remote object you wish to use. Figure 4-2 shows the format of the URL using the values established by the server in the last section.

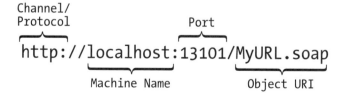

Figure 4-2. Dissecting the parts of a URL

At a high level, the steps for creating the client are as follows:

1. Add a reference to the System.Remoting.Runtime.Remoting.dll.

2. Add a reference to the assembly containing the metadata for the remote type, in this case MathLibrary.dll.

3. Register a channel object using the same channel type as the server.

4. Call the `Activator.GetObject` method, passing the appropriate URL, to retrieve a proxy to the remote object.

5. Cast the proxy to the correct type and start using it as if it were the actual object.

Here is the corresponding code:

```
using System;
using System.Runtime.Remoting;
using System.Runtime.Remoting.Channels;
using System.Runtime.Remoting.Channels.Http;
using MathLibrary;

namespace MathClient
{
    class ClientMain
    {
        static void Main(string[] args)
        {
            // Create and register the channel. The default channel ctor
            // does not open a port, so we can't use this to receive messages.
            HttpChannel channel = new HttpChannel();
            ChannelServices.RegisterChannel(channel);

            // Get a proxy to the remote object
            Object remoteObj = Activator.GetObject(
                            typeof(MathLibrary.SimpleMath),
                            "http://localhost:13101/MyURI.soap"
                        );
```

```
        // Cast the returned proxy to the SimpleMath type
        SimpleMath math = (SimpleMath)remoteObj;

        // Use the remote object
        Console.WriteLine("5 + 2 = {0}", math.Add(5,2));
        Console.WriteLine("5 - 2 = {0}", math.Subtract(5,2));

        // Ask user to press Enter
        Console.Write("Press enter to end");
        Console.ReadLine();
      }
   }
}
```

As before, we first create an HTTP channel object. Note that we do not have to specify a port number in the channel constructor. In fact, if you are using one of the built-in .NET channels, HTTP or TCP, you do not have to register the channel object at all. The runtime will simply use the protocol and port information embedded in the URL to create and register the appropriate channel on your behalf. However, keep in mind that if you do not specify a port number, then the channel cannot act as a server. That is, other applications will not be able to send this application messages. In this particular case, we do not care about this restriction because the program is only meant to be a client.

After the channel is established, the next step is to retrieve a proxy representing the remote object. We accomplish this using the `Activator.GetObject` method, passing in the remote type information and the all-important URL. Finally, we cast the returned proxy to the `SimpleMath` type and use it just as if it were a local object.

To test our code, we first have to start the MathServer application. Then we can start the MathClient project. Figure 4-3 shows the client output.

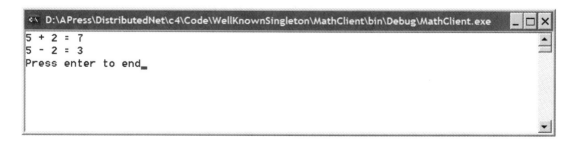

Figure 4-3. The output from the MathClient application

Actually, the output from the MathServer application is more interesting (Figure 4-4). It shows the trace messages that the `SimpleMath` object emits within the method calls, proving that the `SimpleMath` object is running within the MathServer application domain.

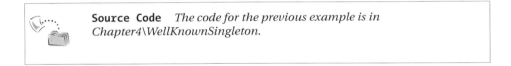

```
D:\APress\DistributedNet\c4\Code\WellKnownSingleton\MathServer\bin\Debug\MathServer.exe
Server started. Press Enter to end
SimpleMath ctor called
SimpleMath.Add(5,2)
SimpleMath.Subtract(5,2)
```

Figure 4-4. The MathServer output shows the `SimpleMath` *object running in the server.*

> **Source Code** *The code for the previous example is in Chapter4\WellKnownSingleton.*

When writing the client code to activate the remote object, you actually have a couple other options beyond the one shown in the previous example. These options vary in syntax, but ultimately provide the same result. The first is to use the static `Connect` method provided by the `RemotingServices` class:

```
SimpleMath math = (SimpleMath)RemotingServices.Connect(
                    typeof(MathLibrary.SimpleMath),
                    http://localhost:13101/MyURI.soap
                  );
```

Another option is to use the `RegisterWellKnownClientType` method provided by the `RemotingConfiguration` class. While this in itself does not return a proxy to the remote object, it does allow you to create a proxy later using the `new` keyword. For example:

```
RemotingConfiguration.RegisterWellKnownClientType(
    typeof(MathLibrary.SimpleMath),
    "http://localhost:13101/MyURI.soap"
);

SimpleMath math = new SimpleMath();
```

All of the preceding techniques share an important characteristic: there is no network activity until a method is called on the remote object. In fact, they all simply generate the appropriate proxy object ready to serialize method calls to the remote object. To "cruft up" this proxy, the runtime must have access to the remote object's type metadata. As mentioned in the previous chapter, this has the unfortunate side effect of requiring that the assembly containing the remote type be distributed to both the client and the server. We will look at various ways to mitigate the consequences of this later in Chapter 5.

Singleton Mode vs. SingleCall Mode

So far, we have been activating the remote object in Singleton mode. This means that the runtime will create one object that serves all client requests. The lifetime of this object is dictated by a leasing policy that is discussed in detail later. For now, know that the object will persist as long as clients are continuously making method calls on it. However, if 5 minutes of inactivity passes, then the runtime frees the object, subjecting it to the next garbage collection. If a client makes a request after the object is freed, the runtime creates a new instance to serve the request. You can override this behavior such that the Singleton object will persist for as long as the server application is running, but the mechanics of this will have to wait for the upcoming section, "Understanding Lease-based Lifetimes."

If multiple clients access a Singleton object at the same time, each request executes on a separate worker thread. The .NET runtime has a built-in thread pooling facility that efficiently dedicates threads to these incoming requests. Since the worker threads execute within the same Singleton object, you may run into concurrency issues if the threads access and modify instance fields on the object. It is your responsibility to ensure synchronized access to instance fields. The CLR defines several thread synchronization constructs within the System.Threading namespace. In addition, C# provides the lock keyword, which establishes a section of code where only one thread at time can enter. A full discussion of thread synchronization techniques is way out of the scope of this text, but here is a quick example of using the lock keyword.

```
// Acquire lock, now no thread can enter this or any other
// code block protected by "lock(this)"
lock(this)
{
    // read or modify instance fields
}
// lock is automatically released when thread leaves the lock scope.
```

Singleton mode is useful if the object contains some state or resource that should be shared between all clients. However, the statefulness of Singleton objects can be a problem in a server farm scenario where the identical application is load balanced between several machines. Therefore, for scalability reasons you will typically use the alternate activation mode: SingleCall.

In SingleCall mode, the runtime creates a new object to service each client request and releases the object after it completes the request. The object is therefore unreachable, and will be destroyed during the next garbage collection. Clearly, no state can be shared between clients or even between method calls—that is, the object is stateless. This mode is ideal for load balancing requests across several server machines.

We can test the behavioral differences between Singleton and SingleCall by making a few simple changes to our current remoting application. First, in the MathClient project we add a user input loop to the main function that allows the user to send multiple SimpleMath.Add method requests to the server.

```
// Use the remote object. Loop until user enters 'q'
do
{
    Console.WriteLine("5 + 2 = {0}", math.Add(5,2));
    Console.Write("Enter q to quit: ");
}while (Console.ReadLine() != "q");
```

Then, in the MathServer project, we register our SimpleMath type to activate in SingleCall mode by changing the RegisterWellKnownServiceType method call as shown here:

```
// Register a type as a well-known type
RemotingConfiguration.RegisterWellKnownServiceType(
    typeof(MathLibrary.SimpleMath), // The type to register
    "MyURI.soap",                   // The well-known name
    WellKnownObjectMode.SingleCall // SingleCall or Singleton
);
```

Now if we run these two programs and use the client to trigger a couple `Add` methods, the server console output shows that a new `SimpleMath` object is constructed with each call (Figure 4-5).

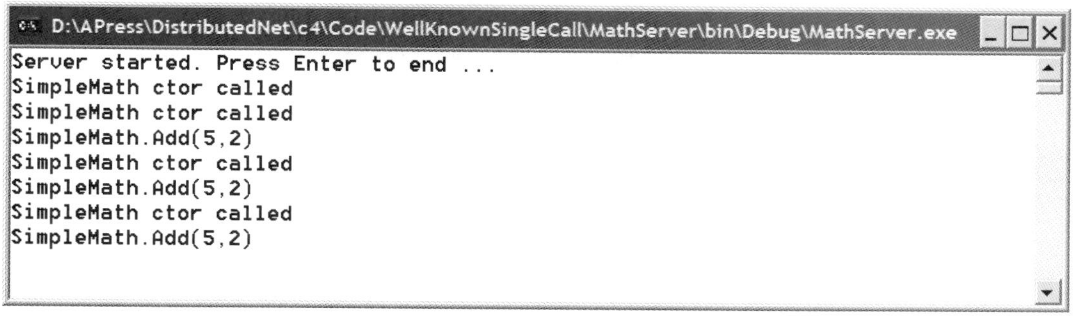

```
D:\APress\DistributedNet\c4\Code\WellKnownSingleCall\MathServer\bin\Debug\MathServer.exe    _ □ ×
Server started. Press Enter to end ...
SimpleMath ctor called
SimpleMath ctor called
SimpleMath.Add(5,2)
SimpleMath ctor called
SimpleMath.Add(5,2)
SimpleMath ctor called
SimpleMath.Add(5,2)
```

Figure 4-5. The MathServer output showing the effect of SingleCall activation

For the sake of comparison, let's change the activation mode to Singleton and look at the results in Figure 4-6. The results show that the `SimpleMath` constructor is indeed only called one time and that the same object is serving the three calls to the `Add` method.

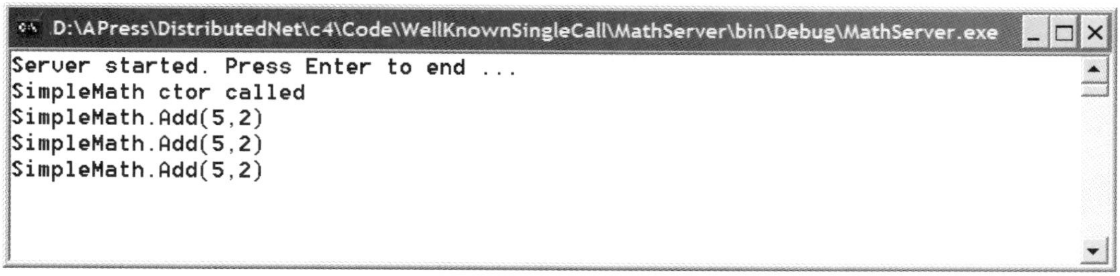

```
D:\APress\DistributedNet\c4\Code\WellKnownSingleCall\MathServer\bin\Debug\MathServer.exe    _ □ ×
Server started. Press Enter to end ...
SimpleMath ctor called
SimpleMath.Add(5,2)
SimpleMath.Add(5,2)
SimpleMath.Add(5,2)
```

Figure 4-6. The MathServer output showing the effect of Singleton activation

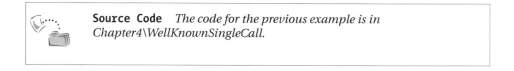

Source Code *The code for the previous example is in Chapter4\WellKnownSingleCall.*

Looking (Briefly) at Some Remoting Issues

Having taught this subject matter to many developers, I know that readers experienced in distributed programming with (D)COM technology are having a heart attack about now. They will rightly point out several issues dealing with location transparency and the need to deploy implementation assemblies to the client. In fact, an honest appraisal of our current remoting sample application exposes three problems.

- There is a significant amount of channel creation, object registration, and other configuration code. If these details change, then we need to recompile.

- For well-known objects, the server must create the object using the default constructor. There is no way for the client to specify a nondefault constructor.

- The client must reference the assembly that contains the well-known type. Therefore, we must distribute the assembly to all client machines. This seems to defeat the purpose of distributed programming if we have to distribute the entire binary image of our object to the clients.

Fear not—the previous examples were intended to highlight these problems. Throughout the rest of this chapter, I will address each issue.

Remoting Configuration

The first issue noted in the previous section can be resolved by providing a remoting configuration file. Much like the application configuration file, this file contains XML that describes the remoting parameters for the application. Therefore, instead of hard-coding the values, the application can read them from the configuration file, allowing you to make changes without rebuilding the application. Furthermore, once you have a proper remoting configuration file established, you can replace all of the channel and object registration code in the previous example with one method call. While it is possible to have two separate configuration files, one for the application configuration settings and the other for remoting settings, it is recommended that you combine them both into the application configuration file.

All remoting configuration settings fall under the <system.runtime.remoting> element. This, in turn, is a child of the <configuration> element, just like the <runtime> element where we place the binding redirects. Therefore, to combine assembly binding and remoting configuration into the same file, you need to structure it as shown here:

```
<configuration>
  <runtime>
    <!-- Put version binding redirects here -->
  </runtime>
  <system.runtime.remoting>
    <!-- Put remoting configuration settings here -->
  </system.runtime.remoting>
</configuration>
```

Configuring the Server

At this time we are only concerned with the remoting section of the configuration file. Basically, the information we specify in this section correlates directly with the information specified in the previous remoting example. That is, we have to specify the channel type and port where the server will listen for requests, the type of the object we want to expose, the URL used as the well-known name, and the activation mode. The following example demonstrates how this information is specified in the configuration file.

```
<configuration>
  <system.runtime.remoting>
    <application>
      <service>
        <wellknown mode="Singleton"
                   type="MathLibrary.SimpleMath, MathLibrary"
                   objectUri="MyURI.soap" />
      </service>
      <channels>
        <!-- NOTE: The following type attribute must actually be
             on a single line! It is broken up into multiple lines
             here for readability. -->
        <channel port="13101"
                 type="System.Runtime.Remoting.Channels.Http.HttpChannel,
                       System.Runtime.Remoting,
                       Version=1.0.3300.0, Culture=neutral,
                       PublicKeyToken=b77a5c561934e089" />
      </channels>
    </application>
  </system.runtime.remoting>
</configuration>
```

The <application> element encapsulates the remoting settings for the application. The <service> element encapsulates information about the types that this application exposes for remoting.

Within <service>, you can specify any number of <wellknown> elements. As you can see, this contains the majority of the configuration information for the exposed type. The mode attribute can be set to Singleton or SingleCall. The type attribute specifies the type to expose. Note that the value contains the fully qualified type name and the assembly name in the format "typename, assemblyname". You cannot provide a path to the assembly. Instead, the runtime locates the specified assembly using the binding mechanism described in the Chapter 2. Finally, the objectURI attribute specifies the well-known name to assign to the object.

The <channel> element allows you to specify the type of channel and the port number on which the application should listen for incoming requests. Note that when specifying the channel type, you must provide its fully qualified name and the assembly where it is defined. Furthermore, since the assembly is strong named, you must also specify the full strong name of the assembly including version, culture, and public key token. Before complaining too much about the amount of information you must provide here, be aware that there is a more convenient mechanism which we cover in the next section. In any event, you can specify multiple <channel> elements within the <channels> element. However, note that only one channel of a specific type is allowed.

Assuming that the previous XML was placed within the application configuration file for the MathServer assembly, we can now replace all the previous configuration code with a simple call to the RemotingConfiguration.Configure method as shown here:

```csharp
using System;
using System.Runtime.Remoting; // General remoting stuff

namespace MathServer
{
    class ServerMain
    {
        static void Main(string[] args)
        {
            // Read remoting info from config file.
            RemotingConfiguration.Configure("MathServer.exe.config");

            // Keep the server alive until Enter is pressed.
            Console.WriteLine("Server started. Press Enter to end ...");
            Console.ReadLine();
        }
    }
}
```

As you can see, the RemotingConfiguration.Configure method simply takes a string representing the name of the file containing the remoting configuration information. This example uses the application configuration file, which is the recommended technique. Also notice that there are fewer required namespaces. We simply need to include the System.Runtime.Remoting namespace to access the RemotingConfiguration type. But the most important benefit of using this style of remoting configuration is that you can make changes to the remoting settings without having to recompile the server application.

Because the server no longer refers to the SimpleMath type, the MathServer project does not have to reference the MathLibrary assembly. However, MathServer must still bind to MathLibrary.dll at runtime, therefore the assembly must be copied to the MathServer application directory or it has to be installed in the GAC. For this reason, it may be more convenient to have the MathServer project reference MathLibrary simply to leverage Visual Studio .NET's automatic copy behavior.

Configuring the Client

Before we cover the remoting configuration file format from the client perspective, keep in mind that we can use our previous client program as is to access the remoted type. Just because the server uses a remoting configuration file to specify remoting settings does not mean that the client must also.

Also keep in mind that the amount of configuration code required on the client is far less than that required by the server. In fact, if you are using one of the built-in channels, then you need only call the Activator.GetObject method. In this case, the runtime uses the information embedded in the provided URL to configure the proper channel.

Still, a remoting configuration file offers a couple advantages. First, as noted earlier, it allows you to make changes to the remoting specifics without requiring you to rebuild the client. Second, and possibly more interesting, it allows you to activate the remote object using the familiar new keyword, thus providing the same level of location transparency as COM.

Here is the remoting configuration file for the client:

```
<configuration>
  <system.runtime.remoting>
    <application>
      <client displayName="MathClient">
        <wellknown type="MathLibrary.SimpleMath, MathLibrary"
                   url="http://localhost:13101/MyURI.soap" />
      </client>
```

```
        <channels>
          <!-- NOTE: The following type attribute must actually be
                on a single line! It is broken up into multiple lines
                here for readability. -->
          <channel type="System.Runtime.Remoting.Channels.Http.HttpChannel,
                        System.Runtime.Remoting, Version=1.0.3300.0,
                        Culture=neutral, PublicKeyToken=b77a5c561934e089" />
        </channels>
      </application>
    </system.runtime.remoting>
</configuration>
```

As is the case on the server side, the remoting settings all fall under the <system.runtime.remoting> element. Under the <application> element, you can specify multiple <client> elements, each with an optional displayName attribute (used only by the .NET Framework Configuration tool, not the runtime). The <wellknown> element specifies the important remoting information. The type attribute provides the full type name of the remote object and the full name of the assembly where it resides. The url attribute specifies the location of the remote object. Channel configuration is the same as in the server, except that we do not need to provide a port number.

Given the previous configuration, whenever the client creates a SimpleMath object, the runtime will activate it in the MathServer's application domain. Here is the client code:

```
using System;
using System.Runtime.Remoting;
using MathLibrary;

namespace MathClient
{
    class ClientMain
    {
        static void Main(string[] args)
        {
            // Load the configuration file
            RemotingConfiguration.Configure("MathClient.exe.config");

            // Get a proxy to the remote object
            SimpleMath math = new SimpleMath();
```

```
        // Use the remote object
        Console.WriteLine("5 + 2 = {0}", math.Add(5,2));
        Console.WriteLine("5 - 2 = {0}", math.Subtract(5,2));

        // Ask user to press Enter
        Console.Write("Press enter to end");
        Console.ReadLine();
      }
    }
}
```

As you can see, the use of the remoting configuration file simplifies the client code significantly by reducing the number of namespaces required and by allowing the remote object to be activated with the new keyword.

Channel Configuration

Although you can specify the channel settings in the remoting configuration file, it does require that you provide the full strong name of the channel's assembly, including the version, culture, and public key token. Not only is this tedious, but if you get one thing wrong, the channel will not load.

To make things easier, the configuration schema allows you to create *channel templates*. A channel template encapsulates all the detailed information regarding the channel and assigns a unique channel ID. Once a channel template is defined, the application's channel settings need only refer to the channel template using the assigned ID.

You specify channel templates under a <channels> element which is a child of <system.runtime.remoting>. This is different from the <channels> child element of <application>. To clarify, consider the following configuration structure:

```
<configuration>
  <system.runtime.remoting>
    <application>
      <channels>
        <!-- Define channels used by the application here -->
      </channels>
    </application>
    <channels>
      <!-- Define channel templates here -->
    </channels>
  </system.runtime.remoting>
</configuration>
```

As the preceding structure shows, the placement of the <channels> element is important. If it is under the <application> element, then it is used to specify the channels to use for remoting. If it is under the <system.runtime.remoting> element, then it is used to define a channel template.

To demonstrate how to use a channel template, let's modify our MathServer's configuration file to define and use a channel template:

```
<configuration>
  <system.runtime.remoting>
    <application>
      <service>
        <wellknown mode="Singleton"
                   type="MathLibrary.SimpleMath, MathLibrary"
                   objectUri="MyURI.soap" />
      </service>
      <channels>
        <channel port="13101" ref="MyHTTPChannel" />
      </channels>
    </application>
    <channels>
      <!-- NOTE: The following type attribute must actually be
           on a single line! It is broken up into multiple lines
           here for readability. -->
      <channel id="MyHTTPChannel"
               type="System.Runtime.Remoting.Channels.Http.HttpChannel,
                     System.Runtime.Remoting, Version=1.0.3300.0,
                     Culture=neutral, PublicKeyToken=b77a5c561934e089" />
    </channels>
  </system.runtime.remoting>
</configuration>
```

The important modifications appear in both the <channels> elements. In the channel template section, the template is defined using the <channel> element and type attribute as before. However, we also set the id attribute to "MyHTTPChannel". In the application channel section, we can simply refer to the channel template using the <channel> element's ref attribute.

Admittedly, this really did not save us any work. We must still enter all the channel assembly's strong name information, albeit in a separate section of the configuration file. But it turns out there is no need to create channel templates for any of the built-in channels, as we did here, because the .NET Framework already defines channel templates for them. In fact, it defines several channel templates in the machine configuration file (machine.config) that you can refer to in your configuration files. Here is the relevant section of the machine.config file:

```
<system.runtime.remoting>
  <channels>
    <channel id="http"
            type="System.Runtime.Remoting.Channels.Http.HttpChannel,
                System.Runtime.Remoting, Version=1.0.3300.0,
                Culture=neutral, PublicKeyToken=b77a5c561934e089" />
    <channel id="http client"
            type="System.Runtime.Remoting.Channels.Http.HttpClientChannel,
                System.Runtime.Remoting, Version=1.0.3300.0,
                Culture=neutral, PublicKeyToken=b77a5c561934e089" />
    <channel id="http server"
            type="System.Runtime.Remoting.Channels.Http.HttpServerChannel,
                System.Runtime.Remoting, Version=1.0.3300.0,
                Culture=neutral, PublicKeyToken=b77a5c561934e089" />
    <channel id="tcp"
            type="System.Runtime.Remoting.Channels.Tcp.TcpChannel,
                System.Runtime.Remoting, Version=1.0.3300.0,
                Culture=neutral, PublicKeyToken=b77a5c561934e089" />
    <channel id="tcp client"
            type="System.Runtime.Remoting.Channels.Tcp.TcpClientChannel,
                System.Runtime.Remoting, Version=1.0.3300.0,
                Culture=neutral, PublicKeyToken=b77a5c561934e089" />
    <channel id="tcp server"
            type="System.Runtime.Remoting.Channels.Tcp.TcpServerChannel,
                System.Runtime.Remoting, Version=1.0.3300.0,
                Culture=neutral, PublicKeyToken=b77a5c561934e089" />
  </channels>
</system.runtime.remoting>
```

Because these templates are defined in the machine configuration file, you need only refer to them in your remoting configuration files. For example, here is the final version of our MathServer configuration file, which refers to the HTTP channel template:

```
<configuration>
  <system.runtime.remoting>
    <application>
      <service>
        <wellknown mode="Singleton"
                type="MathLibrary.SimpleMath, MathLibrary"
                objectUri="MyURI.soap" />
      </service>
```

```
        <channels>
         <channel port="13101" ref="http" />
        </channels>
     </application>
   </system.runtime.remoting>
</configuration>
```

As you can see, this greatly simplifies the task of specifying channels in the configuration file. Also, if any of the HTTP channel assembly details change, then the channel template in the machine.config file could be updated appropriately and all applications referring to the channel template would still work properly.

 Source Code   *Source Code: The code for this section is in Chapter4\RemotingConfig.*

Implementing Client-Activated Objects

So far, we have been focusing on the activation of well-known objects. One of the issues pointed out earlier was that our well-known object had to implement a default constructor, which the server used to construct the object. This also means that a client cannot construct a well-known object using a nondefault constructor.

For example, assume we added the following constructor to the SimpleMath class:

```
public class SimpleMath : MarshalByRefObject
{
    public SimpleMath(int n1, int n2)
    { // constructor implementation
    }
    // ...
}
```

Now assume we tried to call this constructor from the remote client using the following code:

```
class ClientMain
{
   static void Main(string[] args)
   {
      RemotingConfiguration.RegisterWellKnownClientType(
         typeof(MathLibrary.SimpleMath),
         "http://localhost:13101/MyURI.soap"
      );

      // This line causes a runtime exception!!
      SimpleMath math = new SimpleMath(5,2);
   }
}
```

Although this seems like a reasonable thing to do, the preceding code results in the exception shown in Figure 4-7.

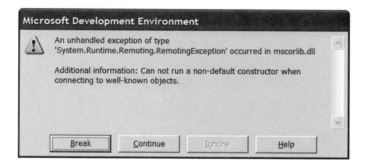

Figure 4-7. Calling a nondefault constructor on a well-known object causes an exception.

Simply put, it is impossible for the client to construct a well-known object with any constructor other than the default constructor. If this is unacceptable, then you have only one choice: register the remote object as a *client-activated* object.

Client-activated objects are similar to well-known SingleCall objects in that each client activates a unique instance of the remote type. However, unlike the well-known SingleCall objects, client-activated objects persist beyond a single method. Therefore, it is possible for a client-activated object to hold state. In other words, client-activated objects are stateful.

Building the Server

Client-activated objects require different configuration and registration methods on both the server and the client. And, just as with a well-known object, you can programmatically register a type for client activation or you use the remoting configuration file.

To demonstrate client activation, we will create a very simple Customer class that implements a single, nondefault constructor and a SayHello method.

```
public class Customer : MarshalByRefObject
{
   string mName;

   public Customer(string name)
   {
      Console.WriteLine("Customer.ctor({0})", name);
      mName = name;
   }

   public string SayHello()
   {
      Console.WriteLine("Customer.SayHello()");
      return "Hello " + mName;
   }
}
```

Since the class does not implement a default constructor, it cannot be registered as a well-known type. While this can be easily remedied by adding a default constructor to the class, there are other reasons why this class is ill suited as a well-known type. Notice that the class is stateful because it maintains the customer name as instance data. Therefore, it does not make sense to configure it as a well-known SingleCall type because the runtime orphans each SingleCall object and all its instance state after completing a method call. Furthermore, it is highly unlikely that multiple clients will want to share the exact same customer state, so it does not make sense to configure the Customer class as a well-known Singleton type.

So that leaves only one option—register it as a client-activated object. The following example shows how to accomplish this programmatically using the RegisterActivatedServiceType method of the RemotingConfiguration class.

```
class ServerMain
{
    static void Main(string[] args)
    {
        // Create a channel specifying the port #
        HttpServerChannel channel = new HttpServerChannel(13101);

        // Register the channel with the runtime remoting services
        ChannelServices.RegisterChannel(channel);

        // Register the Customer class as a client-activated type.
        RemotingConfiguration.RegisterActivatedServiceType(
            typeof(MathLibrary.Customer)
        );

        // Keep the server alive until Enter is pressed.
        Console.WriteLine("Server started. Press Enter to end ...");
        Console.ReadLine();
    }
}
```

As you might expect, you can achieve the same effect using the remoting configuration file:

```
<configuration>
  <system.runtime.remoting>
    <application>
      <service>

        <!-- Register Customer class as client activated -->
        <activated type="MathLibrary.Customer, MathLibrary" />

        <wellknown mode="Singleton"
                   type="MathLibrary.SimpleMath, MathLibrary"
                   objectUri="MyURI.soap" />
      </service>
      <channels>
         <channel port="13101"
                   ref="http" />
      </channels>
    </application>
  </system.runtime.remoting>
</configuration>
```

The only difference between this example and our previous remoting configuration file is the addition of the <activated> element under the <service> element.
This is all that is required to expose the Customer class as a client-activated object.
I kept the well-known SimpleMath entry in the example only to demonstrate that
you can specify multiple well-known and client-activated elements within the
same <service> element.

Building the Client

Clients can use multiple techniques to create a client-activated object. The
RemotingConfiguration class provides one of the easiest techniques in the form of
the RegisterActivatedClientType method. After calling this method and passing it
the type and the server URL, you can use the new keyword to create the remote
object. For example:

```
class ClientMain
{
    static void Main(string[] args)
    {

        RemotingConfiguration.RegisterActivatedClientType(
            typeof(MathLibrary.Customer),
            "http://localhost:13101"
        );

        // Calling a nondefault constructor. No exceptions now because
        // Customer is a client-activated object.
        Customer cust = new Customer("Homer");

        Console.WriteLine(cust.SayHello());
        Console.ReadLine();
    }
}
```

This example provides two interesting points. First, notice that the URL provided in the RegisterActivatedClientType method call ends after the port number.
This is because client-activated objects, unlike well-known objects, do not have a
well-known object URI. Instead the runtime generates a unique GUID-based URI
for each instance of a client-activated type. Second, and more importantly, notice
that the client can invoke a nondefault constructor.

The Activator.CreateInstance method also provides the ability to create a
client-activated object. Actually, this method is overloaded several times and as a

result can be used to create local and remote objects in many different ways. For example, using the CreateInstance method you can create a remote object while specifying the type as a string. Therefore, the client does not need to reference a local assembly containing the remote type information at compile time. However, this also means that you must supply the method with construction parameters as an array of objects.

Once again, the easiest way to configure the client is to use the remoting configuration file. The following example demonstrates how:

```
<configuration>
  <system.runtime.remoting>
    <application>
      <client url="http://localhost:13101">

        <!-- Allows client activation of Customer type at above URL -->
        <activated type="MathLibrary.Customer, MathLibrary" />

        <wellknown type="MathLibrary.SimpleMath, MathLibrary"
                   url="http://localhost:13101/MyURI.soap" />
      </client>
    </application>
  </system.runtime.remoting>
</configuration>
```

There are two important additions here. The first is the <activated> element added under the <client> element. This tells the runtime that the MathLibrary.Customer type should be created remotely as a client-activated object. However, unlike the <wellknown> element, the <activated> element does not allow you to specify the server URL. So how does the runtime know where to find the server? That information is specified in the containing <client> element via its url attribute. The runtime will direct the requests for each of the client-activated types listed under the <client> element to this URL. You can specify multiple <client> elements under the <application> element, so it is possible to have multiple client-activated objects created in multiple servers.

Source Code   *The code for the previous example is in Chapter4\ClientActivated.*

Understanding Lease-based Lifetimes

The fact that client-activated objects persist between method calls (that is, are stateful) raises a difficult issue for the server application hosting the objects. When can the server destroy the object? If the server destroys the object too soon, then it risks losing important state information required by any client still using the object. If the server waits too long before destroying the object, then the object may continue to consume precious server resources after the last client is finished using it.

Currently, DCOM uses reference counting to determine if clients are still using an object. When the reference count goes to zero, DCOM knows it is safe to destroy the object and does so. The Achilles heel of this solution is that each client must explicitly notify the server that it is finished using the object. If a client fails to do this, then the object will persist—potentially forever.

There are two scenarios where this scheme can fail. The first is the relatively benign case where the network connection is lost or the client process crashes before it releases the remote object. To handle this scenario, DCOM periodically pings the client to ensure it is still alive. If the client does not respond, the object's reference count is decremented. While effective, the periodic pinging of many clients can consume network bandwidth on a LAN, and is extremely expensive on a WAN or Internet connection.

The second scenario is the so-called greedy client. This is a client that, either by accident or by design, keeps a reference alive to a remote object even though it is used rarely or not at all. There is little that the server can do to prevent this from happening. Interestingly, middleware services such as COM+ (and MTS before that) address this by promoting the use of stateless objects that are created when the client invokes a method and destroyed when it completes. This is analogous to .NET's well-known SingleCall objects. However, if the object must be stateful, then this approach to solving the greedy client problem does not work.

The .NET Leasing Distributed Garbage Collector addresses both of these issues. Whenever a client-activated object or a well-known Singleton object is created on the server, the runtime gives it a fixed lifetime known as a *lease*. When the lease expires, the runtime releases its reference to the object, thus subjecting it to the next garbage collection. However, whenever the client invokes a method on the object, the runtime renews the object lease. This simple solution provides a way to keep stateful objects alive and active for a reasonable amount of time. Since objects are automatically released after idling for a period of time, it solves the greedy client problem without resorting to the use of stateless objects. Furthermore, the server no longer has to ping the clients to ensure they are still alive.

Investigating Object Lifetime

Exactly how much idle time is reasonable for an object before the runtime should release it varies drastically between applications and even between individual types. So .NET provides the ability to obtain and configure the lease settings for an application or type. However, if you do nothing, a default lease is established that lasts for 5 minutes.

Before jumping into some lease configuration code, let's first see how we can programmatically discover lease information for a type. The MarshalByRefObject class implements a GetLifetimeService method that returns an ILease object. We can use the properties of ILease to discover the lifetime settings. For example, the following Diagnostics class uses the ILease interface to dump various bits of lease information to the console window.

```
public class Diagnostics
{
    public static void ShowLeaseInfo(ILease leaseInfo)
    {
        Console.WriteLine("*** Lease Information ***");
        if (leaseInfo != null)
        {
            // Show the current lease time
            Console.WriteLine("  Current Lease time: {0}:{1}",
                leaseInfo.CurrentLeaseTime.Minutes,
                leaseInfo.CurrentLeaseTime.Seconds
            );

            // Show the initial lease time
            Console.WriteLine("  Initial Lease time: {0}:{1}",
                leaseInfo.InitialLeaseTime.Minutes,
                leaseInfo.InitialLeaseTime.Seconds
            );

            // Show the renew on call time
            Console.WriteLine("  Renew on call time: {0}:{1}",
                leaseInfo.RenewOnCallTime.Minutes,
                leaseInfo.RenewOnCallTime.Seconds
            );

            // Show the current state
            Console.WriteLine("  Current state: {0}", leaseInfo.CurrentState);
        }
```

```
        else
        {
            // No lease information
            Console.WriteLine("  No Lease Info!!");
        }
    }
}
```

Now we can call this static `Diagnostics.ShowLeaseInfo` method from our client-activated `Customer` class to dump lease information about the object. For now, we call the method only from the `Customer.SayHello()` method to display the lease information each time a client calls it:

```
public class Customer : MarshalByRefObject
{
    public string SayHello()
    {
        Console.WriteLine("Customer.SayHello()");

        // Show the lease information for this object
        Diagnostics.ShowLeaseInfo((ILease)this.GetLifetimeService());

        return "Hello " + mName;
    }
    // Snip rest of class implementation ...
}
```

Since `Customer` derives from `MarshalByRefObject`, it inherits a `GetLifetimeServices` method. We call this method and pass the result to `Diagnostics.ShowLeaseInfo`. However, `GetLifetimeServices` technically returns a generic object type, so we must cast the return value to the `ILease` interface before passing it into `ShowLeaseInfo`. When we execute this code, the MathServer application generates the output shown in Figure 4-8.

So what do these values mean? The current lease time shows that the object currently has 4 minutes and 59 seconds left on its lease. The initial lease time shows that the object began life with lease of 5 minutes. Finally, the renew-on-call time shows that the runtime will reset the lease to 2 minutes each time a client invokes a method on the object. These are the default lease values the runtime assigns to client-activated objects.

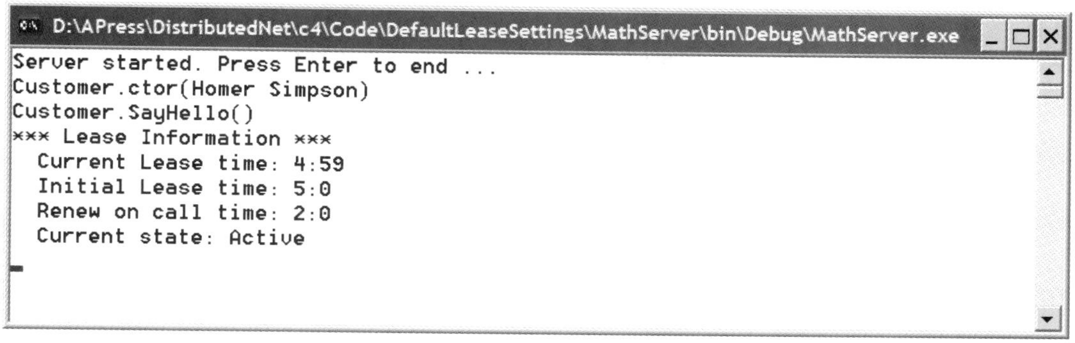

Figure 4-8. Examining the default lease settings

Next, we will make a small change to our MathClient program so that we can invoke the Customer.SayHello method multiple times. Here is the code:

```
class ClientMain
{
    static void Main(string[] args)
    {
        // Load the configuration file
        RemotingConfiguration.Configure("MathClient.exe.config");

        Customer cust = new Customer("Homer Simpson");

        // Loop until user enters "q" to quit
        Console.WriteLine("Enter 'q' to quit: ");

        do
        {
            Console.WriteLine("Server returns: {0}", cust.SayHello());
        }while (Console.ReadLine() != "q");

    }
}
```

Now let's execute the server and the client. Figure 4-9 shows the server output when we press Enter a couple times in the client console window.

Note that the current lease time is decreasing each time we call the method. It may also seem strange that the lease time is not set to 2 minutes after any of the method calls. In fact, the "renew on call time" value does not take effect until the current lease time drops below the renew value.

```
cs  D:\APress\DistributedNet\c4\Code\DefaultLeaseSettings\MathServer\bin\Debug\MathServer.exe   _ □ ×
Server started. Press Enter to end ...
Customer.ctor(Homer Simpson)
Customer.SayHello()
*** Lease Information ***
  Current Lease time: 4:59
  Initial Lease time: 5:0
  Renew on call time: 2:0
  Current state: Active
Customer.SayHello()
*** Lease Information ***
  Current Lease time: 4:48
  Initial Lease time: 5:0
  Renew on call time: 2:0
  Current state: Active
Customer.SayHello()
*** Lease Information ***
  Current Lease time: 4:30
  Initial Lease time: 5:0
  Renew on call time: 2:0
  Current state: Active
```

Figure 4-9. Examining the lease settings after several invocations of the object's methods

Of course, if the client attempts to invoke a method on the object after the lease is expired, the runtime raises the exception shown in Figure 4-10.

```
cs  D:\APress\DistributedNet\c4\Code\DefaultLeaseSettings\MathClient\bin\Debug\MathClient.exe   _ □ ×
Enter 'q' to quit:
Server returns: Hello Homer Simpson


Unhandled Exception: System.Runtime.Remoting.RemotingException: Object </afb438c
9_6719_4540_9ca5_5faa8a2ade43/26660255_1.rem> has been disconnected or does not
exist at the server.
```

Figure 4-10. Invoking a method on an expired object causes an exception.

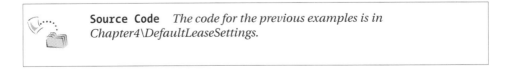

Source Code   *The code for the previous examples is in Chapter4\DefaultLeaseSettings.*

Configuring Object Lifetime

If the default lease settings are inadequate, you can set your own values using (what else) the remoting configuration file. For example, the configuration below sets the initial lease time to 10 seconds and the renew time to 5 seconds:

```
<configuration>
  <system.runtime.remoting>
    <application>

      <!-- Configure the lease for all client-activated objects in the app -->
      <lifetime leaseTime="10s" renewOnCallTime="5s" />

      <!-- Configure server and channels as before ... -->
    </application>
  </system.runtime.remoting>
</configuration>
```

Figure 4-11 shows the server console output with these new lease settings in effect.

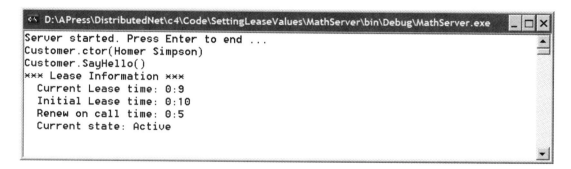

Figure 4-11. The MathServer output after configuring the lease settings

The lease values specified within the <lifetime> element apply to all objects within the application. If you wish to customize these settings for each individual type, then you must write the appropriate code within the type itself. To accomplish this, you can use yet another method inherited from the MarshalByRefObject class: InitializeLifetimeServices. The runtime calls this method as it is creating the object. We can override this method in our Customer class to apply type-specific lease settings. For example:

```
public class Customer : MarshalByRefObject
{
    public override object InitializeLifetimeService()
    {
        // Call base class version
        ILease leaseInfo = (ILease)base.InitializeLifetimeService();

        // Set lease values
        leaseInfo.InitialLeaseTime = TimeSpan.FromSeconds(7);
        leaseInfo.RenewOnCallTime = TimeSpan.FromSeconds(3);
        return leaseInfo;
    }
}
```

In this example, we first call the base class (in this case `MarshalByRefObject`) version of the `InitializeLifetimeService` method. This returns a lease object with the default settings. We then set the `InitialLeaseTime` and `RenewOnCallTime` properties to 7 and 3 seconds respectively, using the `TimeSpan` class. Figure 4-12 shows the server console output after we test this new code.

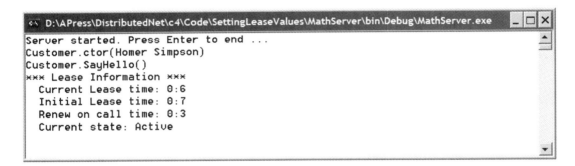

Figure 4-12. The MathServer output after overriding the `InitializeLifetimeService` *method*

 Source Code *The code for the previous example is in Chapter4\SettingLeaseValues.*

Setting Infinite Leases

Recall that well-known Singleton objects also have lease-based lifetimes. Therefore, assuming the default lifetime settings, if a Singleton object idles for 5 minutes, the runtime orphans it and any contained state. Unlike client-activated objects, however, if a client requests a Singleton object after it has been released, the runtime automatically creates a new instance to serve the request. In the case of client-activated objects, this results in an exception.

Even so, if a Singleton object is maintaining important state information and sharing it among clients, you may want it to persist for the length of the application. You can accomplish this by overloading the InitializeLifetimeService method and return null as shown in the following example. Returning null effectively gives the object an infinite lease.

```
public override object InitializeLifetimeService()
{
    return null;
}
```

Building and Registering Sponsors

As mentioned earlier, the runtime renews an object's lease whenever a client invokes a method on it. A lease can also be renewed by a registered *sponsor* object for the remote type. A sponsor object is simply an object that implements the ISponsor interface. When an object's lease has expired, the runtime first checks to see if there are any sponsor objects associated with the remote object. If so, the runtime gives each sponsor an opportunity to renew the lease. The runtime continues through the list of sponsors until one renews the lease. If none do, then the runtime drops its reference to the remote object, thereby subjecting it to the next garbage collection.

Since the ISponsor interface defines only one method, Renewal, it is easy to create a sponsor object. Within this method, you implement whatever logic is needed to determine how much more lease time, if any, to give to the object. For example, the following CustomerSponsor class renews the lease exactly three times.

```
class CustomerSponsor : ISponsor
{
    private int mRenewCount = 0;

    // Implements ISponsor.Renewal
    public TimeSpan Renewal(ILease leaseInfo)
    {
        // Just a trace message for testing
        Console.WriteLine("CustomerSponsor.Renewal()");
        if (mRenewCount < 3)
        {
            mRenewCount++;
            return TimeSpan.FromSeconds(5);
        }
        else
        {
            return TimeSpan.FromSeconds(0);
        }
    }
}
```

The runtime resets the lease time to the value returned from the Renewal method. In the preceding example, that value is 5 seconds for the first three times it is called. After the third call, the Renewal method returns 0, effectively refusing to sponsor the object again. When the runtime sees this, it will remove this sponsor object from the list of registered sponsors, and try the next sponsor in the list.

We can associate this CustomerSponsor object with the Customer object by retrieving the Customer object's lease information and invoking the ILease.Register method. One logical place for this is within the Customer.InitializeLifetimeService method as demonstrated here:

```
public override object InitializeLifetimeService()
{
    // Call base class version
    ILease leaseInfo = (ILease)base.InitializeLifetimeService();

    // Register a CustomerSponsor object as a sponsor.
    leaseInfo.Register(new CustomerSponsor());

    return leaseInfo;
}
```

With this implementation, each `Customer` object creates and registers a `CustomerSponsor` object.

Client-Side Sponsors

Sponsor objects are not strictly server-side. Many times a client application may wish to sponsor the lease of a remote object. .NET makes this possible. In fact, the solution builds upon all the remoting plumbing already discussed, but you must keep one important point in mind: in regards to sponsorship, the client and the server switch roles. In other words, the client becomes the server, and the server becomes the client.

For example, consider the following `CustomerClientSponsor` class defined within the MathClient application:

```
class CustomerClientSponsor : MarshalByRefObject, ISponsor
{
   private int mRenewCount = 0;

   // Just a trace messsage for testing.
   Console.WriteLine("CustomerClientSponsor.Renewal()");
   public TimeSpan Renewal(ILease leaseInfo)
   {
      if (mRenewCount < 3)
      {
         mRenewCount++;
         return TimeSpan.FromSeconds(5);
      }
      else
      {
         return TimeSpan.FromSeconds(0);
      }
   }
}
```

The client can register this sponsor object by calling the remote `Customer` object's `GetLifetimeServices` method and using the returned `ILease` object's `Register` method. In the following example, the client registers the sponsor right after creating the `Customer` object.

```
class ClientMain
{
   static void Main(string[] args)
   {
      // Load the configuration file
      RemotingConfiguration.Configure("MathClient.exe.config");
      Customer cust = new Customer("Homer Simpson");

      // Register the client side sponsor
      ILease leaseInfo = (ILease)cust.GetLifetimeService();
      leaseInfo.Register(new CustomerClientSponsor());

      // Loop until user enters "q" to quit (snipped ...)
   }
}
```

Like our previous server-side sponsor, this sponsor renews the lease only three times. However, there is one subtle but important difference in this class definition: CustomerClientSponsor derives from MarshalByRefObject! And if you think about it, this makes perfect sense. The server runtime will need to invoke this Renewal method when the Customer lease is about to expire. Because the client sponsor object is running in a different application domain, it must be marshaled just like any other remote object. Therefore, the client holds a proxy to the remote Customer object, and the server holds a proxy to the remote CustomerClientSponsor object.

Now that our client application has also become a server, you need to be aware of an important implication. We must explicitly register a client remoting channel either a unique port number or with port 0. If we specify port 0, the runtime will automatically select an unused port. Remember, when a client is just a client the runtime can use the information imbedded in the object URL to determine the proper channel information. But when the client is a client *and* a server, you have to explicitly register the channel information so that the runtime can establish a listener thread at the given port number. To make things easy, we will just add the appropriate channel settings to the application configuration file:

```
<configuration>
  <system.runtime.remoting>
    <application>
      <client url="http://localhost:13101">
        <!-- Allows client activation of Customer type at above URL -->
        <activated type="MathLibrary.Customer, MathLibrary" />
      </client>
```

```
      <!-- Channel must be configured for client side sponsor -->
      <channels>
        <channel port="13102" ref="http" />
      </channels>
    </application>
  </system.runtime.remoting>
</configuration>
```

The server and client output from running this code is shown in Figure 4-13 and Figure 4-14 respectively. If you run this yourself, you will see that the server-side sponsor is notified first since it was the first sponsor added to the list. After it renews the lease three times, it refuses another sponsor query, so the runtime removes it from the sponsor list and queries the next sponsor, which happens to be the client-side sponsor.

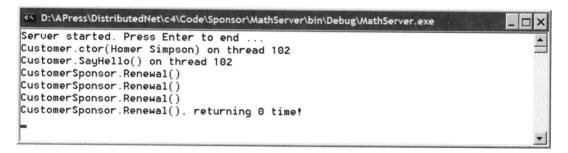

Figure 4-13. The MathServer output shows the server-side sponsor responding to renewal requests.

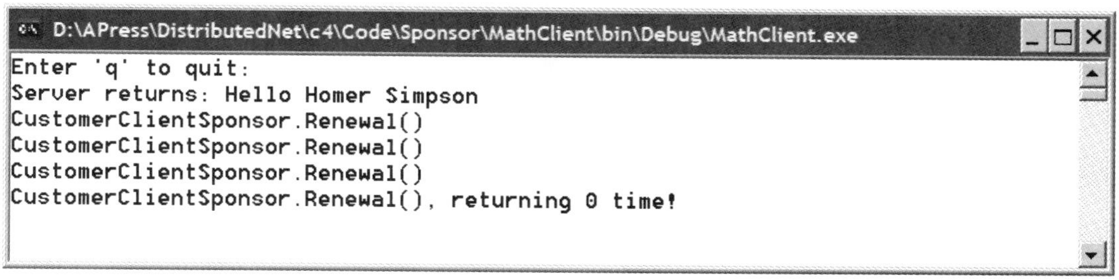

Figure 4-14. The MathClient output shows the client-side sponsor responding to renewal requests.

As mentioned earlier, the server communicates with the client-side sponsor object using the remoting plumbing. But is the client-side sponsor a well-known or client-activated object? The answer is that it behaves more like a client-activated object in that its lifetime is controlled by the LDGC. So you can assign lifetime values to your client-side sponsor objects just as we did earlier with the client-activated objects. It also means that client-side sponsors do eventually expire, unless explicitly set to live forever.

Source Code *The code for the previous example is in Chapter4\Sponsor.*

Other Lifetime Settings

The use of client-side sponsors can introduce other complications. What if the network connection has been lost? Or what if the connection is just slow? What if the sponsor's lifetime lease has expired? Given these possibilities, how long should the server runtime wait for a sponsor to reply? It turns out the default timeout value for a sponsorship reply is 2 minutes. But you can change the default using the <lifetime> element's sponsorshipTimeout attribute in the remoting configuration file.

By default, the runtime evaluates the status of all the leases every 10 seconds. You can change this polling frequency using the <lifetime> element's leaseManagerPollTime attribute. The example here demonstrates how to set both the sponsorship timeout and the polling values.

```
<lifetime leaseTime="10s" renewOnCallTime="5s"
          sponsorshipTimeout="5s" leaseManagerPollTime="5s"/>
```

Managing Resource-Intensive Objects

Recall that when a remote object's lease expires and no sponsor renews it, the runtime clears its reference to the object so that it will be garbage collected in the next sweep. This is adequate for most objects, but some may consume scarce resources and therefore should be destroyed as soon as the lease expires. In the general case, you solve this by implementing the IDisposable interface and its Dispose method. However, this assumes that the client will call this method and thus suffers from the same issues as DCOM's reference counting because it relies on the client to release the remote object.

Sponsorship provides a convenient mechanism to resolve the situation. You can create a sponsor object that actually disposes the remote object when the sponsor's Renewal method is called. To demonstrate, we modify the Customer class to implement the IDisposable interface:

```
public class Customer : MarshalByRefObject, IDisposable
{
    string mName;

    public Customer(string name)
    {
        Console.WriteLine("Customer.ctor({0}) on thread {1}", name,
            Thread.CurrentThread.GetHashCode());
        mName = name;
    }

    public string SayHello()
    {
        Console.WriteLine("Customer.SayHello() on thread {0}",
            Thread.CurrentThread.GetHashCode());

        return "Hello " + mName;
    }

    // Implements IDisposable.Dispose()
    public void Dispose()
    {
        Console.WriteLine("Customer.Dispose() on thread {0}",
            Thread.CurrentThread.GetHashCode()
        );
        // Free all unmanaged resources
        GC.SuppressFinalize(this);
    }

    // The Finalizer
    ~Customer()
    {
        Console.WriteLine("Customer.Finalize()");
    }
    // The rest snipped ...
}
```

You will have to use your imagination a bit and pretend that the Customer class implements Dispose because it allocates a scarce unmanaged resource. In Dispose, we output the current thread hash code to tell what thread is executing the Dispose method. We also update the trace messages from the constructors and the SayHello method to display the thread hash code.

Next we implement a sponsor class that calls Dispose on its sponsored object. Here is the code:

```
class DisposingSponsor : ISponsor
{
    private IDisposable mManagedObj;
    public DisposingSponsor(IDisposable managedObj)
    {
        mManagedObj = managedObj;
    }

    public TimeSpan Renewal(ILease leaseInfo)
    {
        mManagedObj.Dispose();
        return TimeSpan.FromSeconds(0);
    }
}
```

As you can see, the DisposingSponsor class simply disposes the object when its Renewal method is called. The sponsored object is passed into the constructor.

Finally, we can modify the Customer.InitializeLifetimeService method so that it registers this new sponsor object with the current Customer object. Here is the code:

```
public override object InitializeLifetimeService()
{
    ILease leaseInfo = (ILease)base.InitializeLifetimeService();

    // Register a CustomerSponsor object as a sponsor.
    leaseInfo.Register(new CustomerSponsor());

    // Register a DisposingSponsor object
    leaseInfo.Register(new DisposingSponsor(this));

    // RegisterSponsors(leaseInfo);
    return leaseInfo;
}
```

In this example, we first register a `CustomerSponsor` object, which, remember, can renew the lease three times. Then we register the `DisposingSponsor` object. This arrangement allows the object's lease to be renewed three times, and then disposed immediately afterwards. The output is shown in Figure 4-15.

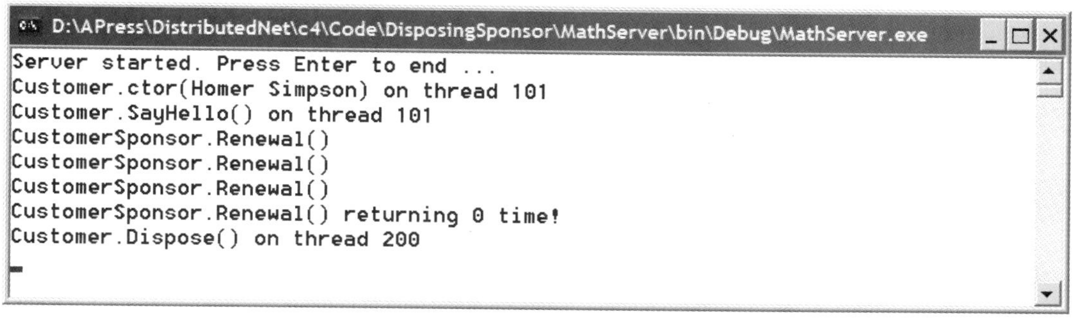

```
D:\APress\DistributedNet\c4\Code\DisposingSponsor\MathServer\bin\Debug\MathServer.exe    _ □ ×
Server started. Press Enter to end ...
Customer.ctor(Homer Simpson) on thread 101
Customer.SayHello() on thread 101
CustomerSponsor.Renewal()
CustomerSponsor.Renewal()
CustomerSponsor.Renewal()
CustomerSponsor.Renewal() returning 0 time!
Customer.Dispose() on thread 200
```

Figure 4-15. Testing the `DisposingSponsor` *class*

The output shows that the remote object is disposed immediately after the `CustomerSponsor` object refuses to renew the lease again. However, note the thread values in the output. Sponsor objects are invoked in a different thread, so this works only if the `Dispose` logic does not need to execute on a particular thread.

Building Remoting Hosts

So far, every server application example has been a simple console application. However, you can use many other types of applications to host remotable objects and serve them to clients. One intriguing option is to host the objects within a Windows service. The advantage of a Windows service is that it can be configured to automatically start whenever the machine is rebooted. In contrast, our previous console applications have to be manually started. Another option is to host remotable objects using IIS and ASP.NET. This is probably the easiest of all hosting options, but ASP.NET can only remote objects over the HTTP channel. The following sections describe how to employ both of these options.

Hosting Remotable Objects in a Windows Service

A Windows service provides the ability to execute a long running application in the background. It does not provide a user interface and therefore does not interfere with other users on the machine. IIS and SQL Server are familiar examples of

Windows services. And like these services, any Windows service can be configured to start automatically whenever the machine is booted and execute with a specific user account. These features make Windows services well suited for hosting remotable objects.

Historically, Windows service development was done almost exclusively in C++. In .NET, however, the CLR contains a number of classes that simplify the creation of a Windows service and (of course) can be used from any .NET language. Visual Studio .NET makes it even easier by providing a Windows service project template (Figure 4-16). When you create a Windows service project, Visual Studio .NET sets the appropriate references and namespaces, and provides some starter code.

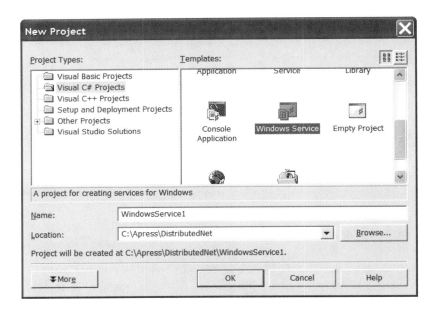

Figure 4-16. Visual Studio .NET provides a Windows Service project template.

When you create a Windows service project, Visual Studio .NET generates a class that derives from `System.ServiceProcess.ServiceBase`. This base class implements the basic necessities of any Windows service and exposes a number of overridable methods. You need only override these methods to define the behavior of your custom Windows service. At a minimum you should override the `OnStart` and `OnStop` methods. Visual Studio .NET also generates a `Main` method that loads your custom service class.

Building a Windows Service

For example, let's return to the earlier MathLibrary assembly and host the remotable SimpleMath object within a Windows service called MathService. To begin, we select the Windows service project template. This will create a project containing a service class with a default name of Service1. The service name can be changed by manually editing the generated code, but you will have to modify the class name, the constructor name, and some code within the Main function. Therefore, it is easier to select the designer view of the service, go to the Property window, and set its Name property to MathService (see Figure 4-17).

Figure 4-17. Setting the Name property for the Windows service

Figure 4-17 also shows a separate ServiceName property that specifies the friendly name of the service displayed by the Services MMC snap-in and other management utilities. So we also set this property to MathService. Here are the highlights of the generated code after performing these steps:

```
public class MathService : ServiceBase
{
    static void Main()
    {
        ServiceBase[] ServicesToRun;

        ServicesToRun = ServiceBase[] { new MathService() };

        ServiceBase.Run(ServicesToRun);
    }
```

```
        private void InitializeComponent()
        {
            components = new System.ComponentModel.Container();
            this.ServiceName = "MathService";
        }

        protected override void OnStart(string[] args)
        {
            // TODO: Add code here to start your service.
        }

        protected override void OnStop()
        {
            // TODO: Add code here to perform any tear-down necessary
        }
}
```

As you can see from this excerpt, the `Main` function constructs the `MathService` object, stores it in an array, and passes the entire array into the `ServiceBase.Run` method. The `Run` method then starts all the services contained in the array. This mechanism provides the ability to run multiple services within the same process—though we do not need this ability now.

The generated code also includes stubs for overriding the `OnStart` and `OnStop` methods. The `OnStart` method is called whenever the service is started and provides the ideal location for custom initialization logic, such as loading a remoting configuration file or performing the equivalent configuration programmatically. For example, the following code registers the proper channels and exposes the SimpleMath type as a well-known Singleton object.

```
protected override void OnStart(string[] args)
{
    // Configure the channel
    HttpChannel channel = new HttpChannel(13101);
    ChannelServices.RegisterChannel(channel);

    // Register SimpleMath as well-known Singleton
    RemotingConfiguration.RegisterWellKnownServiceType(
        typeof(MathLibrary.SimpleMath),
        "SimpleMath.soap",
        WellKnownObjectMode.Singleton
    );
}
```

In this example, we chose to configure the remoting settings programmatically, but we could have read the settings from a configuration file instead using the RemotingConfiguration.Configure method. The key difference to note between this example and earlier console application host examples is that we did not keep the server alive by executing a Console.Readline. This is because a Windows service remains running until it is manually stopped. In any case, a console window is not available in a Windows service, so an attempt to read from or write to the console is ignored.

Since there is no console available, Windows services typically only send trace or error messages to a file or to the Windows event log. The System.Diagnostics.EventLog class provides methods to read and write to the Windows event log. To demonstrate, let's modify the SimpleMath class to write its trace messages to the event log instead of the console window. Here is the code:

```
public class SimpleMath : MarshalByRefObject
{
    public SimpleMath()
    {
        WriteLogEntry("SimpleMath ctor called");
    }

    public int Add(int n1, int n2)
    {
        WriteLogEntry(string.Format("SimpleMath.Add({0},{1})", n1, n2));
        return n1 + n2;
    }

    public int Subtract(int n1, int n2)
    {
        WriteLogEntry(string.Format("SimpleMath.Subtract({0},{1})", n1, n2));
        return n1 - n2;
    }

    private void WriteLogEntry(string msg)
    {
        EventLog.WriteEntry("MathService", msg);
    }
}
```

In this example, we have added a WriteLogEntry method that uses the EventLog class to write a given message to the Windows event log. In this case, we are using a static version of the WriteEntry method, although overloaded instance versions also exist. The first method argument specifies the source of the event and the second argument specifies the message to write to the log. Each of the other `SimpleMath` methods has been updated to call the `WriteLogEntry` method to write the trace messages instead of using the console.

Installing the Windows Service

Now that our logic for the Windows service is complete, the next step is to install the application as a Windows service. Unlike other .NET applications that boast xcopy installation, installing a Windows service requires various registry settings and configuration. A command line tool called InstallUtil (installutil.exe) is provided for this task, but it expects the application to provide a class derived from `System.Configuration.Install.Installer`. InstallUtil calls this class to handle any custom installation details. In a Windows service application, the derived `Installer` class should create an instance of `System.ServiceProcess.ServiceProcessInstaller`. The `ServiceProcessInstaller` class implements the standard requirements for installing a Windows service.

While this may seem somewhat complicated, in Visual Studio .NET we can add an appropriate `Installer` with just a couple mouse clicks. In fact, the Properties window for the service designer contains a link at the bottom of the window entitled Add Installer (this is shown in Figure 4-17). If you click this link, Visual Studio .NET generates an `Installer`-derived class that creates and initializes a `ServiceProcessInstaller` object as described in the previous paragraph. It also adds another designer to the project that allows you to set properties for both of these items via the Properties window. For example, you can configure the `ServiceProcessInstaller` object to install the Windows service such that it runs under a specified user account or under the LocalSystem account (as most services do). In this case, we want MathService to execute under the LocalSystem account, so we set `Account` property as shown in Figure 4-18.

Now that we have added the appropriate installers, we can compile the MathService application and install it using the InstallUtil command line tool as shown here:

```
Installutil mathservice.exe
```

Once installed, we can now start, stop, or reconfigure the MathService service using the Services MMC snap-in (Control Panel | Administration Tools | Services). We can also configure the service to start automatically whenever the machine boots. And since the service executes under a given user account, remote clients can use the service even if a user is not logged into the server machine. Speaking of clients, we can use any of our earlier MathClient examples to test out the new MathService. No special code or additional configuration is required to use the MathService instead of the console-based MathServer application.

Figure 4-18. The ServiceProcessInstaller *Properties window*

 NOTE   *Since the MathService Windows service and the MathServer console application both expose their remotable objects on port 13101, you will not be able to run them at the same time.*

 Source Code   *The code for the previous example is in Chapter4\Windows Service.*

Debugging the Windows Service

Typically, you can take advantage of Visual Studio .NET's advanced debugging capabilities by simply pressing the F5 key or the menu equivalent Debug | Start. However, in the case of a Windows service project, it is not quite as easy. In fact, attempting to start the Windows service from within the IDE will result in the error shown in Figure 4-19.

Figure 4-19. Starting a Windows service in the IDE causes an error.

Therefore, to debug a Windows service, you must use Visual Studio .NET's ability to attach to a running process. For example, to attach to the MathService service, open the MathService project in Visual Studio .NET and select Debug | Processes. This will display a dialog box showing the processes executing on the machine. Check the "Show system processes" check box to display all processes including the services. Then select MathServer.exe from the list of processes and click the Attach button (Figure 4-20).

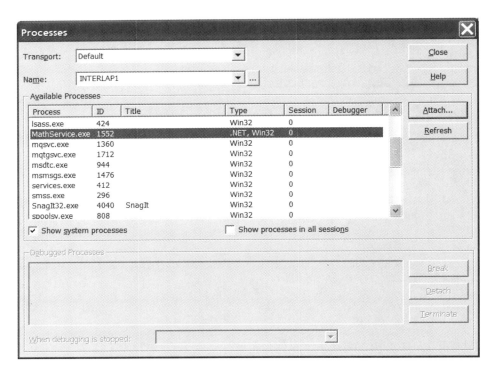

Figure 4-20. Attaching to a running process

Another dialog box will appear asking you to choose the program types you wish to debug. For this example, only the Common Language Runtime option needs to be selected (Figure 4-21).

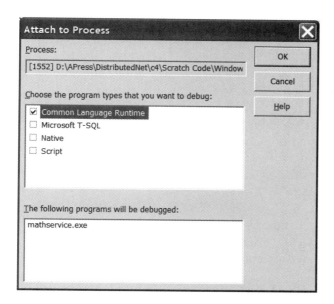

Figure 4-21. Selecting the type of program to debug

After clicking the OK button, the IDE attaches to the specified process and goes into debug mode. From here, you can set breakpoints as needed, trigger them from the client, and step through the code.

Hosting Remotable Objects in ASP.NET

The easiest way to build a host for remotable objects is to use Internet Information Server (IIS) and ASP.NET. IIS is Microsoft's Web server software, but calling IIS a Web server is a bit of an oversimplification. IIS is an application server in its own right, providing a scalable architecture and security services that any IIS hosted application can leverage. IIS exposes a low-level programmatic interface called the *Internet Service API* (ISAPI), which allows any custom application to hook into the functionality of IIS. Such an application is called an *ISAPI extension*. ASP.NET (and classic ASP before that) is fundamentally an ISAPI extension that abstracts the low-level details of ISAPI and encapsulates it into a powerful, easy-to-use framework. Furthermore, as its name suggests, ASP.NET takes full advantage of .NET technologies including assemblies, reflection, the CLR, and managed code.

While ASP.NET provides an easy mechanism for hosting remotable objects, it is only an option if you are willing to use the HTTP channel rather than the faster TCP channel. On the other hand, you can minimize the performance differences by replacing the default SOAP formatter with the binary formatter. More details to come.

Creating the IIS Virtual Directory

When using ASP.NET to host remotable objects, you do not have to write any code. However, you do have to perform some mechanical steps and write a configuration file. Here are the steps:

1. Create a directory to serve as the physical location for the assemblies defining the remotable types and a configuration file.

2. Under the directory, create a web.config file to contain the remoting configuration information.

3. Create a bin subdirectory and copy the assemblies defining the remotable types into the directory. Only assemblies that are not shared need to be copied. IIS will find shared assemblies in the GAC.

4. Using the Internet Services Manager administration tool, create an IIS virtual directory aliasing the directory created in the previous steps.

Let's perform these steps to host the SimpleMath class and create an IIS virtual directory called MathService. We have to copy the MathLibrary assembly to the bin subdirectory and create a web.config file as shown here:

```
<configuration>
  <system.runtime.remoting>
    <application>
      <service>
        <wellknown mode="Singleton"
                   type="MathLibrary.SimpleMath, MathLibrary"
                   objectUri="SimpleMath.soap" />
      </service>
      <channels>
        <channel ref="http" />
      </channels>
    </application>
  </system.runtime.remoting>
</configuration>
```

As you can see, the web.config file follows the same format as any remoting configuration file. But there are a few considerations:

- You cannot specify an application name in the <application> element. Instead, the name of the virtual directory is used as the application name.

- Since ASP.NET can only use the HTTP channel, no channel configuration is required. However, you can add a <channel> element if you require some special channel properties.

- Do not specify a port number in the channel configuration. By default, IIS will listen at port 80. If you need the application to listen on a different port number, then specify it using the Internet Services Manager.

- The object URI must end with a .rem or .soap extension. While I have been doing this throughout all the examples, these extensions are required only when using IIS as a host.

Building the IIS Client

Building a client for the IIS hosted service is like building any other remoting client. You need only remember that the virtual directory is the application name, and modify the URL accordingly. For example, here is a possible client:

```
class ClientMain
{
    static void Main(string[] args)
    {
        // Go get the remote object
        Object remoteObj = Activator.GetObject(
                            typeof(MathLibrary.SimpleMath),
                        "http://localhost/MathService/SimpleMath.soap"
                    );

        // Cast the returned proxy to the SimpleMath type
        SimpleMath math = (SimpleMath)remoteObj;

        // Use the remote object
        do
        {
            Console.WriteLine("5 + 2 = {0}", math.Add(5,2));
            Console.WriteLine("5 - 2 = {0}", math.Subtract(5,2));
        }while(Console.ReadLine() != "q");
    }
}
```

In this example, note the URL specified in the Activator.GetObject method call. First, notice that no port number is specified; therefore it will default to port 80.

Also notice how the MathService virtual directory name is incorporated into the URL. Finally, remember that all the remoting details apply as before, including the fact that the client must have the `SimpleMath` type metadata available locally either in the form of the actual implementation assembly or a metadata-only assembly (as described in Chapter 5).

Using the Binary Formatter in IIS

As noted earlier, the HTTP channel does not perform as well as the TCP channel. Partly, this is caused by the fact that the HTTP channel uses the SOAP formatter by default. Not only does this create a larger payload that taxes the network bandwidth, it also takes longer to serialize and deserialize a SOAP message. However, the channel architecture allows you to associate any channel with any formatter. So you can reduce the HTTP channel overhead by using the binary formatter instead.

We can configure our current example to use the binary formatter with a simple addition to the configuration file. Here is the new web.config file:

```
<configuration>
  <system.runtime.remoting>
    <application>
      <service>
        <wellknown mode="Singleton"
                   type="MathLibrary.SimpleMath, MathLibrary"
                   objectUri="SimpleMath.soap" />
      </service>
      <channels>
        <channel ref="http">
          <serverProviders>
            <formatter ref="binary" />
          </serverProviders>
        </channel>
      </channels>
    </application>
  </system.runtime.remoting>
</configuration>
```

The changes are confined to the <channels> section. The added <serverProviders> element allows us to associate any formatter with the specified channel. Remember, the `ref` attributes shown in this example refer to channel and formatter templates defined in the machine.config file.

The client application must also be modified to use the binary formatter. You can programmatically associate the binary formatter with the HTPP channel using an overloaded version of the `HTTPClientChannel` class constructor. For example:

```
IChannel channel = new HttpClientChannel(
    "HttpAndBinary",  // A friendly name for the channel
    new BinaryClientFormatterSinkProvider() // the binary formatter
);
ChannelServices.RegisterChannel(channel);
```

Or you can accomplish this using a configuration file as shown here:

```
<configuration>
  <system.runtime.remoting>
    <application>
      <channels>
        <channel ref="http">
          <clientProviders>
            <formatter ref="binary" />
          </clientProviders>
        </channel>
      </channels>
    </application>
  </system.runtime.remoting>
</configuration>
```

 Source Code *The code for this example is in Chapter4\IIS Host.*

Debugging ASP.NET-Hosted Services

Debugging a remotable object when it is hosted in ASP.NET presents issues similar to the Windows service scenario. So once again, you must attach the IDE to a running process in order to debug. For ASP.NET-hosted remote objects, the ASP.NET process (aspnet_wp.exe) loads the assemblies and hosts the objects. Therefore, you must attach the debugger to the aspnet_wp.exe process.

IIS Hosting and Web Services

At this point, the inevitable question is, "If I use ASP.NET to host my remoted objects, is that considered a Web service?" The short answer is no. However, the exact definition of Web services was very fluid in the beta stages of .NET, and some books, articles, and even Microsoft documentation confused Web services with

.NET Remoting. This is understandable, given, in the case of ASP.NET hosting, the remote object is accessible over the Web using standard protocols such as HTTP and SOAP.

The reason why this is not Web services will be explained in Chapter 6 after we have covered the full nature of Web services. Fundamentally, however, it is a matter of assumptions. .NET Remoting, regardless of the channel, formatter, or host used, assumes a .NET application is on the other side of the wire, whereas Web services make no such assumption. This makes .NET Remoting far more flexible and powerful in a ".NET everywhere" environment, but Web services more useful in an open environment.

Summary

This chapter has covered many gory details of .NET Remoting. As you will see in the next chapter, there is much more. However, the topics covered here and in the previous chapter comprise the core aspects of remoting. Therefore, the knowledge imparted in this chapter is sufficient for many distributed applications.

To review, here are some of the key points of the chapter:

- Well-known objects are identified by a commonly known and unique name. The server activates a well-known object in one of two modes: Singleton or SingleCall.

- In Singleton mode, a single persistent object serves all client requests. In SingleCall mode, the runtime creates a new object to serve each request, and releases it when the request is completed.

- Client-activated objects allow construction with nondefault constructors. More importantly, they can maintain client-specific state indefinitely.

- The runtime uses a leasing mechanism to manage the lifetime of client-activated objects and well-known Singleton objects. An object's lease is renewed with each client method call, or by registered sponsor objects.

- Any managed application type can host remotable objects. However, hosting in a Windows service or ASP.NET are logical choices in most real-world applications.

Compared to DCOM, .NET Remoting presents a very different model for implementing distributed applications. Although it does expose the inner workings of the network more so than DCOM, the result is a framework that is powerful as is and highly extensible. As a longtime Visual Basic programmer frustrated by the limitations imposed by the language and DCOM, I feel completely empowered when working with .NET Remoting. Even if you don't agree with that now, I think you will after some time working with remoting and absorbing some of the details.

In the next chapter, you will learn some more advanced, but still important, remoting techniques. This should round out your remoting knowledge and leave you ready to explore even more advanced topics as needed.

CHAPTER 5

Additional Remoting Techniques

ONE OF THE FASCINATING ASPECTS of remoting is how many levels of complexity it has. At one level, remoting is as easy as setting some configuration details, creating the remote object, and using it. At the other end of the complexity spectrum, remoting can involve the creation of custom proxies, channels, and formatters. This chapter strikes a balance between these two extremes by examining some more advanced, but still practical, remoting techniques without wandering into the esoteric realms of the topic.

In fact, I was tempted to title this chapter "Advanced Remoting Techniques," but some topics, such as solving the metadata deployment issue are critical and are required knowledge for any developer planning to use remoting. So I like to think of this chapter as covering remoting topics that not everyone is interested in, but should be. Unfortunately, that doesn't make a very good title, so the current one must do.

Solving the Metadata Deployment Issue

In Chapter 4, I pointed out that our very first remoting example suffered from three problems. The first problem, too much hard-coded configuration settings, was solved using a remoting configuration file. The second problem, the inability to create a remote object with a nondefault constructor, was solved using client activation. The third problem, however, proves the hardest to solve.

The third and final problem is the issue of deployment. Whenever a client application connects to a remote object, it will use code like the following:

```
// Go get the remote object
Object remoteObj = Activator.GetObject(
                typeof(MathLibrary.SimpleMath),
                "http://localhost:13101/myURI.soap"
        );
```

You now know that this code does not return the actual object, but a proxy to the remote object. The client runtime generates this proxy such that it impersonates the remote object; in other words, the proxy exposes the same methods and properties. How does the runtime accomplish this? By reflecting over the remote type's metadata. But the runtime can only do this is if it can read the metadata from the remote object's assembly. Therefore, an assembly containing the remotable type must be deployed on both the server (so it can be remoted) and on the client (so the runtime can build a proxy).

DCOM programmers are already familiar with this issue. However, with DCOM, you need only deploy a *type library* to the client. The type library contains only the information necessary to build a proxy for a remote object. Developers can use the Interface Definition Language (IDL) or tools like Visual Basic 6.0 to build type libraries.

You can do the same thing in .NET. In fact, there are three techniques you can use.

- You can create a separate metadata-only assembly by compiling stubbed out versions of the remote types. You then deploy this metadata assembly to the client and keep the full implementation assembly on the server.

- You can split the remote types into interfaces (and/or abstract base classes) and implementations and compile each into a separate assembly. You then deploy only the interface assembly to the client and keep the full implementation assembly on the server.

- You can use the Soapsuds tool (soapsuds.exe) to automatically build a metadata assembly.

Deploying Metadata Assemblies

The first way to solve the type metadata deployment issue is to build a special assembly that contains only the remote type metadata. In essence, this metadata assembly is equivalent to the COM type library, except that you can build it using your .NET language of choice instead of cryptic IDL.

This is a very flexible technique, but you must keep one restriction in mind: the full type name on the server must match exactly with that on the client. Since the assembly name is part of the type name, this also means the client's metadata assembly name and the server's implementation assembly name must match.

Do yourself a favor and read the last paragraph again. Make sure you understand it because it will keep biting us over and over again throughout this section. The reason for this restriction is due to the way the remoting plumbing works. Remember, when an object is returned from the server via a method call, the server actually passes an `ObjRef`. The `ObjRef` contains all the information required to construct the proxy on the client side, including the type name, the URI, type hierarchy, and supported interfaces. Of these, the important piece of information for this discussion is the type name, because it also includes the name of the assembly. The client runtime then attempts to reflect over this assembly to build the proxy. Obviously, if the assembly were named differently on the client, then the runtime cannot build the proxy.

In the next few sections, we will walk through a complete example to demonstrate how to build and use a metadata assembly. However, because we will be juggling several projects, you might find yourself losing your bearings. To help prevent this, Table 5-1 describes each project and the corresponding assemblies.

Table 5-1. Customer Project Descriptions

Project Name	Output Assembly	Project Type	Description
CustomerLibrary	CustomerLibrary.dll	Class Library	Implementation assembly; that is, the assembly containing `CustomerService` and `Customer` class implementations
CustomerMetadata	CustomerLibrary.dll	Class Library	Metadata assembly; that is, the assembly containing the stubbed out class definitions
CustomerServer	CustomerServer.exe	Console Application	The server application hosting the remote types
CustomerClient	CustomerClient.exe	Console Application	The client application

Building the Server

To begin, we will build a Class Library project called CustomerLibrary. This project defines two simple MBR classes: `CustomerService` and `Customer`. To keep things simple, the `CustomerService` class exposes only two methods. The `CreateCustomer` method is the important one. It constructs a `Customer` object using the provided name and returns a `Customer` object. The other method, `Test`, exists only to provide a simple method we can call to test that our remoting settings are correct. It simply returns an integer value to the client. The `Customer` class has only one method, `SayHello`, which returns a string containing a friendly greeting to the customer. Here is the code:

```
namespace CustomerLibrary
{
    public class CustomerService : MarshalByRefObject
    {
        public int Test()
        {
            Console.WriteLine("CustomerService.Test()");
            return 5;
        }
        public Customer CreateCustomer(string name)
        {
            Console.WriteLine("CustomerService.CreateCustomer(\"{0}\")", name);
            return new Customer(name);
        }
    }

    public class Customer : MarshalByRefObject
    {
        string mName;

        public Customer(string name)
        {
            Console.WriteLine("Customer.ctor(\"{0}\")", name);
            mName = name;
        }

        public string SayHello()
        {
            Console.WriteLine("Customer.SayHello");
            return "Hello " + mName;
        }
    }
} // Namespace CustomerLibrary
```

To host these types, we build a server console application called CustomerServer. This looks very much like our previous servers; it simply reads a remoting configuration file and waits for clients to connect.

```
namespace CustomerServer
{
    class CustomerMain
    {
        static void Main(string[] args)
        {
            Console.WriteLine("Customer Server initializing ...");
            RemotingConfiguration.Configure("CustomerServer.exe.config");

            Console.WriteLine("Waiting for clients. Press 'q' to quit");

            string input;
            do
            {
                input = Console.ReadLine();
            }while(input != "q");
        }
    }
}
```

To complete the picture, here is the remoting configuration file used on the server:

```
<configuration>
  <system.runtime.remoting>
    <application>
      <service>
        <wellknown mode="SingleCall"
                   type="CustomerLibrary.CustomerService, CustomerLibrary"
                   objectUri="customer.soap" />
      </service>
      <channels>
        <channel port="13101" ref="http" />
      </channels>
    </application>
  </system.runtime.remoting>
</configuration>
```

So far, nothing is different from our previous remoting examples. If we wish, we could distribute the full CustomerLibrary assembly to any client and have it build the necessary proxies using the metadata within. However, our goal here is not to distribute the implementations, so we create one final class library project called CustomerMetadata. In this project, we redefine the `CustomerService` and `Customer` classes with stubbed out implementations. For example:

```
namespace CustomerLibrary
{
   // The CustomerService class stub code
   public class CustomerService : MarshalByRefObject
   {
      // A basic test to make sure remoting settings are working
      public int Test()
      {
         throw new NotSupportedException("Method cannot be run locally");
      }

      // A factory method to return a Customer object
      public Customer CreateCustomer(string name)
      {
         throw new NotSupportedException("Method cannot be run locally");
      }
   }

   // The Customer class stub code
   public class Customer : MarshalByRefObject
   {
      public string SayHello()
      {
         throw new NotSupportedException("Method cannot be run locally");
      }
   }
}
```

There are a few important items to note about the previous code example. First, notice that the namespace and class names match *exactly* with those in the CustomerLibrary project. Second, note that the signatures of all the methods also match with the corresponding methods in CustomerLibrary. However, the implementations are very different. In fact, since the methods in the CustomerMetadata project should never be executed, they all throw an exception. This way, if a client has incorrect remoting settings and mistakenly creates a local `Customer` object, the `SayHello` method will throw an exception.

Building the Client

Now let's try building a client using the metadata assembly. To start, we create yet another console project called CustomerClient and enter the following code:

```
using System;
using System.Runtime.Remoting;
using CustomerLibrary;

namespace CustomerClient
{
    class CustomerMain
    {
        static void Main(string[] args)
        {
            RemotingConfiguration.Configure("CustomerClient.exe.config");

            // Create a proxy to the remote CustomerService object
            CustomerService custSvc = new CustomerService();

            // Execute the simple Test method
            Console.WriteLine(custSvc.Test());

            // Get a proxy to a remote Customer object
            Customer cust = custSvc.CreateCustomer("Homer");
            Console.WriteLine(cust.SayHello());

            Console.ReadLine();
        }
    }
}
```

As you can see in the previous code, this client reads the remoting setting from the configuration file. Here are the contents of the remoting configuration file:

```
<configuration>
  <system.runtime.remoting>
    <application>
      <client>
        <wellknown type="CustomerLibrary.CustomerService, CustomerLibrary"
                   url="http://localhost:13101/customer.soap" />
      </client>
    </application>
  </system.runtime.remoting>
</configuration>
```

Finally, we set a reference to the CustomerMetadata.dll assembly and compile the client. Everything compiles fine, but when we test this application (running the server and the client), we see the exception shown in Figure 5-1.

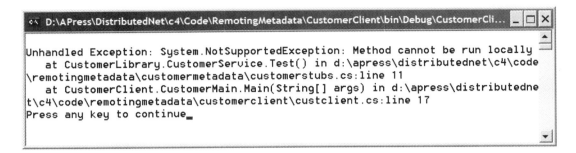

```
Unhandled Exception: System.NotSupportedException: Method cannot be run locally
   at CustomerLibrary.CustomerService.Test() in d:\apress\distributednet\c4\code
\remotingmetadata\customermetadata\customerstubs.cs:line 11
   at CustomerClient.CustomerMain.Main(String[] args) in d:\apress\distributedne
t\c4\code\remotingmetadata\customerclient\custclient.cs:line 17
Press any key to continue_
```

Figure 5-1. Exception caused when client attempts to run CustomerService locally

Apparently, the client attempted to run the CustomerService.Test method locally. Why? *Because we forgot to change the name of the metadata assembly to match the name of the implementation assembly.* As it stands now, the CustomerMetadata project is generating an assembly named CustomerMetadata. We must change this so that it generates an assembly named CustomerLibrary. Using Visual Studio .NET, this can be done by clicking Project | Properties and, in the General tab, changing the Assembly Name setting to CustomerLibrary (see Figure 5-2).

Finally, in the CustomerClient project, we remove the reference to CustomerMetadata and replace it with a reference to the CustomerLibrary assembly emitted by the CustomerMetadata project.

> **NOTE** *Make sure the client project references the correct CustomerLibrary assembly. Do not select the one created by the CustomerLibrary project because it contains the full implementation of the types. Instead, the client should reference the CustomerLibrary assembly generated by the CustomerMetadata project.*

Now we can rebuild the client and test the application. Figure 5-3 shows the client output.

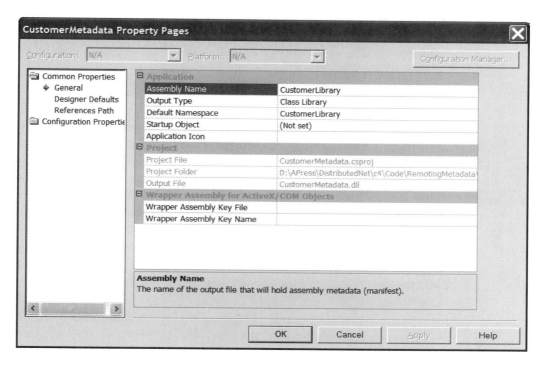

Figure 5-2. You can change the output assembly name in the Project Properties dialog box.

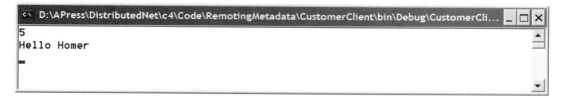

Figure 5-3. The CustomerClient output

In this example, the CustomerService class is the only type exposed to clients as a well-known object. The Customer type is exposed by a factory method of CustomerService. So is Customer a well-known or client-activated type? The answer, really, is neither. Both of these terms describe types that serve as an entry point into a remote application. The Customer object is simply an object marshaled out of the remote application domain. But, like a client-activated type, its lifetime is managed through the leasing mechanism described earlier.

Adding a Client-Activated Object

In the previous example, we used a well-known object as an entry point into the remote application. We can also use metadata assemblies with client-activated objects. For example, let's add a CAOCustomer class to our ClassLibrary project:

```
namespace CustomerLibrary
{
   public class CAOCustomer : MarshalByRefObject
   {
      string mName;

      public CAOCustomer(string name)
      {
         Console.WriteLine("Customer.ctor(\"{0}\")", name);
         mName = name;
      }
      public string SayHello()
      {
         Console.WriteLine("Customer.SayHello");
         return "Hello " + mName;
      }
   }
}
```

Within the CustomerMetadata project, we add a corresponding class with stubbed out methods:

```
namespace CustomerLibrary
{
   // The "dummy" CAOCustomer implementation
   public class CAOCustomer : MarshalByRefObject
   {
      public CAOCustomer(string name)
      {
         throw new NotSupportedException("Method cannot be run locally");
      }
      public string SayHello()
      {
         throw new NotSupportedException("Method cannot be run locally");
      }
   }
}
```

As before, the methods in this class throw an exception if the client attempts to execute them locally. And finally, we update the configuration file to expose the CAOCustomer type as a client-activated object by putting the following <activated> element under the <service> element:

```
<!-- Register Customer class as client activated -->
<activated type="CustomerLibrary.CAOCustomer, CustomerLibrary" />
```

To test our new client-activated object, we update the client's main method to create the CAOCustomer object and invoke the SayHello method.

```
class CustomerMain
    {
        static void Main(string[] args)
        {
            RemotingConfiguration.Configure("CustomerClient.exe.config");

            // Snipped some code here ...

            // Get a proxy to the remote CAO Customer object
            CAOCustomer caoCust = new CAOCustomer("Marge");
            Console.WriteLine(caoCust.SayHello());

            Console.ReadLine();
        }
    }
```

We also have to update the client's configuration file to recognize the client-activated object. The additions are all made under the <client> element:

```
<client url="http://localhost:13101">
  <activated type="CustomerLibrary.CAOCustomer, CustomerLibrary" />

  <wellknown type="CustomerLibrary.CustomerService, CustomerLibrary"
             url="http://localhost:13101/customer.soap" />
</client>
```

Finally, we can compile everything and test our application. When we do, we should see the output shown in Figure 5-4.

 Source Code   *The code for this example is in Chapter5\RemotingMetadata.*

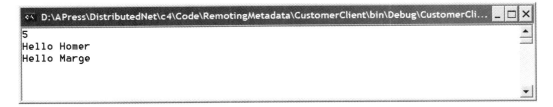

Figure 5-4. The CustomerClient output with client-activated object

Deploying Interface Assemblies

Another way to provide metadata to a client is to deploy an interface assembly. The idea here is that you split each remote object into an interface and an implementation. Then you distribute only the interfaces to the client machines, while leaving the implementations on the server. Technically, you can also include abstract base classes within the interface assembly. In concept, interface assemblies and metadata assemblies are very similar. However, instead of deploying stubbed-out class implementations, we deploy only interfaces. This adds an element of elegance to the solution, but also introduces some issues in regards to client-activated objects.

To demonstrate how to create and use an interface assembly, we will be reworking the previous customer example. And, just as before, we need to manage a number of projects. So Table 5-2 summarizes the projects we will be creating.

Table 5-2. Customer Project Descriptions

Project Name	Output Assembly	Project Type	Description
CustomerLibrary	CustomerLibrary.dll	Class Library	Implementation assembly; that is, the assembly containing the CustomerService and Customer class implementations
CustomerInterfaces	CustomerInterfaces.dll	Class Library	Interface assembly; that is, the assembly containing the ICustomerService and ICustomer interfaces
CustomerServer	CustomerServer.exe	Console Application	The server application
CustomerClient	CustomerClient.exe	Console Application	The client application

Building the Server

Our first step in building the server is to define the appropriate interfaces for the CustomerService and Customer classes. So we create a class library project called CustomerInterfaces and define the interfaces as shown in the following example:

```
namespace CustomerLibrary
{
   public interface ICustomerService
   {
      int Test();
      ICustomer CreateCustomer(string name);
   }

   public interface ICustomer
   {
      string SayHello();
   }
}
```

Other than the use of interfaces, this is quite similar to the earlier CustomerMetadata implementation. Of course, interfaces cannot be executed, so we do not have to worry about a client attempting to run these methods locally. Also note that the CreateCustomer method returns an ICustomer object, instead of a Customer object as before.

Another important distinction is that we do not have to change the name of the emitted assembly. Recall that the ObjRef contains information regarding a remote type's implemented interfaces. Therefore, the client can cast the runtime-generated proxy object to any of the remote object's implemented interfaces.

Now we can create a class library project called CustomerLibrary and set a reference to the CustomerInterfaces assembly. Then we implement the CustomerService and Customer classes as shown here:

```
namespace CustomerLibrary
{
   public class CustomerService : MarshalByRefObject, ICustomerService
   {
      public int Test()
      {
         Console.WriteLine("CustomerService.Test()");
         return 5;
      }
```

```
        public ICustomer CreateCustomer(string name)
        {
            Console.WriteLine("CustomerService.CreateCustomer(\"{0}\")", name);
            ICustomer cust = (ICustomer)new Customer(name);
            return cust;
        }
    }

    public class Customer : MarshalByRefObject, ICustomer
    {
        string mName;
        public Customer(string name)
        {
            Console.WriteLine("Customer.ctor(\"{0}\")", name);
            mName = name;
        }
        public string SayHello()
        {
            Console.WriteLine("Customer.SayHello");
            return "Hello " + mName;
        }
    }
}
```

Again, the implementations shown in this example are very similar to the previous metadata assembly example. This time, however, each class implements the corresponding interface from the interface assembly.

Next, we build a console application called CustomerServer that serves the objects to clients. The code here is straightforward, we just have to remember to copy the implementation CustomerLibrary assembly to the server's application directory so that the server can bind to it when it must create the Customer objects. Or, we can set a reference to the implementation CustomerLibrary assembly and let the Visual Studio .NET IDE copy the assembly automatically. Here is the code:

```
using System;
using System.Runtime.Remoting;

namespace CustomerServer
{
    class CustomerMain
    {
```

```
       static void Main(string[] args)
       {
           Console.WriteLine("Customer Server initializing ...");
           RemotingConfiguration.Configure("CustomerServer.exe.config");

           Console.WriteLine("Waiting for clients. Press 'q' to quit");

           string input;
           do
           {
               input = Console.ReadLine();
           }while(input != "q");
       }
   }
}
```

Probably more importantly, here is the CustomerServer configuration file, which simply exposes the CustomerService object as a well-known SingleCall object.

```
<configuration>
  <system.runtime.remoting>
    <application>
      <service>
        <wellknown mode="SingleCall"
                   type="CustomerLibrary.CustomerService, CustomerLibrary"
                   objectUri="Customer.soap" />
      </service>
      <channels>
        <channel port="13101" ref="http" />
      </channels>
    </application>
  </system.runtime.remoting>
</configuration>
```

Building the Client

Thankfully, the client proves far easier to build than the server. In fact, the steps to build the client are exactly as they were before, except that the assembly used to supply the client with the remote type metadata contains only the interfaces.

To build the client, we create a console application called CustomerClient. Here is the code:

```
using System;
using System.Runtime.Remoting;
using CustomerLibrary;

namespace CustomerClient
{
    class CustomerMain
    {
        static void Main(string[] args)
        {
            ICustomerService custSvc;
            custSvc = (ICustomerService)Activator.GetObject(
                        typeof(ICustomerService),
                        "http://localhost:13101/customer.soap"
                    );

            Console.WriteLine(custSvc.Test());

            ICustomer cust = custSvc.CreateCustomer("Homer");
            Console.WriteLine(cust.SayHello());

            Console.ReadLine();
        }
    }
}
```

Since this code uses the `Activator.GetObject` method, no configuration file is needed. However, note that the client is implemented in terms of the `ICustomerService` and `ICustomer` interfaces. Therefore, the CustomerClient project only needs to reference the CustomerInterfaces assembly, and all the implementation details can remain on the server. The output from the client is shown in Figure 5-5.

 Source Code   *The code for the previous example is in Chapter5\RemotingInterfaces.*

Unfortunately, if the client uses an interface assembly for metadata, then it cannot connect to the remote object with the `new` keyword. This is why the previous example uses the `Activator.GetObject` method instead. Consider the following attempts to use `new`.

```
// Can't construct an interface !!
ICustomerService custSvc2 = new ICustomerService();

// We don't have the type metadata for CustomerService!!
ICustomerService custSvc3 = (ICustomerService) new CustomerService();
```

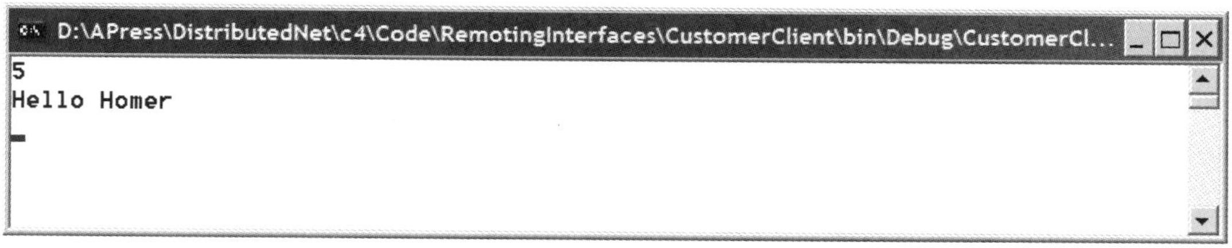

```
D:\APress\DistributedNet\c4\Code\RemotingInterfaces\CustomerClient\bin\Debug\CustomerCl...  _ □ ×
5
Hello Homer
```

Figure 5-5. The output from CustomerClient

Once you see these attempts to use new, the reasons why it does not work become pretty obvious. In the first attempt, we try to instantiate an interface, which is ridiculous and will not compile. In the second attempt, we try to construct a CustomerService object and cast it to an ICustomerService interface. Unfortunately, this requires the type metadata for the concrete CustomerService class. And since we have only deployed the interfaces, this too will not compile.

Although the CustomerService object must be activated using the Activator.GetObject method, we can encapsulate the call within another class which is defined in the CustomerInterfaces assembly and is intended to run in the client application domain. To demonstrate, let's add such a class to the CustomerInterface project and call it CustomerFactory.

```
namespace CustomerLibrary
{
   public class CustomerFactory
   {
      public static ICustomerService CreateCustomerService()
      {
         // Just a trace message to make sure this runs on the client.
         Console.WriteLine("CustomerFactory.CreateCustomerService()");

         ICustomerService custSvc = (ICustomerService) Activator.GetObject(
                                 typeof(ICustomerService),
                                 "http://localhost:13101/customer.soap"
                            );
         return custSvc;
      }
   }
}
```

Now our client code can be simplified by calling this static
CreateCustomerService method:

```
class CustomerMain
{
   static void Main(string[] args)
   {
      RemotingConfiguration.Configure("CustomerClient.exe.config");

      ICustomerService custSvc = CustomerFactory.CreateCustomerService();

      // Call ICustomerService.Test to confirm remoting settings
      Console.WriteLine(custSvc.Test());

      // Get a proxy to a remote Customer object
      ICustomer cust = custSvc.CreateCustomer("Homer");
      Console.WriteLine(cust.SayHello());

      Console.ReadLine();
   }
}
```

Interface Assemblies and Client-Activated Objects

Unfortunately, interface assemblies and client-activated objects do not mix well.
Remember, one of the main benefits of a client-activated object is that a client can
create one by calling a nondefault constructor. However, you cannot invoke any
constructor on an interface. Therefore, the only way to distribute the type
metadata for a client-activated object is to provide a stubbed out version of the
class as we did earlier in the metadata assembly example.

Of course, there is nothing stopping us from putting the stubbed out class
within the interface assembly—creating a hybrid assembly containing both interfaces and stubbed out classes. However, this brings us right back to the assembly
name issue, where the assembly containing the stubbed out class must be named
the same as the assembly containing the actual class implementation. This is not
an insurmountable issue, but it can be a hassle to try to keep track of two very different versions of the same assembly.

Using the Soapsuds Utility

As the previous sections show, correctly building and distributing a metadata or interface assembly can be a little tricky. If you wish to avoid these hassles, you can use the Soapsuds tool (soapsuds.exe) to automatically generate the metadata. Sounds ideal right? Not quite. Like many automation tools, you give up a level of control and flexibility when using Soapsuds. How much flexibility you sacrifice depends on where you are executing the Soapsuds tool: on the client or on the server.

- On the client, you can use Soapsuds to download type metadata from the remote server application itself. However, this only works if the remote server is currently running and uses the HTTP channel to expose remote objects.

- On the server machine, you can use it to generate a metadata assembly for distribution to clients. In this case, the Soapsuds tool is not dependent upon the HTTP channel.

Running Soapsuds on the Client

Using the Soapsuds tool on the client involves connecting to an executing remote application domain and downloading the type metadata directly from the server. The type metadata is transferred over the wire in the form of WSDL (Web Services Description Language). WSDL (pronounced "wiz-dull") is an XML-based language for describing the interface of an object. For example, the following command directs Soapsuds to fetch the WSDL describing the `CustomerService` class and save it in a file called customer.wsdl.

```
soapsuds -url:http://localhost:13101/customer.soap?wsdl -os:customer.wsdl
```

The -url option allows you to specify the URL of a well-known object. Note that the provided URL is the same as that used by clients to connect to the remote object except it has an additional "?wsdl" query string. The presence of this query string causes the remote application domain to download the type metadata in WSDL format. Soapsuds saves the WSDL into the file specified by the -os option.

 TIP *A quick technique for verifying that the remote server is running and configured properly is to enter the URL of a well-known object in a Web browser and append the "wsdl" query string. If everything is working right, then your browser will display the downloaded WSDL.*

While it may be interesting to investigate the WSDL-formatted metadata, our client application cannot reference the WSDL file to read the type metadata at compile time. For that, the client needs a .NET assembly. Luckily, Soapsuds also provides the -oa option, which converts the downloaded WSDL into an assembly with a given name. For example, the following command generates a CustomerProxy.dll metadata based on the WSDL retrieved from the remote application domain.

```
soapsuds -url:http://localhost:13101/customer.soap?wsdl -oa:CustomerProxy.dll
```

Understand that the assembly generated with this command contains more than just metadata. The CustomerProxy assembly completely encapsulates all the client-side remoting tasks. Therefore, a client need only reference this assembly, create a `CustomerService` object using `new`, and start using the remote object. No configuration file or calls to `RemotingConfiguration` are necessary. However, this usage of Soapsuds only works if the server is using the HTTP channel and the SOAP formatter for remoting. In the next section, we will peer into the assembly's source code to understand exactly how it is encapsulating all the remoting details.

 NOTE   *The Soapsuds command shown in the previous examples assumes that the remote server application is executing. Therefore, for this example to work, you must first start the CustomerServer application.*

Examining the Soapsuds-Generated Code

So what exactly is in this assembly built by the Soapsuds tool? We can answer that question by applying another option, -gc, which instructs Soapsuds to generate C# source code. You could compile this source code directly into the client application. However, it is probably more useful as a means to see exactly what magic Soapsuds is performing to generate the assembly.

For example, if we run the following Soapsuds command

```
soapsuds -url:http://localhost:13101/customer.soap?wsdl -gc
```

it generates a CustomerLibrary.cs file containing the resulting code. The following excerpt shows how Soapsuds defines the `CustomerService` type (note that arguments passed to the `SoapTypeAttribute` constructor have been removed for clarity):

```
[SoapType(...)]
 public class CustomerService
    : System.Runtime.Remoting.Services.RemotingClientProxy
 {
     public CustomerService()
     {
         base.ConfigureProxy(this.GetType(),
             @"http://localhost:13101/customer.soap");
     }

     public Object RemotingReference
     {
         get{return(_tp);}
     }

     [SoapMethod(...)]
     public Int32 Test()
     {
         return ((CustomerService) _tp).Test();
     }
     [SoapMethod(...)]
     public Customer CreateCustomer(String name)
     {
         return ((CustomerService) _tp).CreateCustomer(name);
     }
 }
```

As you can see, the Soapsuds tool creates a proxy class for the remote object. This proxy is neither the real proxy nor the transparent proxy discussed in Chapter 3. In fact, it is termed a "wrapped proxy" because it is a wrapper around the transparent proxy. In each method implementation, this CustomerService-wrapped proxy simply forwards the call to the transparent proxy (represented by the _tp variable). Also note the constructor implementation, where the URL passed to the Soapsuds tool is used to configure the client proxy. As a result, the wrapped proxy is "hard coded" to connect to the remote object at the given URL. Therefore, the client does not have to use the Activator.GetObject method or provide a remoting configuration file. Instead, the client can simply instantiate this CustomerService proxy using the new keyword.

Soapsuds and Exposed Custom Types

Any given well-known type may expose other custom types. This occurs whenever the well-known type inherits from a custom base class, implements a custom interface, or returns a custom type from a method call. For example, recall the `CustomerService.CreateCustomer` method:

```
public ICustomer CreateCustomer(string name)
{
    Console.WriteLine("CustomerService.CreateCustomer(\"{0}\")", name);
    return (ICustomer) new Customer(name);
}
```

This method returns a `Customer` object implementing the `ICustomer` interface to clients. Therefore, the type metadata for `ICustomer` must also be available to clients. Soapsuds handles this by generating the `ICustomer` code on the client side:

```
[SoapType(...)]
public interface ICustomer
{
    [SoapMethod(...)]
    String SayHello();
}
```

This works great if the exposed types (for example, `ICustomer`) and the well-known type (for example, `CustomerService`) are all housed within the same server-side assembly. However, if they are defined within different assemblies, then we once again run into the "assembly name is part of the type name" issue. This is because Soapsuds compiles all the types into one client-side assembly, in this case called CustomerLibrary. So when the client makes the following call:

```
CustomerService svc = new CustomerService();
ICustomer cust = svc.CreateCustomer("Homer");
```

the `CreateCustomer` method in the server-side code executes fine, but upon return to the client the runtime raises an `InvalidCastException`.

To illustrate the source of the problem, let's assume the `ICustomer` interface is defined within the CustomerInterfaces assembly. Now imagine if we had to fully qualify type names by placing the assembly name within square brackets (which, by the way, is exactly what the compiler does when generating the IL). For example, the `CreateCustomer` method would then be:

```
// Imaginary code!! Don't try this at home! Assembly name indicated in []
public [CustomerInterface]CustomerLibrary.ICustomer CreateCustomer(string name)
{
   Console.WriteLine("CustomerService.CreateCustomer(\"{0}\")", name);
   return new [CustomerLibary]CustomerLibrary.Customer(name);
}
```

Following the same imaginary syntax, the client-side call would then be

```
// This is fine. CustomerService resides in CustomerLibrary on both the
// client and the server.
[CustomerLibrary]CustomerLibrary.CustomerService svc = new CustomerService();

// Invalid cast!! The CreateCustomer method returns a
// [CustomerInterfaces]CustomerLibrary.ICustomer which cannot be cast to
// [CustomerLibrary]CustomerLibrary.ICustomer as it is defined on the client.
[CustomerLibrary]CustomerLibrary.ICustomer cust = svc.CreateCustomer("Homer");
```

In this example, everything works fine up to the last line, which calls the CreateCustomer method. This method creates a Customer object, but it is marshaled out of the application domain as [CustomerInterfaces]CustomerLibrary.ICustomer. However, on the client side, the ICustomer interface is defined within the CustomerLibrary assembly, so its fully qualified type is [CustomerLibrary]CustomerLibrary.ICustomer. The difference in the assembly name portion of the type causes the InvalidCastException.

Soapsuds and Client-Activated Objects

The previous example used Soapsuds to generate metadata for just a single well-known object and its exposed types. But what about client-activated objects? Can Soapsuds generate metadata for these too? It turns out that it can, but since client-activated types do not have a predefined object URI, you must specify the "RemotingApplicationMetadata.rem" endpoint. For example:

```
soapsuds -url:http://localhost:13101/RemoteApplicationMetadata.rem?wsdl -gc
```

This Soapsuds command fetches the metadata for *all* remoted types exposed by the CustomerServer application, including client-activated types. However, there is an unfortunate limitation: only the default constructor is described in the metadata, even for the client-activated types. Therefore, the generated proxy object exposes a default constructor only, and the client must use the default constructor to connect to the remote type. For this reason, the current Soapsuds tool provides little practical assistance in regards to client-activated objects.

Running Soapsuds on the Server

So far, we have looked at the utility of Soapsuds from the client's perspective. However, it can also be useful for a server programmer. For example, you can use the -ia option to specify an input assembly. Soapsuds will then generate metadata for all types in the specified assembly, which you can then distribute to clients.

```
soapsuds -ia:CustomerLibrary -oa:CustomerLibraryProxy.dll
```

Note that you should not provide an extension when specifying the input assembly. The Soapsuds tool uses the same binding mechanism described in Chapter 2 to resolve the assembly's extension.

The preceding technique generates metadata for all types in the assembly. Alternately, you can use the -types option to generate metadata for specific types only. For example:

```
soapsuds -types:CustomerLibrary.CustomerService,CustomerLibrary
-oa:CustomerLibraryProxy.dll
```

As this example shows, the types are specified in the format *fullTypeName,assemblyName*. Note that there is no space after the comma. You can also specify multiple types by delimiting them with a semicolon, as shown here:

```
soapsuds -types:CustomerLibrary.CustomerService,CustomerLibrary;CustomerLibrary.
CAOCustomer,CustomerLibrary -oa:CustomerLibraryProxy.dll
```

Be aware that, unlike the earlier Soapsuds examples that used the -url option, the previous examples do not embed a URL within the resulting assembly. Therefore, clients using this assembly for remote type information would need to supply the URL through remoting configuration. If you wish Soapsuds to configure each type's wrapped proxy to connect to a specific URL, you can specify the URL after the assembly name as shown here:

```
soapsuds -types:CustomerLibrary.CustomerService,CustomerLibrary,http://localhos
t:13101/customer.soap -oa:CustomerLibraryProxy.dll
```

Turning Off the Wrapped Proxy

By default, Soapsuds generates a wrapped proxy for each remotable type. This provides convenience since the client application does not require any remoting configuration file or code. However, the wrapped proxy works only if the remoting transport is SOAP over the HTTP channel. You can achieve more flexibility if you direct Soapsuds to generate only metadata via the -nowp option (no wrapped proxy). For example, the following Soapsuds command generates only stub code for the well-known CustomerService type (and any exposed types):

```
soapsuds -url:http:/localhost:13101/customer.soap?wsdl -os:CustomerLibrary.wsdl
-gc -oa:CustomerLibrary.dll -nowp
```

This results in the following generated code for the CustomerService class:

```
[Serializable, SoapType(...)]
public class CustomerService : System.MarshalByRefObject, ICustomerService
{
    [SoapMethod(...)]
    public virtual ICustomer CreateCustomer(String name)
    {
        return((ICustomer) (Object) null);
    }
    [SoapMethod(...)]
    public virtual Int32 Test()
    {
        return((Int32) (Object) null);
    }
    [SoapMethod(...)]
    public CustomerService CreateService()
    {
        return((CustomerService) (Object) null);
    }
}
```

As you can see, each CustomerService method simply returns null if executed locally. This is equivalent in spirit to the metadata assembly we manually created earlier that raised exceptions from the methods if executed locally. Clients can reference the Soapsuds-generated metadata assembly just as they did the Soapsuds-generated wrapped proxy assembly. However, since the remoting details are no longer hard coded within the wrapped proxy, the client must configure the remoting settings properly to ensure the object is activated remotely rather than locally. On the other hand, you can use any combination of channels or formatters.

Summary of Deployment Issues

When I started this section, I said that deployment of type metadata was the thorniest of the remoting issues. By now, you probably see what I mean. How you should distribute type information to clients depends greatly on the type of application you are building. There are many possible techniques, but none offer a quick, easy solution in all cases. So here are a few guidelines to help you decide which to use.

If you are using the TCP channel for remoting, then you have three choices:

- Deploy the assembly implementing the remote types.

- Deploy a metadata assembly (manually created or generated with Soapsuds).

- Deploy an interface assembly.

The first option is obviously the easiest solution and works in all cases. However, it may be unacceptable if the implementation contains sensitive data or intellectual property. Deploying a metadata assembly also works in all cases and protects intellectual property, but requires a bit more care on the developer's part to ensure the metadata and implementation assemblies share the same name. To avoid this name issue, you can deploy interface assemblies (which can also contain abstract base classes). However, interface assemblies will not work with client-activated types.

In general, avoid using Soapsuds to generate metadata if the exposed types are defined in separate assemblies. If you do use Soapsuds, specify the -nowp option to make sure it generates a metadata assembly instead of wrapped proxies. This keeps your remoting channel and formatter options open.

Clearly, the number of options and their impact can be very confusing, so let's add a little perspective. The analogous entity to a metadata or interface assembly in the COM universe is a type library. Currently, writing COM type libraries in IDL is common practice, but this requires a deep understanding of IDL and the inner workings of COM. On the other hand, you can write an interface or metadata assembly using any .NET language and you only need to understand basic object-oriented principles.

If you are using the HTTP channel for remoting then, in addition to the three choices listed earlier, you can use Soapsuds to dynamically download the type metadata straight from the server application domain. This is a helpful tool in simple cases, but using it is rather awkward and it does not handle client-activated objects well. The tool may improve, but until that time you really must understand how the remoting plumbing works in case you have to work around the Soapsuds tool's limitations.

Calling Remote Objects Asynchronously

So far, all of the remoting examples shown have used synchronous method calls. That is, the calling code halts while the method call makes its way through the remoting plumbing, then to the remote object for execution, and finally returns back with a return value if any. In the meantime, the user of the client application is unable to work on any other task while the remote call executes.

Because of the overhead associated with remote calls, they are orders of magnitude more time consuming than local calls and therefore make excellent candidates for asynchronous execution. In this case, the calling code continues executing after making the remote method call, allowing the application user to complete other tasks while the remote call is processing in the background. The challenge with asynchronous calls, however, is not just in making it execute in the background. The challenge is also knowing how and when to synchronize again. In other words, how does the client code know when the remote call is finished? How does it receive a return value or error code? As you will learn in this section, .NET has a built-in feature that greatly simplifies the mechanics of calling both local and remote methods asynchronously: *delegates*.

Understanding Delegates

Before jumping into asynchronous method calls, you first need a solid understanding of delegates. Delegates are often described as type-safe function pointers. This definition refers to a common pattern in C/C++ programming where an argument passed to a function is actually the address to another function. The called function can then invoke the function at the given address whenever it needs to "call back" to the client.

Function pointers are extremely powerful and are used extensively throughout the Win32 API. However, since they are simply pointers, C++ allows you to cast a function pointer to any type of function regardless of its signature. In effect, you could pass the address of a function that requires two parameters into a function that only expects it to require one parameter.

Experimenting with Function Pointers

To help clear this up and to demonstrate the fundamental problem with function pointers, here is a C++ code example of a function pointer at work:

```
// FooBar refers to any function that takes a single int
// argument and returns an int.
typedef int FooBar(int);

// Foo returns the given int
int Foo(int i) {return i;}

// Bar adds two ints
int Bar(int i, int j) {return i + j;}

// This is our function that requires a pointer to any
// function matching the FooBar signature
int DoIt(FooBar* f, int value)
{
   return f(value);
}

int main(int argc, char* argv[])
{
   cout << DoIt(Foo, 6) << endl;
   cout << DoIt((FooBar*)Bar, 6) << endl;
}
```

To understand this example, first focus on the DoIt function. Note that the first argument is a pointer to a type called FooBar. Looking up from the DoIt function reveals that FooBar is defined as:

```
typedef int FooBar(int);
```

This C++ syntax is basically defining the FooBar type to represent any function that takes a single integer argument and returns an integer. Therefore, the first argument to DoIt is a pointer to any such function. The implementation of DoIt simply invokes the given function passing the second argument, value, into it.

In the main function, we have the following line:

```
cout << DoIt(Foo, 6) << endl;
```

This is the correct way to use the function pointer because the signature of the passed Foo function matches the signature of FooBar. However, the next line shows the fundamental weakness of function pointers:

```
cout << DoIt((FooBar*)Bar, 6) << endl;
```

Note that the signature of the Bar function does not match that of FooBar. The C++ compiler is smart enough to catch this and will complain unless it is explicitly cast, which is exactly what is done here. Because of this cast, the compiler ignores the signature discrepancy and, at runtime, the Bar function accesses uninitialized stack memory. The results are shown in Figure 5-6. As you can see, the incorrect use of the function pointer causes erroneous results. In other scenarios the outcome could be much worse. For example, it could cause a memory overwrite or an unforeseen exception.

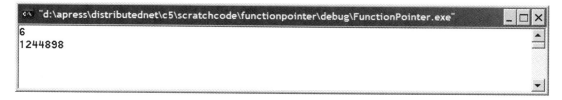

Figure 5-6. The function pointer output

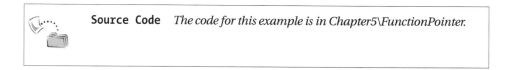

Source Code   *The code for this example is in Chapter5\FunctionPointer.*

Experimenting with Delegates

With delegates, .NET provides the same functionality as function pointers, but without the risk. Earlier I defined a delegate as type-safe function pointer, but it is more accurate to think of it as a dynamically generated class wrapper around a function pointer. This gives the delegate more intelligence at runtime, allowing it to avoid the problems we saw in the earlier function pointer example.

To demonstrate what a delegate is, let's convert the previous C++ code into C# code using a delegate.

```
class DelegateMain
{
    // FooBar delegate refers to any function that takes a
    // single int argument and returns an int.
    delegate int FooBar(int i);
```

```
// Foo returns the given int
static int Foo(int i) {return i;}

// Bar adds two ints
static int Bar(int i, int j) {return i + j;}

// This is our function that requires a delegate to any
// function matching the FooBar signature
static int DoIt(FooBar f, int value)
{
    return f(value);
}

static void Main(string[] args)
{
    Console.WriteLine(DoIt(new FooBar(Foo), 6));

    // No way to "trick" this to compile!!
    // Console.WriteLine(DoIt(new FooBar(Bar), 6));

    Console.ReadLine();
}
}
```

This example implements the exact same functionality as the earlier C++ example. First note the declaration of the delegate:

```
delegate int FooBar(int i);
```

Understand that this line simply defines a custom delegate *type*. And just like any other custom type, to use it we must create an instance of it. This explains the following code in `Main`:

```
Console.WriteLine(DoIt(new FooBar(Foo), 6));
```

This line is creating an instance of the `FooBar` delegate, passing the address of the `Foo` method into its constructor. The resulting object is therefore a wrapper around the `Foo` function pointer.

In `Main`, also note that we must comment out the line attempting to create a `FooBar` delegate instance by passing an address to the `Bar` function. Otherwise the code will not compile. Delegates only allow you to pass the address of a function whose signature exactly matches that of the delegate, and no amount of type casting trickery will change that fact.

Source Code   *The code for this example is in Chapter5\Delegates.*

Dissecting the Delegate

Remember, the following delegate declaration actually defines a custom type.

```
delegate int FooBar(int i);
```

In fact, it is instructive to investigate the IL resulting from this one little line. When this line is compiled, the compiler generates IL that is roughly equivalent to the following C# code:

```
sealed class FooBar : MulticastDelegate
{
    public FooBar(object target, uint funcAddr);
    public int Invoke(int i);
    public IAsyncResult BeginInvoke(int i, AsyncCallback callback,
                                    object state);
    public int EndInvoke(IAsyncResult result);
}
```

As you can see, when you define a delegate, the compiler actually generates a sealed class deriving from the CLR-provided MulticastDelegate class. The compiler uses the signature of the delegate to define the signatures of the generated class methods. For example, note that the signature of the Invoke method is identical to the signature of the FooBar delegate. The runtime calls this method whenever the delegate is used to invoke the function. For example:

```
static int DoIt(FooBar f, int value)
{
    return f(value); // <-- FooBar.Invoke is called here!
}
```

The compiler uses the following pattern to generate the delegate class. It replaces the italicized items with the corresponding items from the delegate declaration.

```
sealed class DelegateName : MulticastDelegate
{
    public DelegateName(object target, uint funcAddr);
    public returnval Invoke(all args);
    public IAsyncResult BeginInvoke(all args,
                                    AsyncCallback callback,
                                    object state);
    public returnval EndInvoke(out and ref args, IAsyncResult result);
}
```

For example, given this delegate declaration:

```
delegate string AnotherDelegate(string msg, out int i, ref int j);
```

the compiler generates the following delegate class:

```
sealed class AnotherDelegate : MulticastDelegate
{
    public AnotherDelegate(object target, uint funcAddr);
    public string Invoke(string msg, out int i, ref int j);
    public IAsyncResult BeginInvoke(string msg, out int i, ref int j,
                                    AsyncCallback callback,
                                    object state);
    public string EndInvoke(out int i, ref int j,
                            IAsyncResult result);
}
```

Hopefully, this in-depth look into the mechanics of delegates has removed any mystique they may have held. Delegates are simply compiler-generated classes that wrap a function pointer in a type-safe container. Before examining how delegates are used to facilitate asynchronous calls, it is worth noting that you cannot manually create the delegate class as shown in the previous examples because the MulticastDelegate base class is reserved for compiler use only. These examples are only meant to illustrate what the compiler does behind the scenes when you declare a delegate.

Using Delegates for Local Asynchronous Calls

A delegate's Invoke method is used to call a function in a synchronous fashion. However, it is the delegate's other methods, BeginInvoke and EndInvoke, that provide asynchronous call capabilities and are the real reason for this extended discussion of delegates. Note that the BeginInvoke method, like the Invoke method, is generated to accept all the delegate function arguments. However, when you call BeginInvoke on a delegate instance, the runtime creates a new thread and executes the delegate function on that thread. Therefore, the call to BeginInvoke is non-blocking; it returns immediately, allowing the calling thread to continue without waiting for the delegate function to complete.

At some point, the calling thread will likely want to know the result of the asynchronous call. To retrieve this information, it must call EndInvoke on the delegate instance. Note that the generated EndInvoke method signature includes all the out and ref arguments and the return value defined by the delegate declaration. However, keep in mind that the EndInvoke method is a blocking call. So if the task is not complete, the thread will stop at the EndInvoke call and wait for it to return.

To demonstrate, let's return to our SimpleMath class and execute its Add method asynchronously. First, to make things more interesting, we make a few modifications to the SimpleMath class:

```
public class SimpleMath
{
    public int Add(int n1, int n2)
    {
        // Display the current thread ID
        Console.WriteLine("SimpleMath.Add() executing on thread {0}",
            Thread.CurrentThread.GetHashCode());

        // Waste some time
        Thread.Sleep(5000);

        return n1 + n2;
    }
    // snip ...
}
```

This SimpleMath.Add implementation writes the current thread ID to the console window, sleeps for 5 seconds to simulate a complex calculation, and then returns the result.

Now for the calling code:

```
class LocalAsyncMain
{
   delegate int BinaryOperatorDelegate(int n1, int n2);

   static void Main(string[] args)
   {
      // Display the primary thread's ID
      Console.WriteLine("Main executing on thread {0}",
         Thread.CurrentThread.GetHashCode());

      SimpleMath math = new SimpleMath();

      // Create the delegate instance
      BinaryOperatorDelegate binOp = new BinaryOperatorDelegate(math.Add);

      // Call SimpleMath.Add(5, 2) asynchronously
      IAsyncResult asyncResult = binOp.BeginInvoke(5, 2, null, null);

      // Do other work while SimpleMath.Add runs in the background ...

      // Get the result from SimpleMath.Add, thread blocks here
      int result = binOp.EndInvoke(asyncResult);
      Console.WriteLine("The result is {0}", result);

      Console.ReadLine();
   }
}
```

This example starts by declaring a BinaryOperatorDelegate:

```
delegate int BinaryOperatorDelegate(int n1, int n2);
```

Remember that this will result in the following generated signatures for BeginInvoke and EndInvoke:

```
public IAsyncResult BeginInvoke(int n1, int n2,
                                AsyncCallback callback,
                                object state);
public int EndInvoke(IAsyncResult result);
```

In this example, we ignore the last two parameters of BeginInvoke by passing null for each. BeginInvoke returns an object that implements the IAsyncResult interface. This object is significant for a couple reasons. First, it provides the calling thread with a couple mechanisms for determining whether or not the asynchronous call has completed. Second, the calling thread must pass the returned `IAsyncResult` object into the `EndInvoke` method.

In this case, the calling thread calls `EndInvoke` immediately after `BeginInvoke`. Therefore, the calling thread blocks on the call to EndInvoke and waits for the asynchronous operation to complete, effectively making the call synchronous again. However, the output (Figure 5-7) does prove that the `SimpleMath.Add` method executes on a different thread.

 NOTE   *Since BeginInvoke and EndInvoke are dynamically generated by the compiler, Visual Studio .NET does not display them in IntelliSense. This is just a limitation of the development environment, not an indication that you did anything incorrectly.*

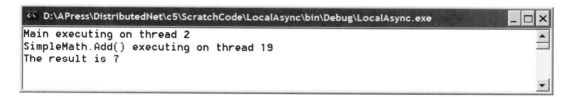

Figure 5-7. Calling BeginInvoke causes the Add *method to run on a different thread.*

Synchronizing the Calling Thread

As mentioned, the `IAsyncResult` object returned from `BeginInvoke` provides a couple ways to determine if the asynchronous call has completed its work. First the calling thread can check the `IAsyncResult.IsCompleted` property. For example, let's update the previous calling code to use this property instead of blocking right away on `EndInvoke`.

```
// Call SimpleMath.Add(5, 2) asynchronously
IAsyncResult asyncResult = binOp.BeginInvoke(5, 2, null, null);

// Do other work ...
while (!asyncResult.IsCompleted)
{
   Console.WriteLine("Main thread working ...");
   Thread.Sleep(1000);
}

// Get the result from SimpleMath.Add
int result = binOp.EndInvoke(asyncResult);
```

Now the calling thread loops (while doing some simulated work) until the asynchronous call completes. The output is shown in Figure 5-8.

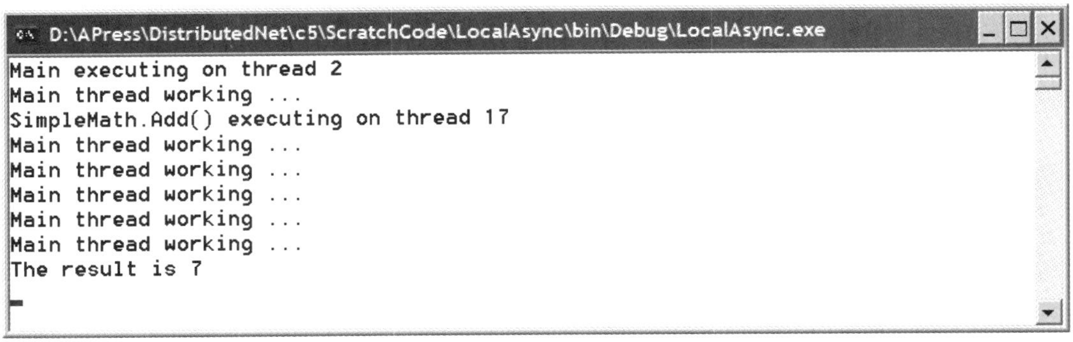

Figure 5-8. Doing simulated work while SimpleMath.Add *executes*

You can achieve similar functionality using the IAsyncResults.AsyncWaitHandle property. This property returns a WaitHandle object that provides various synchronization capabilities, including a WaitOne method. You can use this method to force the calling thread to wait for the asynchronous call to complete. The method is overloaded, allowing you to block the thread indefinitely or to specify a maximum wait time. For example, we can replace the loop in the previous example with the following:

```
while (!asyncResult.AsyncWaitHandle.WaitOne(1000, true))
{
    Console.WriteLine("Main thread working ...");
}
```

With this implementation, the thread waits on the asynchronous call for one second before entering the loop and executing the simulated work. It repeats this process until the asynchronous call completes, at which time the WaitOne method returns true.

Using the AsyncCallback Delegate

Another option for signaling the calling thread when the asynchronous call is complete is to provide a callback when calling the BeginInvoke method. The *callback* is a method that the delegate calls when the asynchronous task completes. Historically, callbacks were implemented as function pointers, but of course in .NET these are replaced with delegates. Therefore, when using this technique, you are essentially passing a delegate into the delegate's BeginInvoke method! In this case, however, the delegate you pass is not a custom one that you define. Instead you pass an AsyncCallback delegate that is defined by the CLR.

The third parameter of the BeginInvoke method allows you to pass an instance of AsyncCallback. The CLR defines this delegate as follows:

```
delegate void AsyncCallback(IAsyncResult ar)
```

So to use AsyncCallback, you must define a callback method with this signature, but you can implement the callback method to do whatever you like. For example, the following code alters the previous example to use the AsyncCallback functionality.

```
class AsyncCallbackMain
{
   delegate int BinaryOperatorDelegate(int n1, int n2);

   static void Main(string[] args)
   {
      // Display the primary thread's ID
      Console.WriteLine("Main executing on thread {0}",
         Thread.CurrentThread.GetHashCode());

      SimpleMath math = new SimpleMath();

      // Create the delegate instance
      BinaryOperatorDelegate binOp = new BinaryOperatorDelegate(math.Add);

      // Call SimpleMath.Add(5, 2) asynchronously and specify callback
      IAsyncResult asyncResult = binOp.BeginInvoke(5, 2,
         new AsyncCallback(AddCallback), null);

      // This will block the main thread. Pressing "Enter" before the
      // async call completes will end the entire application.
      Console.ReadLine();
   }

   static void AddCallback(IAsyncResult ar)
   {
      // Display the current thread ID
      Console.WriteLine("AddCallback executing on thread {0}",
         Thread.CurrentThread.GetHashCode());

      Console.WriteLine("SimpleMath.Add completed!");
   }
}
```

This example is very similar to the previous asynchronous call example, except that the BeginInvoke call in Main now passes an AsyncCallback delegate. This delegate is constructed to refer to the AddCallback method, which simply displays the current thread ID and a message indicating that the add task has completed. When examining the output (Figure 5-9), note that the callback method actually executes on the same thread as the asynchronous call instead of the main thread.

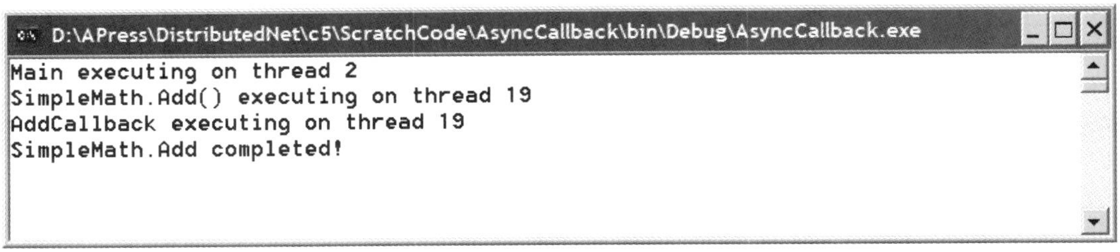

Figure 5-9. The callback method executes on the delegate's thread.

Of course, our current callback implementation is not very useful. Since the callback method is invoked when the asynchronous call completes, the typical action would be to determine the outcome of the asynchronous call. This requires a call to the asynchronous delegate's EndInvoke method, but the callback method is not passed a reference to the asynchronous delegate. Or is it? Although the callback method must accept one parameter of type IAsyncResult, the runtime actually passes an object of type AsyncResult (note no "I" prefix, therefore this is a class). The AsyncResult class provides an AsyncDelegate property that returns a reference to the asynchronous delegate. Therefore, you can use this property (and some clever casting) to retrieve the asynchronous delegate and call EndInvoke.

To demonstrate, the following example shows a new implementation of the AddCallback method that uses this technique for retrieving the asynchronous call results. The output from this code is shown in Figure 5-10.

```
static void AddCallback(IAsyncResult ar)
{
    // Display the current thread ID
    Console.WriteLine("AddCallback executing on thread {0}",
        Thread.CurrentThread.GetHashCode());

    Console.WriteLine("SimpleMath.Add completed!");

    // Cast IAsyncResult to the AsyncResult class
    AsyncResult asyncResult = (AsyncResult)ar;
```

```
   // Use AsyncResult.AsyncDelegate property to retrieve delegate
   BinaryOperatorDelegate binOp;
   binOp = (BinaryOperatorDelegate)asyncResult.AsyncDelegate;

   // Call EndInvoke on delegate to get results
   int result = binOp.EndInvoke(ar);

   Console.WriteLine("Add result is {0}", result);
}
```

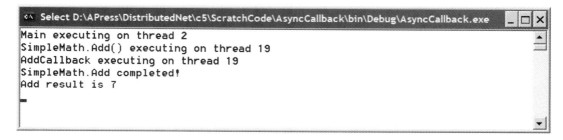

```
 Select D:\APress\DistributedNet\c5\ScratchCode\AsyncCallback\bin\Debug\AsyncCallback.exe    _ □ ×
Main executing on thread 2
SimpleMath.Add() executing on thread 19
AddCallback executing on thread 19
SimpleMath.Add completed!
Add result is 7
```

Figure 5-10. Retrieving asynchronous results in the callback method

The final parameter to the BeginInvoke method is typed as object. The purpose of this parameter is to allow the calling thread to pass information to the callback method. Since it is typed as an object, you can pass anything you want, so long as the callback method knows what to expect. In the callback method, you can retrieve the information using the IAsyncResult.AsyncState property.

For example, imagine we want to pass a string to the callback method that it should display when the asynchronous task finishes. To accomplish this, we can change the BeginInvoke call in Main to this:

```
IAsyncResult asyncResult = binOp.BeginInvoke(5, 2,
   new AsyncCallback(AddCallback), "Async call complete");
```

Now we can rewrite AddCallback to retrieve the string and display it.

```
static void AddCallback(IAsyncResult ar)
{
   // Display the current thread ID
   Console.WriteLine("AddCallback executing on thread {0}",
      Thread.CurrentThread.GetHashCode());
```

```
    // Retrieve the informational object and cast it to string
    string msg = (string)ar.AsyncState;
    Console.WriteLine(msg);

    // Cast IAsyncResult to the AsyncResult class
    AsyncResult asyncResult = (AsyncResult)ar;

    // Use AsyncResult.AsyncDelegate property to retrieve delegate
    BinaryOperatorDelegate binOp;
    binOp = (BinaryOperatorDelegate)asyncResult.AsyncDelegate;

    // Call EndInvoke on delegate to get results
    int result = binOp.EndInvoke(ar);

    Console.WriteLine("Add result is {0}", result);
}
```

 Source Code *The source code for this example is in Chapter5\AsyncCallback.*

Using Delegates for Remote Asynchronous Calls

The catalyst for this examination of delegates was to learn how to invoke remote methods asynchronously. So far, however, all the examples have been local calls. Fortunately, all the techniques used to run local methods asynchronously also apply in the remote case. One of the powerful aspects of the delegate concept is that it allows the caller to decide whether a call should be synchronous or asynchronous. Therefore, the server application does not require any special modifications to support asynchronous calls.

Let's assume we have a remote server exposing the SimpleMath class as a client-activated object (this should be second nature by now, so I won't bore you with the details). The following client code executes the SimpleMath.Add method asynchronously.

```
class ClientMain
{
    delegate int BinaryOperatorDelegate(int n1, int n2);

    static void Main(string[] args)
    {
        // Load the configuration file
        RemotingConfiguration.Configure("MathClient.exe.config");

        // Create the remote object.
        SimpleMath math = new SimpleMath();

        // Create the delegate
        BinaryOperatorDelegate binOp;
        binOp = new BinaryOperatorDelegate(math.Add);

        // Call SimpleMath.Add(5, 2) remotely and asynchronously
        IAsyncResult ar = binOp.BeginInvoke(5, 2, null, null);

        // Do other work while waiting for Add to complete ...
        while (!ar.IsCompleted)
        {
            Console.WriteLine("Client main thread working ...");
            Thread.Sleep(1000);
        }

        // Get the result from SimpleMath.Add
        int result = binOp.EndInvoke(ar);
        Console.WriteLine("The result is {0}", result);

        // Ask user to press enter
        Console.Write("Press enter to end");
        Console.ReadLine();
    }
}
```

If you examine this code example closely, you find that it differs from our original local asynchronous example by one line only! And that line is just a call to load the remoting configuration file. This demonstrates the power of delegates and the transparency you can achieve with .NET Remoting.

Source Code *The code for this example is in Chapter5\RemoteAsync.*

Using the OneWay Attribute

When a remote application domain processes an incoming method call, the runtime establishes the return plumbing for ref and out parameters and return values. Even if the method has no such parameters and no return value, the plumbing is still established in case the method causes an exception. In this case, the exception is serialized to the client as an implicit return value.

If a method has no out parameters (ref or out), no return value, and does not raise an exception (or you don't care about the exception), then you can apply the OneWayAttribute. This has two important side effects. First, on calls from remote clients, the runtime does not bother establishing any return plumbing, which greatly reduces the overhead of a remote call. Second, from the client's point of view the call occurs asynchronously automatically—no delegate code required.

For a simple example, let's add the following WriteToConsole method to the SimpleMath class.

```
public class SimpleMath : MarshalByRefObject
{
    // snip ...

    [OneWay()]
    public void WriteToConsole(string msg)
    {
        // Waste some time
        Thread.Sleep(5000);
        Console.WriteLine("The message from client is {0}", msg);
    }
}
```

The code to asynchronously call the WriteToConsole method is shown in the following example. Note that no delegate is required.

```
static void Main(string[] args)
{
    // Load the configuration file
    RemotingConfiguration.Configure("MathClient.exe.config");
```

```
// Create the remote object.
SimpleMath math = new SimpleMath();

// Call the OneWay WriteToConsole method
Console.WriteLine("Calling the OneWay method ...");
math.WriteToConsole("Hello server!");

// Ask user to press enter
Console.Write("Press enter to end");
Console.ReadLine();
}
```

Source Code   *The code for this example is in Chapter5\OneWay.*

Implementing Remote Callbacks

In an earlier example, you saw how to establish a callback method that the runtime invokes as soon as the asynchronous task completed. This allows the calling thread to continue work without having to periodically check if the asynchronous task has completed. Although the earlier example was for a local method call, the same concept can also be applied to remote method calls.

You can choose from three different techniques for establishing a remote callback.

- **Use AsyncCallback.** This is the easiest technique, but places the burden on the client code. This technique has no special metadata deployment requirements.

- **Pass a custom delegate to the server.** This technique requires some specialized support by the server application, but minimizes the client's responsibility. However, it complicates the metadata deployment requirements.

- **Pass a callback interface to the server.** This technique also requires specialized server support. Like the previous technique, it minimizes the client's responsibility, but does not require you to deploy any additional metadata.

Implementing Remote Callbacks with AsyncCallback

By far, the easiest of these callback options is the first: using AsyncCallback. In this case, calling a remote method with a callback is no different than calling a local method with a callback. For example, the following client code asynchronously invokes the remote SimpleMath.Add method and establishes a callback.

```
class ClientMain
{
    delegate int BinaryOperatorDelegate(int n1, int n2);

    static void Main(string[] args)
    {
        // Display the primary thread's ID
        Console.WriteLine("Main executing on thread {0}",
            Thread.CurrentThread.GetHashCode());

        // Load the configuration file
        RemotingConfiguration.Configure("MathClient.exe.config");

        // Create the remote object.
        SimpleMath math = new SimpleMath();

        // Create the delegate
        BinaryOperatorDelegate binOp;
        binOp = new BinaryOperatorDelegate(math.Add);

        // Call SimpleMath.Add(5, 2) asynchronously and specify callback
        IAsyncResult asyncResult = binOp.BeginInvoke(5, 2,
            new AsyncCallback(AddCallback), "Async call complete");

        // This will block the main thread. Pressing "Enter" before the
        // async call completes will end the entire application.
        Console.ReadLine();
    }

    static void AddCallback(IAsyncResult ar)
    {
        // Display the current thread ID
        Console.WriteLine("AddCallback executing on thread {0}",
            Thread.CurrentThread.GetHashCode());

        // Retrieve the informational object and cast it to string
        string msg = (string)ar.AsyncState;
        Console.WriteLine(msg);
```

```
        // Cast IAsyncResult to the AsyncResult class
        AsyncResult asyncResult = (AsyncResult)ar;

        // Use AsyncResult.AsyncDelegate property to retrieve delegate
        BinaryOperatorDelegate binOp;
        binOp = (BinaryOperatorDelegate)asyncResult.AsyncDelegate;

        // Call EndInvoke on delegate to get results
        int result = binOp.EndInvoke(ar);

        Console.WriteLine("Add result is {0}", result);
    }
}
```

Again, the only difference between this example and the previous local callback example is the need to load the remoting configuration file. However, this technique requires a significant amount of client-side code to create the delegate and implement the callback to retrieve the results. The client code can be simplified if you implement the server to directly support asynchronous calls. This technique is examined in the upcoming sections.

Implementing Remote Callbacks with Custom Delegates

To simplify the client code, you can implement the remote object to support asynchronous operations. The moment you do this, however, you must consider how to notify the client when an asynchronous operation completes. You can solve this by following the same pattern used by the delegate's BeginInvoke method. Namely, create a separate method for asynchronous operation that accepts all the standard arguments plus a delegate to a client-defined callback method.

For example, let's modify the SimpleMath class by adding an asynchronous add method called AsyncAdd. The following code excerpt shows the key concepts.

```
public class SimpleMath : MarshalByRefObject
{
    // This delegate is used by the client to establish a callback
    // which the server calls when the async operation is finished.
    public delegate void ClientCallbackDelegate(int result);

    public void AsyncAdd(int n1, int n2, ClientCallbackDelegate callback)
    { // implementation ...
    }
    // snip ...
}
```

The SimpleMath class now defines a public delegate called ClientCallbackDelegate. The intent is that the client creates an instance of this delegate and passes it to the AsyncAdd method. The server then uses the delegate to notify the client when the Add task is complete.

Here is complete implementation of AsyncAdd.

```
public class SimpleMath : MarshalByRefObject
{

   // This delegate is used on the server to call the Add and
   // Subtract methods asynchronously.
   private delegate int BinaryOperatorDelegate(int n1, int n2);

   public void AsyncAdd(int n1, int n2, ClientCallbackDelegate callback)
   {
      // Display the current thread ID
      Console.WriteLine("SimpleMath.AsyncAdd() executing on thread {0}",
         Thread.CurrentThread.GetHashCode());

      // Create the delegate to execute Add asynchronously
      BinaryOperatorDelegate binOp;
      binOp = new BinaryOperatorDelegate(Add);

      // Call Add(n1, n2) async. Also pass server callback,
      // and client callback
      binOp.BeginInvoke(n1, n2, new AsyncCallback(DoClientCallback), callback);
   }
   // Snip ...
}
```

In this example, we are using another delegate, BinaryOperatorDelegate, to facilitate the asynchronous call to Add. However, unlike ClientCallbackDelegate, this delegate is private; it is only intended for use by members of the SimpleMath class.

Take a closer look at the BeginInvoke call:

```
binOp.BeginInvoke(n1, n2, new AsyncCallback(DoClientCallback), callback);
```

Note that this call uses the AsyncCallback delegate to establish a server-side callback called DoClientCallback. We will look at that implementation in a moment. For now, understand that this call tells the runtime to call DoClientCallback when the Add operation completes. For the last argument to BeginInvoke, we pass the ClientCallbackDelegate instance originally passed to the AsyncAdd method. Therefore, when DoClientCallback is invoked, the method can retrieve the client callback delegate using the IAsyncResult.AsyncState property.

Before examining the DoClientCallback method, it is also important to note that this operation does not become truly asynchronous until the call to BeginInvoke. When a client calls SimpleMath.AsyncAdd, it must wait for the call to travel through the remoting plumbing to the server. Therefore, any server-side asynchronous support only makes sense if the operation itself is more time consuming than the overhead associated with the remote call.

With that in mind, here is the DoClientCallback implementation:

```
public class SimpleMath : MarshalByRefObject
{
   // Snip ...
   private void DoClientCallback(IAsyncResult ar)
   {
      // Display the current thread ID
      Console.WriteLine("DoClientCallback executing on thread {0}",
         Thread.CurrentThread.GetHashCode());

      // Cast IAsyncResult to the AsyncResult class
      AsyncResult asyncResult = (AsyncResult)ar;

      // Use AsyncResult.AsyncDelegate property to retrieve delegate
      BinaryOperatorDelegate binOp;
      binOp = (SimpleMath.BinaryOperatorDelegate)asyncResult.AsyncDelegate;

      // Call EndInvoke on delegate to get results
      int result = binOp.EndInvoke(ar);

      // Retrieve the client callback from the AsyncState property
      ClientCallbackDelegate callback = (ClientCallbackDelegate)ar.AsyncState;
      callback(result);
   }
}
```

The DoClientCallback method first retrieves the result of the asynchronous Add operation using the EndInvoke method. Then it retrieves the client callback delegate from the IAsyncResult.AsyncState property and uses it to invoke the client's callback method.

Although this is a lot more server-side code than before, it translates into easier client-side code. The client must create a class derived from MarshalByRefObject and implement a method to serve as the callback. The method signature must match the signature of the ClientCallbackDelegate. For example:

```
public class SimpleMathResult : MarshalByRefObject
{
    public void MathCallback(int result)
    {
        // Display the current thread ID
        Console.WriteLine("MathCallback executing on thread {0}",
            Thread.CurrentThread.GetHashCode());

        Console.WriteLine("Add result is {0}", result);
    }
}
```

Since the server passes the result to the callback, all the client implementation needs to do is display the result.

· With this SimpleMathResult class established, the client's Main function can use it to instantiate the delegate and pass it to the server. For example:

```
class ClientMain
{
    static void Main(string[] args)
    {
        Console.WriteLine("Main executing on thread {0}",
            Thread.CurrentThread.GetHashCode());

        // Load the configuration file
        RemotingConfiguration.Configure("MathClient.exe.config");

        // Create the remote object.
        SimpleMath math = new SimpleMath();

        // Create the object used for the client callback
        SimpleMathResult mathResult = new SimpleMathResult();

        // Call async version of Add. Pass the callback delegate.
        math.AsyncAdd(5, 2,
            new SimpleMath.ClientCallbackDelegate(mathResult.MathCallback));

        // Ask user to press Enter
        Console.WriteLine("Press enter to end");
        Console.ReadLine();
    }
}
```

Delegates are marshaled by value. Therefore, when this client code passes the callback delegate to the server, the runtime copies it to the server application domain. However, since the callback itself must execute in the client domain, it is important that the delegate target refer to a method on a marshal by reference class. In this case, the server application domain receives the delegate target as an ObjRef, which is used to build a proxy and channel back to the object running on the client. In effect, the server and client swap roles—the client becomes the server and the server becomes the client.

The fact that the client is also a server has two important side effects. First, the client must open a channel port. Second, you must deploy the type metadata for the callback class (for example, SimpleMathResult) to the server. Remember, since the server domain receives an ObjRef, it requires the type metadata to correctly construct a proxy. In this example, the SimpleMathResult class is implemented in a separate assembly called ClientLibrary to make this deployment task easier. Still, it would be simpler from a development and maintenance point of view if no client metadata was required on the server. This can be accomplished using a callback interface instead of a delegate, as shown in the next section.

Source Code   *The code for this example is in Chapter5\RemoteCallbackDelegate.*

Implementing Remote Callbacks with Interfaces

The third and final technique for implementing a remote callback is to use an interface instead of a custom delegate. Like the custom delegate solution, this solution also involves creating a server method designed specifically for asynchronous execution. However, instead of passing an instance of a callback delegate, the client passes an object implementing a callback interface.

The callback interface is defined by the server assembly. The intent, however, is that the client creates a class that implements this interface and passes it to the asynchronous method along with the standard arguments. For example, let's modify our AsyncAdd method to use a callback interface.

```
// The callback interface
public interface IClientCallback
{
   void ResultCallback(int result);
}

public class SimpleMath : MarshalByRefObject
{
   // snip ...

   public void AsyncAdd(int n1, int n2, IClientCallback callback)
   {
      // Display the current thread ID
      Console.WriteLine("SimpleMath.AsyncAdd() executing on thread {0}",
         Thread.CurrentThread.GetHashCode());

      // Create the delegate to execute Add asynchronously
      BinaryOperatorDelegate binOp;
      binOp = new BinaryOperatorDelegate(Add);

      // Call Add(n1, n2) async. Also pass server callback,
      // and client callback
      binOp.BeginInvoke(n1, n2, new AsyncCallback(DoClientCallback), callback);
   }
}
```

This example is only slightly different from the callback delegate example. Note that the third argument to AsyncAdd is a reference to an IClientCallback object. The following DoClientCallback method is also very similar.

```
private void DoClientCallback(IAsyncResult ar)
{
   // Display the current thread ID
   Console.WriteLine("DoClientCallback executing on thread {0}",
      Thread.CurrentThread.GetHashCode());

   // Cast IAsyncResult to the AsyncResult class
   AsyncResult asyncResult = (AsyncResult)ar;

   // Use AsyncResult.AsyncDelegate property to retrieve delegate
   BinaryOperatorDelegate binOp;
   binOp = (BinaryOperatorDelegate)asyncResult.AsyncDelegate;
```

```
// Call EndInvoke on delegate to get results
int result = binOp.EndInvoke(ar);

// Retrieve the client callback from the AsyncState property
IClientCallback callback = (IClientCallback)ar.AsyncState;

    // Invoke the callback method
  callback.ResultCallback(result);
}
```

Much like the callback delegate example, this version uses the `IAsyncResult.AsyncState` property to retrieve the callback object the client originally passed to the `AsyncAdd` method. Then the `ResultCallback` method is invoked on the object. Of course, since the callback object lives in the client domain, this is actually a remote call from the server to client.

The client code is very straightforward. It simply needs to create a callback object that derives from `MarshalByRefObject` and implements the `IClientCallback` interface. For example:

```
public class ClientCallbackSink : MarshalByRefObject, IClientCallback
{
   public void ResultCallback(int result)
   {
      // Display the current thread ID
      Console.WriteLine("ResultCallback executing on thread {0}",
         Thread.CurrentThread.GetHashCode());

      Console.WriteLine("Add result is {0}", result);

      // Simulate a long running callback
      Thread.Sleep(5000);
   }
}
```

This `ResultCallback` method implementation simply displays the result in the console. It also sleeps for a while to simulate a long running callback (which may prompt some special handling on the server as you will see later). Now, all the client code must do is create a `ClientCallbackSink` object and pass it into `SimpleMath.AsyncAdd`, as shown in the following example.

```
class ClientMain
{
    static void Main(string[] args)
    {
        Console.WriteLine("Main executing on thread {0}",
            Thread.CurrentThread.GetHashCode());

        // Load the configuration file
        RemotingConfiguration.Configure("MathClient.exe.config");

        // Create the remote object.
        SimpleMath math = new SimpleMath();

        // Create the object used for the client callback
        ClientCallbackSink callback = new ClientCallbackSink();

        // Call async version of Add. Pass the callback interface.
        math.AsyncAdd(5, 2, callback);

        // Ask user to press Enter
        Console.WriteLine("Press enter to end");
        Console.ReadLine();
    }
}
```

Just as is the case with callback delegates, when using a callback interface the client must open a channel port. However, unlike the callback delegate technique, you do not have to deploy any of the client's type metadata to the server. The server code only calls methods defined by the callback interface. And since this interface is defined in the server assembly, no additional type metadata is required.

Finally, there is one other detail to consider. Recall that the ClientCall-backSink.ResultCallback method sleeps for five seconds to simulate a long running task occurring in the callback method. Note that in the current implementation, the callback itself executes synchronously. That is, the server thread blocks while waiting for the callback to complete. In this case, the server waits at least 5 seconds, but does nothing with the results upon return. This is typical of most callback scenarios—the server does not need any response or results from the callback so it is more efficient to execute it asynchronously. You can accomplish this using a delegate, but a far easier solution is to apply the OneWay attribute to each method in the callback interface. For example:

```
public interface IClientCallback
{
    [OneWay]
    void ResultCallback(int result);
}
```

 Source Code   *The code for this example is in*
Chapter5\RemoteCallbackInterface.

Summarizing Asynchronous Remoting

Although I've covered several options for executing remote calls asynchronously
with callbacks, in practice you will probably only use two of these (or some minor
variations): AsyncCallback or a custom callback interface.

Using the AsyncCallback delegate in conjunction with a custom client-side delegate to invoke the remote method asynchronously has the following characteristics:

- The solution is completely client-side; the remote object does not need to
be implemented any differently.

- The entire operation occurs asynchronously, including the remoting
overhead to transport the method call to the server.

- The client application does not need to open a channel port.

- You do not need to deploy any client type metadata to the server.

- It requires the most client-side code, some of which can be confusing if the
programmer is not familiar with delegates.

To eliminate some of the client coding burden, you can add specially designed
asynchronous methods to the remote type. The best solution, in this case, is to
design the method to accept a callback argument implemented as an interface.
This has the following characteristics:

- The required client-side code is minimized and simplified by removing the
need for delegates. The client must implement the callback interface, but
this task is more familiar to most developers than implementing delegates.

- You do not need to deploy any client type metadata to the server.

- The call is synchronous until it arrives at the remote object, where the server-side code makes it asynchronous.

- The client must open a channel port to listen for the callbacks.

Understanding Call Context

At times, it may be desirable to pass data to a remote object that is separate from the method parameters. For example, the remote object may require the client to pass a security token that it uses to perform authentication before executing a method. For stateful remote objects, the client can set the token by calling a specific method or property on the remote object, which then caches the value in a field. Subsequent method calls are then authenticated using the cached token. Many remoting scenarios, however, call for stateless objects. In this case, each method would require an additional parameter to accept the token. This clutters method signatures with a parameter that is not directly associated with the semantics of the method.

Consider the following SimpleMath class and its method signatures:

```
public class SimpleMath : MarshalByRefObject
{
    public int Add(int n1, int n2, string securityToken)
    { ... }
    public int Subtract(int n1, int n2, string securityToken)
    { ... }
    // etc ...
}
```

The key point here is that the securityToken parameter has nothing at all to do with adding or subtracting numbers. The fact that this class requires security authentication is an implementation detail, but it is being mixed into the interface, which can minimize the advantages gained through interface-based programming. For example, you may wish to define a generic interface for any object that supports simple math behavior. The logical solution for this would be as follows:

```
public interface ISimpleMath
{
    int Add(int n1, int n2);
    int Subtract(int n1, int n2);
}
```

Although the SimpleMath class supports this ISimpleMath interface in spirit, the extra security parameter keeps it from implementing this interface in reality. Therefore, clients written purely in terms of the ISimpleMath interface would not be able to use the SimpleMath class.

The .NET runtime implements a memory storage area named *call context* and defines a CallContext class that you can use to set and retrieve call context data. This provides a convenient way to pass information like the security token as "out-of-band" data. Using call context, you can pass the token as an implicit parameter and keep the actual method signatures consistent with the ISimpleMath interface. The CallContext class provides a SetData method for setting the data and a GetData method for retrieving the data. All CallContext methods are static.

Call Context vs. Thread Local Storage

Call context data looks and acts very much like thread local storage. Like thread local storage, the CallContext class allows you to establish data that is global to a single thread. Therefore, if a thread sets some call context data in one method, it can retrieve the data in another. For example:

```
class CallContextMain
{

    static void Main(string[] args)
    {
        // Look ma! No parameter passing!
        SetName();
        GetName();
        Console.ReadLine();
    }

    static void SetName()
    {
        CallContext.SetData("FirstName", "Homer");
    }

    static void GetName()
    {
        string firstName = (string)CallContext.GetData("FirstName");
        Console.WriteLine("The name is: {0}", firstName);
    }
}
```

This example uses `CallContext` to establish a first name in one method and retrieve it from another without using a class field or method parameter. Note that the `SetData` method takes two parameters that together define a name/value pair. The `GetData` method allows you to retrieve the value given the name. If multiple threads were executing in this example, each would have its own copy of the first name value.

> **Source Code**   *The code for this example is in Chapter5\SimpleCallContext.*

While call context is similar to thread local storage, the difference is that you can use call context to flow data through a *logical* thread, even if the execution passes across multiple *physical* threads. Consider the function call sequence where function f1 calls function f2. If f2 were actually a method on a remote object, it would execute in a separate application domain and thus on a different *physical* thread relative to f1. However, if you look at the sequence from a logical perspective, it is still a single sequential flow of execution, in other words a logical thread of execution.

There is a catch, however. The runtime only flows call context data across application domains if the data type implements the `IlogicalThreadAffinative` interface. "Implements" is a bit too strong, however, since this interface is empty. The runtime simply checks for the existence of this interface to determine if the data should be marshaled across the domain. Since the runtime copies the data from the calling context to the receiving context, you should also make sure the types you store in call context are serializable; each type should be decorated with the `Serializable` attribute or implement the `ISerializable` interface.

Using Call Context with Remoting

For an example of using call context, let's return to the previous secure `SimpleMath` scenario. Remember, the goal is to pass a security token as a string to the `SimpleMath` class without cluttering the interface. First, since strings and all other runtime types do not implement `ILogicalThreadAffinative`, we need to define a container class that does.

```
using System.Runtime.Remoting.Messaging;   // For ILogicalThreadAffinative

[Serializable]
public class CallContextData : ILogicalThreadAffinative
{
   private object mData;
   public CallContextData(object data)
   {
      mData = data;
   }

   public object Data
   {
      get { return mData; }
   }
}
```

This class is a marshal by value type because we've marked it serializable. Since this class stores any object, it can be used for any serializable type. Now let's use this in the SimpleMath class.

```
using System.Runtime.Remoting.Messaging;   // For CallContext

public class SimpleMath : MarshalByRefObject, ISimpleMath
{
   public int Add(int n1, int n2)
   {
      // Get call context
      CallContextData ctxData = (CallContextData)CallContext.GetData("token");
      string token = (string)ctxData.Data;

      //Validate security token
      Console.WriteLine("Call context data: {0}", token);

      return n1 + n2;
   }
   // ...
}
```

This SimpleMath.Add method calls the CallContext.GetData method to retrieve the value named "token". GetData returns a generic object, so it is cast to CallContextData to retrieve the string inside. Also note that the SimpleMath class implements the ISimpleMath interface. This is possible because the Add method's signature does not include the security token. Furthermore, clients can be implemented in terms of the ISimpleMath interface, which can simplify metadata deployment and versioning.

Here is the client code. We will assume the SimpleMath class is remoted as a well-known SingleCall object.

```
using System.Runtime.Remoting.Messaging;   // For CallContext

class ClientMain
{
    static void Main(string[] args)
    {
        // Load the configuration file
        RemotingConfiguration.Configure("MathClient.exe.config");

        ISimpleMath math = (ISimpleMath) Activator.GetObject(
            typeof(MathLibrary.SimpleMath),
            "http://localhost:13101/SimpleMath.soap");

        // Store security token info in the call context
        CallContextData ctxData = new CallContextData("MyToken");
        CallContext.SetData("token", ctxData);

        int result = math.Add(5, 2);
        Console.WriteLine("5 + 2 = {0}", result);

        // Ask user to press enter
        Console.Write("Press enter to end");
        Console.ReadLine();
    }
}
```

This client example also uses the CallContextData type defined earlier. Therefore, the CallContextData type needs to be deployed for both the client and the server. Since the client uses only the ISimpleMath interface, however, only it needs to be deployed to the client.

 Source Code   *The code for this example is in Chapter5\CallContextRemoting.*

Using Call Context with Asynchronous Calls

Calls to remote application domains are not the only scenario where a logical thread of execution can span across two or more physical threads. Remember, using a delegate's BeginInvoke method executes the target method on another thread. In this scenario, the runtime still flows the call context to the new thread. Even better, on the call to EndInvoke, the runtime populates the calling thread's call context with the original call context data.

To demonstrate, let's modify the previous example to call the Add method asynchronously using the AsyncCallback delegate technique. First, here is the client's Main function:

```
class ClientMain
{
    private delegate int BinaryOperatorDelegate(int n1, int n2);

    static void Main(string[] args)
    {
        // Load the configuration file
        RemotingConfiguration.Configure("MathClient.exe.config");

        ISimpleMath math = (ISimpleMath) Activator.GetObject(
            typeof(MathLibrary.SimpleMath),
            "http://localhost:13101/SimpleMath.soap");

        CallContextData ctxData = new CallContextData("MyToken");
        CallContext.SetData("token", ctxData);

        BinaryOperatorDelegate binOp = new BinaryOperatorDelegate(math.Add);
        binOp.BeginInvoke(5, 2, new AsyncCallback(AddCallback), null);

        // Ask user to press Enter
        Console.WriteLine("Press enter to end");
        Console.ReadLine();
    }
```

This implementation is similar to the previous except for additional delegate logic. The method uses a custom delegate, BinaryOperatorDelegate, to invoke the Add method asynchronously. It also uses the AsyncCallback delegate to establish a callback method named AddCallback. Most of the interesting code is in this callback method:

```
        static void AddCallback(IAsyncResult ar)
        {
            // Display the current thread ID
            Console.WriteLine("AddCallback executing on thread {0}",
                Thread.CurrentThread.GetHashCode());

            // Cast IAsyncResult to the AsyncResult class
            AsyncResult asyncResult = (AsyncResult)ar;

            // Use AsyncResult.AsyncDelegate property to retrieve delegate
            BinaryOperatorDelegate binOp;
            binOp = (BinaryOperatorDelegate)asyncResult.AsyncDelegate;

            // Call EndInvoke on delegate to get results
            int result = binOp.EndInvoke(ar);

            // Get the security token from the call context
            CallContextData ctxData;
            ctxData = (CallContextData)CallContext.GetData("token");
            string token = (string)ctxData.Data;

            // Get the server's return message from the call context
            ctxData = (CallContextData)CallContext.GetData("message");
            string msg = (string)ctxData.Data;

            Console.WriteLine("The token is {0}", token);
            Console.WriteLine("The server says {0}", msg);

            Console.WriteLine("Add result is {0}", result);
        }
}
```

Note that after the call to EndInvoke, this method gathers the information from the call context. In addition to the security token, this callback method expects the server to populate a call context value named "message". Here is the SimpleMath.Add implementation that does exactly that.

```
public class SimpleMath : MarshalByRefObject, ISimpleMath
{
    public int Add(int n1, int n2)
    {
        // Get call context
        CallContextData ctxData = (CallContextData)CallContext.GetData("token");
        string token = (string)ctxData.Data;
```

```
    //Validate security token
    Console.WriteLine("Call context data: {0}", token);

    // Set some context data for return
    ctxData = new CallContextData("Hello from server");
    CallContext.SetData("message", ctxData);

    return n1 + n2;
}
```

During execution of this example, the call context information travels over three physical threads: the primary thread in the client domain, the client-side thread facilitating the asynchronous call, and the primary thread of the server domain. The runtime, however, faithfully carries the call context information across all these threads, allowing you to treat the sequence as a single logical thread.

 Source Code *The code for this example is in Chapter5\CallContextAsync.*

Using Call Context Headers

In addition to call context data, the runtime provides another way to pass out-of-band data to a method, known as *call context headers.* The advantage with headers is that the runtime propagates header data across application domains without checking for ILogicalThreadAffinative. The disadvantage is that the header data is available for one method call only. It does not flow through the entire logical thread like call context data.

To define header data, you use the Header class provided by the runtime. The CallContext class provides a SetHeaders method that accepts an array of Header objects. The following example demonstrates how to use this method to set the header data.

```
Header[] headers = {new Header("token", "Another token")};
CallContext.SetHeaders(headers);
```

The CallContext class provides a GetHeaders method that returns the array of Header objects. The following example demonstrates how to use this method to retrieve the header data.

```
Header[] headers = CallContext.GetHeaders();
string token = (string)(headers[0].Value);
```

Summary

This concludes coverage of the .NET Remoting Framework. A journey that began way back in Chapter 3 has come to an end. In this final remoting chapter, you have learned some valuable, real-world remoting facts and techniques including the following:

- How to deploy remote type metadata: implementation assemblies, metadata assemblies, and interface assemblies.

- How to use the Soapsuds tool to automatically generate type metadata. And why you many never want to use it.

- How you can use delegates to facilitate asynchronous calls on local and remote methods. And how to synchronize the calling thread when the asynchronous call completes.

- Why call context can clean up your interfaces and be used to flow data across a logical thread of execution.

In the next chapter, we will turn to the most hyped aspect of .NET programming: XML Web services. While Web services are an important innovation, in many ways they represent a subset of .NET Remoting. Therefore, you already know many of the fundamental concepts.

CHAPTER 6

Understanding XML Web Services

RARELY HAVE I SEEN a new technology hyped as much as Web services. Microsoft even describes .NET as a "platform for building Web services," though it is so much more than that. And it seems every new technical book I pick up nowadays has a chapter on Web services. Are Web services really that revolutionary? Read on to find out.

Interestingly, what Microsoft now calls XML Web services were once called ASP.NET Web services in the early Beta documentation. I suppose many people thought it was a Microsoft proprietary technology, so Microsoft changed the name to XML Web services to stress the fact it uses open standards (like XML). Regardless, in this chapter I refer to the technology as simply Web services, without any additional qualification.

Web Services Overview

When I was fresh out of college, I worked for a company that had a successful integrated database/4GL product. I was experimenting with a new technology called the World Wide Web and had successfully "Web-enabled" the product, which meant only that its data could be queried from and displayed in a browser. Being the only Web "expert" at that company, I was called into a high-level strategy meeting where the original architects of the product were brainstorming more significant ways to leverage its strengths for the Web. The idea they presented to me was this: since the Web contained large amounts of data, and the product's strength was its data processing engine, could this engine be used to dynamically query, correlate, and report on data retrieved from Web sites?

I almost laughed but had to stifle it when I realized they were serious. What they did not realize was that the Web is not structured into neat little tables with well-defined relationships for consumption by computerized data engines. Instead, the Web is a chaotic jumble of sites that deliver information designed for human consumption. Each site is organized very differently, and each has its own unique way of presenting the data. Furthermore, Web sites are constantly changing. We humans are incredibly flexible parsers, so we can make sense out of the chaos. We easily adjust when Amazon.com changes its page layout, but it would take an AI application of immense complexity for a computer to do the same. I had to break this bad news to the architects with a straight face.

It turns out that the joke is on me. This vision of a queriable Web is exactly where we are heading. Though we have a long ways to go, Web services are a giant step forward. I think of this vision as a queriable Web, but the working technical term is the *semantic* Web, which refers to a Web containing structured information with well-defined meaning. In other words, it refers to a Web that you can query.

Why Web Services?

Technologies such as COM popularized the notion of component-based programming. In this style of programming, developers write small, discrete programs and connect them to compose an application. Other technologies, including DCOM and now .NET Remoting, allow you to build an application by connecting components executing on separate networked machines. These technologies assume a homogeneous environment. For example, .NET Remoting assumes that a .NET application exists on both ends of the communication channel.

Web services make it possible for Web sites and applications to interact like components. Like any component, a Web service exposes its functionality through a set of methods. Unlike DCOM or .NET Remoting, however, Web services are designed for a heterogeneous environment. That is, a client running on any platform can invoke a method on a Web service running on any platform. The Web service responds with data stripped of unnecessary details, allowing the client to use the data in whatever manner it wishes. Therefore, the typical Web service client is *not* a Web browser. Instead, Web service clients are Windows applications, application servers, other Web sites, PDA software, and so on. In other words, the end user of a Web service is a computer program, not a human.

The application of Web services is limitless. In one scenario, data can be gathered from totally unrelated Web sites and correlated in imaginative ways without human intervention. For example, let's say I start a Web site called The VikingsReport.com, which follows the ups and downs of the Minnesota Vikings football team. My theory is that the Vikings have good seasons when the economy is strong, but struggle when the economy is bad. To support my hypothesis, I could write a program that contacts Web services hosted by sites such as NYSE.com, Nasdaq.com, ESPN.com, and FederalReserve.gov, download statistical data ranging from economic reports to passing yards, correlate the data into a series of graphs, charts, and reports, and then post it all on my site for the benefit of Vikings fans. This scenario is summarized in Figure 6-1.

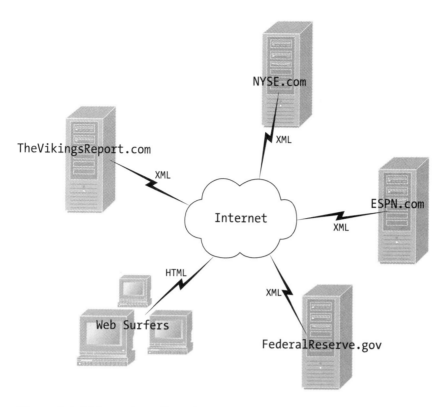

Figure 6-1. Web services allow data to be correlated from various sites.

Other uses of Web services include B2B scenarios in which companies can conduct business using nothing more than the Internet and some agreed-upon protocols. Because Web services are platform agnostic, you can also use them to integrate a diverse back office environment consisting of a variety of modern platforms and legacy mainframe applications.

Web Service Composition

Web services achieve platform interoperability because they are built using industry standards and widely supported protocols such as these:

- **Extensible Markup Language (XML).** The foundation of Web services is XML. It provides a platform-agnostic way to mark up data and is the grammar upon which SOAP and WSDL are built.

- **HyperText Transfer Protocol (HTTP).** This is the networking protocol used by the Web. The popularity of the Web ensures all but the most ancient platforms have rich support for the HTTP networking stack.

- **Simple Object Access Protocol (SOAP).** The preferred, but not required, Web service messaging protocol is SOAP. It is quickly being adopted throughout the industry.

- **Web Service Description Language (WSDL).** This is an XML-based grammar that describes the layout of the SOAP messages accepted by a particular Web service.

- **Universal Description, Discovery, and Integration (UDDI).** This is an XML-based grammar that allows Web service providers to advertise the existence of their Web services.

Using these standards, Web services provide three critical infrastructure services:

- **Discovery.** With UDDI, Web services provide a mechanism by which client programs or client programmers can locate a Web service that provides the required functionality.

- **Description.** Once the Web service is located, the client downloads a WSDL document that details the Web service functionality and how to use it. This includes method names, parameter types, and return types.

- **Wire Format.** When the client invokes a Web service method, the method call must be serialized into some format that can be transported to and understood by the Web service. The most common serialized format is SOAP, although you can also use the query-string mechanism supported by HTTP.

The Role of XML and XML Schema

The popularity of the Web has driven vendors to create more and more powerful Web server products, until the Web server itself has become the application server. However, Web server-based applications generally return HTML. Although HTML is adept at defining page layout, colors, text emphasis, and so on, it surrounds the raw data with these presentation details. In other words, HTML mixes the data and the presentation. For example, consider the following excerpt from the class schedule page of the Intertech, Inc. Web site:

```
<TR name ='only row for data'>
    <TD WIDTH='40%' VALIGN='top'>
        <A href='/courses/CourseDetails.asp?LOC=details&ID=99115'>
        <P ALIGN='left'>Extreme .NET</p></a></TD>
    <TD align='Center' WIDTH='10%' VALIGN='TOP'>
        <Font class='whitefont'> __ </font> </TD>
    <TD align='Center' WIDTH='10%' VALIGN='TOP'>
        <Font class='whitefont'>
        <A href='https://www.intertech-inc.com/enroll.asp?CourseDateID=889'>
        <font class='Bold75'>6-10</font></A>
        </font> </TD>
    <TD align='Center' WIDTH='10%' VALIGN='TOP'>
        <Font class='whitefont'>   __      </font></TD>
    <TD align='Center' WIDTH='10%' VALIGN='TOP'>
        <Font class='whitefont'>   __      </font></TD>
</TR>
```

In all this text, only the items in bold constitute data. The rest is presentation detail. If you had a program that periodically went to this Web page, fetched the course schedule, and updated your Outlook calendar, then it would have to parse through all this presentation detail to retrieve the data. Furthermore, if the page layout changed, you would have to update your program's parsing logic.

In contrast, Web services use XML to transmit pure data mixed only with metadata. For example, the data in the previous excerpt can be represented in XML as follows:

```
<courseSchedule>
    <course id="99115">
        <name>Extreme .NET</name>
        <date id="889">2002-6-10</date>
    </course>
</courseSchedule>
```

Obviously, this is much more concise than the HTML example. Furthermore, this layout only changes if the data schema itself changes, which is far less frequent than updates to the look and feel of a Web site. As a result, your parsing code remains valid for much longer. Luckily, if you use .NET to consume Web services, you rarely need to write any parsing code because .NET can convert XML into data that your .NET language of choice can understand. In other words, it can take the following line:

```
<date id="889">2002-6-10</date>
```

and turn it into an instance of the CLR's `DateTime` type. Web services themselves, however, know nothing about the Common Type System (CTS) used by the CLR and all .NET languages. Instead, Web services use a type system that is native to XML and is part of the XML Schema specification. .NET simply translates the XML Schema types to the corresponding CTS types. On the server side, if you use .NET to build the Web service, then the runtime automatically converts CLR types to the corresponding XML Schema types.

The Role of UDDI and Disco

If you open a new business, you need to make potential customers aware of it through advertising. The first place businesses advertise is in the Yellow Pages, because it provides a resource that all potential customers are familiar with and can use to look up phone numbers and addresses of businesses offering the required services.

Likewise, if I built a Web service for the Intertech class schedule, I would want people to use it and would therefore advertise its existence and general functionality. UDDI provides a standard XML-based grammar that describes the general services and location of a Web service. Gather these UDDI descriptions into one repository, and you essentially have the Yellow Pages for Web services. Such UDDI sites are already beginning to arrive on the scene. For example, Microsoft provides a UDDI Web site at `http://uddi.microsoft.com`.

Ironically, UDDI is itself a Web service. In theory, a program that needs the current weather report, for example, can query a UDDI repository, retrieve the locations of several such Web services, and use whichever one it wants. This brings us much closer to the vision of the semantic Web I mentioned earlier. In the short term, however, most Web service clients will just "know" the location of the Web service, or a human will find it by the usual means—surfing the Web. For example, the most effective way for me to advertise the Intertech class schedule Web service would be to provide a link on the Intertech home page. Customers surfing to the Web site could then see that the service is available and choose to build a client program to consume it.

UDDI is in its infancy stages. Because of this, when Microsoft was designing its Web service support, it included its own discovery mechanism called *disco*. Like UDDI, disco is XML-based, but it is much simpler. Unlike UDDI, the intent of disco is just to allow the discovery of Web services hosted by a given Web site. To muddle the issue even more, Visual Studio .NET Web service projects contain files with the .vsdisco extension that are called *dynamic discovery files*, not to be confused with files with the .disco extension that are called *static discovery files*. Dynamic discovery allows ASP.NET to investigate each virtual directory of a Web site in order to find and report on any available Web services. For security reasons, the release version of .NET cripples this feature. Though it is not recommended, you can follow the instructions in Microsoft Knowledge Base article Q307303 (search for it at `http://support.microsoft.com`) to enable dynamic discovery on a Web site.

The Role of WSDL

Once you find a Web service, how do you use it? This question is addressed by WSDL. To understand its role, consider the information required to use any CLR-defined class. First, you need the name of each of its methods. Then, for each method, you need the list of input parameters it expects, and the type of data it returns in response. This is exactly the same information required to consume a Web service. A WSDL document contains this information for a given Web service and, because it is formatted using a standard XML grammar, it can be interpreted by any program on any platform.

For example, consider the following Web service:

```
public class ClassSchedule
{
   [WebMethod] // <-- This attribute described in the next section!
   public DateTime GetNextClassDate(string className)
   { ... }
}
```

A *small* portion of the WSDL for this Web service is shown here:

```
<s:element name="GetNextClassDate">
  <s:complexType>
    <s:sequence>
      <s:element minOccurs="0" maxOccurs="1" name="className" type="s:string" />
    </s:sequence>
  </s:complexType>
</s:element>
<s:element name="GetNextClassDateResponse">
  <s:complexType>
    <s:sequence>
      <s:element minOccurs="1" maxOccurs="1" name="GetNextClassDateResult"
                 type="s:dateTime" />
    </s:sequence>
  </s:complexType>
</s:element>
```

This portion of the WSDL document describes the parameter types required to call the GetNextClassDate method and the type of data it returns. The actual WSDL document is much longer and quite complex. Luckily .NET provides a tool called Wsdl.exe that builds a .NET proxy class based on this WSDL document. Other development platforms provide similar tools. Thus you can think of a WSDL document as the type metadata for a given Web service.

When writing the client code, you simply call methods on the generated proxy. The proxy class uses the WSDL to determine how to serialize each method call into a message format the Web service understands (typically SOAP) and transmits the message to the Web service.

The Role of SOAP

SOAP provides a standard XML-based message format to represent a method call and its response. Because SOAP is an industry standard, a client built on any platform can compose a SOAP message to invoke a method on a Web service running on any platform. By design, SOAP is a very simple specification, defining only three parts: the envelope, the header, and the body. The relationship between these SOAP sections is described here and illustrated in Figure 6-2.

- The SOAP body contains the information required to execute the method call such as its name and the parameters.

- The SOAP header contains other out-of-band data such as security or transactional information. This section is optional.

- The SOAP envelope encapsulates the body and the header.

Figure 6-2. The layout of a SOAP message

For example, the following code invokes the GetNextClassDate method on a client-side proxy to the ClassSchedule Web service:

```
// Create the Web service proxy
ClassSchedule proxy = new ClassSchedule();

// Call a method on the Web service
DateTime next = proxy.GetNextClassDate("Extreme .NET");
```

As a result, the proxy class serializes the GetNextClassDate call into the following SOAP message:

```
<soap:Envelope xmlns:xsi="http://www.w3.org/2001/XMLSchema-instance"
               xmlns:xsd="http://www.w3.org/2001/XMLSchema"
               xmlns:soap="http://schemas.xmlsoap.org/soap/envelope/">
  <soap:Body>
    <GetNextClassDate xmlns="http://www.intertech-inc.com">
      <className>Extreme .NET</className>
    </GetNextClassDate>
  </soap:Body>
</soap:Envelope>
```

Because this SOAP message is formatted as indicated by the WSDL document, the Web service can interpret it, execute the requested method, and return the result. The result, too, must be serialized into an understood message format. Here is the SOAP result message:

```
<soap:Envelope xmlns:xsi="http://www.w3.org/2001/XMLSchema-instance"
               xmlns:xsd="http://www.w3.org/2001/XMLSchema"
               xmlns:soap="http://schemas.xmlsoap.org/soap/envelope/">
  <soap:Body>
    <GetNextClassDateResponse xmlns="http://www.intertech-inc.com">
      <GetNextClassDateResult>2002-6-10</GetNextClassDateResult>
    </GetNextClassDateResponse>
  </soap:Body>
</soap:Envelope>
```

The client-side proxy reads this SOAP message and converts the date data (in bold) to a CLR DataTime object.

The SOAP specification defines the following formatting styles for both the overall contents of the body section and for each individual method parameter:

- **RPC style.** This term refers to the format of the SOAP body. A message that uses RPC style follows the format defined in section 7 of the SOAP specification.

- **Encoded style.** This term refers to the format of the method parameters within the SOAP body. A message falls in the encoded style category if it formats parameters according to section 5 of the SOAP specification.

However, the SOAP specification does allow for some variation. Of course, both the client and the Web service must understand and expect any variation from the specification.

WSDL defines two such variations. These variations use XML Schema as the underlying specification rather than SOAP sections 5 and 7.

- **Document style.** This refers to an alternate format for the SOAP body. In other words, it is an alternate to RPC style.

- **Literal style.** This represents an alternate format for the method parameters within the SOAP body, that is, an alternate to encoded style.

Before this discussion of RPC style, document style, section 5, and section 7 drives you Section 8, keep in mind that you rarely need to know anything other than what the Web service supports. The WSDL document for a Web service defines which styles it uses. So .NET reads the WSDL to determine the appropriate message format. All .NET Web services default to document style with literal parameters, but can also support document style with encoded parameters and RPC style with encoded parameters. RPC style only supports encoded parameters. See Table 6-1 for a summary of these supported combinations.

Table 6-1. The Body and Parameter Formatting Combinations

	Supported Parameter Formats	
BODY FORMAT	*ENCODED*	*LITERAL*
RPC	Yes	No
Document	Yes	Yes

NOTE *Although SOAP was originally an acronym for Simple Object Access Protocol, once it was handed to the W3C standards committee, the committee renamed it XML Protocol. Due to the popularity of the name, however, it is still referred to as SOAP. So like OLE before it, SOAP has become a name unto itself rather than an acronym.*

SOAP was specifically designed as a transport-agnostic message format. That is, it does not care what underlying network protocol is used to transport the SOAP message. Web services, however, rely exclusively on HTTP for SOAP transport. In fact, if a Web service method only consists of parameters with simple types, you can invoke it using nothing more than the standard HTTP GET and POST verbs instead of SOAP. SOAP, however, allows for the serialization of complex types and thus is the preferred messaging format.

The World Wide Web Consortium

As noted, Web services derive their usefulness from the fact that they are based on widely supported standards. The World Wide Web Consortium (W3C) is the organization that reviews, establishes, and documents many of these standards. You can browse their site (http://www.w3.org) for information regarding XML, XML Schema, WSDL, and SOAP.

With all the hype surrounding Web services, a key fact has been overlooked; at the time of this writing, WSDL and SOAP have *not* reached the recommendation stage—that is, these are not official standards endorsed by the W3C. In particular, the WSDL specification is currently only a "note," which means it has not even been reviewed yet. The bottom line is that these specifications can change, so your projects should not rely too heavily on their current incarnations. As you will see in the next section, .NET provides several tools that abstract most of the details of SOAP and WSDL and thus isolate your application code from specification changes. Even so, you must consider any Web service development inherently risky due to these fluid standards.

WARNING *SOAP, WSDL, and UDDI have not yet been finalized by standards committees.*

Building and Consuming Web Services in .NET

So far, I have been discussing Web services very generically. The details in the previous section apply regardless of the platform you are using to develop Web services. In this section, however, you learn how to build Web services in .NET. As you will see, .NET does provide several handy tools that isolate you from the ugly details of XML serialization and generating WSDL documents.

The IIS to ASP.NET to Web Service Relationship

Until .NET is ported to other platforms, you will use ASP.NET to build Web services in .NET. Therefore, it is important to understand the relationships between IIS, ASP.NET, and the Web service code you write.

The key software components to ASP.NET are an ISAPI extension (aspnet_isapi.dll) and a separate ASP.NET worker process (aspnet_wp.exe). IIS routes requests for files with certain extensions (.aspx, .asmx, .asax, and others) to this ISAPI DLL. The ASP.NET DLL then forwards the request through a named pipe to the ASP.NET worker. Responses are also sent back through the named pipe. Figure 6-3 illustrates this architecture.

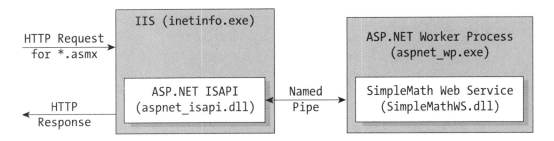

Figure 6-3. The relationship between IIS, ASP.NET, and Web services

In its simplest form, Web service code resides within a file with an .asmx extension and includes a directive at the top of the file indicating the programming language. For example, the following code defines a Web service. Assume this code resides in SimpleMathWS.asmx.

```
<%@ WebService Language="c#" Class="SimpleMath.SimpleMathWS" %>
using System;
using System.Web.Services;

namespace SimpleMath
{
    public class SimpleMathWS
    {
        [WebMethod]
        public int Add(int n1, int n2)
        {
            return n1 + n2;
        }
    }
}
```

This code represents the minimum required to create a Web service in .NET. Notice that it looks like any other .NET class except for the directive at the top of the file and the use of the WebMethodAttribute. Only those methods decorated with this attribute are exposed as Web service methods to clients. On the first request for this file, the ASP.NET ISAPI DLL compiles this code and caches the results. All subsequent requests can then use the compiled version of the code.

To test this Web service, you must create a virtual directory aliasing its physical path. Next, open IE and enter the URL to the SimpleMathWS.asmx file. When the ASP.NET ISAPI DLL receives a simple request for an asmx file without any other information, it automatically generates HTML you can use to test the Web service (see Figure 6-4). Note that you do not have to use Visual Studio .NET to build or test the Web service. All of the previous steps can be accomplished with a text editor and a Web browser.

Using Code-Behind

There are a couple problems with placing the Web service code directly within the asmx file. First, the code is not compiled until the first request—even little typos in the code are not caught until you test it. Second, Visual Studio .NET does not recognize the asmx files as code files and therefore does not provide syntax color-coding and IntelliSense.

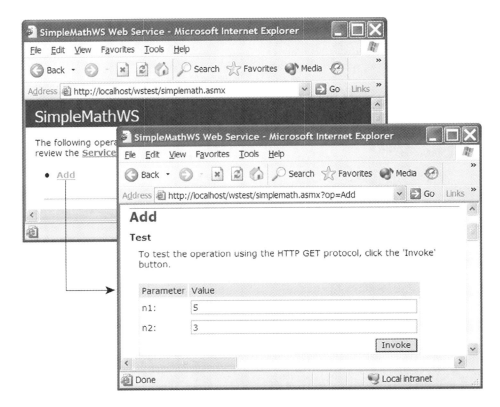

Figure 6-4. Testing the SimpleMathWS *Web service*

ASP.NET offers a more attractive option called *code-behind*. With this, you move all the Web service code into a separate file and compile it into a normal .NET assembly. The directive at the top of the asmx page is typically altered to refer to the file that contains the Web service code. As a result, the only item left in the asmx file is the directive itself. For example, here is the SimpleMathWS.asmx page using code-behind:

```
<%@ WebService Language="c#" Class="SimpleMath.SimpleMathWS"
    CodeBehind="SimpleMath.cs" %>
```

That's it! Note the additional `CodeBehind` attribute is referring to the source file, but it is only used by development environments such as Visual Studio .NET to allow you to toggle between editing the asmx page and the code-behind file. Here is the resulting SimpleMath.cs file:

```
using System;
using System.Web.Services;

namespace SimpleMath
{
   public class SimpleMathWS
   {
      [WebMethod]
      public int Add(int n1, int n2)
      {
        return n1 + n2;
      }
   }
}
```

To test this version of the Web service, we must compile SimpleMath.cs into an assembly and place it in a bin subdirectory, then test it as before. Because the actual Web service code is already compiled, ASP.NET can simply load the DLL located in the bin subdirectory when the first request for the Web service arrives.

Building Web Services with Visual Studio .NET

Again, you can implement and test this Web service without using Visual Studio .NET, though doing so is far easier. Visual Studio .NET provides a project specifically for creating Web services. When you select this project, Visual Studio .NET automatically generates a virtual directory, an asmx file, a code-behind file, and several other files.

Let's walk through the creation of a simple Web service using Visual Studio .NET so you see what files it creates and where it places them. First, we start a new project and select the ASP.NET Web Service project template (see Figure 6-5).

When we click the OK button in the New Project dialog box, Visual Studio .NET does the following:

- Creates a physical directory called MathService under c:\inetpub\wwwroot (or wherever IIS is installed on your machine).

- Generates several files and places them in the c:\inetpub\wwwroot\ MathService directory. The generated files include a project file, the asmx file, the code-behind file, and more.

- Creates an IIS virtual directory called MathService that aliases the c:\inetpub\wwwroot\MathService directory.

- By default, generates the solution file (which sports an .sln extension) and places it within your MyDocuments\Visual Studio Projects directory. This location is, however, configurable.

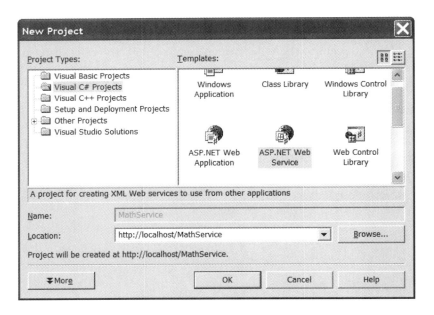

Figure 6-5. The ASP.NET Web Service project template in Visual Studio .NET

When finished, Visual Studio .NET presents a Solution Explorer with some key files hidden by default. You can click an icon in the Solution Explorer to force it to show all files (see Figure 6-6). Table 6-2 describes the purpose of each file.

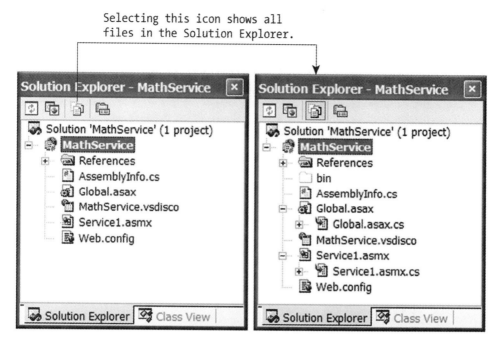

Figure 6-6. *You can force the Solution Explorer to show all project files.*

Table 6-2. *Examining the Web Service Project Files*

Filename	Meaning in Life
Service1.asmx	The default Web service file. You can change this to a more appropriate name.
Service1.asmx.cs	The code-behind file for the Service1.asmx Web service. If you change the name of the Web service file, Visual Studio .NET automatically updates this file's name, too.
Global.asax	The equivalent to ASP's Global.asa file.
Global.asax.cs	The code-behind file for Global.asax. Application code for initial request or new session goes here.

Table 6-2. Examining the Web Service Project Files (Continued)

Filename	Meaning in Life
Web.config	The application configuration file for the Web service. Web applications use files named Web.config instead of a file named after the assembly (for example, client.exe.config).
MathService.vsdisco	A dynamic discovery file. For security reasons, the release version of .NET cripples dynamic discovery, making this file useless.

Once we have the project started, the first task is to change the name of the Service1.asmx file to something more appropriate like SimpleMath.asmx. Note that this also updates the code-behind filename. Next, we open the code-behind file and change the generated code to the following:

```
using System;
using System.Web.Services;

namespace MathService
{
   public class SimpleMath
   {
      [WebMethod]
      public int Add(int n1, int n2)
      {
         return n1 + n2;
      }
      [WebMethod]
      public int Subtract(int n1, int n2)
      {
         return n1 - n2;
      }
   }
}
```

This example shows that we can remove much of the original code, including some namespaces and the component designer generated code, and still have a valid Web service. At this point, we can test the Web service by running it directly from Visual Studio .NET, which simply directs IE to the asmx page, as shown earlier in Figure 6-4.

Consuming the Web Service

As you can see, building a Web service in .NET is straightforward. .NET also provides numerous tools to consume Web services. The most important feature, however, is the ability to automatically generate a managed client-side proxy class that represents the Web service. Like the remoting proxies, the Web service proxy mimics the Web service by exposing the same interface as the Web service. When the client invokes a method on the proxy, it serializes the method call into the proper SOAP format, and forwards it to the Web service. It also deserializes the returned SOAP message and converts the XML Schema types into their corresponding CTS types. In other words, the proxy class takes care of all the grunge work.

.NET provides a couple tools to generate the Web service proxy class. Both require a WSDL document as input. Luckily, ASP.NET creates WSDL for a Web service on demand. Simply enter the URL to the asmx file and append the "?wsdl" query string. For example, the following URL will retrieve the WSDL for the SimpleMath Web service:

```
http://localhost/wstest/simplemath.asmx?wsdl
```

Setting a Web Reference

.NET provides a command line tool called Wsdl.exe that generates the proxy class in either C# or VB .NET. However, most developers will likely use Visual Studio's Add Web Reference feature. This tool presents a GUI interface for selecting a Web service and building the proxy.

To demonstrate, let's walk through the creation of a client for the SimpleMath Web service. First, we must create another Visual Studio .NET project. This can be any type of project, but to keep it simple we will just use a console application. Once the project is established, we add a reference to the Web service by right-clicking the Reference node in the Solution Explorer and selecting the Add Web Reference menu item (see Figure 6-7). Visual Studio then presents a browser-like interface that we can use to enter the URL to the desired Web service, view the WSDL, and test the functionality of the Web service. When we are satisfied that this is the service we want, we simply click the Add Reference button.

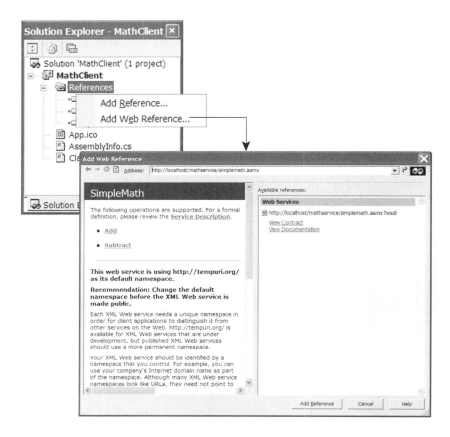

Figure 6-7. Visual Studio .NET makes it easy to build a Web service proxy.

When we click the Add Reference button, Visual Studio .NET

- Creates a subdirectory named Web References under the project directory.

- Creates a subdirectory under Web References named the same as the domain hosting the Web service. In this example a localhost subdirectory is created.

- Generates a proxy class in the References.cs file. The full name of the class follows the convention *clientname.domain.webservice*. The proxy in this example is named `MathClient.localhost.SimpleMath`.

- Stores the WSDL in the SimpleMath.wsdl file.

Using the Generated Proxy

Once this reference is set, we can use the proxy class like any other, as shown in the following example:

```
using System;
using MathClient.localhost;

namespace MathClient
{
    class ClientMain
    {
        static void Main(string[] args)
        {
            SimpleMath math = new SimpleMath();

            Console.WriteLine("5 + 3 = {0}", math.Add(5,3));
            Console.WriteLine("5 - 3 = {0}", math.Subtract(5,3));

            Console.ReadLine();
        }
    }
}
```

The generated proxy looks complicated at first glance. But you can see the basic structure if you can ignore the XML namespace and serializing details added by various attributes. The following excerpt shows the generated proxy with just the core details:

```
namespace MathClient.localhost
{
    public class SimpleMath : SoapHttpClientProtocol
    {
        public SimpleMath()
        {
            this.Url = "http://localhost/mathservice/simplemath.asmx";
        }
        public int Add(int n1, int n2)
        {
            object[] results = this.Invoke("Add", new object[] {n1, n2});
            return ((int)(results[0]));
        }
```

```
                public IAsyncResult BeginAdd(int n1, int n2,
                   AsyncCallback callback, object asyncState)
                {
                   return this.BeginInvoke("Add", new object[] {n1, n2},
                      callback, asyncState);
                }
                public int EndAdd(System.IAsyncResult asyncResult)
                {
                   object[] results = this.EndInvoke(asyncResult);
                   return ((int)(results[0]));
                }

                // Etc ...
         }
   }
```

Calling Web Services Asynchronously

Notice that the proxy constructor establishes the URL to the Web service. Also notice that each exposed Web method has three corresponding methods in the proxy: a synchronous method, Add, plus two additional methods, BeginAdd and EndAdd, that provide asynchronous functionality. As you can see, this follows the same pattern used by delegates as described in Chapter 5. The following code example shows how to use these methods for an asynchronous Web service call:

```
namespace MathClient
{
   class ClientMain
   {
      static void Main(string[] args)
      {
         SimpleMath math = new SimpleMath();

         // Invoke the aynchronous BeginAdd method. The proxy
         // object (math) is passed as the state parameter so it
         // can be retrieved in the callback method.
         math.BeginAdd(5, 3, new AsyncCallback(MathCallback), math);

         Console.ReadLine();
      }
```

```
   static void MathCallback(IAsyncResult ar)
   {
      // Retrieve the Web service proxy from the AsyncState property
      SimpleMath math = (SimpleMath)ar.AsyncState;

      int result = math.EndAdd(ar);
      Console.WriteLine("The result is: {0}", result);
   }
 }
}
```

The most interesting aspect of this example is found in the call to `BeginAdd`. Note how the `SimpleMath` proxy reference is passed into the `BeginAdd` method as the `asyncState` parameter. This allows the callback method, `MathCallback`, to retrieve a reference to the proxy using the `IAsyncResult.AsyncState` property. The code then invokes `EndAdd` on this proxy.

This differs somewhat from the asynchronous delegate example in Chapter 5. Remember, with a callback from a delegate you can cast the passed `IAsyncResult` reference to an `AsyncResult` type and use its `AsyncDelegate` property. However, this scheme doesn't work with Web services because the type of object passed to the callback method is `WebClientAsyncResult` (instead of `AsyncResult`). This class does *not* have an `AsyncDelegate` property. Therefore, you must either pass the Web service proxy as shown or scope it such that the callback method can access it.

Returning Custom Types from the Web Service

So far, the Web service examples have returned simple data types. Things get a little more interesting, however, when you wish to return custom types or more complex types like objects and arrays. Here, you will find many key differences between Web services and .NET Remoting. First, unlike .NET Remoting, method return values and output parameters are *always* marshaled by value in Web services, even if the parameter type derives from `MarshalByRefObject`. Furthermore, types do not have to be marked with a special attribute (for example, `SerializableAttribute`) to be marshaled. Finally, Web services do not use either of the remoting formatters (binary or SOAP) to serialize types. Instead, they use the `XmlSerializer` found in the `System.Xml.Serializaton` namespace.

Using the XmlSerializer

Since the XmlSerializer class plays such an important role in Web services, let's turn from the discussion of Web services for a minute to consider it. This class is analogous to the BinaryFormatter and SoapFormatter found in the remoting world, but with a few differences:

- The XmlSerializer cannot serialize private data. It can serialize public fields and properties.

- The XmlSerializer does not serialize any type information.

- The XmlSerializer allows you to specify the generated XML tags using various attributes.

For example, the following code creates a simple Customer class and uses the XmlSerializer to save it as XML to a file:

```
using System;
using System.Xml.Serialization;
using System.IO;

namespace XmlTest
{
   class XmlMain
   {
      static void Main(string[] args)
      {

         // Create the customer and set the first name
         Customer cust = new Customer();
         cust.FirstName = "Homer";

         // Initialize XML Serializer to serialize a customer type
         XmlSerializer xs = new XmlSerializer(typeof(Customer));

         // Serialize customer to file
         Stream s = File.OpenWrite("Customer.xml");
         xs.Serialize(s, cust);
         s.Close();
      }
   }
```

```
   public class Customer
   {
      private string mFirstName;

      public string FirstName
      {
         get { return mFirstName;}
         set { mFirstName = value;}
      }
   }
}
```

After executing this code, the Customer.xml file contains the following text. Note how the XMLSerializer maps the class and property names to elements in the XML text.

```
<?xml version="1.0"?>
<Customer xmlns:xsd="http://www.w3.org/2001/XMLSchema"
          xmlns:xsi="http://www.w3.org/2001/XMLSchema-instance">
  <FirstName>Homer</FirstName>
</Customer>
```

You can add attributes to the Customer class to explicitly define the element names the XmlSerializer uses. You can also map properties to XML attributes. For example, the following is a modified version of the previous Customer class that defines some custom XML elements and an ID attribute:

```
[XmlRoot("MyCustomRoot")]
public class Customer
{
   private string mFirstName;
   private int mID;

   [XmlElement("MyCustomElement")]
   public string FirstName
   {
      get{ return mFirstName;}
      set{ mFirstName = value;}
   }
```

```
      [XmlAttribute()]
      public int ID
      {
         get{ return mID; }
         set{ mID = value;}
      }
   }
```

When serialized, this results in the following XML:

```
<?xml version="1.0"?>
<MyCustomRoot xmlns:xsd="http://www.w3.org/2001/XMLSchema"
              xmlns:xsi="http://www.w3.org/2001/XMLSchema-instance"
              ID="4">
   <MyCustomElement>Homer</MyCustomElement>
</MyCustomRoot>
```

Source Code *The code for this example is in Chapter6\XML Serialization.*

XmlSerializer in Web Services

Through the XmlSerializer class, Web services provide an easy mechanism to return custom types. Consider the following EmployeeService Web service:

```
namespace Employees
{
   public class EmployeeService : System.Web.Services.WebService
   {
      [WebMethod]
      public EmployeeData GetEmployee(int Id)
      {
         return new EmployeeData(Id, "Homer", "333-33-3333");
      }
   }
```

```
public class EmployeeData
{
    public string Name;
    public string SSN;

    [XmlAttribute()]
    public int Id;

    public EmployeeData(int id, string name, string ssn)
    {
        Id= id; Name = name; SSN = ssn;
    }

    public override string ToString()
    {
        return string.Format("ID={0};Name={1};SSN={2}", Id, Name, SSN);
    }

    //Required by XmlSerializer
    public EmployeeData(){}
  }
}
```

When a client calls the EmployeeService.GetEmployee method, the XmlSerializer serializes the returned EmployeeData object to the following XML:

```
<?xml version="1.0" encoding="utf-8" ?>
<EmployeeData xmlns:xsd="http://www.w3.org/2001/XMLSchema"
              xmlns:xsi="http://www.w3.org/2001/XMLSchema-instance"
              xmlns="http://tempuri.org/"
          Id="2" >
  <Name>Homer</Name>
  <SSN>333-33-3333</SSN>
</EmployeeData>
```

In order for the client to understand this, it will need to know the data structure of an EmployeeData type. Luckily, this information is part of the WSDL contract downloaded when you set a reference to the Web service. Using this WSDL, Visual Studio .NET generates a client-side type to represent the EmployeeData. Here is the generated client-side EmployeeData type:

```
public class EmployeeData
{
   public string Name;
   public string SSN;

   [System.Xml.Serialization.XmlAttributeAttribute()]
   public int Id;

   [System.Xml.Serialization.XmlIgnoreAttribute()]
   public bool IdSpecified;
}
```

Notice that the client-side implementation does not include any of the EmployeeData methods! In particular, the ToString method is missing. Unlike the type metadata generated by .NET Remoting's Soapsuds tool, Web service metadata does not include method information, just information about the object's state. Therefore, the client can use the generated EmployeeData class to retrieve only the employee ID, name, and SSN. If the client calls ToString on the EmployeeData object, the default System.Object version is executed locally.

For example, the following client code retrieves an EmployeeData object from the Web service and invokes its ToString method. The output is shown in Figure 6-8. Note that the ToString method call returns the type name, which is the default behavior inherited from System.Object.

```
class ClientMain
{
   static void Main(string[] args)
   {
      EmployeeService empService = new EmployeeService();
      EmployeeData emp = empService.GetEmployee(1);
      Console.WriteLine("Employee name: {0}", emp.Name);
      Console.WriteLine("Employee ToString: {0}", emp.ToString());

      Console.ReadLine();
   }
}
```

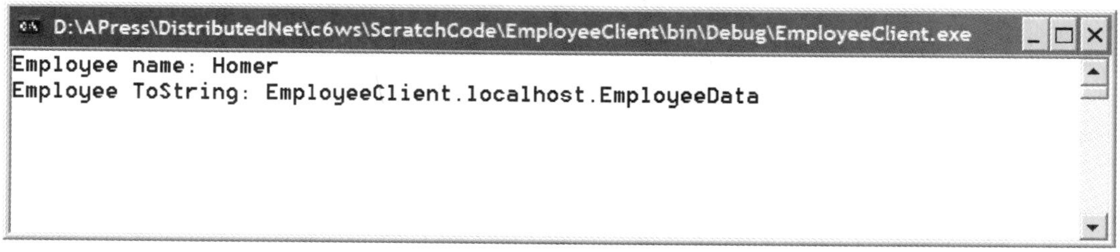

Figure 6-8. Calling `EmployeeData.ToString` *runs the* `System.Object` *version locally.*

Returning Generic Types

Now we will look at a more complicated scenario. Let's say we have a class hierarchy of employees with `EmployeeData` being the topmost class, and two derived classes called `WageEmployee` and `Boss`. Here is the `EmployeeData` code:

```
public abstract class EmployeeData
{
    public string Name;
    public string SSN;

    [XmlAttribute()]
    public int Id;

    public EmployeeData(int id, string name, string ssn)
    {
        Id = id; Name = name; SSN = ssn;
    }

    public override string ToString()
    {
        return string.Format("ID={0};Name={1};SSN={2}", Id, Name, SSN);
    }

    public abstract double ComputePay();

    //Required by XmlSerializer
    public EmployeeData(){}
}
```

Because `EmployeeData` is now a base class, we make it abstract. We also include a polymorphic method called `ComputePay`. Here are the two derived classes that override `ComputePay`:

```
public class WageEmployee : EmployeeData
{
   public double Wage;
   public double Hours;

   public override double ComputePay()
   { return Wage * Hours; }

   internal WageEmployee(int  id, string name, string ssn)
      : base(id, name, ssn)
   {Wage = 10; Hours = 40;}

   public WageEmployee(){}
}

public class Boss : EmployeeData
{
   public double Salary;

   public override double ComputePay()
   { return Salary; }

   internal Boss(int id, string name, string ssn)
      : base(id, name, ssn) {Salary = 9999; }

   public Boss(){}
}
```

Next, we update the Web service's `GetEmployee` method so that it creates and returns a `Boss` object if the ID is 1, otherwise it creates and returns a `WageEmployee`:

```
public class EmployeeService : System.Web.Services.WebService
{
   [WebMethod]
   public EmployeeData GetEmployee(int Id)
   {
      if (Id == 1)
      {
         return new Boss(Id, "Marge", "333-33-3333");
      }
      else
      {
         return new WageEmployee(Id, "Homer", "444-44-4444");
      }
   }
}
```

The interesting item in this example is that the GetEmployee method returns the generic EmployeeData type. Since that is the only type exposed to the outside world, ASP.NET does not include the subclasses when it generates the WSDL contract, and therefore clients will not recognize them when they are returned. As a result, when we run the client code, we see the exception shown in Figure 6-9.

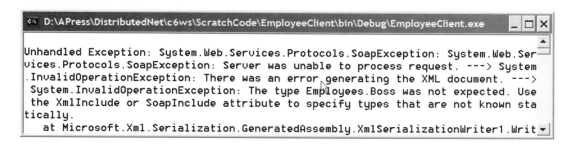

Figure 6-9. Running the client causes this exception.

To fix this, we must explicitly tell ASP.NET to include the Boss and WageEmployee definitions in the WSDL contract. We can do this by decorating the EmployeeData with the XmlInclude attribute as shown here:

```
[XmlInclude(typeof(WageEmployee)), XmlInclude(typeof(Boss))]
public abstract class EmployeeData
{ ... }
```

Now, whenever ASP.NET generates WSDL for this Web service, it will include definitions for Boss and WageEmployee any time the generic EmployeeData type is returned. Therefore, the client runs successfully, generating the output shown in Figure 6-10.

Figure 6-10. The Web service client output

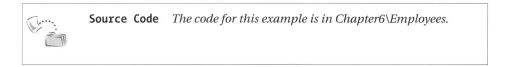

> **Source Code**   *The code for this example is in Chapter6\Employees.*

Using the ASP.NET Session Object

Web services are inherently stateless. However, because they run within ASP.NET, they can use the state management services that it provides, namely the HttpSessionState and the HttpApplicationState objects.

The easiest way to access these objects is to derive the Web service from the System.Web.Services.WebServices class, which provides properties that return the session and application object. You can start using the application object with no other modifications. However, you must explicitly enable session management using the WebMethod attribute as shown here:

```
public class SessionTest : System.Web.Services.WebService
{
   [WebMethod(EnableSession = true)]
   public void SaveInSession(string msg)
   {
      Session["Msg"]=msg;
   }
```

```
   [WebMethod(EnableSession = true)]
   public string GetFromSession()
   {
      return (string)Session["Msg"];
   }
}
```

ASP.NET, by default, uses cookies to manage the session state. Therefore, it assumes the client stores the session cookie and sends it back with each request. Although most browsers do this automatically, if you are consuming the Web service in a Windows or console application, then you must configure the Web service proxy to hold the cookies. This turns out to be straightforward, as the following client code demonstrates:

```
// This is the Web service proxy
SessionTest testProxy = new SessionTest();

// Establish the container for cookies
testProxy.CookieContainer = new System.Net.CookieContainer();

// Save some session data
testProxy.SaveInSession("Another test");

// Retrieve the session data
Console.WriteLine(testProxy.GetFromSession());
```

If you cannot derive the Web service class from WebService (for example, because it already derives from another class), then you can use the System.Web.HttpContext class to access the session and application objects:

```
public class SessionTest : SomeOtherBaseClass
{
   [WebMethod(EnableSession = true)]
   public void SaveInSession(string msg)
   {
      HttpContext.Current.Session["Msg"]=msg;
   }

   [WebMethod(EnableSession = true)]
   public string GetFromSession()
   {
      return (string)HttpContext.Current.Session["Msg"];
   }
}
```

Remoting vs. Web Services

What is the difference between .NET Remoting and Web services? When would you use one over the other? These are some of the most common questions in the .NET universe. Part of the confusion is a result of some misleading Beta documentation that lumped the two technologies together. However, most of the confusion is technical in nature. Remoting and Web services share many components such as SOAP and WSDL. Furthermore, ASP.NET can host remotable objects and expose them over the HTTP channel using SOAP serialization, making the remoted object look a lot like a Web service.

In spite of all these similarities, there are some real differences. The most fundamental difference takes us way back to the opening of Chapter 2 and the importance of type. .NET Remoting uses serialization mechanisms that maintain CTS type fidelity, whereas Web services use a serialization mechanism that maintains XML Schema type fidelity. Because of this difference, .NET Remoting is suitable when you know the clients will only be .NET clients. However, if you have to support a variety of client platforms, then using Web services is the better choice.

Flexibility is also an issue. As Chapter 4 demonstrates, you can create a variety of remoting objects, from stateless well-known `SingleCall` objects to stateful client-activated objects. You can also use a variety of transport protocols and formatters. Finally, you can host remoted objects in several different types of applications such as console applications, Windows services, or within ASP.NET. A Web service, on the other hand, is strictly stateless. In that regard, it is comparable to a well-known `SingleCall` object in remoting. And Web services are hosted only by ASP.NET. Table 6-3 summarizes these differences.

Table 6-3. .NET Remoting vs. Web Services

Characteristic	.NET Remoting	Web Services
Type system	CTS	XML Schema
Expected client platform	.NET	Any
Serialization stack	`System.Runtime.Serialization`	`System.Xml.Serialization`
Message format	Binary, SOAP, or custom	HTTP query string or SOAP
State model	Stateful or stateless	Stateless only
Marshaling	By value or by reference	By value only
Possible hosts	Any managed application: console, Windows service, ASP.NET	ASP.NET
Proxy building tool	Soapsuds.exe	Wsdl.exe

These differences add up to a simple conclusion. If you need to support clients on a variety of platforms, then the best solution is Web services. However, if all clients are .NET clients, then .NET Remoting offers better performance (with binary formatting) and more flexibility.

Summary

Once you've been through the details and flexibility of .NET Remoting, Web services pale in comparison. However, remember that each technology has different goals. In this chapter, you have learned the role Web services play in the distributed architecture. Chapter highlights include the following:

- Web services are a step toward the semantic Web, in which there is meaning and structure to all Web data. UDDI is the next step.

- ASP.NET is an ISAPI extension that forwards Web service requests to the ASP.NET worker process.

- You can build Web services in .NET without using Visual Studio .NET.

- SOAP provides a messaging protocol between the Web service consumer and the application.

- .NET Remoting is far more powerful than Web services; however, Web services make no assumptions regarding the platform the consumer is using.

In the next chapter, we will shift gears a bit and examine COM interop. While this in itself has little to do with distributed programming, you need to have a grounding in COM interop before tackling Chapter 8, which discusses how to build serviced components in managed code.

CHAPTER 7

Understanding
COM Interop

WHAT DOES COM INTEROPERABILITY have to do with distributed programming? Good question. In a perfect world where all code is managed by the .NET runtime and there is infinite time to complete projects, this chapter would not be needed. I don't have to tell you that this is not a perfect world. And not even Microsoft has infinite time to complete projects. Therefore, for the initial release of .NET, Microsoft decided to leverage the existing COM+ code instead of rewriting it in managed code. So when hosting managed objects, COM+ must use the COM interoperability services provided by .NET. To be sure, you can skip this chapter and go directly to the sexier COM+ material. However, when you start implementing COM+ components in managed code, some COM+ behavior may surprise and confound you if you are not familiar with the concepts presented here.

The Need for COM Interop

As mentioned earlier, .NET leverages the existing COM+ runtime in order to provide services such as Just-In-Time activation and distributed transactions. And, as its name suggests, COM+ is based on COM technology. Therefore, we need to take a fairly large tangent and examine the COM interoperability (henceforth shortened to COM interop) services provided by .NET. Entire books can be written about COM interop. Luckily, we do not need to approach that level of detail in order to write managed code components that leverage COM+.

The first thing to understand regarding COM interop is that it works. Really. Microsoft and its customers have made large investments in COM technology since its introduction in 1993, and Microsoft knew that .NET would never be a success if it could not interact with legacy COM-based applications.

The second thing to understand about COM interop is that the runtime provides two-way communication between .NET and COM components. Unmanaged code (that is, COM components) can call into managed code (that is, .NET components) using the runtime's *COM Callable Wrapper* (CCW). In the other direction, managed code can call into unmanaged code using the *Runtime Callable Wrapper* (RCW).

Managed to Unmanaged Interop

The ability to call unmanaged code from managed code is clearly important if you wish to extend your existing COM-based application with some .NET capabilities. For example, many companies have thousands of development hours invested in middleware business objects implemented using VB 6.0/COM technology, but wish to replace their current ASP-based front end with a new and improved ASP.NET front end. Of the two directions of interop, this direction is less of a factor when building COM+ objects in managed code. Still, it does play an important role in certain situations.

Understanding the Runtime Callable Wrapper

In order to call a COM component from .NET, there needs to be a proxy that wraps the COM component and understands how to transform a .NET method call into a COM call. This capability is provided by an RCW (see Figure 7-1). An RCW performs the following tasks:

- **Marshals data between managed and unmanaged code.** The RCW knows how to convert method arguments and return values from .NET types to COM types and vice versa. For example, it converts the BSTR type used to represent strings in COM to .NET's System.String type. The default RCW implementation can marshal all automation-compliant (also known as variant-compliant) data types. If you are building COM components in VB 6.0, then your objects use only automation-compliant data types.

- **Manages the COM object's lifetime.** As mentioned in Chapter 2, COM and .NET have very different lifetime management schemes. COM uses reference counting, while .NET uses garbage collection. All COM objects implement an interface called IUnknown that defines an AddRef and a Release method. These methods are called to increment and decrement the object's reference count respectively. When a .NET client uses the new keyword to create a COM object, both an RCW and the COM object are created. The RCW is a managed object, therefore it is garbage collected. However, its finalizer method is implemented to call the Release method on the wrapped COM object.

- **Consumes some standard COM interfaces.** The RCW does not expose all interfaces implemented by the COM object to the managed client. Some standard COM interfaces are consumed by the RCW itself. These interfaces include IUnknown, IDispatch, IProvideClassInfo, and IConnectionPoint.

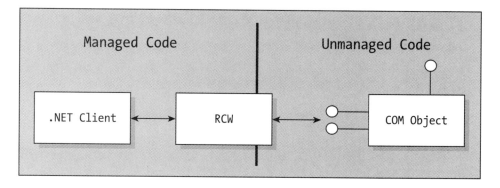

Figure 7-1. Managed code calling into unmanaged code

Building an Interop Assembly

The code for an RCW can be generated in several ways. However, the two most common techniques involve using either the Type Library Importer or the Visual Studio.NET IDE. Regardless of the technique you choose, the output is always an *interop assembly*. This is an assembly that contains the RCW implementations wrapping the COM objects in a given COM server. Managed clients reference this assembly to activate and use the COM objects.

The interop assembly is generated by reading the COM server's type library. Recall that a COM server keeps all its type metadata within the type library. Many times the type library is embedded within the COM server itself. Otherwise it can reside in a separate .tlb file.

Building an Interop Assembly with Visual Studio .NET

The easiest way to create an interop assembly is through the Visual Studio .NET IDE. The Project | Add Reference dialog box contains a COM tab that allows you to select any COM server registered on the machine (see Figure 7-2).

When you select one of the COM servers in the list box, the IDE first looks in the GAC for a *primary* interop assembly. This is a strong-named interop assembly generated by the publisher of the COM server. If a primary interop assembly is not found, then the IDE asks if you wish to create a *wrapper,* which is just a synonym for an interop assembly. The interop assembly is placed in the project's debug subfolder, which allows the client to bind to the assembly at runtime using the probing mechanism described in Chapter 2.

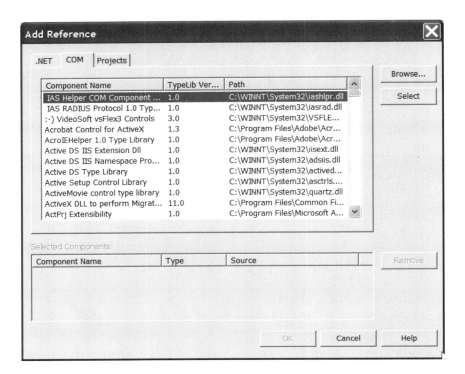

Figure 7-2. Creating an interop assembly using Visual Studio .NET

Building an Interop Assembly with the Type Library Importer

The .NET Framework also provides a command line tool called the Type Library
Importer (tlbimp.exe), which can generate interop assemblies. This tool has
several options, but its typical usage is shown here:

```
tlbimp /out:Interop_COMMathLibrary.dll COMMathLibrary.dll
```

In this example, we are telling the tool to read the type library contained
within COMMathLibrary.dll and generate an interop assembly called
Interop_COMMathLibrary.dll.

Unmanaged to Managed Interop

COM+ is a COM-based runtime designed to host COM objects and provide them
with important middleware services. In other words, COM+ is unmanaged code.
Therefore, to provide these services to .NET objects, COM+ must use the interop
services that allow unmanaged code to call into managed code. You must have a

good understanding of this direction of interop to develop COM+-serviced objects in .NET.

Understanding the COM Callable Wrapper

Like the RCW, the COM Callable Wrapper (CCW) provides a bridge between the .NET universe and the COM universe. However, the CCW facilitates interop in the reverse direction: unmanaged code calling managed code (see Figure 7-3). The CCW performs the following tasks:

- **Marshals data between unmanaged and managed code.** Like the RCW, the CCW knows how to convert method arguments and return values from .NET types to COM types and vice versa.

- **Manages the .NET object's lifetime.** The CCW runs under the COM runtime and is therefore unmanaged. And like any other COM object, its lifetime is dictated by a reference count. Therefore, when its reference count is zero, the CCW clears its reference to the associated managed object, which is then collected during the next garbage collection sweep.

- **Exposes the appropriate custom interfaces.** COM is completely interface-based. A client never holds a reference to a COM object; instead it holds a reference to an interface implemented by the COM object. The CCW exposes all interfaces explicitly implemented by the .NET object to the COM client. By default, members of the managed class are exposed to COM clients through IDispatch only, so clients cannot early bind to the class methods. However, any explicitly implemented interface is exposed as a dual interface, meaning it supports both IDispatch and IUnknown. Therefore, clients can early bind or late bind to the interface. Optionally, the CCW can associate the members of a .NET class with a default interface in order to expose them to COM clients.

- **Provides standard COM interfaces.** The COM universe expects an object to support at a minimum the IUnknown interface and usually many more. For example, all VB 6.0 COM objects are dual interface, meaning they support both IUnknown and IDispatch. IDispatch provides late binding capabilities to scripting clients such as ASP. However, managed objects cannot explicitly implement these interfaces. Instead the CCW provides these on behalf of the managed object.

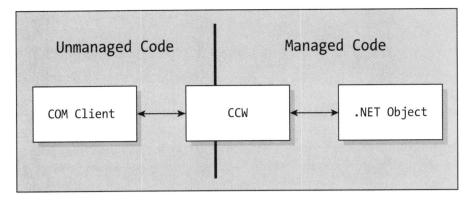

Figure 7-3. Unmanaged code calling into managed code

Although the CCW handles these tasks seamlessly, there are a few restrictions worth mentioning:

- Only default constructors are exposed to COM clients. If a managed class does not have a default constructor, it cannot be created from a COM client. VB 6.0 programmers may equate this to a PublicNotCreateable class.

- Only public types and public members are exposed to COM. If you wish to hide a public type or member, then you can apply the ComVisibleAttribute and set it to false.

- Static members and constant fields are not exposed to COM.

Registering an Assembly for COM Interop

In the COM universe, servers must be registered for use. This involves placing several bits of information in different system registry locations. Likewise, in order for a COM client to access types in a .NET assembly, the assembly must also be registered in typical COM fashion. Actually, to be precise, you must register a COM type library that is generated by reflecting over the assembly's type metadata. You can generate the type library using the Type Library Exporter (tlbexp.exe) console tool provided by .NET, but this tool does not register the type library. For this reason, the Assembly Registration Tool (regasm.exe) proves more useful. It can generate a type library and register it appropriately.

Like the other .NET console tools, regasm has many options. However, the following example demonstrates its typical usage:

```
regasm /tlb:MathLibrary.tlb MathLibrary.dll
```

The /tlb option instructs regasm to generate a type library with the provided name. This is followed by the name of the assembly to register for COM interop. Regasm then reads the assembly metadata to construct the type library and registers it, its classes, and its interfaces in the system registry. This allows any COM client to use the managed type without even realizing that it resides within a .NET assembly.

The .NET assembly must be loaded in the client process following the normal .NET binding rules. Therefore, the assembly must either reside in the same directory as the COM client, or it must be shared (that is, installed in the GAC). For integrating with COM+, you will always want to create a strong-named .NET assembly and install it in the GAC. Otherwise you would have to copy the assembly to the System32 directory where the COM+ executable, dllhost.exe, resides.

Writing Managed Code for COM Interop

When you are developing a managed class and know it will be called from a COM client (as is the case for any serviced component), you can take a number of actions to ensure seamless interop. One of the primary concerns is how to expose the members of a managed class to COM. Since COM is purely an interface-based system, it cannot directly access the members of a class. Visual Basic 6.0 hides this issue by automatically creating a *default interface,* which exposes the public members of a class. The name of the default interface is always the name of the class preceded by an underscore (for example, _SimpleMath).

Consider the following SimpleMath class:

```
namespace MathLibrary
{
    public class SimpleMath
    {
        public int Add(int n1, int n2)
        { return n1 + n2; }

        public int Subtract(int n1, int n2)
        { return n1 - n2; }
    }
}
```

During the export process, the `SimpleMath` class is converted to a COM coclass. Here is how it appears in the generated type library:

```
coclass SimpleMath {
    [default] interface IDispatch;
    interface _Object;
};
```

There are two issues to note with this. First, the type library contains no information regarding the `Add` or `Subtract` methods. Second, the default interface is `IDispatch`. As a result, clients can only late bind to the `SimpleMath` object, which means that method calls cannot be validated at compile time. Worse, since call validation must happen at runtime, late bound calls are always significantly slower than early bound calls.

You can solve this in one of two ways. First, you can create an interface and explicitly implement it in the `SimpleMath` class. Or, you can use the `ClassInterfaceAttribute` to instruct the Type Library Exporter tool to automatically generate a default interface (much like what occurs in Visual Basic 6.0). Both of these techniques are examined in the following sections.

Explicitly Implementing Interfaces

The recommended technique for exposing a .NET class to COM clients is to use interfaces exclusively. In other words, all of the class' public members should be members of an implemented interface. This technique provides the most robust versioning. Also, it follows COM's notion of pure interface-based programming and therefore provides relatively seamless interop.

For example, let's add an `ISimpleMath` interface to the previous example:

```
namespace MathLibrary
{
    public interface ISimpleMath
    {
        int Add(int n1, int n2);
        int Subtract(int n1, int n2);
    }

    public class SimpleMath : ISimpleMath
    {
        public int Add(int n1, int n2)
        { return n1 + n2;}
```

```
        public int Subtract(int n1, int n2)
        { return n1 - n2; }
    }
}
```

When this code is exported to COM, the type library now looks as follows (some IDL attributes have been removed for clarity):

```
interface ISimpleMath : IDispatch {
    [id(0x60020000)]
    HRESULT Add(
                    [in] long n1,
                    [in] long n2,
                    [out, retval] long* pRetVal);
    [id(0x60020001)]
    HRESULT Subtract(
                    [in] long n1,
                    [in] long n2,
                    [out, retval] long* pRetVal);
};

coclass SimpleMath {
    [default] interface IDispatch;
    interface _Object;
    interface ISimpleMath;
};
```

Now, clients capable of early binding can do so against the ISimpleMath interface. However, the IDispatch interface is still marked as the default interface of the SimpleMath coclass. Therefore, late bound clients still cannot validate method calls at compile time. For example, the following Visual Basic 6.0 code will compile even though the Add method is called incorrectly:

```
'VB6 Client Code!!
Private Sub Command1_Click()
    Dim math As SimpleMath
    Set math = CreateObject("MathLibrary.SimpleMath")

    'Invoke Add with too many arguments!
    MsgBox math.Add(5, 2, 3)
End Sub
```

But this Visual Basic 6.0 code will not compile (which is the desired behavior):

```
'VB6 Client Code!!
Private Sub Command1_Click()
    Dim math As ISimpleMath
    Set math = CreateObject("MathLibrary.SimpleMath")

    'Invoke Add with too many arguments!
    MsgBox math.Add(5, 2, 3)
End Sub
```

Note that the only difference between these two examples is that the first creates a variable of type SimpleMath, and the second creates a variable of type ISimpleMath. This is unintuitive to Visual Basic 6.0 programmers who usually assume any explicitly typed object reference (that is, any non Object typed reference) is early bound. In this case, however, it is late bound.

You can resolve this issue by applying the ClassInterfaceAttribute to the SimpleMath class as shown here:

```
namespace MathLibrary
{
    // The ClassInterfaceAttribute lives in the following namespace
    using System.Runtime.InteropServices;

    [ClassInterface(ClassInterfaceType.None)]
    public class SimpleMath : ISimpleMath
    {
        public int Add(int n1, int n2)
        { return n1 + n2;}

        public int Subtract(int n1, int n2)
        { return n1 - n2; }
    }
}
```

With the ClassInterfaceType.None enumeration value specified in the ClassInterfaceAttribute constructor, the type library export process does not expose IDispatch as the default interface for the SimpleMath coclass. Instead, the first interface in the list of implemented interfaces is used as the default interface. In fact, the export process defines the SimpleMath coclass as follows:

```
coclass SimpleMath {
    interface _Object;
    [default] interface ISimpleMath;
};
```

Using this definition, both of the previous Visual Basic 6.0 code examples result in a compile error. In other words, both the SimpleMath and ISimpleMath typed references are early bound.

> **NOTE** *If you wish, you can follow COM's default interface naming convention by simply changing the name of the* ISimpleMath *interface to* _SimpleMath.

Finally, if you intend to use the explicit interface implementation technique on all classes within an assembly, you can apply the ClassInterfaceAttribute to the assembly as shown in the following example. If you do this, the attribute applies to all the public classes in the assembly and you do not need to add it to each one.

```
// In AssemblyInfo.cs
[assembly: ClassInterface(ClassInterfaceType.None)]
```

Generating the Class Interface Automatically

Admittedly, explicitly implementing interfaces can be tedious. To make things a little easier, the ClassInterfaceAttribute also accepts the ClassInterfaceType.AutoDual enumeration value. This instructs the Type Library Exporter to automatically generate a default interface containing all the public members of a class.

To see how this works, let's modify the SimpleMath class with this new attribute setting:

```
namespace MathLibrary
{
   // The ClassInterfaceAttribute lives in the following namespace
   using System.Runtime.InteropServices;

   [ClassInterface(ClassInterfaceType.AutoDual)]
   public class SimpleMath
   {
      public int Add(int n1, int n2)
      { return n1 + n2;}

      public int Subtract(int n1, int n2)
      { return n1 - n2; }
   }
}
```

Note that the ISimpleMath interface is no longer required. Instead, the Type Library Exporter generates a default interface for the SimpleMath coclass called _SimpleMath as shown in the following type library excerpt:

```
interface _SimpleMath : IDispatch {
    [id(00000000), propget]
    HRESULT ToString([out, retval] BSTR* pRetVa
    [id(0x60020001)]
    HRESULT Equals(
                    [in] VARIANT obj,
                    [out, retval] VARIANT_BOOL* pRetVal);
    [id(0x60020002)]
    HRESULT GetHashCode([out, retval] long* pRetVal);
    [id(0x60020003)]
    HRESULT GetType([out, retval] _Type** pRetVal);
    [id(0x60020004)]
    HRESULT Add(
                    [in] long n1,
                    [in] long n2,
                    [out, retval] long* pRetVal);
    [id(0x60020005)]
    HRESULT Subtract(
                    [in] long n1,
                    [in] long n2,
                    [out, retval] long* pRetVal);
};

coclass SimpleMath {
    [default] interface _SimpleMath;
    interface _Object;
};
```

As this type library excerpt shows, the generated default interface follows the COM naming conventions. But if you look closely at the _SimpleMath interface definition, you see that it contains more than just the Add and Subtract methods. It also contains the methods inherited from System.Object. In fact, when you apply the AutoDual setting, the Type Library Exporter includes all public class members in the default interface. This includes members inherited from all base classes and members from implemented interfaces.

Managed Code and COM Versioning

In Chapter 2, you learned that the way .NET and COM handle versioning are worlds apart. You also learned how to take full advantage of the sophisticated .NET versioning capabilities. Unfortunately, when interoperating with COM clients, your .NET assemblies are forced to comply with COM versioning rules. Therefore, this section reviews COM versioning and presents techniques for handling changing versions in managed code exposed to COM clients.

Reviewing COM Versioning Rules

COM versioning is based on the idea that items in a type library are identified by a 128-bit number termed a *globally unique identifier* (GUID). When you compile an early bound client, the COM server's GUIDs are included in the executable. At runtime, the client passes these GUIDs to the COM runtime, which uses them to find and activate the types. The bottom line is this: if a GUID changes in the type library, then any early bound clients compiled against the old GUID are broken.

COM programmers are familiar with the notion of *binary compatibility*. This refers to the case where a newly compiled COM server retains the same GUIDs as the old version of the COM server. Therefore, existing clients can immediately use the new server. Of course, if one of the COM server's interfaces changes (for example, if the signature of a method changes), then it should be assigned a new GUID. In fact, one of the fundamental rules of COM is that interfaces are immutable. If this were not so, then existing clients could pass the wrong number or the incorrect type of arguments to the server, causing logic and fatal memory errors.

Developers building COM servers in C++ need to exercise discipline in regards to versioning. If they change an interface, then they should also change its IID (when a GUID is applied to an interface it is called an IID, or Interface ID). On the other hand, the Visual Basic 6.0 compiler automatically detects if changes were made to an interface, and prompts you to "break compatibility." If you choose to break compatibility, VB 6.0 generates and applies new GUIDs automatically. In contrast, when writing managed code for COM consumption, you can choose between automatic generation and application of GUIDs (like VB 6.0) or manual generation and application of GUIDs (like C++).

Using Automatic GUID Generation

If you do nothing to manually apply GUIDs to your assemblies and managed types, then the type library export tool automatically generates them. The method used to generate a GUID depends on whether it will identify an assembly (TLBID), class (CLSID), or interface (IID).

- For an assembly, the export process generates the TLBID by hashing the assembly's friendly name (for example, MathLibrary) and version. If the assembly is strong named, then the strong name is hashed to generate the TLBID.

- For a class, the export process generates the CLSID by hashing the full classname (including namespace) and the assembly version.

- For an interface, the export process generates the IID by hashing the interface name and the complete signatures of all its members. Reordering the members within the interface results in a different IID.

Applying GUIDs Manually

Like C++, .NET also lets you take complete control over how GUIDs are generated and applied. The CLR provides the GuidAttribute, which you can use to decorate an assembly, class, or interface. If this attribute is present, the export process does not generate a GUID for the item. Instead it uses the GUID passed to the GuidAttribute constructor.

For example, in the following code, we decorate the SimpleMath class with a GuidAttribute to manually set the CLSID:

```
[Guid("2E2EE280-936D-4790-8EB1-8946A34ABCCC")]
public class SimpleMath : IAdvancedMath
{
  // ...
}
```

In the type library, the class is now represented as follows:

```
[
  uuid(2E2EE280-936D-4790-8EB1-8946A34ABCCC),
  version(1.0),
  custom({0F21F359-AB84-41E8-9A78-36D110E6D2F9}, "MathLibrary.SimpleMath")
]
coclass SimpleMath {
    [default] interface IDispatch;
    interface _Object;
    interface IAdvancedMath;
};
```

In the type library, the CLSID is represented by the UUID attribute applied to the SimpleMath coclass. Note that it matches the CLSID specified in the GuidAttribute constructor.

 NOTE *If you choose to manually apply GUIDs, then you must determine if changes to the assembly cause incompatibility and change the GUIDs as necessary. Unlike Visual Basic 6.0, .NET compilers do not warn you if your modifications affect compatibility.*

To manually generate the GUID, you can use the uuidgen.exe command line utility that ships with earlier versions of Visual Studio and the .NET SDK. Or, in the Visual Studio .NET IDE, you can select Tools | Create GUID, and then copy and paste the resulting GUID into your code.

Contrasting Versioning Options

It is important to understand that the versioning concerns noted earlier apply to early bound clients only. When you compile a late bound client, GUIDs from the type library are not embedded within the resulting executable. Therefore, changing GUIDs does not break late bound clients. Of course, changing method signatures of interfaces can still break clients, but the outcome of a bad method call is a relatively benign runtime error (as compared to the memory errors that occur with early bound clients).

Remember, a simple managed class with no applied attributes is exposed to COM clients through IDispatch only. Therefore, clients can only late bind to it. This results in slower execution and the inability to validate method calls at compile time. However, it is also the most flexible option in regards to versioning.

In contrast, the least flexible option in regards to versioning is to allow the exporter to automatically generate the default interface via the ClassInterfaceType.AutoDual setting. Given that the default interface is generated, you cannot set the IID by applying a GuidAttribute. Instead, the IID is automatically generated by hashing the signature of all the interface members. Therefore, if you add a new method to your class, existing early bound clients will be broken even though they never call the new method.

For this reason, it is recommended that COM-exposed managed classes explicitly implement interfaces instead of relying on the ClassInterfaceType.AutoDual setting. This way, you can fix IIDs by applying the GUIDAttribute to the interfaces. Also, if you need to change a method signature, you can define the method in a new interface. This leaves the existing interface and its method intact for backwards compatibility with existing clients, while new clients can call the changed method in the new interface.

Summary

In this chapter, I introduced you to the essentials of COM interop. With this knowledge, you are empowered to take full advantage of COM+ services from managed code.

Here are a few of the main ideas from the chapter:

- COM+ is a COM-based technology. However, it can host managed objects through COM interop.

- COM interop must be considered in two different directions. The Runtime Callable Wrapper (RCW) provides interop from managed code to unmanaged code, allowing legacy COM components to be reused from .NET. The COM Callable Wrapper (CCW) provides interop from unmanaged code to managed code.

- You can generate interop assemblies using the Type Library Importer tool (tlbimp.exe) or the Visual Studio.NET IDE.

- The Assembly Registration Tool (regasm.exe) can generate a COM type library by reflecting over a given assembly and register it.

- You can influence the exact behavior of the export process by applying various attributes including the `GuidAttribute` and the `ClassInterfaceAttribute`.

In the next chapter, you will see how COM interop is used by the COM+ runtime to host objects written in managed code. And we will get back on track discussing technologies that directly relate to distributed programming.

CHAPTER 8

Leveraging Component Services

WITH ALL THE NEW technologies available in .NET, it is nice to know that at least one thing remains the same: COM+. But since "COM" is a dirty word these days, we now use the more politically correct "Component Services" term. Despite the different terminology, everything you have learned about Component Services is still true, and you can apply your knowledge in .NET. This is particularly good news for the many VB and C++ developers who have invested considerable amounts of time and money learning how to make the best use of Component Services. Having read the previous COM interoperability chapter (you didn't skip it, did you?), you are now ready to learn how to build .NET objects that can be hosted and serviced by COM+. So let's begin.

Component Services Overview

The technology now known as Component Services has changed many times over the past few years. Unfortunately, one of those changes is its name. Originally, it was called Microsoft Transaction Server (MTS). Then, with the introduction of Windows 2000, it was renamed to COM+. Now, with the release of .NET, it can go by several names: COM+, Component Services, or even Enterprise Services.

Regardless of its name, the basic idea remains the same: application developers have better things to do than to write custom solutions for distributed transactions, security, thread pooling, and object pooling. These are fundamental infrastructures services that all scalable distributed applications require, but they are not trivial to implement. Microsoft recognized the need for a generic solution for these issues and originally provided it with MTS. Refined it with COM+. And leveraged it in .NET.

Just to be clear, I'll refer to the technology as *Component Services* or *COM+*. Objects written in managed code designed to use Component Services will be called *serviced components* or *serviced objects*.

Component Services Motivation

The primary motivation behind Component Services is the need for a generic solution for common infrastructure problems in distributed applications. All distributed applications, if they are to scale at all, need an intelligent way to handle pools of worker threads. They also need a way to squeeze as much use as possible out of scarce resources such as database connections. Distributed applications may also need to coordinate transactions that span many databases, even databases from different vendors. Finally, the distributed application environment can change significantly over time. For example, you may add new hardware, or purchase additional database connections. These changes can make previous settings obsolete since they were optimized for the old environment. So distributed applications must allow administrators to easily adjust thread pooling or object pooling settings to take full advantage of new hardware or software.

This is a tall order for a company that, for example, just wants to sell books over the Internet. What does all this have to do with selling a book? Luckily, these services are all provided by COM+. So you can worry about your business application, rather than worrying about implementing object pooling.

Revisiting Context

In Chapter 3, I introduced the notion of a context. Recall that the .NET context serves two primary purposes: 1) to contain objects that share similar runtime requirements, and 2) to provide a layer of interception that allows the runtime to provide the required services. It turns out that this concept is not new in .NET. In fact, it originated with COM+.

The COM+ context serves the same purpose as the .NET context, but there are a few differences. Earlier you learned that the .NET runtime determines an object's context by investigating the type metadata in the assembly. If the information in the metadata includes context properties, then the runtime creates the object in a context that has those properties set. As developers, we can affect the type metadata by applying attributes to the type definition. Finally, recall that .NET objects requiring context are referred to as *context bound objects*.

In contrast to the .NET runtime's handling of context, the COM+ runtime determines an object's context by examining a machine-wide database called the *COM+ catalog*. This catalog maintains information regarding an object's context requirements. As developers, we can update the values in the COM+ catalog using the Component Services administration tool. This tool allows you to configure an object's context settings via an easy-to-use graphical user interface and can be used by both developers and system administrators. Any object that you configure via this tool is called a *configured object* to indicate that it requires Component Services. Figure 8-1 illustrates the relationship between the Component Services administration tool, the COM+ catalog, and the COM+ context.

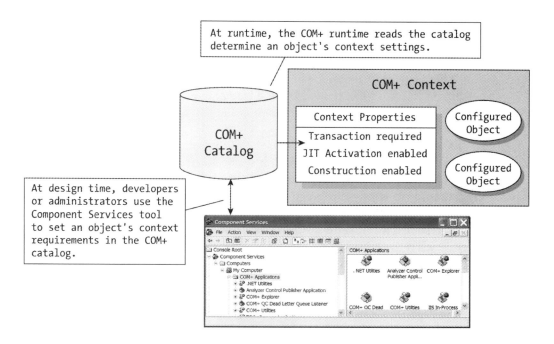

Figure 8-1. The administration tool to COM+ catalog to context relationship

Survey of Component Services

So what services does COM+ provide to configured objects? Here is a short summary:

- **Role-based security.** This service allows you to group application users into logical roles such as Administrator, Customer Service Representative, Manager, and so on. Once you associate a role or roles with an object, interface, or method, COM+ ensures only those users in the roles can access the item. Since creating and associating roles is done through the Component Services administration tool, you do not have to write security code within the object. Furthermore, you can change the role security details without recompiling the component.

- **Object pooling.** This service provides the ability to pool objects and share them among many clients. When the application begins, COM+ can create a number of objects, initialize them, and store them in the pool to be retrieved when needed. To serve an incoming client request, COM+ removes the object from the pool and places it back in the pool when the request is finished. With object pooling the server does not need to waste processor cycles to create an object with each request, and relatively few objects can serve a large number of clients.

- **Automatic transactions.** This service allows you to execute a transaction that spans multiple data sources. Furthermore, there is minimal code involved; you only need to implement the object to vote on the outcome of the transaction.

- **Just-In-Time (JIT) activation.** This service works hand-in-hand with object pooling and automatic transactions. With this service, COM+ does not activate an object until a client calls a method on it. Furthermore, COM+ deactivates the object as soon as the method call completes, which ensures that scarce resources consumed by the object are released. JIT activation prevents the greedy client scenario, where a client retrieves a reference to a remote object early and holds it for an excessive amount of time.

- **Queued components.** This service provides an easy way to implement methods that execute asynchronously. The service is built upon Microsoft Message Queuing (MSMQ), but provides a much simpler programming model for developers.

- **Loosely coupled events.** This service provides *publish and subscribe* communication between objects. Subscriber objects may subscribe to certain registered events. When an event is raised by another object (the publisher), COM+ ensures that all subscribers are notified. Unlike the normal COM tightly coupled events, the publisher and the subscriber require no knowledge about each other.

It is important to understand that little or no code is required to take advantage of the preceding services. Instead, you simply configure the object using the Component Services tool (or, in .NET, using attributes), and COM+ does the rest.

Survey of COM+ Configuration Settings

With the unveiling of MTS, Microsoft introduced the notion of *declarative attributes.* Instead of requesting services using a set of API calls, a component uses attributes set at design time to advertise and specify the exact set of services required at runtime. Declarative attributes allow programmers or administrators to reconfigure components without recompiling, even after they are put into production.

COM+ not only continues this declarative attribute model, it expands on it. Compared to MTS, COM+ provides many more services and allows a finer grained level of control over these services. For example, COM+ supplies security attributes that can be applied down to the method level.

Do not confuse the COM+ style of declarative attributes with .NET attributes. While the concepts are similar, the mechanics are very different. You apply .NET attributes to types using the attribute syntax of your chosen .NET language. When compiled, these attributes become type metadata stored within the assembly. On the other hand, you apply COM+ attributes using the Component Services tool, and the values are stored in the COM+ catalog.

COM+ attributes can be applied to an entire COM+ application, a single component, an interface, or a method. As shown in Figure 8-2, the Component Services tool displays all of these items in a tree view control. You simply drill down to the application, component, interface, or method you need to configure and right-click to bring up the Properties dialog box. By setting values in a node's Properties dialog box, you are applying COM+ attributes to the item.

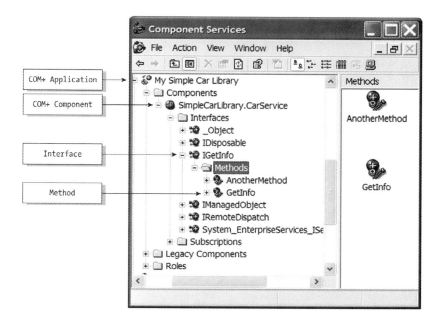

Figure 8-2. Drill down into the tree view to see the COM+ item you wish to configure.

Many books have gone to great lengths to describe each and every attribute in COM+. This is not one of them. However, given that .NET provides attributes that mirror the COM+ attributes, it is worthwhile to cover a few of the commonly used settings.

COM+ Application Settings

All components installed in COM+ must belong to a COM+ application. The purpose of a COM+ application is to maintain the configuration settings for related components. It also provides settings that are scoped to the entire application. In other words, the settings apply to all its contained components.

There are three primary application-scoped configuration settings:

- **Security.** You can turn COM+ role–based security off or on for all components residing in the application. You can also define how often security is validated: per call, per packet, and so on.

- **Activation.** You can choose between server and library activation mode. If the application is set to server activations, then all components in the application are executed in the COM+ server process (dllhost.exe). In library activation mode, the components are executed within the client's process.

- **Identity.** If the activation mode is set to server, then you can specify the user account that COM+ will use to execute all the components in the application. Thus, the credentials of this user account are used to access databases, files, and other operation system resources.

You may be tempted to think that there is always a one-to-one relationship between COM+ applications and .NET assemblies. While this is true in most cases, it is not always true. In fact, you can install managed classes from many different assemblies into a single COM+ application.

COM+ Component Settings

When a class is installed in a COM+ application, the class is represented by a COM+ component. Unfortunately, the term *component* is highly overloaded. Depending on the context, it can refer to an entire COM DLL or it can refer to just one COM object. In the case of COM+, it refers to a single COM class or a single .NET class.

Most COM+ attributes are applied at the component level. Here are the general categories of settings:

- **Transactions.** You can configure a component to require or participate in COM+ automatic transactions. This is discussed in detail later.

- **Security.** You can assign predefined security roles to the component. If authorization is enabled at the COM+ application level, then only those users belonging to assigned roles can activate the component. Others will receive a security error.

- **Activation.** You can configure the component to participate in object pooling and set values for the minimum and maximum number of objects in the pool. You can also specify a string that COM+ passes to the component during activation. The passed string can contain information required to correctly activate the component, such as a database connection string.

- **Concurrency.** Although COM+ is a multithreaded environment, the COM+ synchronization services allow you to implement classes without regard to thread safety. By configuring the component to use COM+ synchronization, you ensure that only one thread is executing within a component at a time.

COM+ Interface and Method Settings

By the time you drill down to the interface or method level, the number of COM+ attributes you can apply gets very small. In fact, there are only a couple:

- **Queuing.** This applies to interfaces only. Marking an interface for queuing allows its methods to be called asynchronously. The interface must consist entirely of methods that return void (or Subs in VB) and have parameters that are only pass by value.

- **Security.** This applies to interfaces and methods. Like components, you can apply predefined security roles to an interface or method. This allows methods within a given component to accept calls from users in different roles.

Building Serviced Components in Managed Code

As mentioned earlier, .NET does not replace COM+. Instead, Microsoft chose to leverage the existing COM+ code by enabling it to host managed objects via the COM interop layer. Eventually, a future version of .NET will provide all the COM+ services using managed code, but for now developers must contend with both the managed and unmanaged world when building serviced components. The good news is that the manner in which managed objects request the services remains the same regardless of whether the service is provided by a managed or unmanaged host. Therefore, once the transition is made to a pure managed code solution, your existing code will require little or no modifications.

Populating the COM+ Catalog

Recall that the COM+ runtime determines an object's context properties by examining the COM+ catalog. This is also true for managed objects. However, .NET developers do not need to use the Component Services administration tool to configure the object. Instead, you decorate managed classes with attributes to specify the COM+ configuration settings. To be clear, the attributes you use to decorate classes are not COM+ attributes, but .NET attributes that mirror those defined by COM+.

For example, the following code defines a CarService class that requires COM+ Just-In-Time activation services:

```
// All the important enterprise service types are contained here.
using System.EnterpriseServices;

namespace SimpleCarLibrary
{
    // Class requires JIT activation
    [JustInTimeActivation()]
    public class CarService : ServicedComponent
    {
        // Implementation
    }
}
```

This code example demonstrates the pattern for writing serviced components in managed code. All COM+ configuration settings have corresponding CLR attributes that you can use to configure your classes for COM+ services. In this case, I am applying the JustInTimeActivation attribute, thus requesting this service from COM+. As is the case for all .NET attributes, these COM+-associated attributes become part of the assembly's metadata when compiled.

However, the COM+ runtime knows nothing about assembly metadata. Therefore, after the assembly is compiled, the COM+ configuration information stored in the metadata must somehow be copied into the COM+ catalog. You can do this in three ways:

- You can manually populate the COM+ catalog using the .NET Services Installation tool (regsvcs.exe). This tool reads the metadata and copies any COM+-related settings into the COM+ catalog.

- You can rely on the .NET runtime to automatically populate the COM+ catalog using *lazy registration.*

- You can programmatically populate the COM+ catalog using the RegistrationHelper class provided by the CLR. In fact, the regsvcs tool uses this class to perform its duties.

The first two techniques are described in detail in the following sections. I'll leave the third option for the ambitious reader to investigate. Regardless of the technique employed, Figure 8-3 illustrates how the assembly metadata is used to populate the COM+ catalog.

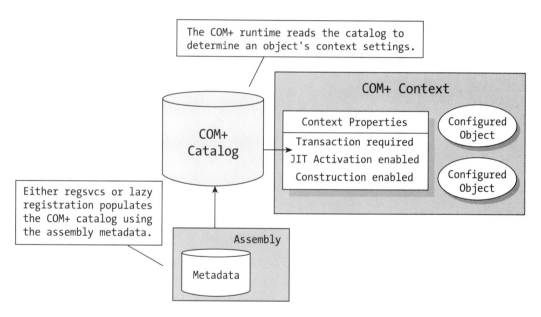

Figure 8-3. The assembly metadata to COM+ catalog to COM+ context relationship

Using the .NET Services Installation Tool (Regsvcs)

In all likelihood, you will use the .NET Services Installation tool (henceforth regsvcs) to populate the COM+ catalog. The example here demonstrates the typical use of this tool:

```
regsvcs CarLibrary.dll
```

This simple command performs several tasks:

1. It generates and registers a COM type library using the same process as the regasm.exe utility discussed in Chapter 7. In this case, the resulting type library is named CarLibrary.tlb, but you can specify a different name using the /tlb option.

2. Within the COM+ catalog, it searches for a COM+ application named CarLibrary. If not found, it is created. You can change the COM+ application name using the /appname option. You can also specify the target COM+ application name in code using the ApplicationNameAttribute.

3. It reads the CarLibrary assembly's metadata and copies any COM+ settings to the COM+ catalog in the application found or created in the previous step.

There are a few important things to keep in mind when running the regsvcs tool:

• The assembly must be strong named. And though it is not required in all situations, the assembly should be installed in the GAC. This is certainly true if the COM+ application is server activated.

• You must have administrative rights to write to the COM+ catalog. Therefore, you must have administrative rights to run the regsvcs tool.

Lazy Registration

Serviced components built in .NET actually have the ability to automatically install themselves within COM+. When a managed client calls a managed serviced component, the .NET runtime determines whether the serviced component is installed in COM+ or not. If not, the .NET runtime dynamically performs the steps listed in the previous section.

While convenient, this technique works in only a few scenarios. Remember, administrative rights are required to write to the COM+ catalog. Therefore, if the caller does not have administrative rights, then lazy registration will fail. Furthermore, lazy registration only works if the client is a managed client. An unmanaged client requires a registered type library to locate the requested class in the registry. Finally, if there are problems registering a component, these will not be discovered until a client attempts to connect.

Experimenting with a Simple Serviced Component

To make sure the mechanics of building a serviced component in .NET are clear, let's walk through the creation of a very simple serviced class. In the simplest of cases, creating a serviced class requires the following steps:

1. Build a class library assembly and implement a class derived from the ServicedComponent class.

2. Decorate the class with one or more attributes that define the required COM+ services.

3. Install the assembly in COM+ using the .NET Services Installation tool (regsvcs.exe) or rely on lazy registration.

Implementing the Serviced Component

To implement the serviced component, first open a class library project in your .NET language of choice. Then implement a class deriving from ServicedComponent. This type and all of the other COM+-related types reside in the System.EnterpriseServices namespace. For example, let's revisit the CarService class defined earlier:

```
// All the important enterprise service types are contained here.
using System.EnterpriseServices;

namespace SimpleCarLibrary
{
   // Class requires Just-In-Time (JIT) activation
   [JustInTimeActivation()]
   public class CarService : ServicedComponent
   {
      // Serviced components require a default constructor.
      public CarService() {}
   }
}
```

The abstract ServicedComponent base class serves a number of purposes. First, tools such as regsvcs look for this base class to determine which classes require COM+ services. Second, the ServicedComponent class provides default implementations for two COM+ interfaces: IObjectControl and IObjectConstruct (which will be discussed in detail later). Finally, as Figure 8-4 shows, ServicedComponent derives from ContextBoundObject, which in turn derives from MarshalByRefObject. Therefore, all classes extending `ServicedComponent` are also marshaled by reference and context bound.

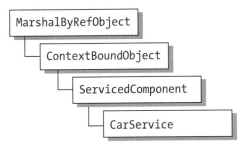

Figure 8-4. The `ServicedComponent` *hierarchy*

Another item to note in the previous example is the existence of a public default constructor. This is required by all classes deriving from `ServicedComponent`, otherwise the regsvcs utility will fail when attempting to install the class into COM+. Also, note that serviced classes must be public and cannot be abstract.

The next step is to compile the preceding code into an assembly, which we will call SimpleCarLibrary.dll. Remember that this assembly must be strong named, so we need to apply the `AssemblyKeyFile` attribute as described in Chapter 2.

```
[assembly: AssemblyKeyFile(@"D:\MyKey.snk")]
```

Also, remember that if the serviced class is server activated (that is, activated within a COM+ server process instead of within the client process), then you must also install the assembly in the GAC. However, for this first attempt, we will accept the default library activation setting. So, for now, we do not need to share the assembly.

After you compile the assembly, the next step is to run the regsvcs tool, which installs the component within COM+ and creates a type library for COM interop.

```
regsvcs SimpleCarLibrary.dll
```

Figure 8-5 shows the results of this command in the Component Services administration tool. Note that there now exists a COM+ application named SimpleCarLibrary.

Granted, our serviced class does not do much, so let's modify the class a little to give us something to test. We will add the following `GetInfo` method, which will eventually return useful information regarding the current object. For now, however, it will simply return a hard coded message as shown here:

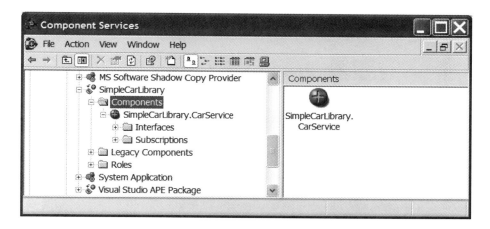

Figure 8-5. The SimpleCarLibrary application after running regsvcs

```
[JustInTimeActivation()]
public class CarService : ServicedComponent
{
   public CarService(){}

   public string GetInfo()
   {
      return "Testing the CarService component!";
   }
}
```

The Trouble with GUIDs

Now we can recompile the assembly and run regsvcs again. However, note the result in Figure 8-6. The SimpleCarService application now has two CarService components!

Unfortunately, that is not the only problem. If we view the registered type libraries using the OLE/COM Object Viewer, we see that two SimpleCarLibrary.tlb files are now registered (see Figure 8-7). One registration refers to the newly created type library, while the other refers to the old one we just overwrote. And, if we dig further, we discover that there are two SimpleCarLibary.CarService classes registered too: once for the old implementation and again for the new. To rid the registry of these now orphaned registry items, we would have to manually remove the items or use a utility like RegClean.

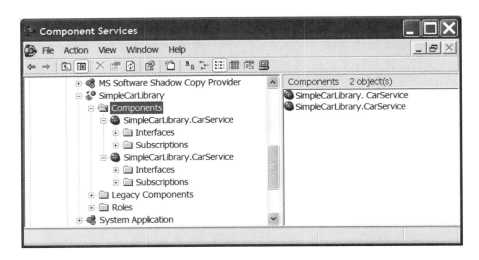

Figure 8-6. After running regsvsc again, there are two `CarService` *components.*

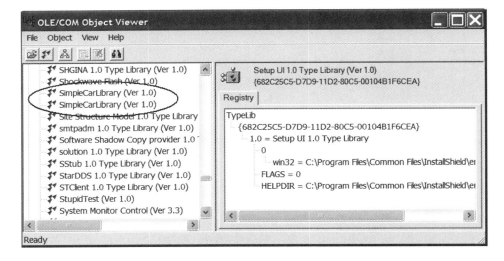

Figure 8-7. After running regsvcs again, there are two SimpleCarLibrary type libraries registered.

What is the cause of all this? The short answer is GUIDs. Since COM+ is based on COM, it uses GUIDs to distinguish between components and interfaces. The regsvcs utility uses the same mechanism as the regasm tool discussed in the last chapter to automatically generate GUIDs and create the type library for COM interop. Recall that regasm generates the TLBID by hashing the assembly's strong name, including the version number. By default, Visual Studio .NET adds the following line to the AssemblyInfo.cs file, which causes the compiler to automatically update the build and revision parts of the version number with each compile:

```
[assembly: AssemblyVersion("1.0.*")]
```

Therefore, recompiling and reregistering this assembly will always result in a different TLBID and leave the old TLBID orphaned within the registry. The easiest solution for this problem is to set the entire version number to some value as follows:

```
[assembly: AssemblyVersion("1.0.0.0")]
```

This solves the issue of multiple type library registrations, but what about the issue of the multiple CarService components? Yet again, differing GUIDs are the cause. In this case, the regsvcs tool generates a new CLSID for the CarService component, causing COM+ to interpret the newly compiled component as a different component. However, as discussed in the previous chapter, CLSIDs are generated by hashing the full name of the class and the assembly version. Therefore, applying a fixed assembly version number solves both the TLBID and CLSID issues.

Of course, another way to solve both these issues is to turn off automatic GUID generation by manually applying your own GUIDs to both the assembly and the class as shown in the previous chapter. This way, you can change the assembly version without affecting the GUIDs in COM+. In other words, you can keep the versioning characteristics of .NET and COM separate. For a refresher, the following code applies a GUID to the assembly and the CarService class:

```
using System.EnterpriseServices
using System.Runtime.InteropServices;  // Required for GUIDAttribute

[assembly: Guid("932B6A4D-FCC2-48a9-966A-9BE4794CB562")]

namespace SimpleCarLibrary
{
   [JustInTimeActivation(), Guid("00E1160C-F65B-45fa-A92D-C24AB92831C8")]
   public class CarService : ServicedComponent
   { }
}
```

Building a Simple Managed Client

Now that our serviced class is correctly installed in COM+, the next step is to build a client. For the time being, we will build a simple client to test our serviced class. In the next section, I will discuss other client issues.

Fortunately, there is not much difference between building a client for a serviced component and building any other client. The client must reference the assembly containing the serviced class, in this case SimpleCarLibrary.dll, and it must reference the System.EnterpriseServices.dll assembly. The code that follows is for a console application client called SimpleCarClient.

```
using System;
using SimpleCarLibrary;

namespace SimpleCarClient
{
   class CarMain
   {
      static void Main(string[] args)
      {
         CarService carSvc = new CarService();
         Console.WriteLine(carSvc.GetInfo());

         Console.ReadLine();
      }
   }
}
```

Note that instantiating the serviced object is no different than any other object. We simply use the new keyword. The runtime determines the requested class is a serviced class and creates the object within a COM+ context. For a more thorough explanation of the interaction between COM+ and the serviced object, see the upcoming section titled "Examining COM+ and .NET Interaction."

Interacting with the COM+ Context Using ContextUtil

Currently, we are acting on faith by assuming our CarService class is activated and executed under COM+. How can we prove it? One way is to fetch and display information regarding the COM+ context, such as the context ID. The CLR provides the ContextUtil class for the purpose of interacting with the COM+ context. This class exposes a number of static members that allow you to retrieve various bits of context information. Later, we will see that it also provides methods for controlling the behavior of a transaction.

To try this class out, we will modify our CarService.GetInfo method to return a string containing context information.

```
public string GetInfo()
{
   StringBuilder ctxInfo = new StringBuilder();

   // Use ContextUtil to fetch context information
   ctxInfo.AppendFormat("Context ID: {0}\n", ContextUtil.ContextId);
   ctxInfo.AppendFormat("Activity ID: {0}\n", ContextUtil.ActivityId);

   // If in transaction, get transaction ID
   string txId = "No Tx";
   if (ContextUtil.IsInTransaction)
      txId = ContextUtil.TransactionId.ToString();

   ctxInfo.AppendFormat("Transaction ID:    {0}\n", txId);
   ctxInfo.AppendFormat("Security Enabled?: {0}\n",
      ContextUtil.IsSecurityEnabled);

   return ctxInfo.ToString();
}
```

From this code, you can see that the ContextUtil class provides access to the COM+ context ID, activity ID, and transaction ID (if present). The output (Figure 8-8) proves the CarService object is running within a COM+ context.

Figure 8-8. The client output proves the CarService *object is running under COM+.*

The preceding result shown is not quite as gratifying as the famous "spinning ball" that the Component Services administration tool shows when a component is activated within COM+. More importantly, it does not show the usage statistics in the component status view. As you can imagine, these features consume server resources. Therefore, they are turned off by default with .NET serviced classes. To turn them on, we can apply the EventTrackingEnabledAttribute to the serviced class.

```
[JustInTimeActivation(), EventTrackingEnabled()]
public class CarService : ServicedComponent
{
    // ...
}
```

 Source Code   *The code for this example is in Chapter8\SimpleComponent.*

Figure 8-9 shows the CarService component's status view after compiling and reregistering with the event tracking enabled. Note that the administration tool is now able to show component usage statistics.

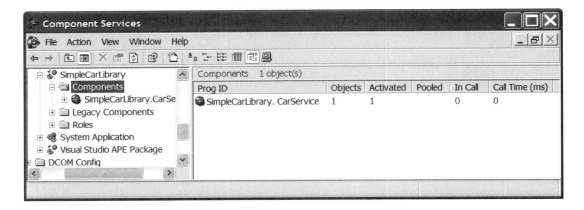

Figure 8-9. The CarService *component's status view*

Using Server Activation

Currently, the CarService component activation setting is set to Library, which means the object is activated within the caller's process. This is the default activation for serviced components, but it is easy to change our component to server activation. We can simply set server activation using the administration tool, or, within our code, we can apply the `ApplicationActivationAttribute` to the assembly. We want this setting to persist even if the assembly is reregistered with COM+, so we will take the latter approach:

```
[assembly: ApplicationActivation(ActivationOption.Server)]
```

Note that the `ApplicationActivationAttribute` constructor takes an `ActivationOption` enumeration that has values for Server and Library activation.

The activation attribute is one of a few attributes in the `System.EnterpriseServices` namespace that apply to an assembly. Two other handy ones are `ApplicationNameAttribute` and `ApplicationIDAttribute`. The first attribute allows you to specify the COM+ application name generated by regsvcs, which uses the assembly name by default. The second allows you to specify a GUID that COM+ will use to identify the COM+ application. For example, here we apply both of these attributes to our SimpleCarLibrary assembly:

```
[assembly: ApplicationName("My Simple Car Library")]
[assembly: ApplicationID("F449B097-52ED-4a5d-A408-E5880E10FD29")]
```

 NOTE *Applying the* `ApplicationIDAttribute` *to the assembly is different than applying the* `GuidAttribute`. *The regsvcs utility uses the former to identify the COM+ application and uses the latter to identify the type library.*

Now we can recompile and run regsvcs. However, when we run the application, we now get the exception shown in Figure 8-10. The reason? We forgot to install the SimpleCarLibrary assembly in the GAC. Remember, with server activation, the COM+ process (dllhost.exe) must load the assembly using the assembly binding mechanism described in Chapter 2. Therefore, since the dllhost.exe file resides in the Winnt\System32 directory, the SimpleCarLibrary assembly must either be copied to the Winnt\System32 directory or installed in the GAC. Seeing as we don't want to clutter the System32 directory, the best option is to install the assembly into the GAC.

Once we install the SimpleCarLibrary assembly in the GAC, our application runs as before. Figure 8-11 shows the CarService component's status view after compiling, reregistering, and running the client application. Note that the application name is now listed as "My Simple Car Library" due to applying the `ApplicationNameAttribute`.

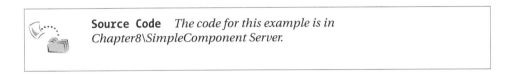

Figure 8-10. Using server activation without installing assembly in the GAC causes an exception.

Source Code   *The code for this example is in Chapter8\SimpleComponent Server.*

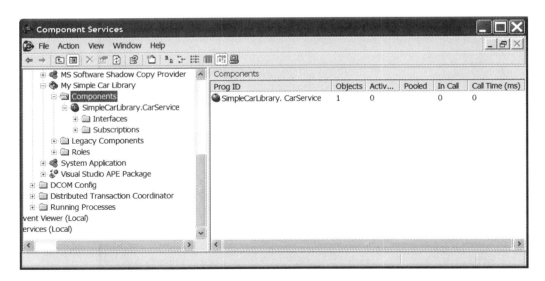

Figure 8-11. The application name is now "My Simple Car Library."

Avoiding Server Activation Frustrations

With server activation, the COM+ process loads the assembly and retains it in memory even after all clients have shut down. This can cause a variety of frustrating behavior while you are developing and testing the application, including the inability to compile your application and the impression that, when you can recompile, your changes have no effect.

The first problem, the inability to recompile, occurs only when you are compiling debug versions of the assembly. Unlike the days of COM, a COM+ server application loads the .NET assembly from the GAC, not the assembly you are writing when you rebuild the application. This means you do not get the annoying "permission denied" messages when attempting to overwrite your copy of the DLL. However, the COM+ process also loads the debugging symbols contained in the PDB file (for example, SimpleCarLibrary.pdb). The IDE attempts to write the same PDB file with every rebuild. Therefore, you DO get the annoying "permission denied" error for the PDB file (see Figure 8-12 for the actual error message). To recompile the project, you either have to wait until the COM+ process releases it (after 3 minutes of inactivity by default) or manually shut down the process using the Component Services administration tool.

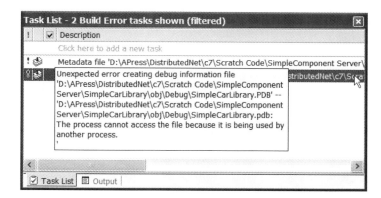

Figure 8-12. Build error when trying to overwrite the PDB file

The fact that the COM+ process loads the assembly from the GAC can cause another potential problem. If you do recompile, but fail to install the new assembly in the GAC, COM+ loads the GAC assembly instead of the one you just built. Another subtlety at work is that the GAC allows you to install a rebuilt assembly over an old assembly even if a process is currently using the old assembly. Many seasoned COM developers would expect the GAC install to fail if the assembly is in use. Therefore, they are under the false impression that the COM+ server process has released the old assembly, and any new tests will exercise the rebuilt assembly.

Instead, the GAC has "shadow copied" the assembly, meaning the rebuilt assembly is installed, but will only take effect for new bind requests. The COM+ server process thus must unload the old assembly from memory and bind to the rebuilt assembly in the GAC. Again, you can force this to happen by stopping the COM+ server process via the Component Services administration tool.

The bottom line is that you have to be on your toes when developing components with server activation. The following build sequence may be overkill in many situations, but I have found it to be surefire way to avoid the issues noted in this section.

1. Before rebuilding the assembly, uninstall the current assembly from COM+ using the regsvcs utility. This will force the COM+ server process to shut down. For example:

```
regsvcs /u simplecarlibrary.dll
```

2. Rebuild the assembly.

3. Reinstall the assembly into COM+ using the regsvcs utility.

```
regsvcs simplecarlibrary.dll
```

4. Install the assembly in the GAC.

```
gacutil /i simplecarlibrary.dll
```

5. Test the application.

This may seem like a large number of steps, but if you keep a command prompt window open, you can quickly reissue these commands using the history feature of the command prompt and the arrow keys. Also note that the steps assume that all COM+ configuration details are included within the assembly metadata. Any configuration administered via the Component Services tool is lost since the entire COM+ application is removed and then reinstalled.

Where Are My Methods?

For the experienced COM+ developer, everything may now seem fairly normal—until we use the Component Services administration tool to drill a little deeper into the component. As Figure 8-13 shows, the administration tool is not displaying the CarService.GetInfo method!

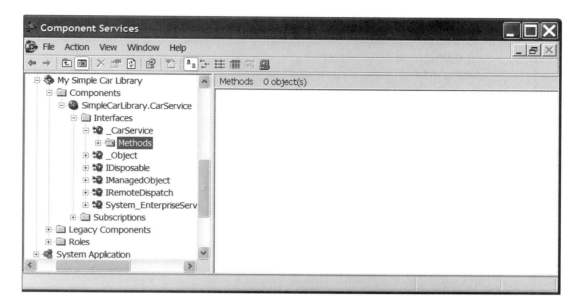

Figure 8-13. The GetInfo *method is not listed under the the* CarService *component.*

Once again, we have to go back to the last chapter to understand why this is happening. COM+ reflects over the type library to display the interfaces and methods of the component. However, recall that unless we tell it otherwise, the assembly to type library export process creates a late bound only class as shown here:

```
coclass CarService {
  [default] interface _CarService;
  interface _Object;
  interface IRemoteDispatch;
  interface IDisposable;
  interface IManagedObject;
  interface System_EnterpriseServices_IServicedComponentInfo;
};

interface _CarService : IDispatch {
};
```

As you can see, this list of interfaces is exactly what is shown in the administration tool. And since the _CarService interface does not list any methods, neither does the administration tool.

Displaying the Methods the Easy Way

There are two ways to fix this: the easy way, and the right way. The easy way is to apply the ClassInterfaceAttribute with the ClassInterfaceType.AutoDual setting. Recall that this instructs the assembly exporter to generate an interface containing the class members. So all we need to do is apply the attribute as follows:

```
[JustInTimeActivation(), EventTrackingEnabled(),
 ClassInterface(ClassInterfaceType.AutoDual)]
public class CarService : ServicedComponent
{
    // ...
}
```

After compiling and running regsvcs, the type library now looks like the following (some attributes removed for clarity):

```
coclass CarService {
   [default] interface _CarService;
   interface _Object;
   interface IRemoteDispatch;
   interface IDisposable;
   interface IManagedObject;
};

interface _CarService : IDispatch {
   HRESULT ToString([out, retval] BSTR* pRetVal);
   HRESULT Equals([in] VARIANT obj, [out, retval] VARIANT_BOOL* pRetVal);
   HRESULT GetHashCode([out, retval] long* pRetVal);
   HRESULT GetType([out, retval] _Type** pRetVal);
   HRESULT GetLifetimeService([out, retval] VARIANT* pRetVal);
   HRESULT InitializeLifetimeService([out, retval] VARIANT* pRetVal);
   HRESULT CreateObjRef([in] _Type* requestedType,
                        [out, retval] IDispatch** pRetVal);
   HRESULT Activate();
   HRESULT Deactivate();
   HRESULT CanBePooled([out, retval] VARIANT_BOOL* pRetVal);
   HRESULT Construct([in] BSTR s);
   HRESULT Dispose();
   HRESULT GetInfo([out, retval] BSTR* pRetVal);
};
```

This type library defines a default interface called _CarService, which includes all public members exposed by the CarService class, including those inherited from base classes. Therefore, the Component Services administration tool displays these members as shown in Figure 8-14.

Source Code   *The code for this example is in Chapter8\Displaying-Methods Easy.*

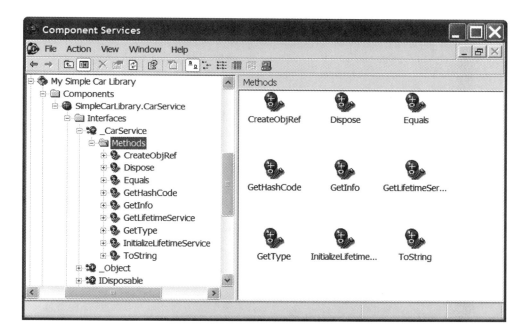

Figure 8-14. Now all methods, including those inherited, are displayed.

So why is this easy way not the right way? I think you can probably guess the first reason. Out of all the methods listed under the _CarService interface node, we only really care about one: GetInfo. The rest are inherited from base classes and clutter the view. The second reason is a little less obvious, but more serious. To demonstrate, let's add another method to our CarService class named AnotherMethod.

```
[JustInTimeActivation(), EventTrackingEnabled(),
 ClassInterface(ClassInterfaceType.AutoDual)]
public class CarService : ServicedComponent
{
    public void AnotherMethod() {...}
    public CarService()  {...}
    public string GetInfo() {...}
}
```

After we compile and run regsvcs, the Component Services administration tool now lists two _CarService interfaces (Figure 8-15)! And once again, the root cause of this unfortunate situation is automatic GUID generation. Remember, unless directed otherwise, the regsvcs tool generates IIDs (interface GUIDs) by hashing the signatures of the members. Typically, we could apply the GuidAttribute to the interface to assign our own fixed GUID. In this case, however, the interface is also automatically generated, so it is impossible to apply the GuidAttribute in code.

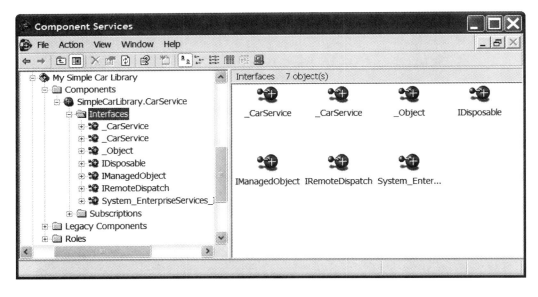

Figure 8-15. After recompiling with AutoDispatch, two _CarService *interfaces are displayed.*

Displaying the Methods the Right Way

If you care to see your component's methods listed in the Component Services administration tool, then the best way is to define interfaces and implement them within the serviced class. For example, we can define an `IGetInfo` interface and implement it as shown here:

```
[Guid("5A1BB09D-8D4B-481a-A441-DC6D8D48F396")]
public interface IGetInfo
{
    string GetInfo();
}


[JustInTimeActivation(), EventTrackingEnabled(),
 ClassInterface(ClassInterfaceType.None)]
public class CarService : ServicedComponent, IGetInfo
{
    public CarService()  {...}
    public string GetInfo() {...}
}
```

Note the change in the `ClassInterfaceAttribute` in this example; this time we are using the `ClassInterfaceType.None` value. Remember, this enumeration value turns off the default behavior of exposing the `IDispatch` interface as the default interface for the class (see the previous chapter for a full explanation). After we compile and run regsvcs, we see that the resulting type library is greatly simplified:

```
interface IGetInfo : IDispatch {
    HRESULT GetInfo([out, retval] BSTR* pRetVal);
};

coclass CarService {
    interface _Object;
    interface IRemoteDispatch;
    interface IDisposable;
    interface IManagedObject;
    [default] interface IGetInfo;
};
```

And, as shown in Figure 8-16, we see that this results in a much cleaner view within the Component Services administration tool. We can expand the `IGetInfo` node to view the `GetInfo` method, and not have to look at all the other inherited methods.

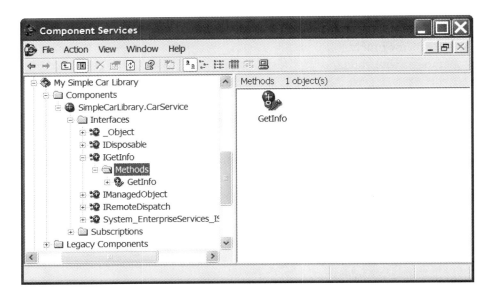

Figure 8-16. Using custom interfaces results in a cleaner view.

Perhaps more importantly, using this technique we can add another method and reinstall in COM+ without generating two duplicate named interfaces in the administration tool. For example, in the following code, we add AnotherMethod to the interface and implemented it in the CarService class:

```
[Guid("5A1BB09D-8D4B-481a-A441-DC6D8D48F396")]
public interface IGetInfo
{
   string GetInfo();
   void AnotherMethod();
}
[JustInTimeActivation(), EventTrackingEnabled(),
 ClassInterface(ClassInterfaceType.None)]
public class CarService : ServicedComponent, IGetInfo
{
   public void AnotherMethod() {...}
   public CarService()  {...}
   public string GetInfo() {...}
}
```

Figure 8-17 shows the results in the Component Services administration tool after compiling and running regsvcs on the preceding code. As expected, it shows only one IGetInfo node with two method nodes underneath: GetInfo and AnotherMethod.

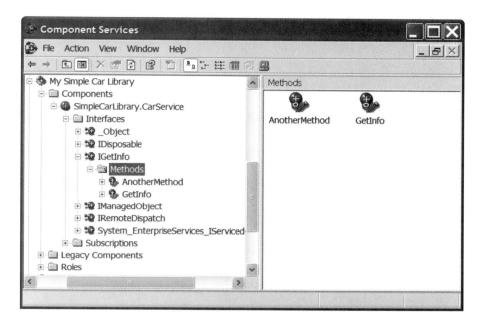

Figure 8-17. Using interfaces also makes it easier to add methods.

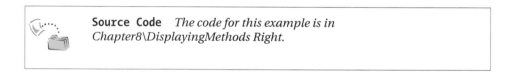

Source Code   *The code for this example is in Chapter8\DisplayingMethods Right.*

Examining COM+ and .NET Interaction

The interaction between the managed world of the .NET runtime and the unmanaged world of the COM+ runtime differs depending on whether the application uses library or server activation. One primary concept is used in both cases, however: context.

Because the ServicedComponent class derives from ContextBoundObject, all serviced objects are context bound. As you know, context provides an interception layer for the .NET runtime. Therefore, when the client code creates a ServicedComponent type, the runtime activates the object within a managed context and returns a proxy reference to the client code. This interception infrastructure can be customized; you can create your own proxy implementation for a given context bound type and define custom interception behavior. The .NET runtime uses this customization mechanism to interact with COM+. When a serviced object is created, the .NET runtime creates a specialized proxy called the *serviced component proxy* (SCP).

In the case of library activation and a managed client, the SCP facilitates the interaction between COM+ and .NET. When the serviced object is activated, COM+ reads the object's required services from the COM+ catalog and establishes the proper COM+ context. However, instead of housing the actual serviced object, the COM+ context maintains only a reference to the managed SCP. Likewise, the SCP contains a reference to the COM+ context. The SCP intercepts each method call on the serviced object, and routes it to the COM+ context so that it can perform its preprocessing duties as defined by the COM+ context properties. When this is finished, the SCP then invokes the method on the actual serviced object. Upon return, the SCP also contacts the COM+ context, allowing it to perform any required post-processing. Figure 8-18 illustrates the role of the SCP.

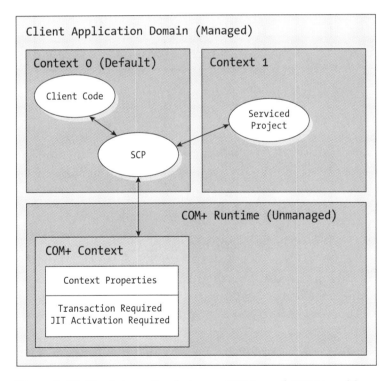

Figure 8-18. The interaction between COM+ and .NET in a library-activated application

Technically speaking, a library-activated COM+ application does *not* use COM interop to host the serviced object when accessed by a managed client. As Figure 8-18 shows, at no time does this interaction involve an RCW or CCW. On the other hand, it still requires a COM type library built from the assembly metadata, and it still requires the type library to be registered just as it does with any other COM type library. For this reason, I don't believe it is entirely inaccurate to say that library-activated applications use COM interop to host managed serviced objects. All the mechanical steps are the same, and you still have to worry about GUID generation, class interfaces, and other COM interop details such as versioning.

In the case of server activation, full COM+ interop is used. For details, see the upcoming section titled "Exposing Objects with DCOM."

Just-In-Time Activation

To run our experiments in the last section, our `CarService` object used the JIT activation service. This service provides an important benefit in itself, and is critical for other services such as automatic transactions and object pooling.

With JIT activation enabled, COM+ activates the object only when a method is called. Typically, the object is deactivated as soon as the method completes. What it means for the object to be "activated" or "deactivated" depends on whether the object is pooled or not. If the object is pooled, then activation means the object is taken from the pool and deactivation means the object is placed back into the pool. If the object is not pooled, then activation is the same as creation, and deactivation is similar to destruction. Regardless, the client is not aware that COM+ is activating and deactivating the object between method calls. From the client's perspective, it is calling methods on a single persistent object.

The primary motivation behind JIT activation is to prevent greedy clients. A *greedy client* is one that holds a long-lived reference to a COM+ object even while it is not using the object. If the object consumes scarce resources while alive, then a greedy client can block other clients from using the resources. JIT activation splits the responsibility of object deactivation and associated resource cleanup between the object and the COM+ runtime. Therefore, a greedy client has no impact.

JIT Activation and Stateless Objects

Even though clients are generally unaware of JIT activation objects, these types of objects do have a distinctive look and feel. For example, a client should never use a JIT activation object in the following fashion:

```
// How NOT to use a JIT activation object!!
CarService carSvc = new CarService();
carSvc.Model = "Honda";
carSvc.Color = "Red";
carSvc.Save();
```

Why is this incorrect? Remember, JIT activation objects are typically released between method calls. Therefore, in this example, the call to the Color property would likely be serviced by a different object than the Save method call.

For this reason, the use of a JIT activation object looks more like the following:

```
// How TO use a JIT activation object!!
CarService carSvc = new CarService();
carSvc.Save("Honda", "Red");
carSvc.Save("Toyota", "White");
```

In the preceding example, it does not matter if the second call to Save is served by a different object, because all the information required to complete the save operation is passed into the method. The object does not rely on any information that must persist between method calls, such as object instance data. In other words, it is stateless.

To be clear, JIT activation is not required to implement a stateless object. For that, all you need are class methods that complete their operations without using instance data. One reason stateless objects are used is to minimize the consumption of resources. You can implement each method to allocate the required resources and deallocate them before the method returns. JIT activation, however, provides a more structured and convenient approach through the IObjectControl interface.

Implementing IObjectControl

The IObjectControl interface defines three methods: Activate, Deactivate, and CanBePooled. Through this interface, the COM+ runtime can notify the object that it has just been activated or that it is about to be deactivated, giving the object the opportunity to complete any associated tasks. Typically, you would implement the Activate method to allocate resources and release them within Deactivate.

In COM programming, each configured class implements the IObjectControl interface through standard COM mechanisms. However, in .NET, the interface is implemented by the ServicedComponent base class. Therefore, you can do nothing and accept the default implementations in the base class, or you can override them within the serviced class. The default implementations of both Activate and Deactivate do nothing, while the default implementation of CanBePooled returns false.

To demonstrate, let's override these methods in our CarService class. Since this class currently has no special requirements at activation or deactivation time, we will implement the methods to simply write an entry in the Windows event log. This will help us confirm that COM+ executed the methods.

```
[JustInTimeActivation(), EventTrackingEnabled(),
 ClassInterface(ClassInterfaceType.None)]
public class CarService : ServicedComponent
{
   public CarService()
   {
      string logMsg = string.Format("Created Object: {0}", this.GetHashCode());
      EventLog.WriteEntry("CarService.ctor()", logMsg);
   }
   protected override void Activate()
   {
      string logMsg = string.Format("Activated Object: {0}",
                        this.GetHashCode());
      EventLog.WriteEntry("CarService.Activate", logMsg);
   }
   protected override void Deactivate()
   {
      string logMsg = string.Format("Deactivated Object: {0}",
                        this.GetHashCode());
      EventLog.WriteEntry("CarService.Deactivate", logMsg);
   }
   protected override bool CanBePooled()
   {
      string logMsg = string.Format("Object {0} not pooled",
                        this.GetHashCode());
      EventLog.WriteEntry("CarService.CanBePooled", logMsg);
      return false;
   }
   ~CarService()
   {
      string logMsg = string.Format("Object {0} Finalized",
         this.GetHashCode());
      EventLog.WriteEntry("CarService.Finalize", logMsg);
   }
}
```

As you can see, we have also implemented a finalizer so that it too writes a message to the event log. To test this, we must recompile, reinstall the assembly in the GAC, and finally execute the client. Figure 8-19 shows the resulting windows event log.

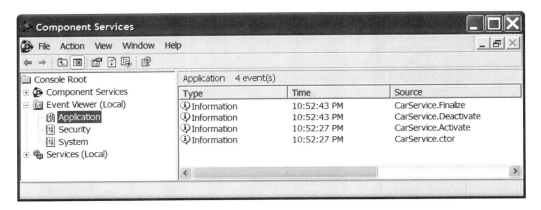

Figure 8-19. The event log shows that the Activate *and* Deactivate *methods are called.*

There are two things worth noting in the event log. First, the CanBePooled method never executed. This is because we haven't yet configured the class for object pooling. Second, the Deactivate method executed several seconds after the Activate method. However, we expected the method to execute almost immediately after the GetInfo method returned. What happened? It turns out the method must tell the COM+ runtime to deactivate the object. Otherwise it will persist like any other object. In this case, it persisted until the client shut down several seconds later.

As Soon As Possible Deactivation

To achieve As Soon As Possible (ASAP) deactivation along with Just-In-Time activation, you have to inform the COM+ runtime that it should deactivate the object when the method returns. This can be done in several different ways. Most techniques involve using the ContextUtil class, which we used earlier to gather COM+ context values. The COM+ context maintains a boolean flag called the *done bit*. Using the ContextUtil class, you can set the context's done bit to true. The COM+ runtime examines the done bit when the method returns. If it is true, then the COM+ runtime immediately deactivates the object and executes the finalizer. It also suppresses finalization so that the finalizer is not executed again when the object is garbage collected.

The ContextUtil class exposes three static members that can set the done bit to true: SetComplete, SetAbort, and DeactivateOnReturn. SetComplete and SetAbort actually affect another context flag too, called the *happy bit*, which will come into play later when we look at transactions. Calling SetComplete sets both the happy and done bits to true. Calling SetAbort sets the done bit to true, but the happy bit to false. The following is an example of using the SetComplete method to force ASAP deactivation:

```csharp
public string GetInfo()
{
   StringBuilder ctxInfo = new StringBuilder();

   // Use ContextUtil to fetch context information
   ctxInfo.AppendFormat("Context ID:  {0}\n", ContextUtil.ContextId);
   ctxInfo.AppendFormat("Activity ID: {0}\n", ContextUtil.ActivityId);

   // If in transaction, get transaction ID
   string txId = "No Tx";
   if (ContextUtil.IsInTransaction)
      txId = ContextUtil.TransactionId.ToString();

   ctxInfo.AppendFormat("Transaction ID:    {0}\n", txId);
   ctxInfo.AppendFormat("Security Enabled?: {0}\n",
      ContextUtil.IsSecurityEnabled);

   // Tell COM+ to deactivate the object upon return
   ContextUtil.SetComplete();

   return ctxInfo.ToString();
}
```

As you can see in Figure 8-20, when this code is executed, the Deactivate method runs immediately after the Activate method.

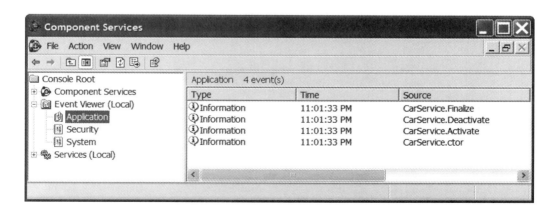

Figure 8-20. With JIT activation and ASAP deactivation, runs immediately after the method returns.

Alternately, you can set the context done bit by setting the `DeactivateOnReturn` property. Unlike `SetComplete` or `SetAbort`, this property only affects the done bit. By default, the property is false, so as the following code demonstrates, you need only set it to true to achieve ASAP deactivation:

```
public string GetInfo()
{
   StringBuilder ctxInfo = new StringBuilder();

   // Use ContextUtil to fetch context information
   ctxInfo.AppendFormat("Context ID:  {0}\n", ContextUtil.ContextId);
   ctxInfo.AppendFormat("Activity ID: {0}\n", ContextUtil.ActivityId);

   // If in transaction, get transaction ID
   string txId = "No Tx";
   if (ContextUtil.IsInTransaction)
      txId = ContextUtil.TransactionId.ToString();

   ctxInfo.AppendFormat("Transaction ID:   {0}\n", txId);
   ctxInfo.AppendFormat("Security Enabled?: {0}\n",
      ContextUtil.IsSecurityEnabled);

   // Tell COM+ to deactivate the object upon return
   ContextUtil.DeactivateOnReturn = true;

   return ctxInfo.ToString();
}
```

The final way to achieve ASAP deactivation does not involve the `ContextUtil` class at all. Instead, you simply apply the `AutoCompleteAttribute` to the method. By applying this attribute, the done bit will automatically be set to true. It also affects the happy bit, as we will see later when transactions are discussed. With this attribute, our `GetInfo` method now looks like the following:

```
[AutoComplete()]
public string GetInfo()
{
   StringBuilder ctxInfo = new StringBuilder();

   // Use ContextUtil to fetch context information
   ctxInfo.AppendFormat("Context ID:  {0}\n", ContextUtil.ContextId);
   ctxInfo.AppendFormat("Activity ID: {0}\n", ContextUtil.ActivityId);
```

```
   // If in transaction, get transaction ID
   string txId = "No Tx";
   if (ContextUtil.IsInTransaction)
      txId = ContextUtil.TransactionId.ToString();

   ctxInfo.AppendFormat("Transaction ID:    {0}\n", txId);
   ctxInfo.AppendFormat("Security Enabled?: {0}\n",
      ContextUtil.IsSecurityEnabled);

   return ctxInfo.ToString();
}
```

 Source Code   *The code for this example is in Chapter8\JITA.*

ASAP Deactivation vs. Dispose

Given that the COM+ runtime calls the Deactivate method before deactivating an object, it makes a good location for resource cleanup logic. This sounds much like another well-known method described in Chapter 2, Dispose. In fact, you can consider ASAP deactivation an alternative to implementing Dispose.

Unlike Dispose, ASAP deactivation requires no action by the client, instead it happens automatically. But this convenience comes at a price. Consider the following client code:

```
static void SomeClientFunction()
{
   CarService carSvc = new CarService();
   carSvc.GetInfo();
   carSvc.AnotherMethod();
}
```

If the CarService object used ASAP deactivation in both the GetInfo and Another-Method methods, then the object would be activated and deactivated with each method call, causing unnecessary overhead.

However, if we forego JIT activation and ASAP deactivation, then we must rely on the client to call Dispose when finished with the object. For all serviced classes, Dispose is inherited from the ServicedComponent base class, so you do not need to implement it. In fact, you cannot override it because it is not defined as overrideable in the ServicedComponent class.

So what happens when the client calls Dispose on a serviced object? The answer depends on what COM+ services the object uses. Table 8-1 summarizes the different possibilities.

Table 8-1. Summary of Dispose *Behavior in Serviced Objects*

COM+ Services	Default Behavior of Dispose
No object pooling, no JIT activation	Immediately executes the finalizer. The finalizer is not executed again when the object is garbage collected.
Object pooling (without JIT activation)	Executes Deactivate, then CanBePooled. If CanBePooled returns false, then the finalizer is immediately executed. It is not executed again when the object is garbage collected. If CanBePooled returns true, then the finalizer is not executed and the object is returned to the pool.
Object pooling and JIT activation	Behaves just like object pooling without JIT activation. However, clients should avoid calling Dispose if the object uses ASAP deactivation (that is, sets the context done bit to true).
JIT activation (without object pooling)	Executes Deactivate and the finalizer. The finalizer is not executed again when the object is garbage collected. Clients should avoid calling Dispose if the object uses ASAP deactivation.

Consider the following client code:

```
static void SomeClientFunction()
{
   using (CarService carSvc = new CarService())
   {
      carSvc.GetInfo();
      carSvc.AnotherMethod();
   } // Dispose is called automatically here.
}
```

NOTE *Remember that the* using *statement ensures* Dispose *is called even in the event of an exception.*

This solution is more efficient than the previous because the object is activated and deactivated only once, rather than for each method call. Of course, the difference in efficiency increases the more times the client invokes methods on the object.

Unfortunately, it is bad practice to mix the Dispose and ASAP deactivation techniques for resource management. In other words, a client should never call Dispose on an object that uses ASAP deactivation in its methods. Why? Because the Dispose method call itself causes the COM+ runtime to activate and deactivate the object an additional time. Since the object is already deactivated, this additional activation and deactivation is simply wasted overhead. Therefore, it is best for client developers to know if the serviced class uses ASAP deactivation so that they can avoid calling Dispose. Likewise, client developers should also know if the object does not use ASAP deactivation, so that they know to call Dispose when finished with the object.

To confuse matters some more, there is a caveat to this. In the case of library activation, if a client calls Dispose on a deactivated object, it has no effect. So no extra overhead is incurred when calling Dispose.

Overriding Dispose

As mentioned earlier, the ServicedComponent base class provides a default implementation for Dispose that cannot be overridden. However, it also provides an overloaded version of Dispose that takes a single Boolean parameter (hereafter referred to as Dispose(bool)). You can override this method in your derived ServicedComponent classes to clean up resources. The Dispose(bool) method is called in two scenarios:

- When the garbage collector finds an unreachable serviced object, it calls the finalizer on the ServicedComponent base class. This finalizer calls the Dispose(bool) method, passing false.

- When a nonpooled serviced object is deactivated, or when a client calls Dispose directly, the ServicedComponent base class Dispose method invokes the Dispose(bool) method, passing true.

If you choose to override the Dispose(bool) method, the code must read the incoming Boolean parameter to determine which of these two scenarios caused the invocation of the method. If the parameter is false, then Dispose(bool) has been called from the finalizer, and the method should *not* try to dispose managed resources. Otherwise, it has not been called from the finalizer and it can safely dispose managed resources. This leads to the implementation pattern shown here:

```
protected override void Dispose(bool disposing)
{
   if(disposing)
   {
      // Not called from finalizer, ok to dispose managed resources
   }
   // free unmanaged resources ...
}
```

If your serviced class implements a finalizer, it will get called whenever the object is destroyed. However, it is more efficient to not implement a finalizer and instead place the finalization logic within the overloaded Dispose(bool) method.

If you must override the no-argument version of Dispose, you can by declaring a new Dispose method. If you do this (and I recommend that you don't), make sure you call the base class Dispose method after you complete the custom logic. Here is an example:

```
public new void Dispose()
{
   // Perform custom dispose tasks ...

   // Call ServicedComponent.Dispose
   base.Dispose();
}
```

Note the use of the new modifier in this method declaration. In C#, this hides the inherited Dispose method, allowing you to redefine it as necessary.

Summarizing Just-In-Time Activation

It is important to remember that JIT activation and ASAP deactivation work together to prevent a greedy client from monopolizing server resources, a heavy-handed approach that can sometimes cause the objects to be activated and deactivated unnecessarily. It is always more efficient to avoid JIT activation and implement altruistic clients that call Dispose when appropriate. However, JIT activation and ASAP deactivation make an excellent safety net for when the client development is outside of your influence.

That said, the cost of JIT activation diminishes when combined with object pooling, as we will see in the next section. Also, JIT activation is required for objects that use COM+ automatic transactions.

Understanding Object Pooling

As mentioned earlier, if a JIT activation object is not pooled, then each method call results in a new object being created and activated. For some objects, however, this can prove to be very expensive. For example, an object may need to acquire a resource that takes a long time to initialize. Furthermore, after initialization, the resource could possibly be shared among many different clients. In this situation, constantly creating and destroying the object is extremely costly.

The object described in this scenario is an ideal candidate for object pooling. With object pooling enabled, the COM+ runtime creates a specified number of objects when the application starts. At creation time, each object can acquire and initialize the required resources. When a client requests the object, COM+ chooses one out of the pool. When the client request is complete, COM+ places the object back in the pool. During the pooled object's lifetime, the required resources remain initialized. Therefore, the cost of initializing them is paid only once when the application begins instead of being paid with each method call.

Advantages of Object Pooling

The previous introductory paragraphs already described one of the advantages of object pooling, but there are several more. Here, then, is a complete list of advantages:

- **Spreads initialization cost across many clients.** If an object initializes resources in the constructor, and if that object and its resources are then shared by many clients, then the cost of initialization is effectively shared by all the clients that use the object over the course of its lifetime.

- **Improves JIT activation efficiency.** This is the advantage described in the introductory paragraphs. The disadvantage of JIT activation and ASAP deactivation is the cost of creating and destroying an object with each method call. Clearly, object pooling eliminates a majority of the cost since an existing pooled object is used instead of a new one being created.

- **Allows allocation of objects at application startup.** You can start the COM+ application before any clients access it. The COM+ runtime creates the specified minimum number of objects, ensuring that these objects are immediately available when the first client request arrives.

- **Establishes resource usage thresholds.** The minimum and maximum number of pooled objects can be specified through the Component Services administration tool or through attributes. Pooled objects often wrap resources that only exist in small, fixed numbers due to software licensing or hardware limitations. By setting the minimum and maximum number of objects in the pool, you can tune the application to make the most efficient use of available resources. Also, if the resource increases from the purchase of additional licenses or hardware, then you can easily increase the maximum number as appropriate.

As you can see, object pooling has many advantages. However, this does not mean that any application can be improved simply by using object pooling. In fact, the types of objects that benefit most from object pooling are those that take a large amount of time to create and initialize relative to the amount of time spent executing any one method. The benefits of object pooling are minimal when the object is cheap to create. In this case, the extra memory and the processing required to manage the pool may actually outweigh the benefits.

Object Pooling Requirements

Not every object can be pooled. In fact, an object must meet several requirements in order for COM+ to effectively pool the object. In the past, only one programming language, C++, could be used to write an object that met all of these requirements. However, with .NET, all managed languages, including VB .NET, can be used to write poolable objects.

In order to be pooled effectively by COM+, an object

- **Must be stateless.** Stateless is a loaded word in today's development. The meaning here is that a pooled object should not hold *client-specific* state information after being deactivated. To understand this requirement, let's consider what would happen if this were not the case. While serving the client request, the object saves the results or partial results within instance fields. Then the object is placed back in the pool without clearing these fields. When the object is activated again for the next client, the fields still hold the results from the previous activity. This could compromise security (imagine if one of the fields held a credit card number), or could corrupt the results of the new request. To meet this stateless requirement, you should make sure all client-specific state information is cleared within the Deactivate method.

- **Must not exhibit thread affinity.** Thread affinity refers to the scenario in which an object must execute within the thread where it was created. Objects created in VB 6.0 are the most common example of this, but any object marked to run under the COM Apartment threading model suffers from thread affinity. Pooled objects, however, must be able to execute on multiple threads. On a related note, you should make sure your pooled object does not use thread local storage. Any such use would again bind the object to a particular thread.

- **Must support aggregation.** The object pool itself is actually a COM object that aggregates all the pooled objects. In COM, there are a number of implementation steps and considerations to allow aggregation. However, in .NET, all classes deriving from ServicedComponent support aggregation automatically. To be more precise, the generated CCW is the object that is actually pooled by COM+ and supports aggregation.

Enabling Object Pooling

Configuring a serviced class for object pooling is actually very easy. As you may have already guessed, the System.EnterpriseServices namespace provides an ObjectPoolingAttribute for that purpose. This attribute's constructor accepts values for the minimum and maximum number of pooled objects.

For example, let's apply this attribute to our CarService class:

```
[EventTrackingEnabled()]
[ClassInterface(ClassInterfaceType.None)]
[ObjectPooling(5, 10)]
public class CarService : ServicedComponent, IGetInfo
{ }
```

Notice that we have not applied JIT activation to the class. Before testing this, there is another important change we must make. Currently, our CanBePooled implementation returns false. So we'll modify it to return true:

```
protected override bool CanBePooled()
{
   // Return true if the object can be pooled.
   // Base class implementation returns false.
   string logMsg = string.Format("Object {0} can be pooled",
      this.GetHashCode());
   EventLog.WriteEntry("CarService.CanBePooled", logMsg);
   return true;
}
```

Finally, in the client, we will execute a couple methods. Since the object is not using JIT activation and ASAP deactivation, the client calls `Dispose` when finished.

```
static void SomeClientFunction()
{
   using (CarService carSvc = new CarService())
   {
      carSvc.GetInfo();
      carSvc.AnotherMethod();
   } // Dispose is called automatically here.
}
```

The result of all this is shown in Figure 8-21. Note that the COM+ runtime creates five objects, the specified minimum, immediately upon application startup. Also note that the `CanBePooled` method is now executing after the object is deactivated.

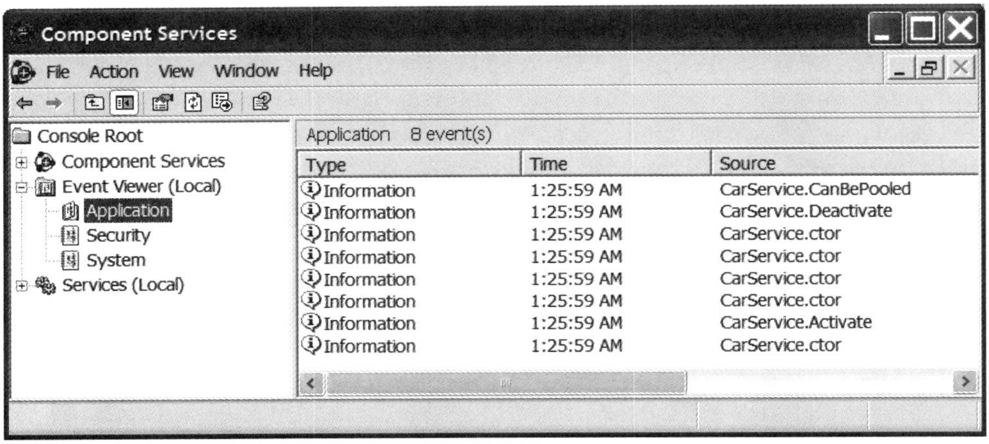

Figure 8-21. The event log shows five objects are created when the application begins.

Of course, if we apply JIT activation and ASAP deactivation to the `CarService` class, then each method call causes the object to activate and deactivate. To test this, we will update our `CarService` class to use JIT activation and apply the `AutoComplete` attribute to the methods. Then we modify the client so that it does not call `Dispose` as follows:

```
static void SomeClientFunction()
{
    CarService carSvc = new CarService();
    carSvc.GetInfo();
    carSvc.AnotherMethod();
}
```

The event log results are shown in Figure 8-22. As expected, the results show that after the first method call, the object is not destroyed but placed in the pool instead. Also note that a new object is not constructed to serve the second method call. Instead, an existing object is used from the pool.

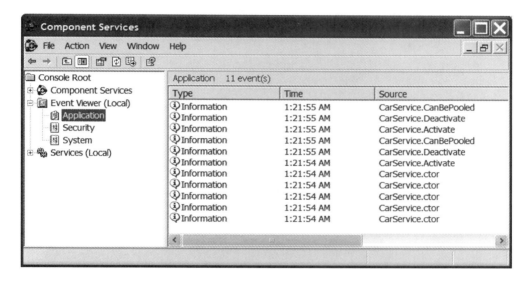

Figure 8-22. Object pooling with JIT activation and ASAP deactivation

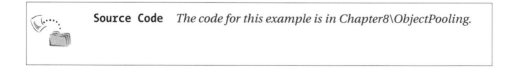

Source Code   *The code for this example is in Chapter8\ObjectPooling.*

Using Object Construction

Another service COM+ provides is called *object construction*. With this service, administrators can specify a string that the COM+ runtime passes to the object during construction. Administrators can set the string value using the Component Services administration tool. The setting options are under the Activation tab of the component's Properties dialog box (Figure 8-23).

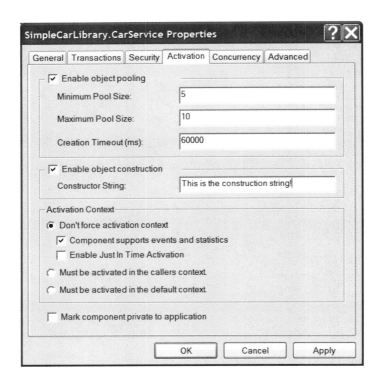

Figure 8-23. Administrators can set the construction string using Component Services tool.

Of course the example string shown in Figure 8-23 is not very useful. But the mechanism is very flexible, allowing you to pass a variety of information in a string which you can then parse and use from within the component. One of the most common uses of the construction string is to pass a database connection string. Keep in mind, however, that the construction string is stored in clear text within the COM+ catalog, so sensitive information should be encrypted before being entered into the construction string field.

In order to receive this string within our serviced objects, there are just a couple steps we must perform. First, we need to apply the ConstructionEnabledAttribute to our serviced class. This attribute class has a Default property that we can use to set a default construction string if one is not provided through the administration tool. The C# attribute syntax allows us to set any attribute's property in the constructor as shown in the following example:

```
[ConstructionEnabled(Default="This is a default string")]
public class CarService : ServicedComponent, IGetInfo
{}
```

The second step is to override the Construct method that is inherited from the ServicedComponent base class. The COM+ runtime calls this method after the constructor runs and passes the construction string. From that point, it is up to us to determine how our class will use the string. In the following example, we simply write the provided string to the event log:

```
[ConstructionEnabled(Default="This is a default string")]
public class CarService : ServicedComponent, IGetInfo
{
    protected internal override void Construct(string s)
    {
        string logMsg = string.Format("Constructed object using string {0}", s);
        EventLog.WriteEntry("CarService.Construct()", logMsg);
    }
}
```

Automatic Transactions

Given that COM+ was in large part derived from a technology known as Microsoft *Transaction* Server, it follows that the transaction service is a key feature. However, many technologies provide transaction abilities. The ADO Connection object, for example, allows you to begin, commit, and roll back a transaction. So what makes the COM+ transaction services so special? There are two answers: simplicity, and the ability to run distributed transactions.

Unlike other transaction technologies, COM+ transactions demand very little extra code—hence the term *automatic* transaction. The transaction is started automatically and is committed or aborted automatically based on the outcome. To support this, each object participating in the transaction need only vote on the outcome.

The other advantage that COM+ transactions have over other transaction methods is the ability to execute a distributed transaction (that is, one which spans multiple data sources). In contrast, the ADO Connection object represents a connection to a single data source. Therefore, its transactional capabilities are limited to updates that occur within that data source. If a transaction consists of updates against many data sources, then your best solution is to use a middleware transaction monitor like COM+.

The Distributed Transaction Coordinator

The COM+ ability to coordinate distributed transactions is quite an achievement. As you are probably aware, transactions must meet strict requirements known as the ACID rules (Atomic, Consistent, Isolated, and Durable). Meeting these requirements in a distributed environment involves the cooperation of several pieces of software, including the participating data sources. The most impressive aspect of COM+, however, is how little you need to understand about these underlying complexities as you are developing your business application. However, it is worthwhile to discuss some of the magic behind it all.

The key piece of the puzzle is a service called the *Distributed Transaction Coordinator* (DTC), which is Microsoft's implementation of a transaction monitor. Each data source participating in the transaction has its own associated DTC. The DTC, like all transaction monitors, is responsible for communicating with the data sources participating in the transactions. For any given distributed transaction, one DTC is the *coordinating DTC*. The job of the coordinating DTC is to determine the overall success or failure of the transaction and inform the other DTCs (called *participating DTCs*) to either commit or abort their transactions. This process is known as *two-phase commit*. Figure 8-24 illustrates the relationship between coordinating and participating DTCs.

Although Figure 8-24 shows only SQL Server databases participating in the transaction, other data sources, such as Oracle, can also interoperate with the DTC as long as they follow a protocol called *OLE Transactions*. Bridging software exists for data sources that implement other protocols, such as the X/Open standard.

You can start and stop the DTC using the Component Services administration tool. Simply right-click a computer node (such as My Computer), and a pop-up menu appears with an option to stop or start the DTC. Under each computer node, you will also find a child node titled Distributed Transaction Coordinator, which you can use to view transaction statistics (Figure 8-25).

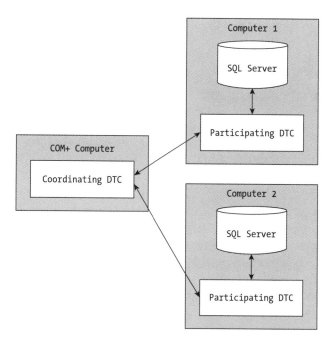

Figure 8-24. The coordinating DTC controls the distributed transaction.

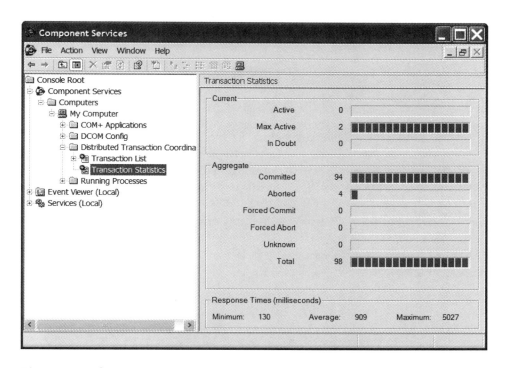

Figure 8-25. The DTC statistics view

Enabling Transactions

The DTC exposes a programmatic interface through which you can start, commit, and abort transactions. However, COM+ makes the process much easier. In fact, there are really only two things a COM+ object must do to run a transaction: advertise its need for COM+ transactional services, and vote on the transaction's outcome.

For the first task, advertising the need for transaction services, you apply the `TransactionAttribute` to your serviced class. This attribute's constructor accepts a `TransactionOption` enumeration parameter that describes the transactional support required by the class. The enumeration's values are described here:

- **Required.** This value informs the COM+ runtime that the object requires a transaction. When the object is created, the COM+ runtime determines whether the caller is already running within a transaction. If so, then the object shares this transaction. Otherwise, COM+ starts a new transaction for the object.

- **RequiresNew.** This value is much like Required, except the object is always placed within a new transaction, even if the caller is already running within a transaction.

- **Supported.** An object with this setting shares the caller's transaction if one exists. If there is no existing transaction, then the object runs without a transaction.

- **NotSupported.** This value informs the COM+ runtime that the object does not support transactions. If a transaction is already running for the caller, the object cannot vote on the transaction's outcome.

- **Disabled.** This is the default value. Use this setting if the object does not access a data source and thus has no transactional requirements. This differs from NotSupported in that the object may be activated in the caller's context, saving the overhead of cross-context calls.

The following example demonstrates how to apply these settings to a class:

```
[Transaction(TransactionOption.Required)]
public class CarService : ServicedComponent
{}
```

Determining the Transaction's Outcome

In COM+ programming, you never explicitly commit or roll back a transaction. Instead, all objects participating in the transaction simply vote for success or failure. Of course, this is not a democracy; the majority does not win. Even if only one object votes for failure, then COM+ will roll back the transaction.

The object's vote is maintained by the COM+ context using a boolean flag called the happy bit. This is similar to the done bit discussed in the JIT activation section. In addition to these context flags, the COM+ transaction also maintains another flag called the *doomed bit*. A transaction always begins with its doomed bit set to false. However, if it ever becomes true, then the transaction cannot be recovered and it must be rolled back. Figure 8-26 shows the transaction state immediately following the activation of a transaction required object.

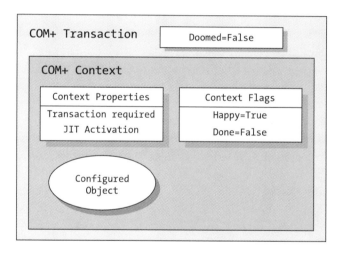

Figure 8-26. The COM+ context maintains the happy and done bits for the object.

The Role of the Root Object

When does COM+ investigate the doomed bit and complete the transaction? The answer lies with the *root object*. Every COM+ transaction is started by virtue of a client activating a transaction required (or requires new) object. This object, the initial object in the transaction, is called the root object.

The lifetime of the transaction is bound to the lifetime of the root object. If the root object persists, the transaction remains active. When the root object deactivates, the COM+ either commits the transaction if the doomed bit is false, or aborts the transaction if the doomed bit is true. All transactional objects are assigned a timeout value so that an object that does not deactivate voluntarily within the timeout period is forced to deactivate. The default timeout value is 60 seconds, but this value is configurable per object.

Voting on the Transaction's Outcome

You now know that the doomed bit determines the outcome of the transaction. But what sets the doomed bit? Whenever a transactional object is deactivated, the COM+ runtime investigates the associated context's happy bit. If the happy bit is true, then the runtime does nothing. However, if it is false, then the runtime sets the transaction's doomed bit to true, effectively dooming the transaction.

It is important to remember two things from this. First, COM+ does not investigate the happy bit until the object is deactivated. Therefore, the object can set the happy bit many times without dooming the transaction. Second, once the COM+ runtime sets the doomed bit to true, there is nothing any object can do to save the transaction.

Recall from the discussion of JIT activation that we used the ContextUtil class to set the context done bit. Similarly, we can also use the class to set the happy bit. In fact, many of the techniques we used earlier to deactivate the object upon returning from the method also affect the happy bit. For example, calling the SetComplete method sets both the happy and done bits to true, while calling SetAbort sets the done bit to true but the happy bit to false. As you can see, calling SetAbort effectively dooms the transaction. This leads to a fairly common method implementation pattern in all COM+ transactional objects. For example:

```
public void UpdateCar(DataSet carData)
{
    try
    {
        // Use ADO.NET to update car database
        // then vote for success
        ContextUtil.SetComplete();
    }
    catch
    {
        // Something went wrong, so vote for failure
        ContextUtil.SetAbort();
    }
}
```

In the preceding example, if the car database is updated without incident, then the SetComplete method is called. However, if an exception is raised while updating the database, then the finally block is executed, calling SetAbort.

The `SetComplete`/`SetAbort` methods have been available to developers since MTS. However, COM+ also allows the object to set the context bits individually. The `ContextUtil` class exposes this ability through the `DeactivateOnReturn` and `MyTransactionVote` properties. These properties lend themselves to a slightly easier pattern as demonstrated here:

```
public void UpdateCar(DataSet carData)
{
    // Set done bit to true. Object will deactivate when method completes
    ContextUtil.DeactivateOnReturn = true;

    // Set happy bit to false so that any exception causes the
    // transaction to fail.
    ContextUtil.MyTransactionVote = TransactionVote.Abort;

    // Use ADO.NET to update the car database ...

    // If we get here, we are successful, so vote to commit
    ContextUtil.MyTransactionVote = TransactionVote.Commit;
}
```

Finally, there is one other technique you can use to vote on the transaction, which is to use the `AutoCompeteAttribute` just as we did earlier in the JIT activation section. In this case, if the method completes normally, both the done and the happy bits are set to true. However, if the method causes an exception, then the done bit is still set to true, but the happy bit is set to false.

```
[AutoComplete()]
public void UpdateCar(DataSet carData)
{
    // Use ADO.NET to update the car database ...
}
```

Transactions with Worker Objects

So far, we have been assuming that only one object, the root object, is participating in the transaction. However, in the typical COM+ transaction, the root object creates other objects, called *worker objects*, to perform the actual database updates. In this scenario, the root objects and all the worker objects can vote on the transaction's outcome using any of the techniques shown previously.

When a root object creates another transaction object, COM+ enlists the worker object into the current transaction. However, each worker object is activated within its own context, including its own happy and done bits. This is illustrated in Figure 8-27, which shows a root object creating two worker objects. The additional objects add a bit more complexity to the way COM+ determines the final outcome, so let's walk through a couple scenarios to understand how it all works.

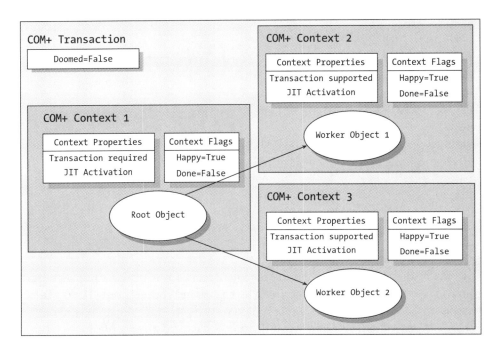

Figure 8-27. Root objects and worker objects participate within a transaction.

First, let's look at the scenario where the transaction completes successfully. After completing its update, worker object 1 sets its happy and done bits to false. When the method returns, COM+ investigates the done bit and, since it is true, deactivates the object. Then COM+ investigates the happy bit, which is also true, so it does not modify the transaction's doomed bit. Control then returns to the root object, which creates worker object 2 and executes a method. It too completes successfully and is deactivated without modifying the doomed bit. Having completed its work, the root object also sets the happy and done bits to true and returns. COM+ then deactivates the root object and commits the transaction.

The second scenario, in which a worker object fails and votes to abort the transaction, is more interesting and complicated. Let's assume that worker object 1 has succeeded and worker object 2 is executing its update. Something goes wrong, so worker object 2 sets the happy bit to false and the done bit to true. When COM+ deactivates the object, it sees that the object is not happy and sets the doomed bit to true. However, the transaction does not end here; remember it only ends when the root object is deactivated.

When control returns to the root object, it is very important that it does not attempt to commit the transaction by setting the happy bit to true. This means the root object must know if one of its workers has voted for failure. Unfortunately, there is no way for the root object to investigate the worker object's happy bit, nor can it access the transaction's doomed bit. Therefore, the worker object must somehow inform the root object that it is not happy. This can be done either by returning an error code from the method, or by raising an exception.

When the root object realizes a worker object has failed, it should set its happy bit to false and its done bit to true. It should also return from the method as soon as possible. Since the transaction is doomed, it does not make sense to continue with any other part of the transaction by creating and executing other worker objects. When the method returns, COM+ deactivates the root object, investigates the doomed bit, and rolls back the transaction.

Using Worker Objects

With all this in mind, let's implement a couple worker objects and a root object to execute them. We will start with worker object 1 first:

```
[Transaction(TransactionOption.Supported)]
public class Worker1 : ServicedComponent
{
    public void DoWork()
    {
        try
        {
            // Perform database update ...

            // Everything is fine. Vote for success.
            ContextUtil.SetComplete();
        }
        catch
        {
            // Something went wrong. Vote for abort.
            ContextUtil.SetAbort();

            // rethrow exception to root object.
            throw;
        }
    }
}
```

As you can see, this worker object calls SetAbort if the update causes an exception. It also raises the exception to the root object so that it too can call SetAbort.

For worker object 2, we'll take a slightly different, but just as valid approach. Here, we will simply apply the AutoCompleteAttribute. This attribute not only ensures the happy bit is set to false if an exception occurs, it also raises the exception to the root object.

```
[Transaction(TransactionOption.Required)]
public class Worker2 : ServicedComponent
{
    [AutoComplete()]
    public void DoWork()
    {
        // Perform database update ...
    }
}
```

It may surprise you that this worker object's transaction support is set to Required instead of Supported. Remember, a transaction required object uses the caller's transaction if it exists. Therefore, a transaction required object can be used as a worker object.

Finally, we can implement the root object:

```
[Transaction(TransactionOption.Required)]
public class Root : ServicedComponent
{
    public void Update()
    {
        try
        {
            Worker1 worker1 = new Worker1();
            Worker2 worker2 = new Worker2();

            worker1.DoWork();
            worker2.DoWork();

            ContextUtil.SetComplete();
        }
```

```
        catch
        {
            ContextUtil.SetAbort();
            // Possibly log error and/or raise error to client.
        }
    }
}
```

As you can see, the root object simply creates the worker objects and invokes their methods. If any object raises an exception, then the root object calls SetAbort and returns.

Using EnableCommit and DisableCommit

It is important that a root object deactivates as soon as the transaction is doomed or when the updates complete successfully so that the transaction can finish and release its locks. However, the same is not true for a worker object. In fact, deactivating a worker object may prematurely doom a transaction. Or, in another scenario, the root object may need to execute several methods on a single worker object, so activating and deactivating the worker object with each method call results in unnecessary overhead. In either of these situations, you should consider setting the happy bit as appropriate, but set the done bit to false. This is exactly what ContextUtil's EnableCommit and DisableCommit methods are designed to do.

Imagine a situation where a worker object must contend with an unreliable network. The worker object's task may fail, not because of a serious database error, but because the network was overloaded at that instant. Instead of dooming the transaction by calling SetAbort, a better option would be to call DisableCommit and raise an exception. Calling DisableCommit sets both the happy and done bits to false. But since the object does not deactivate, COM+ never investigates the done bit and the transaction is not doomed. This gives the root object the opportunity to fix the situation. For example, the root object may be implemented to handle the flaky network by retrying the worker's method three times before giving up and calling SetAbort.

If a class calls EnableCommit or DisableCommit, then it should not be used as a root object. Remember, while the object lives the transaction is also alive and holding precious database locks. Therefore, root objects should deactivate as soon as the final outcome of the transaction is known.

Consuming Serviced Components

Implementing the serviced component is only part of the battle; you must also decide how clients will connect to the component. As you know, COM+ is still based on COM technology. Therefore, if your managed serviced objects are running in a server application, COM+ exposes these to clients using DCOM. If you wish to expose your serviced objects using the new .NET Remoting Framework (and who wouldn't), then you must take some extra steps to build a special listener application.

In order to expose the your serviced objects to clients, you must decide on the type of client (managed or unmanaged) and the remoting protocol (DCOM or .NET Remoting) you wish to support. This will determine the proper steps needed, if any.

Exposing Objects with DCOM

DCOM is the current remoting protocol used by COM+. Any managed object running within a COM+ server application is exposed to clients using DCOM by default. This applies to both managed and unmanaged clients.

Using the Component Services administration tool, you can create an installation file called an *application proxy* that can be deployed to all client machines. When this file is executed on the client machine, it copies and registers a type library describing the serviced object. It also registers the information required to direct client calls to the proper server where the COM+ application is actually running. To create the application proxy, simply right-click any server application in the Component Services tool, and then choose Export from the context menu. A wizard appears that will lead you through the rest of the process (see Figure 8-28). This will generate two files. The Microsoft installation file (.msi) is the file you would copy to a client and execute. The cab file (.cab) is for Internet downloads.

While all this is very simple, it is important to understand that the application proxy is a COM component. Therefore, a managed client must use the COM interop layer just to access the application proxy. Remember, the COM+ runtime is already forced to use COM interop to access your serviced object, so any managed client must call through two layers of interop when you expose the object via DCOM. Figure 8-29 illustrates this scenario. On the other hand, unmanaged clients can call the application proxy directly, and are blissfully unaware that the actual serviced object is implemented in managed code.

NOTE *To use the application proxy, client machines must have the .NET Framework installed, even if the client application is unmanaged. Also, Windows 2000 machines must have Service Pack 3 installed.*

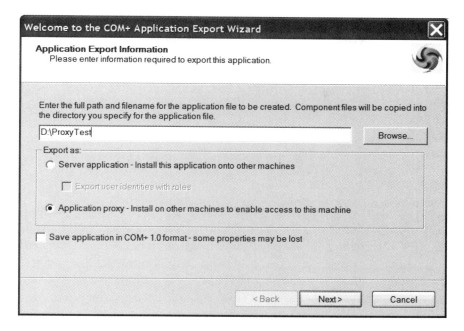

Figure 8-28. The Application Export Wizard creates a client installation.

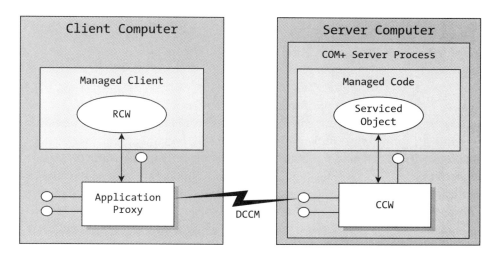

Figure 8-29. COM+ exposes object to clients using DCOM.

Despite these layers of indirection, DCOM is still useful in some scenarios. Currently, .NET Remoting technology does not have any built-in way to represent security information regarding the client. As a result, if your serviced objects use COM+ role–based security, you must remote the objects using DCOM. Also, only DCOM can flow COM+ context information, including transaction context, to another COM+ machine. So if you have to perform a complex distributed transaction involving several COM+ machines, you must use DCOM.

Exposing Objects with .NET Remoting

As you discovered in Chapters 3 and 4, .NET offers a vast remoting infrastructure that can be used in place of DCOM. You also learned that any object derived from `MarshalByRefObject` can be remoted by this framework. As it happens, all serviced objects derive from `ServicedComponent`, which in turn derives from `MarshalByRefObject`. Therefore, all serviced objects can be remoted. However, to expose serviced objects using this framework you must implement an application that listens for incoming .NET Remoting messages from clients and passes them to the serviced object.

You can build such a listener application using any of the hosting techniques discussed in Chapter 4, such as a console application, a Windows service, or an ASP.NET host. Remember, all the limitations noted in Chapter 4 apply as before. For example, using ASP.NET as a listener is very convenient, but limits you to using the HTTP channel.

Implementing a Listener

Implementing a listener application is just like implementing any remoting server; you configure the object URI, channel, and port number either programmatically or within an application configuration file, and then wait for clients to activate the object. This time, however, the well-known object happens to also be a serviced object. For example, the following code implements a server console application that exposes the `CarService` class we have been experimenting with:

```
using System.Runtime.Remoting;
using System.Runtime.Remoting.Channels;
using System.Runtime.Remoting.Channels.Tcp;

namespace CarListener
{
   class CarListenerMain
   {
      static void Main(string[] args)
      {
         // Create a TCP channel specifying the port #
         TcpChannel channel = new TcpChannel(13101);

         // Register the channel with the runtime remoting services
         ChannelServices.RegisterChannel(channel);

         // Register CarService as a well known type
         RemotingConfiguration.RegisterWellKnownServiceType(
            typeof(SimpleCarLibrary.CarService), // The type to register
            "CarService",                        // The objectURI
            WellKnownObjectMode.SingleCall
         );

         // Keep the server alive until enter is pressed.
         Console.WriteLine("Press Enter to end");
         Console.ReadLine();
      }
   }
}
```

In this example, we have programmatically registered the CarService object as a well-known object exposed via the TCP channel on port 13101.

Implementing a Managed Client

Now, any managed client can activate the object using the proper URL as the well-known name. Here is an example client:

```
using System;
using SimpleCarLibrary;
using System.Runtime.Remoting;

namespace SimpleCarClient
{
    class CarMain
    {
        static void Main(string[] args)
        {

            // Activate the well-known object
            CarService carSvc = (CarService) Activator.GetObject(
                            typeof(SimpleCarLibrary.CarService),
                            "tcp://localhost:13101/CarService"
                        );

            // Invoke a method
            Console.WriteLine(carSvc.GetInfo());
        }
    }
}
```

In this example, we create the object using the `Activator.GetObject` method call and passing the appropriate URL. Keep in mind that all the remoting details apply as before, including the fact that the client must have the `CarService` type metadata available locally either in the form of the actual implementation DLL or an interface-only DLL. See Chapters 3 and 4 for further details.

Source Code   *The code for this example is in Chapter8\ConsoleListener.*

Using Library Activation with Listeners

Regardless of what kind of listener you choose to create, you should pay attention to the COM+ application's activation setting. The activation is relative to the caller, which in this case is not the actual client, but our listener application. If activation is set to server, then the object is activated in a separate process from the listener. This means the original call must pass over one process to the listener, and then another to the target object. It is far more efficient to set the activation to library. In this case, the object is activated within the listener's process space, thereby saving a wasteful cross-process trip.

Investigating New Features in COM+ 1.5

Currently, COM+ is widely available in two versions. The Windows 2000 operating systems contain COM+ version 1.0. The Windows XP operating system (Professional edition and up) ships with COM+ version 1.5. While the techniques covered in the previous sections work in both versions of COM+, version 1.5 adds some intriguing new features, which we will investigate in this section. However, keep in mind the following features are not available in COM+ 1.0.

Application Recycling and Pooling

Applications that execute for extended periods tend to be problematic. No matter how careful the application developers may be, memory leaks occur, resources are allocated and never released, and performance suffers over time as the process memory footprint continues to grow. Eventually, the application may crash, leaving data in a corrupt state. A short-lived application can also leak resources, but since it shuts down relatively quickly, forcing the release of all resources (including leaked resources), the impact on system performance is minimal.

Server applications are typically long-lived applications—the extreme case being an e-commerce application that must run 24/7. In this situation, it is very common to periodically "recycle" (that is, shut down and restart) the application. Of course, .NET should greatly minimize the need for this, but many legacy applications will never be rewritten using .NET technology. Therefore, COM+ provides a way to automatically recycle applications based on configured criteria such as memory usage and execution time.

However, COM+ cannot simply shut down an application as soon as it hits some configured criteria. What if it is busy processing a client request? To account for this, COM+ actually starts another instance of the application. All new client requests are directed to the new application while COM+ waits for the old application to finish its requests. When it does, COM+ shuts down the old application.

You can configure recycling via the COM+ Application property page in the Component Services administration tool (see Figure 8-30). Most of the settings are self-explanatory, except for the Expiration Timeout value. This refers to the amount of time COM+ will wait for the old application to finish processing any outstanding client requests before forcing a shutdown.

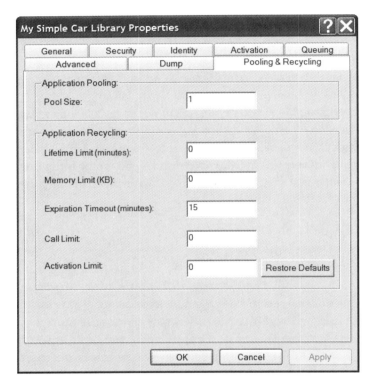

Figure 8-30. Configuring application pooling and recycling

Figure 8-30 also shows another new feature: the ability to pool applications. This is useful if the COM+ application actually wraps a single threaded application for remote access. For example, if you have an existing single threaded COM EXE server (such as those created by the ActiveX EXE project in Visual Basic 6.0), then you can use COM+ to pool multiple instances of the application and expose them as one to clients. This provides better scalability because more applications can be added to the pool to support more clients and leverage more powerful hardware. Application pooling also provides greater stability because if one application crashes, the other applications in the pool can pick up the load. A COM EXE application can be configured in COM+ using the new Legacy Component node found under each COM+ application node.

Configurable Transaction Isolation Levels

As you know, a transaction must, by definition, adhere to the strict ACID rules. The *I* in this acronym stands for *isolated*, which means that if two transactions are executing simultaneously, neither one can see the other's uncommitted updates. Of all the rules, this is the one with the most latitude, because, in reality, there are several different levels of isolation. The highest level of isolation, called *serializable*, guarantees data consistency at the expense of overall throughput. On other hand, the lowest level of isolation, called *read uncommitted*, provides the best performance, but could allow one transaction to read the uncommitted updates of another transaction, leading to data inconsistencies.

By default, COM+ transactions always use an isolation level of serializable. While this is always the safest choice, it is also the most expensive. Therefore, version 1.5 allows you to set the isolation level. You can choose among the following levels, listed in order of lowest level of isolation to highest:

1. **Read uncommitted.** This allows a transaction to view the uncommitted updates made by another transaction, otherwise known as a *dirty read*.

2. **Read committed.** This isolation level forces a transaction to wait before it reads data that another transaction has locked for writing. This is the default isolation level used by SQL Server transactions.

3. **Repeatable read.** This isolation level guarantees that a transaction can read data items multiple times and each time it will get the same values. However, this does not completely guarantee data consistency due to a subtle problem called *phantom inserts*. For example, a transaction may be calculating an average across many rows of data. During this period, another transaction can insert a row, thus the data items read by the first transaction remain the same, but the average is changed due to the new row of data.

4. **Serializable.** This isolation level is like repeatable read except that it also guards against phantom inserts, thus guaranteeing data consistency.

You can set the isolation level using the Component Services administration tool and the Component property page. Or you can set it in code using the `Transaction` property as shown in the following example.

```
[Transaction(TransactionOption.Supported,
             Isolation=TransactionIsolationLevel.ReadCommitted)]
public class CarService : ServicedComponent
{ ... }
```

SOAP Services

As noted earlier, you can expose serviced classes via .NET Remoting using ASP.NET as
a listener. In Chapter 4, you learned that hosting remotable objects in ASP.NET
required just a few mechanical steps. COM+ version 1.5 makes it even easier, requiring
only that you check the appropriate box in the COM+ Application property page,
or (of course) apply the correct attribute in code.

You can see this magic check box in the Component Services administration
tool via the COM+ Application property page (see Figure 8-31). When you check
this, COM+ creates the virtual directory specified in the SOAP VRoot text box, and
generates the proper web.config file to expose the components in the COM+ application using .NET Remoting. In addition, it creates a default.asmx file and a
default.disco file, effectively exposing the component as a Web service.

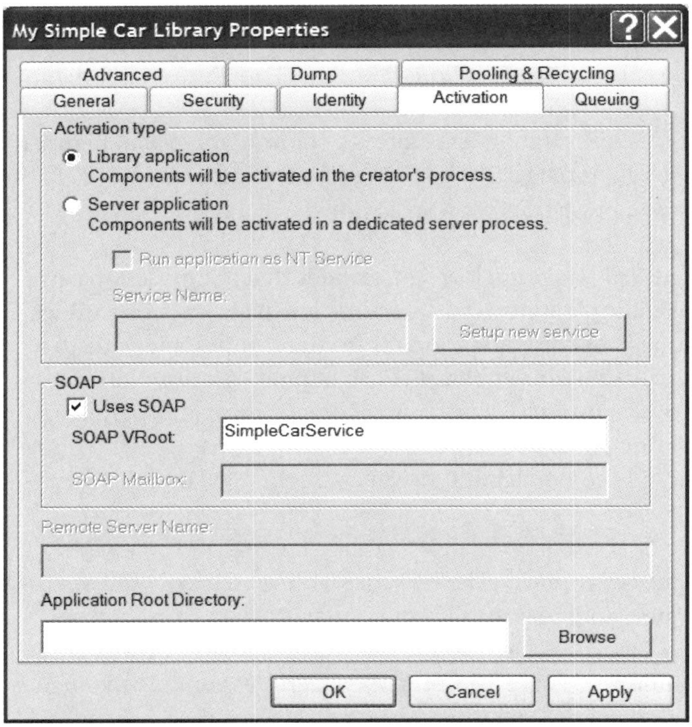

Figure 8-31. Specifing SOAP access in the Component Services tool

With the settings shown in Figure 8-31, COM+ creates an IIS virtual directory called SimpleCarService. It also generates the following web.config file:

```
<?xml version="1.0" encoding="utf-8"?>
<configuration>
  <system.runtime.remoting>
    <application>
      <service>
        <wellknown mode="SingleCall" type="SimpleCarLibrary.CarService,
                   SimpleCarLibrary, Version=1.0.0.0, Culture=neutral,
                   PublicKeyToken=7329edc6dfae6b15"
                   objectUri="SimpleCarLibrary.CarService.soap" />
        <activated type="SimpleCarLibrary.CarService, SimpleCarLibrary" />
      </service>
    </application>
  </system.runtime.remoting>
</configuration>
```

As you can see, this configuration file exposes the CarService class as both a well-known SingeCall object and a client-activated object. You can modify these settings by simply editing the web.config file.

You can also specify SOAP activation in code using the ApplicationActivationAttribute. This attribute provides a SoapVRoot property that allows you to set the virtual directory name when applying the attribute to an assembly. For example:

```
[assembly: ApplicationActivation(ActivationOption.Library,
           SoapVRoot="SimpleCarService")]
```

Summary

This completes a fairly long chapter on Component Services. However, this is a dense topic, and much more could be said on the subject. Luckily, COM+ has been around for a while and is well documented, so I wanted to focus more on the techniques you use to access Component Services from managed code. Armed with these, you can now use any of the services, even if they were not detailed in this chapter.

As time goes on, COM+ and .NET will become more and more integrated. The SOAP Activation feature in COM+ version 1.5 is an example of the integration we can expect in the future. And although we currently must contend with COM interop issues, the mechanism for specifying required COM+ services (that is, attributes) will remain consistent even when the services are finally incorporated into the .NET runtime.

The main ideas to take away from this chapter are as follows:

- Since COM+ is based on COM technology, it uses .NET's COM interop capabilities to host objects written in managed code.

- The CLR provides the `System.EnterpriseServices` namespace, which contains types for building serviced classes, including the common base class `ServicedComponent`.

- The CLR provides many attributes that mirror the settings available in the Component Services administration tool. These attributes are compiled into the assembly manifest, and copied into the COM+ catalog using the regsvcs tool.

- The Component Services architecture is based on context. All classes that derive from `ServicedComponent` are context bound and marshaled by reference.

- In a COM+ transaction, the root object plays the pivotal role. When it is deactivated, the transaction is either committed or aborted.

- COM+ exposes objects to clients using DCOM. Therefore, to use .NET Remoting, you must write a custom listener application or leverage IIS as your listener.

- COM+ version 1.5 provides application recycling, application pooling, configurable transaction isolation, and SOAP activation.

In the next chapter, you will learn how to use another important "DNA" technology from managed code: Message Queuing (MSMQ).

CHAPTER 9

.NET Message Queuing

IN THE LAST CHAPTER, you learned that .NET interacts with existing COM+ code to provide various enterprise services. Likewise, .NET leverages an existing product to provide message queuing functionality: Microsoft Message Queuing (MSMQ). Unlike COM+, however, MSMQ is not a runtime; it is a service that integrates into the Windows operating system and exposes functionality through a simple API. Therefore, the machinations required to interoperate between two entirely different runtimes are not needed. Instead, .NET simply wraps the MSMQ API with a few types residing in the System.Messaging namespace.

In this final chapter, you will learn how to use the types in this namespace. More importantly, the chapter examines why and when you might want to use MSMQ instead of .NET Remoting or Web services.

Message Queuing Overview

Message queuing is commonly described as e-mail for applications. This analogy is entirely accurate—as long as you understand that it is only an analogy. Message queuing allows an application to place information in a message, send it to a well-known queue, and then forget about it. The queue stores the message until another application reads it, ostensibly to take some action based on its contents. Just as you might do with the messages in your e-mail inbox, the receiving application can read the queued messages when it has no other work to do. And just like your e-mail inbox, the queue faithfully persists messages for long periods of time. During periods of heavy activity, the queue can persist the incoming messages and allow the receiving application to catch up during periods of low activity.

The concept of message queuing is not new. It has been used for decades in industries such as telecommunications, airline, and finance. Before diving into the details of .NET message queuing and MSMQ, it is helpful to first understand where this technology fits within the grand scheme of distributed programming. To that end, this section describes the problems that message queuing solves in the distributed world.

Why Message Queuing?

Distributed programming is effective because it allows an application to process requests using several machines executing in parallel. In many cases, the best approach is to duplicate the entire application and load balance it across several machines. However, sometimes this is simply impossible. One of the realities of distributed programming is that many times you are building upon or extending legacy applications. Typically, these legacy applications are large, complicated, and have been developed and tested over several years. As a result, it is better to leverage these systems rather than rewrite them.

For example, consider an e-commerce application built upon a legacy order processing system. Although the original order processing system may have been developed for employees to enter orders received over the phone, the vast majority of the functionality can be reused in an e-commerce environment. The challenge, however, is getting the e-commerce application, built on modern technology, to communicate effectively with the ordering system, built on ancient mainframe technology.

In this case, synchronous communication is usually out of the question. Order processing is generally a time-consuming task, and there is no reason to keep the Web customer waiting while the legacy order processing application checks inventories, calculates shipping costs, verifies credit, and so on. Furthermore, the mainframe may be under a heavy load as a rush of orders come in, causing more delays. Thus, it is better to perform these tasks asynchronously and e-mail the final order details to the customer at a later time.

To provide asynchronous communication, the e-commerce application may write each order to a staging area, such as a well-known file system directory or a specialized and nonnormalized database table. Another application periodically reads the orders from the staging area and uploads them to the mainframe to initiate order processing. Although this is effective, making sure the staging area and upload mechanism is fast, secure, and robust in the face of network failures and transaction rollbacks is your responsibility. Plus, in the case of a database table staging area, such a setup places additional strain on the most likely bottleneck of an application: the database.

Message queuing provides a tested infrastructure to solve these problems so you don't have to. Using message queuing, the e-commerce application can place the order information within a message, send it to a queue, and then continue taking other orders. The receiving application reads the messages as each arrives and uploads the information to the mainframe for processing. This is all accomplished using a simple API or, in the case of .NET, a few simple classes.

This is only one example of message queuing's utility. In general, it is useful whenever safe, robust messaging is required between applications.

Message Queuing Architecture

The primary actors in any message queuing system are senders, queues, and receivers (see Figure 9-1). *Senders* create messages and write them to the queue. *Receivers* monitor the queue and read the messages as they arrive. Typically the messages are read in the order that they arrive—in other words, queues exhibit first in, first out (FIFO) behavior. However, most message queuing systems also allow messages to be assigned a priority, such that the higher priority messages bubble to the top of the queue for quicker processing.

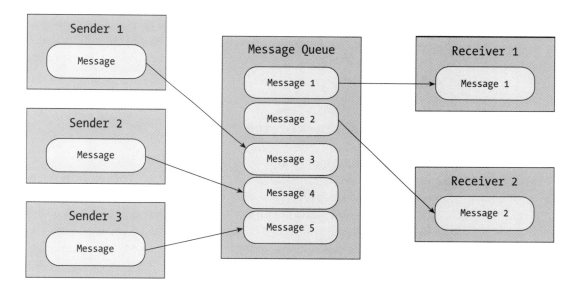

Figure 9-1. The message queuing architecture consists of senders, queues, and receivers.

As shown in Figure 9-1, multiple senders and multiple receivers can share the same queue. This provides an easy way to scale the application; if the receivers fall behind, additional receiver applications can be started to handle the increased load.

Relating this back to the order-processing example mentioned earlier, each sender represents a Web server or application server in the e-commerce application. Each receiver represents a program that monitors the queue for order messages and uploads the order to the legacy mainframe application for processing.

Message Queuing vs. Remoting vs. Web Services

In Chapter 5, you learned how to use delegates to asynchronously execute a method on a remote object. In Chapter 6, you learned how to do the same with Web services. So why do we need message queuing? The problem with asynchronous access in remoting and Web services is that both of these technologies are designed primarily for synchronous calls. The asynchronous techniques learned in Chapters 5 and 6 amount to workarounds. With message queuing, on the other hand, the exact opposite is true. It is designed primarily for asynchronous calls, and you have to apply workarounds to use message queuing in a synchronous manner.

The first class status of asynchronous calls allows message queuing to provide features that would be difficult to implement using remoting or Web services. For example, if the server or network is down, message queuing can store messages locally and send them automatically when the situation is resolved, without losing any messages.

Installing and Administering MSMQ

Many vendors supply message queuing solutions. Microsoft's message queuing technology is aptly named Microsoft Message Queueing. MSMQ has gone through several iterations over the past few years. With each new operating system release, Microsoft has extended and improved upon the product, giving us MSMQ 1.0 with Windows NT, MSMQ 2.0 with Windows 2000, and now MSMQ 3.0 with Windows XP Professional. The following discussion assumes you are using MSMQ 3.0, though most of the details also apply to version 2.0.

MSMQ Installation Options

To get the most out of MSMQ, you should first install it on your network domain's Active Directory server. Once installed, MSMQ integrates with Active Directory to allow computers on the network to publish queues and query for queues on other computers. This mode of MSMQ operation is called *domain mode*. Don't despair, however, if your network doesn't have an Active Directory server, or if the network administrator simply laughs at your request to install MSMQ on it. You can use MSMQ without Active Directory, in which case MSMQ operates in *workgroup mode*.

After you install MSMQ on the Active Directory server, you can install MSMQ on any computer in the domain. To install MSMQ, place the Windows CD-ROM in the CD-ROM drive and navigate to Control Panel | Add or Remove Programs | Add/Remove Windows Components. In the list of optional components, select Message Queuing. On Windows XP, you can click the Details button to configure the subcomponents you wish to install (see Figure 9-2). Table 9-1 describes these subcomponents. The Common subcomponent has two additional subcomponents, which are described in Table 9-2.

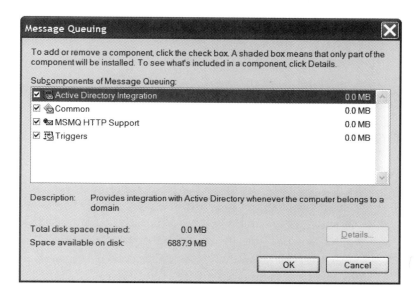

Figure 9-2. Installing and configuring MSMQ

Table 9-1. Message Queuing Subcomponents

Subcomponent	Meaning in Life
Active Directory Integration	When this is selected, MSMQ operates in domain mode. Otherwise, MSMQ operates in workgroup mode. For details, see "Domain Mode vs. Workgroup Mode."
Common	See Table 9-2.
MSMQ HTTP Support	This option allows MSMQ messages to be sent and received using HTTP and IIS. This feature is available only on Windows XP (MSMQ 3.0).
Triggers	This allows you to configure MSMQ to automatically invoke a component or start an executable when a message arrives on a queue. For Windows 2000, this option is available only as a separate add-on component. It is standard on Windows XP (MSMQ 3.0).

Table 9-2. *Common Subcomponents*

Subcomponent	Meaning in Life
Core functionality	Represents the basic MSMQ functionality.
Local Storage	When this is selected, MSMQ is installed as an *independent client*. Otherwise, MSMQ is installed as a *dependent client*. For details, see "Independent Client vs. Dependent Client."

Domain Mode vs. Workgroup Mode

When you install MSMQ, you must configure it to run in domain mode or workgroup mode. Domain mode is available only if you have previously installed MSMQ on the domain's Active Directory server and the target computer is a member of the network domain. In domain mode, the MSMQ computer can create *public queues*. Public queues are published in the domain's Active Directory, allowing MSMQ applications on other computers to dynamically query for and use the queues on your machine. Of course, in domain mode, your MSMQ applications can also query the Active Directory for all queues or for queues matching a given criteria.

In workgroup mode, however, the MSMQ computer can only create *private queues*. Private queues are not published in the domain's Active Directory, and thus applications cannot dynamically discover them. Instead, private queues must be accessed using a well-known full path name. You will see examples of using both public and private queues in the upcoming section titled "Using .NET Message Queuing."

Independent Client vs. Dependent Client

In addition to choosing between domain and workgroup mode, you must also configure the MSMQ computer as either an independent client or a dependent client. If you choose independent client, MSMQ applications running on the computer can send messages even if the computer is disconnected from the network. In this case, MSMQ stores the messages in a temporary local queue and automatically sends them when the connection is reestablished. Obviously, this type of installation is ideal for laptop computers and also provides robustness in the event of a network failure. Furthermore, an independent client can host its own local private or public queues (the latter only if the MSMQ computer is running in domain mode).

Dependent clients, on the other hand, are far more limited. First, dependent clients cannot host local queues. Instead, they are entirely dependent upon the Active Directory server and therefore must be connected to the network domain to send messages. This also means that dependent clients can only run in domain mode. In contrast, independent clients can run in domain or workgroup mode.

For MSMQ experimentation and development, independent client is definitely the preferred configuration. If possible, you should also run your MSMQ workstation in domain mode. The examples that follow assume these settings.

Creating and Managing Queues

If you have configured your workstation as an independent client, you will find it easy to create and manage the local queues. The MSMQ installation provides a MMC snap-in that you can use by navigating to Control Panel | Administrative Tools | Computer Management. In the Computer Management tool, expand the Services and Application node to reveal the Message Queuing node. You can add a public or private queue by right clicking the appropriate node and selecting New from the context menu (see Figure 9-3).

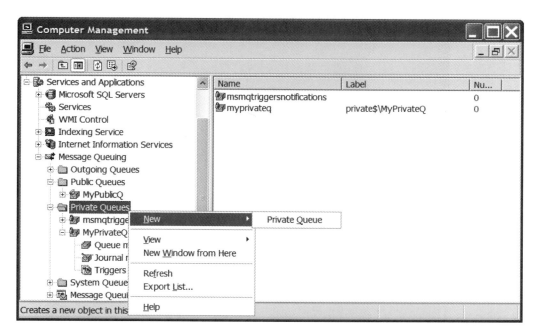

Figure 9-3. Creating a private queue using the Computer Management tool

Once you create a queue, MSMQ applications can begin sending messages to it. To view messages stored in a queue, expand the queue node (for example, the MyPrivateQ node) in Computer Management and click the Queue messages node. You can double-click a message to view its contents and other properties (see Figure 9-4).

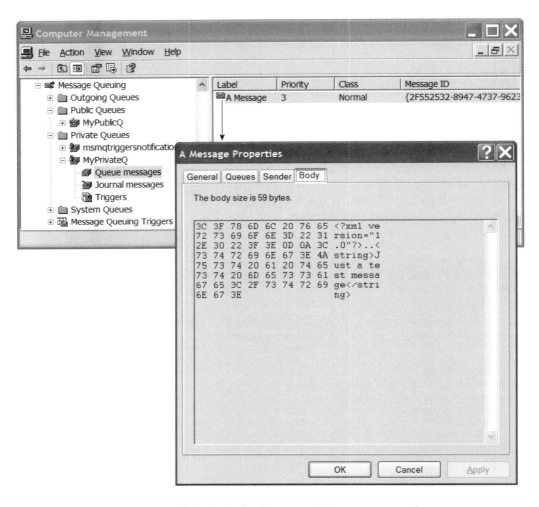

Figure 9-4. Viewing a message's body in the Computer Management tool

You can also manage a computer's queues using the Visual Studio .NET Server Explorer (see Figure 9-5). This tool may be more convenient while you are developing an MSMQ application, because it saves you from having to switch to a different program to view or configure queues. Using either tool, you can delete queues, purge (delete) all messages in a queue, configure queue security, and so on. The management tools are intuitive, so let's move on and examine how to create applications in .NET that send and receive MSMQ messages.

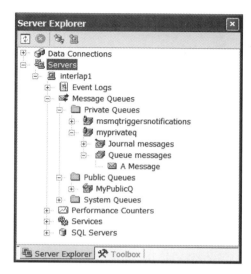

Figure 9-5. *Queues can also be managed using Visual Studio .NET's Server Explorer.*

Using .NET Message Queuing

As mentioned, .NET messaging leverages MSMQ. The CLR provides the System.Messaging namespace, which contains types that wrap the core functionality of the MSMQ API. This namespace is contained within the System.Messaging.dll assembly, so to start using these messaging types you must set a reference to this assembly. To get a feel for these types, let's walk through the creation of several sender and receiver applications.

Building the Sender

The primary class in the System.Messaging namespace is MessageQueue. It exposes several static methods that provide the ability to create and delete queues, or search for queues in the Active Directory matching specified criteria. You can also instantiate a MessageQueue object that refers to an existing queue by providing a queue path in the constructor. The class also has instance members for sending messages, receiving messages, purging all existing messages, and retrieving various bits of information regarding the queue.

The following example demonstrates how to use the `MessageQueue` class to verify the existence of, create, and delete a private queue.

```
using System;
using System.Messaging;

namespace Sender
{
   class SenderMain
   {
      static void Main(string[] args)
      {
         MessageQueue mq;

         // Does the queue already exist?
         if(MessageQueue.Exists(@".\private$\NewPrivateQ"))
         {
            // Yes, then create an object representing the queue
            mq = new MessageQueue(@".\private$\NewPrivateQ");
         }
         else
         {
            // No, create the queue and cache the returned object
            mq = MessageQueue.Create(@".\private$\NewPrivateQ");
         }

         // Now use queue to send messages ...

         // Close and delete the queue
         mq.Close();
         MessageQueue.Delete(@".\private$\NewPrivateQ");

         Console.ReadLine();
      }
   }
}
```

As this example shows, you refer to queues using a path. In the case of a private queue, the path takes this form:

```
<machinename>\private$\<queuename>
```

where `private$` is a required literal. For example, the following line constructs a `MessageQueue` object referring to a private queue named NewPrivateQ on the local machine:

```
mq = new MessageQueue(@".\private$\NewPrivateQ");
```

To specify a public queue, simply leave out the `private$` literal. For example, the following line constructs a `MessageQueue` object referring to a public queue named NewPublicQ on the local machine:

```
mq = new MessageQueue(@".\NewPublicQ");
```

Sending a Simple Message

Once a `MessageQueue` object is instantiated, you can call the `Send` method to send a message to the queue. For example:

```
static void Main(string[] args)
{
    // Create the queue instance
    MessageQueue mq = new MessageQueue(@".\private$\MyPrivateQ");

    // Send a message - XmlMessageFormatter used by default.
    mq.Send("The body of the message", "A message label");
}
```

This example sends a message to a private queue named MyPrivateQ. Because the first parameter of `Send` is typed as `object`, you can pass any CLR type as the message body. In this case, a simple string is passed. Figure 9-6 shows the contents of the MyPrivateQ queue after this code is executed.

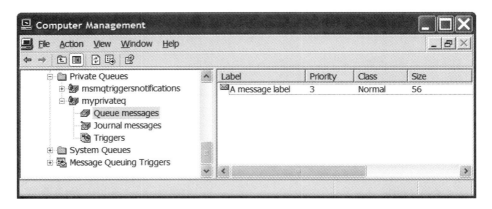

Figure 9-6. Using Computer Manager to confirm the message was sent to the queue.

Specifying More Complex Messages

The CLR also provides a Message class that allows you to construct a message and set several message properties. Once the Message object is constructed and configured, you can pass it to an overloaded version of MessageQueue.Send as shown in this example:

```
static void Main(string[] args)
{
    // Create the queue instance
    MessageQueue mq = new MessageQueue(@".\private$\MyPrivateQ");

    Message msg = new Message();
    msg.Label = "A message label";
    msg.Body = "The message body";

    // This message waits on the queue for a max of 20 seconds.
    msg.TimeToBeReceived = TimeSpan.FromSeconds(20);

    // If the message times out, delete it from destination queue and
    // add and entry to the dead letter queue.
    msg.UseDeadLetterQueue = true;
    mq.Send(msg);
}
```

This example constructs a Message object and sets several properties, including Body and Label. By setting the TimeToBeReceived property, this message will remain on the destination queue for a maximum of 20 seconds. If it is not read from the queue in 20 seconds, the queue deletes the message. Setting the UseDeadLetter property to true instructs MSMQ to copy the message to a system queue named "Dead-letter messages" before removing it from the destination queue. This feature is useful if you need to track messages that timeout while waiting to be read from the queue.

Referencing Queues with Direct Paths

Using simple paths to refer to public message queues on the network works only if the sending computer is running MSMQ in domain mode. In this case, the request to open the queue first consults the Active Directory server to verify the existence of the queue and resolve its location on the network.

However, you can refer to public or private queues in workgroup mode or even when disconnected from the network by using a *direct path*. When you open a queue using a direct path, MSMQ does not consult the Active Directory server. Instead, the message goes directly to the queue specified in the path.

Direct paths can take many forms. However, in all cases you prefix the direct path with the string "FORMATNAME:DIRECT=". For example, the following code refers to a private queue on a machine named interlap1:

```
MessageQueue mq;
mq = new MessageQueue(@"FORMATNAME:DIRECT=OS:interlap1\private$\MyPrivateQ");
```

Consider these other direct path examples:

```
string directPath;

// Refer to a private queue. Use the underlying OS network
// computer naming scheme
directPath = @"FORMATNAME:DIRECT=OS:interlap1\private$\MyPrivateQ";

// Refer to a public queue. Refer to machine using IP address
directPath = @"FORMATNAME:DIRECT=TCP:157.13.8.1\MyPublicQ";

// Refer to queue using a URL (Windows XP only)
directPath = @"FORMATNAME:DIRECT=HTTP://thewebserver/msmq/PublicQ";
```

The last example is interesting. If a queue is hosted on a Windows XP machine, you can send messages to it using HTTP. This can be useful if you need to send the message through a firewall.

Building the Receiver

Building an application that monitors the queue and reads messages as they arrive is more complicated than building the message sender. Two issues complicate matters. First, the receiver must know how to interpret the body of the message. MSMQ does not dictate the structure of the message body, which allows you to use any body format so long as both the sender and the receiver understand it.

Second, the receiver needs to employ an efficient queue monitoring mechanism. Several monitoring options are available, ranging from blocking on the queue read operation until a message arrives to responding to an event when a message arrives.

Using the XmlMessageFormatter

Regarding the first issue, interpreting the message body, .NET messaging provides three message formatters that serialize CLR types into the message body: XmlMessageFormatter, BinaryMessageFormatter, and ActiveXMessageFormatter. When you send a message, the default formatter is XmlMessageFormatter, thus all the previous examples sent messages using this formatter. When receiving the message, however, you must explicitly specify the formatter as shown here:

```
class ReceiverMain
{
    static void Main(string[] args)
    {
        // Open queue
        MessageQueue mq = new MessageQueue(@".\private$\MyPrivateQ");

        // Create an array of types expected in the message body
        Type[] expectedTypes = new Type[] {typeof(string), typeof(float)};

        // Construct formatter with expected types
        mq.Formatter = new XmlMessageFormatter(expectedTypes);

        // Loop forever reading messages from the queue
        while (true)
        {
            Message msg = mq.Receive(); // <-- blocks until message arrives
            Console.WriteLine(msg.Body.ToString());
        }
    }
}
```

In this example, the lines of code in bold establish the proper XmlMessageFor-matter, which is constructed with an array of expected types. When the message body is retrieved, the XmlMessageFormatter compares the data in the message body with the types provided in this array. It deserializes the body if it finds a match, otherwise it raises the exception shown in Figure 9-7. Therefore, this receiver implementation can only deserialize a message containing a string or floating point number in the body.

```
D:\APress\DistributedNet\c9\ScratchCode\CreatingQs\Receiver\bin\Debug\Receiver.exe    _ □ ×

Unhandled Exception: System.InvalidOperationException: Cannot deserialize the me
ssage passed as an argument. Cannot recognize the serialization format.
   at System.Messaging.XmlMessageFormatter.Read(Message message)
   at System.Messaging.Message.get_Body()
   at Receiver.ReceiverMain.Main(String[] args) in d:\apress\distributednet\c9\s
cratchcode\creatingqs\receiver\class1.cs:line 23
Press any key to continue_
```

Figure 9-7. The XmlMessageFormatter raises this exception if it does not recognize the message body format.

Alternately, you can construct the XmlMessageFormatter by passing an array of strings representing the type names of the expected types. For example:

```
string[] expectedTypeNames;
expectedTypeNames = new String[] {"System.String", "System.Single"};
mq.Formatter = new XmlMessageFormatter(expectedTypeNames);
```

The upcoming section titled "Sending Custom Types in Messages" will examine other serialization details including the use of the two other message formatters.

Source Code   *The code for this example is in Chapter9\SimpleMessaging.*

Polling the Queue

The second issue you must contend with on the receiving side is how to monitor the queue. Currently, the receiving application uses the following code to read the queue:

```
// Loop forever reading messages from the queue
while (true)
{
    Message msg = mq.Receive(); // <-- blocks waiting for a message to arrive
    Console.WriteLine(msg.Body.ToString());
}
```

As the comments indicate, the MessageQueue.Receive method call blocks the calling thread until a message arrives on the queue. Meanwhile, the application does nothing. In many cases, of course, you would want the application to do other work while waiting for a message. You can handle this situation by either periodically reading the queue (a process called *polling*) or by using the MessageQueue.BeginReceive method to perform an asynchronous read.

The MessageQueue class does not directly support polling. However, it is easy to implement using other runtime classes, namely the System.Threading.Timer class. Using the Timer class, you can establish a thread that periodically calls a function. In this case, the function should read the queue for new messages. For example, the following code implements this polling mechanism:

```
static void Main(string[] args)
{
    // Open queue
    MessageQueue mq = new MessageQueue(@".\private$\MyPrivateQ");

    // Set up the formatter (removed) ...

    // Construct timer to fire every 5 seconds. Note the message queue
    // reference is passed as the state object.
    Timer tm = new Timer(new TimerCallback(OnTimer), mq, 5000, 5000);

    // Simulate doing other work
    while (true)
    {
        Console.WriteLine("Doing other work on thread {0}",
            Thread.CurrentThread.GetHashCode());
        Thread.Sleep(1000);
    }
}
```

In this example, the key addition is the line that constructs the `Timer` object:

```
Timer tm = new Timer(new TimerCallback(OnTimer), mq, 5000, 5000);
```

This establishes a thread that will call the `OnTimer` function every 5 seconds. It also passes a reference to the `MessageQueue` object, which the `OnTimer` function receives as a parameter. To implement `OnTimer`, you must follow the signature defined by the `TimerCallback` delegate. For example:

```
static void OnTimer(object state)
{
   // Show current thread id
   Console.WriteLine("Checking queue for messages on thread {0}",
      Thread.CurrentThread.GetHashCode());

   // Time to check the queue, first get the queue from the state param
   MessageQueue mq = (MessageQueue)state;

   // Read queue, but only block for 1 second
   try
   {
      Message msg = mq.Receive(TimeSpan.FromSeconds(1));
      Console.WriteLine(msg.Body.ToString());
   }
   catch
   {
      // No Messages, timeout occurred
      Console.WriteLine("No new messages");
   }
}
```

This `OnTimer` implementation casts the incoming state parameter to a `MessageQueue` object and uses it to read the queue. But note the call to the `Receive` method:

```
Message msg = mq.Receive(TimeSpan.FromSeconds(1));
```

Here, a timeout value of 1 second is passed to the `Receive` method. If the queue contains a message, the method reads it and returns immediately. Otherwise, it waits for up to 1 second for a message to arrive. While this does block the calling thread, understand that the `OnTimer` function executes on separate thread relative to the main thread. The main thread can therefore continue doing other work. If no message arrives during the specified timeout period, then the `Receive` method raises a `MessageQueueException`.

Source Code   *The code for this example is in Chapter9\PollingReceiver.*

Reading Messages Asynchronously

The MessageQueuing class follows the delegate pattern to provide asynchronous message reading. That is, it provides BeginReceive and EndReceive methods that mimic a delegate's BeginInvoke and EndInvoke. The BeginReceive method starts a new thread that monitors the queue for incoming messages. When a new message arrives, the thread either raises an event or invokes a specified callback method, depending on the parameters supplied to the BeginReceive method. You can call EndReceive within the callback or event handler to read the message from the queue.

The following code calls BeginReceive using a callback function:

```
static void Main(string[] args)
{
    // Open queue
    MessageQueue mq = new MessageQueue(@".\private$\MyPrivateQ");
    // Set up formatter ... (removed)

    IAsyncResult ar = mq.BeginReceive(
        TimeSpan.FromSeconds(5),        // Timeout value
        mq,                             // State object, the message queue
        new AsyncCallback(OnMessageArrival) // Callback
    );

    // Simulate doing other work
    while(true)
    {
        Console.WriteLine("Doing other work ...");
        System.Threading.Thread.Sleep(1000);
    }
}
```

In this example, the call to the BeginReceive method starts a thread which monitors the queue for five seconds (the specified timeout value). If a message arrives or if the time expires, then the thread invokes the callback function, OnMessageArrival, passing the supplied MessageQueue reference.

The OnMessageArrival method implementation must handle both the timeout and the message arrival situation. This is easily done using exception handling code as demonstrated in the following example:

```
static void OnMessageArrival(IAsyncResult ar)
{
   // Cast the state object to MessageQueue
   MessageQueue mq = (MessageQueue)ar.AsyncState;
   try
   {
      Message msg = mq.EndReceive(ar);
      Console.WriteLine(msg.Body.ToString());
   }
   catch
   {
      Console.WriteLine("Timeout!");
   }
   finally
   {
      mq.BeginReceive( TimeSpan.FromSeconds(5), mq,
         new AsyncCallback(OnMessageArrival));
   }
}
```

Recall from Chapter 5 that the incoming IAsyncResult type provides a property to retrieve a reference to the state object passed into BeginReceive. In this case, the state object is simply the MessageQueue. Then EndReceive is invoked on this MessageQueue object to retrieve the new message. If OnMessageArrival was called due to a timeout, the EndReceive method raises a MessageQueueException.

In either case, you must call BeginReceive again to continue monitoring the queue. This example places the call in the finally block to ensure it is called regardless of what happens in the try or catch blocks.

> **NOTE**   *A section in MSDN erroneously states that the*
> IAsyncResult.IsCompleted *property is set to false if the callback method or event handler is invoked due to a timeout. In fact, the property is set to true in both cases. The only way to distinguish between a timeout and a message arrival is to invoke* EndReceive *and use exception handling to catch the timeout scenario.*

Source Code   *The code for this example is in Chapter9\AsynchReceiver*

Sending Custom Types in Messages

The previous examples used simple types to demonstrate the fundamentals of message queuing. You realize the true power of message queuing, however, when you send messages containing application-specific data, such as customer data, order data, employee data, and so on. The built-in message formatters allow you to easily translate the managed objects containing application data into messages and vice versa. .NET message queuing provides the following formatters:

- XmlMessageFormatter. This is the default formatter and the one used in all the previous examples. As its name suggests, it serializes your custom type into an XML representation using the XML Schema data types. This formatter is slow and creates relatively large messages. However, the messages can be shared and understood by other applications running on different platforms.

- BinaryMessageFormatter. This formatter serializes your custom type into a proprietary binary format. It is faster than the XmlMessageFormatter and generates compact messages. However, only a receiver running on .NET can easily translate the message contents.

- ActiveXMessageFormatter. Like the BinaryMessageFormatter, this serializes your custom types into a proprietary binary format. In this case, the format is the same employed by MSMQ COM components. These legacy COM components expose MSMQ-based functionality to COM languages such as Visual Basic 6. Therefore, you can use this formatter to send messages to or read messages from MSMQ applications written in Visual Basic 6.

In addition, the System.Messaging namespace supplies an IMessageFormatter interface that you can use to create custom formatters. The built-in formatters implement this interface.

The upcoming sections will explain how you can use each of these formatters. To help demonstrate, the examples serialize the following Customer class. We'll assume the class is compiled into an assembly named CustomerLibrary.dll.

```
namespace CustomerLibrary
{
   public class Customer
   {
      public string Name;          // Public field
      private string mCreditCard;  // Private field
      private string mEmail;       // Private field with public property

      public string Email
      {
         get {return mEmail;}
         set {mEmail = value;}
      }

      public Customer(string name, string email, string ccNum)
      {
         Name = name; mEmail = email; mCreditCard = ccNum;
      }

      // Required for serialization
      public Customer(){}
   }
}
```

Using the XmlMessageFormatter

The XmlMessageFormatter behaves very much like the XmlSerializer class associated with Web services. They both serialize CLR objects into XML text. The XmlMessageFormatter, however, is optimized for serializing MSMQ messages. It can serialize public data or private data exposed with public properties. In the latter case, the property must support reads and writes (that is, implement a get and set block).

The following example shows the message sender code that serializes the Customer class into an MSMQ message body:

```
static void Main(string[] args)
{

    // Create the queue instance
    MessageQueue mq = new MessageQueue(@".\private$\MyPrivateQ");

    Message msg = new Message();
    msg.Label = "A Customer Message";

    do
    {
        // Construct Customer and send to queue
        msg.Body = new Customer("Homer", "hsimpson@atomic.com", "5555");
        mq.Send(msg);
    } while(Console.ReadLine() != "q");
}
```

As you can see, this code simply assigns the Message.Body property to the Customer reference. As a result, the XmlMessageFormatter automatically serializes the object into the message body. The serialized customer data is shown here:

```
<?xml version="1.0"?>
<Customer xmlns:xsd="http://www.w3.org/2001/XMLSchema"
          xmlns:xsi="http://www.w3.org/2001/XMLSchema-instance">
  <Name>Homer</Name>
  <Email>hsimpson@atomic.com</Email>
</Customer>
```

Notice that the private mCreditCard field is *not* serialized.

To deserialize this message, the receiving code must construct the XmlMessage-Formatter so that it expects messages containing serialized customers. Just as with simple types, you can specify the expected Customer type using the typeof operator as shown in this example:

```
static void Main(string[] args)
{
    // Open queue
    MessageQueue mq = new MessageQueue(@".\private$\MyPrivateQ");

    // Create an array of types expected in the message body
    Type[] expectedTypes = new Type[] {typeof(CustomerLibrary.Customer)};
```

```
    // Construct formatter with expected types
    mq.Formatter = new XmlMessageFormatter(expectedTypes);

    // Receive message and
    Message msg = mq.Receive();

    // Deserialized body into customer object
    Customer cust = (Customer)msg.Body;

    // Process customer data ...
}
```

Because this code directly refers to the Customer type, it compiles only if the project references the CustomerLibrary assembly. As a result, you must deploy the assembly to both the sender and the receiver. Alternately, you can specify the expected message types as an array of strings, where each string contains the full name of the type:

```
// Create and array of expected type names
string[] expectedTypeNames =
    new String[] {"CustomerLibrary.Customer,CustomerLibrary"};

// Construct formatter with expected type names
mq.Formatter = new XmlMessageFormatter(expectedTypeNames);
```

The advantage of this technique is that it allows the application to bind to the assembly dynamically at runtime rather than at compile time. It also enables you to programmatically determine incoming types and construct the appropriate XmlMessageFormatter. For example, the following sender code uses the Message.Label property to indicate the type of data contained in the message body:

```
Message msg = new Message();

// Place Customer type name (including assembly details) in message label
msg.Label = typeof(Customer).AssemblyQualifiedName;

msg.Body = new Customer("Homer", "hsimpson@atomic.com", "5555");
mq.Send(msg);
```

Now the receiving code can retrieve the message, read its label, and establish the expected type for the formatter.

```
// read the message
Message msg = mq.Receive();

// Get the message type from the label, and set expected type names
string[] expectedTypeNames = new String[] {msg.Label};

// Set the formatter object for deserializing this message
msg.Formatter = new XmlMessageFormatter(expectedTypeNames);

// Retrieve the message
object o = msg.Body;

// Use Customer object in a late bound fashion ...
```

 Source Code   *The code for this example is in Chapter9\XmlFormatter.*

Even though the XmlMessageFormatter is relatively slow, it does have a couple of distinct advantages. Because the message is simply XML, it can be read and interpreted by any XML parser. In other words, the receiving application does not have to use the XmlMessageFormatter to deserialize the message. Instead, the receiver can simply read the raw message data into any XML parser. Because the Message.Body property always attempts to deserialize the message contents, you must use the Message.BodyStream property to retrieve the raw message data. The property returns a System.IO.Stream object that can be passed into a variety of parsers for processing. For example, the following code uses the System.Xml.XmlTextReader to list all the nodes in the message:

```
// Receive message
Message msg = mq.Receive();

// Read the message body stream using the XML text reader.
XmlTextReader xtr = new XmlTextReader(msg.BodyStream);

xtr.WhitespaceHandling = WhitespaceHandling.None;
while(xtr.Read())
{
    Console.WriteLine("{0} = {1}", xtr.Name, xtr.Value);
}
```

Another advantage of the XmlMessageFormatter is that it is not finicky regarding type. Yes, you do have to give it a list of expected types, but it only verifies that the message can be read using the provided type information. It does *not* validate the assembly name, version number, strong name, and so on. For example, assume the following type exists in the receiver assembly:

```
public struct Customer
{
    public string Name;
    public string Email;
}
```

This Customer type differs from the original Customer type in many ways, starting with the fact that this type is a structure, whereas the original is a class. In terms of data schema, however, this Customer structure and the original Customer class are identical. Therefore, the structure can be used to read messages containing Customer data.

By applying attributes in the System.Xml.Serialization namespace, you can define an even more radically different type and use it to deserialize the Customer message:

```
[System.Xml.Serialization.XmlRoot("Customer")]
public struct FooBar
{
    [XmlElement("Name")]
    public string Foo;

    [XmlElement("Email")]
    public string Bar;
}
```

As the following example shows, the receiving code no longer needs to reference the original Customer type and therefore does not need to bind to the CustomerLibrary assembly.

```
// Create an array of types expected in the message body
Type[] expectedTypes = new Type[] {typeof(FooBar)};

// Construct formatter with expected type names
mq.Formatter = new XmlMessageFormatter(expectedTypes);

// Receive message
Message msg = mq.Receive();
FooBar foo = (FooBar)msg.Body;
Console.WriteLine(foo.Bar);
```

Although this example is a bit far fetched, it demonstrates the flexibility of the XmlMessageFormatter. With this flexibility, the sender and the receiver need only agree on the Customer data schema. As long as this remains constant, either application can modify its version of the Customer type without affecting the other application.

 Source Code *The code for this example is in Chapter9\MoreXmlFormatting.*

Using the BinaryMessageFormatter

Unlike the XmlMessageFormatter, the BinaryMessageFormatter uses a compact binary format to serialize the object into the message body. In fact, it leverages the same runtime serialization mechanism used by .NET Remoting, which means you must adorn types with the Serializable attribute. Furthermore, every field in the type is serialized unless it is decorated with the NonSerialized attribute. This includes private fields.

Thus, the BinaryMessageFormatter can serialize the following Customer class, including its private mCreditCard field:

```
[Serializable]
public class Customer
{
    public string Name;         // Public field
    private string mCreditCard; // Private field

    private string mEmail;   // Private field with public property
    public string Email
    {
       get {return mEmail;}
       set {mEmail = value;}
    }

    public Customer(string name, string email, string ccNum)
    {
       Name = name; mEmail = email; mCreditCard = ccNum;
    }

    // Required for serialization
    public Customer(){}
}
```

To send a `Customer` message using this formatter, simply construct a `BinaryMessageFormatter` and associate it with either the `MessageQueue` or with each `Message` object:

```
class BinarySenderMain
{
    static void Main(string[] args)
    {
        // Create the queue instance
        MessageQueue mq = new MessageQueue(@".\private$\MyPrivateQ");

        Message msg = new Message();
        msg.Label = "A Customer object";
        msg.Formatter = new BinaryMessageFormatter();

        do
        {
            // Construct Customer and send to queue
          msg.Body = new Customer("Homer", "hsimpson@atomic.com", "333-33-3333");
            mq.Send(msg);
        } while(Console.ReadLine() != "q");
    }
}
```

Here is the receiving code:

```
class BinaryReceiverMain
{
    static void Main(string[] args)
    {
        // Open queue
        MessageQueue mq = new MessageQueue(@".\private$\MyPrivateQ");

        // Construct formatter with expected type names
        mq.Formatter = new BinaryMessageFormatter();

        // Receive message
        Message msg = mq.Receive();

        // Deserialized body into customer object
        Customer cust = (Customer)msg.Body;

        // Use the object
        Console.WriteLine(cust.Email);
    }
}
```

Source Code   *The code for this example is in Chapter9\BinaryFormatter.*

Although the `BinaryMessageFormatter` is faster and creates a more compact message than the `XmlMessageFormatter`, it is far less flexible. Both the sender and the receiver must have a copy of the CustomerLibrary assembly.

Using the ActiveXMessageFormatter

Before .NET, many MSMQ applications were built using a set of COM objects that wrapped the MSMQ API. In particular, Visual Basic programmers relied on these objects to build messaging applications. To allow compatibility with these applications, .NET provides the `ActiveXMessageFormatter`. This formatter employs the same serialization scheme used by the MSMQ COM objects, so you can build a sender in .NET that sends messages to a receiver built in Visual Basic 6 or vice versa.

The code to use this formatter follows the same pattern as the previous two, so an example is not needed. However, to close this discussion on MSMQ, I would like to offer some thoughts to help you choose the proper formatter. In most cases, MSMQ is applied to backend operations that are not time sensitive. To use the order-processing example again, because the Web customer is not forced to wait for the order processing to complete, it does not matter if it takes 5 milliseconds or 5 minutes. For these backend operations, flexibility trumps raw performance—and the most flexible formatter is the `XmlMessageFormatter`. If the messages contain large amounts of data (as in megabytes), the `XmlMessageFormatter` may overly tax the network. In this case, choose the compact serialization of the BinaryMessageFormatter. Finally, if interoperability with a COM-based MSMQ application is required, then you must to use the `ActiveXMessageFormatter`.

Writing Queued Components in Managed Code

After you've implemented a couple message queuing senders and receivers, you will notice that you write the same boilerplate code each time. On the sender side, you have to open the queue, construct the message, and write it to the queue. On the receiver side, you have to open the queue and design an efficient mechanism to monitor the queue while waiting for messages to arrive. Things get more mundane if message queuing is used to facilitate asynchronous calls to remote objects. In this case, the boilerplate code includes sender-side mechanisms for serializing the method call and receiver-side code for deserializing and executing it.

However, this boilerplate code is unnecessary if you use a *queued component*. This COM+ technology is basically a layer of abstraction over MSMQ that alleviates the need to implement sender and receiver logic. But there is a trade-off: like all abstractions, you give up the fine-grained level of control you have when using MSMQ directly.

The Queued Component Architecture

Recall that the MSMQ architecture includes sender, queue, and receiver components (see Figure 9-1 for a refresher). Queued component technology builds upon this architecture by adding three new participants: Recorder, ListenerHelper, and Player. Figure 9-8 depicts this new architecture.

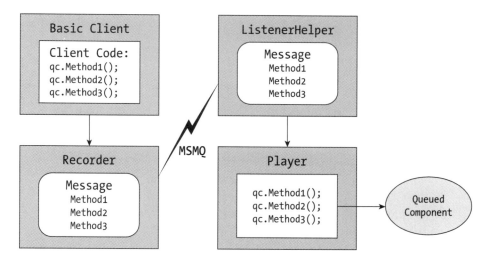

Figure 9-8. The queued component architecture provides several components to abstract the details of MSMQ.

To help understand Figure 9-8, let's step through a typical queued component execution sequence. Assume we've created and configured a queued component named QCLogging.Logger and are now focused on the client-side usage of the component. Here is the client-side code:

```
class ClientMain
{
    static void Main(string[] args)
    {
        // Interfaces are key with QC
        IQueueableLogger logger;

        // Grab a reference to the QC's interface. This returns a recorder
        // object which implements the IQueueableLogger interface.
        logger = (IQueueableLogger)Marshal.BindToMoniker
                    ("queue:/new:QCLogging.Logger");

        // Use the queued component. The recorder is simply saving these
        // method calls. The methods do not execute (yet).
        logger.Write("Log message one");
        logger.Write("Log message two");

        // Release the recorder, which packages the method calls into
        // an MSMQ message.
        Marshal.ReleaseComObject(logger);
    }
}
```

The following steps explain this code example and the role of each of the participants:

1. First, the client code instantiates the `QCLogging.Logger` queued component using the `Marshal.BindToMoniker` method (from the `System.Runtime.InteropServices` namespace). In reality, this doesn't return the `Logger` type. Instead, it creates a `Recorder` object that impersonates the `Logger`.

2. The `Recorder` serializes and caches each method call. *The methods themselves are not executed (yet).*

3. When the `Recorder` object is deactivated via `Marshal.ReleaseComObject`, it packages the cached method calls into an MSMQ message and sends that message to a queue being monitored by the `ListenerHelper`.

4. Upon receiving the message, the `ListenerHelper` creates the `Player` object and passes it the MSMQ message.

5. The Player constructs the Logger object, deserializes the message contents into method calls, and invokes the methods on the Logger in the order they were recorded.

Note that the Recorder and the ListenerHelper play the roles of sender and receiver, respectively. The COM+ runtime provides these components, saving us the trouble of implementing them ourselves.

Implementing a Queued Component

The process of implementing a queued component is much like implementing any other serviced component. You derive the queued class from ServicedComponent and decorate it with the appropriate attributes to configure the required services. Let's see how to build the Logger component referenced in the previous example. The first task is to start a class library project and configure the proper assembly level attributes:

```
[assembly: ApplicationQueuing(QueueListenerEnabled = true)]

[assembly: AssemblyVersion("1.0.0.0")]
[assembly: ApplicationActivation(ActivationOption.Server)]
[assembly: ApplicationName("QCLogging")]

[assembly: ClassInterface(ClassInterfaceType.None)]
[assembly: AssemblyKeyFile(@"d:\Mykey.snk")]
```

The next step is to define the interface for the queued component. Because of their asynchronous nature, however, queued component interfaces have a few important restrictions.

*   All methods must return void.

*   All method parameters must be input parameters; ref or out parameters are not allowed.

With these guidelines in mind, here is the IQueuableLogger interface:

```
public interface IQueuableLogger
{
   void Write(string msg);
}
```

And finally, we implement this interface in a serviced class. As the following code shows, the implementation simply writes the message to the event log:

```
[InterfaceQueuing(Interface="QCLogging.IQueuableLogger,QCLogging")]
public class Logger : ServicedComponent, IQueuableLogger
{
   public void Write(string msg)
   {
      EventLog.WriteEntry("Logger", msg);
   }
}
```

Note the application of the InterfaceQueuing attribute. This tells the COM+ runtime that the IQueuableLogger interface of the Logger class can be queued. When we compile this code and run regsvcs, COM+ creates several new MSMQ queues to support the queued component (see Figure 9-9). Note that the queue names correspond with the COM+ application name. The public qclogging queue is the primary queue used to transfer the messages from the client to the COM+ listener. The private qclogging_n queues facilitate exception handling, which is examined in the following section.

For the final step, we must manually start the COM+ application, QCLogging, from the Component Services administration tool. This can be done by right-clicking the application node and selecting Start from the context menu. This starts the ListenerHelper that monitors the qclogging queue for incoming messages.

Handling Queued Component Exceptions

If an unhandled exception occurs while the Player is executing the method calls on the queued component, an interesting series of events occur:

1. The message is moved to the first of several retry queues. These are the private queues named qclogging_0, qclogging_1, and so on as shown in Figure 9-9. After one minute, the COM+ runtime attempts to execute the methods in the message again. COM+ retries the message three times, waiting a minute between each attempt. If it is still unsuccessful, then the message is moved to the next retry queue.

2. The message continues to move through the retry queues. Each queue defines a maximum number of retries and a wait period between each attempt.

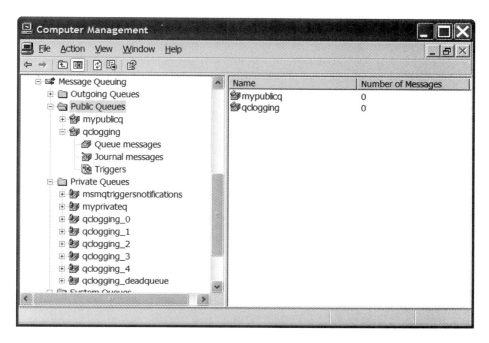

Figure 9-9. COM+ generates queues when you add a queued component.

3. If the message is still unsuccessful, it ends up in the dead queue (called qclogging_deadqueue in this case). At this time, COM+ checks for an associated exception class. If present, the exception object is created and yet another sequence begins. The exception class sequence is examined next.

4. If the exception class sequence completes without error, then the message is removed from the dead queue. Otherwise, if an error occurred during the exception class sequence, or if there is no exception class associated with the component, then the message remains on the queue until it is manually removed.

As indicated in this sequence, once the problematic message lands on the dead queue, the COM+ runtime checks for an associated exception class. The exception class must support two interfaces: IPlaybackControl and the queued interface of the component (in this case IQueuableLogger). Here is an example of an exception class for the Logger:

```
public class LoggerException : IPlaybackControl, IQueuableLogger
{
   public void FinalClientRetry()
   { // This is called on the client side if the message fails
     // to reach the queue
   }

   public void FinalServerRetry()
   { // This is called when the message lands on the dead queue.
   }

   public void Write(string msg)
   {   // After FinalServerRetry, the methods in the message are
     // invoked on this exception class. This allows you to log
     // detailed information or attempt to undo the operation.
   }
}
```

You associate the exception class with the queued component using the
ExceptionClass attribute, as shown here:

```
[InterfaceQueuing(Interface="QCLogging.IQueuableLogger,QCLogging")]
[ExceptionClass("QCLogging.LoggerException")]
public class Logger : ServicedComponent, IQueuableLogger
{  ... }
```

Now, if a message to this queued component lands in the dead queue due to a
series of exception, the following sequence occurs:

1. When the message arrives on the dead queue, COM+ creates
   the associated exception objects and invokes the
   IPlaybackControl.FinalServerRetry method.

2. COM+ invokes the methods saved in the message on the exception object.
   You can use this behavior to log detailed information regarding the error
   or to undo updates that may have been completed before the exception
   occurred.

The IPlaybackControl interface is a COM interface defined within the
comsvcs.dll library. Therefore, to use this interface with your managed code, you
must create an interop assembly (as described in Chapter 7) and reference it from
the queued component project. Because the queued component assembly is

strong named, however, the interop assembly must be strong named too. Unfortunately, when you add a reference to a COM component using Visual Studio .NET's Add Reference dialog box, a strong named interop assembly is not created. Instead, you have to use the tlbimp.exe command line tool as shown here:

```
tlbimp c:\winnt\system32\comsvcs.dll /keyfile:d:\mykey.snk
```

This will create a strong-named interop assembly using the mykey.snk key file. Once you set a reference to this assembly, you can implement the COMSVSCLib.IPlaybackControl interface on the exception class.

Summary

In my experience, messaging technologies such as MSMQ are not utilized enough in distributed applications, whereas COM+ is sometimes used too often. Hopefully, this chapter has removed some of the mystery that surrounds MSMQ and has shown you how it can be effective in creating a scalable and robust application.

Here are a few of the important points to remember from this chapter:

- Message queuing technology is useful whenever you need dependable asynchronous communication. It can often replace a custom implementation that uses the file system or a database table as an input queue for a legacy application.

- MSMQ provides a full-featured, robust message queuing infrastructure. The CLR comes with the System.Messaging namespace, which contains types that wrap the MSMQ API.

- MSMQ can be installed in either domain mode or workgroup mode. Domain mode is preferred because it allows you to create public queues and query the Active Directory server for public queues on the network.

- The System.Messaging namespace provides the MessageQueue class with methods for opening queues, sending messages, receiving messages, finding public queues, and so on.

- Queued components provide an easy-to-use abstraction of MSMQ. Using queued components, you can avoid writing custom message sender and receiver logic.

This concludes the chapter and the book. As I stated in the beginning, this book is intended as a guided tour through the .NET technologies used for distributed programming—and now the tour bus is returning to the home base. As you have seen, .NET introduces a few brand new tools, such as .NET Remoting and Web services, and changes the way you use some existing tools, such as COM+ and MSMQ. It is my hope that you now understand the role each plays and can confidently apply them in your next project.

To round out your knowledge, I now leave you in the capable hands of my colleague, Andrew Troelsen, who has graciously contributed an appendix describing the exciting new capabilities of ADO.NET.

Well, I don't really think that the end can be assessed as of itself as being the end because what does the end feel like? It's like saying when you try to extrapolate the end of the universe, you say, if the universe is indeed infinite, then how—what does that mean? How far is all the way, and then if it stops, what's stopping it, and what's behind what's stopping it? So, what's the end, you know, is my question to you.

—David St. Hubbins (*This Is Spinal Tap*)

Data Access with ADO.NET

by Andrew Troelsen

This is Chapter 13 of *C# and the .NET Platform* (Apress, 2001). From this point on, all references to other chapters and appendixes are to those from Troelsen and not to chapters and appendixes within *Distributed .NET Programming in C#*.

Unless you are a video game developer by trade, you are probably interested in database manipulation. As you would expect, the .NET platform defines a number of types (in a handful of related namespaces) that allow you to interact with local and remote data stores. Collectively speaking, these namespaces are known as ADO.NET, which as you will see is a major overhaul of the classic ADO object model.

This chapter begins by examining some core types defined in the System.Data namespace—specifically DataColumn, DataRow, and DataTable. These classes allow you to define and manipulate a local in-memory table of data. Next, you spend a good deal of time learning about the centerpiece of ADO.NET, the DataSet. As you will see, the DataSet is an in-memory representation of a *collection* of interrelated tables. During this discussion, you will learn how to programmatically model table relationships, create custom views from a given table, and submit queries against your in-memory DataSet.

After discussing how to manipulate a DataSet in memory, the remainder of this chapter illustrates how to obtain a populated DataSet from a Database Management System (DBMS) such as MS SQL Server, Oracle, or MS Access. This entails an examination of .NET "managed providers" and the OleDbDataAdapter and SqlDataAdapter types.

The Need for ADO.NET

The very first thing you must understand when learning ADO.NET is that it is *not* simply the latest and greatest version of classic ADO. While it is true that there is some symmetry between the two systems (e.g., each has the concept of "connection" and "command" objects), some familiar types (e.g., the Recordset) no longer exist. Furthermore, there are a number of new ADO.NET types that have no direct equivalent under classic ADO (e.g., the DataSet).

In a nutshell, ADO.NET is a new database access technology specifically geared at facilitating the development of disconnected systems using the .NET platform. *N*-tier applications (especially Web-based applications) are fast becoming the norm, rather than the exception, for most new development efforts.

Unlike classic ADO, which was primarily designed for tightly coupled client/server systems, ADO.NET greatly extends the notion of the primitive ADO disconnected recordset with a new creature named the DataSet. This type represents a *local* copy of any number of related tables. Using the DataSet, the client is able to manipulate and update its contents while disconnected from the data source and submit the modified data back for processing using a related "data adapter."

Another major difference between classic ADO and ADO.NET is that ADO.NET has full support for XML data representation. In fact, the data obtained from a data store is internally represented, and transmitted, as XML. Given that XML is transported between layers using standard HTTP, ADO.NET is not limited by firewall constraints.

As you might be aware, classic ADO makes use of the COM marshaling protocol to move data between tiers. While this was appropriate in some situations, COM marshaling poses a number of limitations. Specifically, most firewalls are configured to reject COM RPC packets, which makes moving data between machines tricky.

Perhaps the most fundamental difference between classic ADO and ADO.NET is that ADO.NET is a managed library of code and therefore plays by all the same rules as any managed library. The types that comprise ADO.NET use the CLR memory management protocol, adhere to the same programming model, and work with many languages. Therefore, the types (and their members) are accessed in the same exact manner, regardless of which .NET-aware language you use.

ADO.NET: The Big Picture

The types that compose ADO.NET work together for a common goal: populate a DataSet, disconnect from the data store, and return the DataSet to the caller. A DataSet is a very interesting data type, given that it represents a local collection of tables (as well as the relationships between these tables) used by the client application. In some respects, this may remind you of the classic ADO disconnected recordset. The key difference is that a disconnected recordset represents a single table of data, whereas ADO.NET DataSets can model a collection of related tables. In fact, it is completely possible to have a client-side DataSet that represents the *entire* remote database.

Once you have obtained a DataSet, you can perform queries against the local tables to obtain specific subsets of information as well as navigate between related tables programmatically. As you would expect, you can add new rows to a given table in the DataSet as well as remove, filter, or update existing records. Once the modifications have been made, the client then submits the modified DataSet back to the data store for processing.

An obvious question at this point is "How do I get the DataSet?" Under the ADO.NET model, DataSets are populated through the use of a managed provider, which is a collection of classes that implement a set of core interfaces defined in the System.Data namespace; specifically IDbCommand, IDbDataAdapter, IDbConnection, and IDataReader (see Figure 13-1).

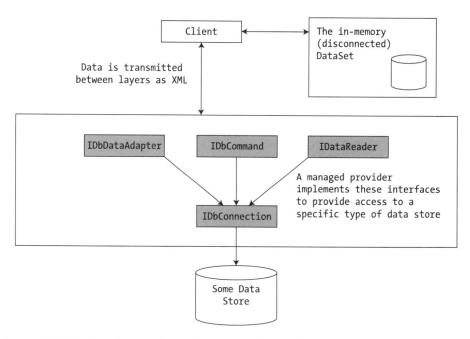

Figure 13-1. Clients interacting with managed providers

ADO.NET ships with two managed providers out of the box. First is the SQL provider, which provides highly optimized interactions with data stored in MS SQL Server (7.0 or higher). If the data you desire is not in an SQL Server data file, you can use the OleDb provider, which allows access to any data store that supports the OLE DB protocol. Be aware, however, that the OleDb provider uses native OLE DB (and therefore requires COM Interop) to enable data access.

As you might suspect, this is always a slower process than talking to a data store in its native tongue. Other vendors will soon begin shipping custom-managed providers for their proprietary data stores. Until then, the OleDb provider does the trick.

Understanding ADO.NET Namespaces

Like other aspects of the .NET universe, ADO.NET is defined in a handful of related namespaces. Table 13-1 gives a quick rundown of each.

Table 13-1. ADO.NET Namespaces

ADO.NET NAMESPACE	MEANING IN LIFE
System.Data	This is the core namespace of ADO.NET. It defines types that represent tables, rows, columns, constraints, and DataSets. This namespace does not define types to connect to a data source. Rather, it defines the types that represent the data itself.
System.Data.Common	This namespace contains the types shared between managed providers. Many of these types function as base classes to the concrete types defined by the OleDb and SqlClient managed providers.
System.Data.OleDb	This namespace defines the types that allow you to connect to an OLE DB–compliant data source, submit SQL queries, and fill DataSets. The types in this namespace have a look and feel similar (but not identical) to that of classic ADO.
System.Data.SqlClient	This namespace defines the types that constitute the SQL-managed provider. Using these types, you can talk directly to Microsoft SQL Server and avoid the level of indirection associated with the OleDb equivalents.
System.Data.SqlTypes	These types represent native data types used in Microsoft SQL Server. Although you are always free to use the corresponding CLR data types, the SqlTypes are optimized to work with SQL Server.

All of these ADO.NET namespaces are in a single assembly named System.Data.dll (Figure 13-2). Thus, like in any project referencing external assemblies, you must be sure to set a reference to this .NET binary.

Of all the ADO.NET namespaces, System.Data is the lowest common denominator. You simply cannot build ADO.NET applications without specifying this namespace in your data access applications. In addition, to establish a connection with a data store, you also need to specify a using directive for the System.Data.OleDb or System.Data.SqlClient namespaces. The exact reasons for this are discussed soon. For now, get to know some of the core types defined in System.Data.

The Types of System.Data

As mentioned, this namespace contains types that represent the data you obtain from a data store, but not the types that make the literal connection. In addition to a number of database-centric exceptions (NoNullAllowedException,

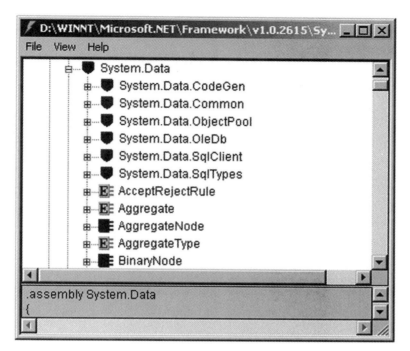

Figure 13-2. The System.Data.dll assembly

RowNotInTableException, MissingPrimaryKeyException, and the like), these types are little more than OO representations of common database primitives (tables, rows, columns, constraints, and so on). Table 13-2 lists some of the core types, grouped by related functionality.

To get the ball rolling, the first half of this chapter discusses how to manipulate these items in a disconnected mode by hand. Once you understand how to build a DataSet in the raw, you should have no problem manipulating a DataSet populated by a managed provider.

Examining the DataColumn Type

The DataColumn type represents a single column maintained by a DataTable. Collectively speaking, the set of all DataColumn types bound to a given DataTable represents the table's schema. For example, assume you have a table named Employees with three columns (EmpID, FirstName, and LastName). Programmatically, you would use three ADO.NET DataColumn objects to represent them in memory. As you will see in just a moment, the DataTable type maintains an internal collection (which is accessed using the Columns property) to maintain its DataColumn types.

Table 13-2. Types of the System.Data Namespace

SYSTEM.DATA TYPE	MEANING IN LIFE
DataColumnCollection DataColumn	DataColumnCollection is used to represent all of the columns used by a given DataTable. DataColumn represents a specific column in a DataTable.
ConstraintCollection Constraint	ConstraintCollection represents all constraints (foreign key constraints, unique constraints) assigned to a given DataTable. Constraint represents an OO wrapper around a single constraint assigned to one or more DataColumns.
DataRowCollection DataRow	These types represent a collection of rows for a DataTable (DataRowCollection) and a specific row of data in a DataTable (DataRow).
DataRowView DataView	DataRowView allows you to carve out a predefined view from an existing row. DataView represents a customized view of a DataTable that can be used for sorting, filtering, searching, editing, and navigating.
DataSet	Represents an in-memory cache of data, which may consist of multiple related DataTables.
ForeignKeyConstraint UniqueConstraint	ForeignKeyConstraint represents an action restriction enforced on a set of columns in a primary key/foreign key relationship. The UniqueConstraint type represents a restriction on a set of columns in which all values must be unique.
DataRelationCollection DataRelation	This collection represents all relationships (i.e., DataRelation types) between the tables in a DataSet.
DataTableCollection DataTable	DataTableCollection represents all the tables (i.e., DataTable types) for a particular DataSet.

If you have a background in relational database theory, you know that a given column in a data table can be assigned a set of constraints (e.g., configured as a primary key, assigned a default value, configured to contain read-only information, and so on). Also, every column in a table must map to an underlying data type (int, varchar, and so forth). For example, the Employees table's schema may demand that the EmpID column maps to an integer, while FirstName and LastName map to an array of characters. The DataColumn class has numerous properties that allow you to configure these very things. Table 13-3 provides a rundown of some core properties.

Table 13-3. Properties of the DataColumn

DATACOLUMN PROPERTY	MEANING IN LIFE
AllowDBNull	Used to indicate if a row can specify null values in this column. The default value is true.
AutoIncrement AutoIncrementSeed AutoIncrementStep	These properties are used to configure the autoincrement behavior for a given column. This can be helpful when you wish to ensure unique values in a given DataColumn (such as a primary key). By default, a DataColumn does not support autoincrementation.
Caption	Gets or sets the caption to be displayed for this column (for example, what the end user sees in a DataGrid).
ColumnMapping	This property determines how a DataColumn is represented when a DataSet is saved as an XML document using the DataSet.WriteXml() method.
ColumnName	Gets or sets the name of the column in the Columns collection (meaning how it is represented internally by the DataTable). If you do not set the ColumnName explicitly, the default values are Column with (n+1) numerical suffixes (i.e., Column1, Column2, Column3, and so forth).
DataType	Defines the data type (boolean, string, float, and so on) stored in the column.
DefaultValue	Gets or sets the default value assigned to this column when inserting new rows. This is used if not otherwise specified.
Expression	Gets or sets the expression used to filter rows, calculate a column's value, or create an aggregate column.
Ordinal	Gets the numerical position of the column in the Columns collection maintained by the DataTable.
ReadOnly	Determined if this column can be modified once a row has been added to the table. The default is false.
Table	Gets the DataTable that contains this DataColumn.
Unique	Gets or sets a value indicating whether the values in each row of the column must be unique or if repeating values are permissible. If a column is assigned a primary key constraint, the Unique property should be set to true.

Building a DataColumn

To illustrate the basic use of the DataColumn, assume you need to model a column named FirstName, which internally maps to an array of characters.

Furthermore, assume this column (for whatever reason) must be read only. Pro-grammatically, you can write the following logic:

```
protected void btnColumn_Click (object sender, System.EventArgs e)
{
    // Build the FirstName column.
    DataColumn colFName = new DataColumn();

    // Set a bunch of values.
    colFName.DataType = Type.GetType("System.String");
    colFName.ReadOnly = true;
    colFName.Caption = "First Name";
    colFName.ColumnName = "FirstName";

    // Get a bunch of values.
    string temp =      "Column type: " + colFName.DataType + "\n" +
                       "Read only? " + colFName.ReadOnly + "\n" +
                       "Caption: " + colFName.Caption + "\n" +
                       "Column Name: " + colFName.ColumnName + "\n" +
                       "Nulls allowed? " + colFName.AllowDBNull;

    MessageBox.Show(temp, "Column properties");
}
```

This gives the result shown in Figure 13-3.

Figure 13-3. Select properties of the DataColumn

Given that the DataColumn provides several overloaded constructors, you can specify a number of properties directly at the time of creation, as shown here:

```
// Build the FirstName column (take two).
DataColumn colFName = new DataColumn("FirstName",
                                     Type.GetType("System.String"));
colFName.ReadOnly = true;
colFName.Caption = "First Name";
```

In addition to the properties already examined, the DataColumn does have a small set of methods, which I assume you will check out on your own.

Adding a DataColumn to a DataTable

The DataColumn type does not typically exist as a stand-alone entity, but is instead inserted in a DataTable. To do so, begin by creating a new DataTable type (fully detailed later in the chapter). Next insert each DataColumn in the DataTable.DataColumnCollection type using the Columns property. Here is an example:

```
// Build the FirstName column.
DataColumn myColumn = new DataColumn();

// Create a new DataTable.
DataTable myTable = new DataTable("MyTable");

// The Columns property returns a DataColumnCollection type.
// Use the Add() method to insert the column in the table.
myTable.Columns.Add(myColumn);
```

Configuring a DataColumn to Function as a Primary Key

One common rule of database development is that a table should have at least one column that functions as the primary key. A primary key constraint is used to uniquely identify a record (row) in a given table. In keeping with the current Employees example, assume you now wish to build a new DataColumn type to represent the EmpID field. This column will be the primary key of the table and thus should have the AllowDBNull and Unique properties configured as shown here:

```
// This column is functioning as a primary key.
DataColumn colEmpID = new DataColumn(EmpID, Type.GetType("System.Int32"));
colEmpID.Caption = "Employee ID";
colEmpID.AllowDBNull = false;
colEmpID.Unique = true;
```

Once the DataColumn has been correctly set up to function as a primary key, the next step is to assign this DataColumn to the DataTable's PrimaryKey property. You will see how to do in just a bit during the discussion of the DataTable, so put this on the back burner for the time being.

Enabling Autoincrementing Fields

One aspect of the DataColumn you may choose to configure is its ability to autoincrement. Simply put, autoincrementing columns are used to ensure that when a new row is added to a given table, the value of this column is assigned automatically, based on the current step of the incrementation. This can be helpful when you wish to ensure that a column has no repeating values (such as a primary key). This behavior is controlled using the AutoIncrement, AutoIncrementSeed, and AutoIncrementStep properties.

To illustrate, build a DataColumn that supports autoincrementation. The seed value is used to mark the starting value of the column, where the step value identifies the number to add to the seed when incrementing, as shown here:

```
// Create a data column.
DataColumn myColumn = new DataColumn();
myColumn.ColumnName = "Foo";
myColumn.DataType = System.Type.GetType("System.Int32");

// Set the autoincrement behavior.
myColumn.AutoIncrement = true;
myColumn.AutoIncrementSeed = 500;
myColumn.AutoIncrementStep = 12;
```

Here, the Foo column has been configured to ensure that as rows are added to the respective table, the value in this field is incremented by 12. Because the seed has been set at 500, the first five values should be 500, 512, 524, 536, and 548.

To prove the point, insert this DataColumn in a DataTable. Then add a number of new rows to the table, which of course automatically bumps the value in the Foo column, as shown here:

```
protected void btnAutoCol_Click (object sender, System.EventArgs e)
{
    // Make a data column that maps to an int.
    DataColumn myColumn = new DataColumn();
    myColumn.ColumnName = "Foo";
    myColumn.DataType = System.Type.GetType("System.Int32");
```

```
// Set the autoincrement behavior.
myColumn.AutoIncrement = true;
myColumn.AutoIncrementSeed = 500;
myColumn.AutoIncrementStep = 12;

// Add this column to a new DataTable.
DataTable myTable = new DataTable("MyTable");
myTable.Columns.Add(myColumn);

// Add 20 new rows.
DataRow r;
for(int i =0; i < 20; i++)
{
    r = myTable.NewRow();
    myTable.Rows.Add(r);
}

// Now list the value in each row.
string temp = "";
DataRowCollection rows = myTable.Rows;
for(int i = 0;i < myTable.Rows.Count; i++)
{
    DataRow currRow = rows[i];
    temp += currRow["Foo"] + " ";
}
MessageBox.Show(temp, "These values brought ala auto-increment");
}
```

If you run the application (and click the corresponding Button), we see the message shown in Figure 13-4.

Figure 13-4. An autoincremented column

Configuring a Column's XML Representation

While many of the remaining DataColumn properties are rather self-explanatory (provided you are comfortable with database terminology), I would like to discuss the ColumnMapping property. The DataColumn.ColumnMapping property is used to configure how this column should be represented in XML, if the owning DataSet dumps its contents using the WriteXml() method. The value of the ColumnMapping property is configured using the MappingType enumeration (Table 13-4).

Table 13-4. Values of the MappingType enumeration

MAPPINGTYPE ENUMERATION VALUE	MEANING IN LIFE
Attribute	The column is mapped to an XML attribute.
Element	The column is mapped to an XML element (the default).
Hidden	The column is mapped to an internal structure.
TableElement	The column is mapped to a table value.
Text	The column is mapped to text.

The default value of the ColumnMapping property is MappingType.Element. Assume that you have instructed the owning DataSet to write its contents to a new file stream as XML. Using this default setting, the EmpID column would appear as shown here:

```
<Employee>
     <EmpID>500</EmpID>
</Employee>
```

However, if the DataColumn's ColumnMapping property is set to MappingType.Attribute, you see the following XML representation:

```
<Employee EmpID = "500"/>
```

This chapter examines the ADO.NET/XML integration in greater detail when discussing the DataSet. Nevertheless, at this point, you understand how to create a stand-alone DataColumn type. Now for an examination of the basic behavior of the DataRow.

SOURCE CODE   *The DataColumn application is included under the Chapter 13 subdirectory.*

Examining the DataRow Type

As you have seen, a collection of DataColumn objects represents the schema of a table. A DataTable maintains its columns using the internal DataColumnCollection type. In contrast, a collection of DataRow types represents the actual data in the table. Thus, if you have 20 listings in a table named Employees, you can represent these entries using 20 DataRow types. Using the members of the DataRow class, you are able to insert, remove, evaluate, and manipulate the values in the table.

Working with a DataRow is a bit different from working with a DataColumn, because you do not create a direct instance of this type, but rather obtain a reference from a given DataTable. For example, assume you wish to insert a new row in the Employees table. The DataTable.NewRow() method allows you to obtain the next slot in the table, at which point you can fill each column with new data, as shown here:

```
// Build a new Table.
DataTable empTable = new DataTable("Employees");

// ...Add EmpID, FirstName and LastName columns to table...

// Build a new Employee record.
DataRow row = empTable.NewRow();
row["EmpID"] = 102;
row["FirstName"] = "Joe";
row["LastName"] = "Blow";

// Add it to the Table's DataRowCollection.
empTable.Rows.Add(row);
```

Notice how the DataRow class defines an indexer that can be used to gain access to a given DataColumn by numerical position as well as column name. Also notice that the DataTable maintains another internal collection (DataRowCollection) to hold each row of data. The DataRow type defines the following core members, grouped by related functionality in Table 13-5.

Understanding the DataRow.RowState Property

Most of the methods of the DataRow class only make sense in the context of an owning DataTable. You will see the process of inserting, removing, and updating rows in just a moment; first, however, you should get to know the RowState property. This property is useful when you need to programmatically identify the set of all rows in a table that have changed, have been newly inserted, and so forth. This property may be assigned any value from the DataRowState enumeration (Table 13-6).

Table 13-5. Members of the DataRow

DATAROW MEMBER	MEANING IN LIFE
AcceptChanges() RejectChanges()	Commits or rejects all the changes made to this row since the last time AcceptChanges was called.
BeginEdit() EndEdit() CancelEdit()	Begins, ends, or cancels an edit operation on a DataRow object.
Delete()	Marks a row to be removed when the AcceptChanges() method is called.
HasErrors GetColumnsInError() GetColumnError() ClearErrors() RowError	The HasErrors property returns a boolean value indicating if there are errors in a column's collection. If so, the GetColumnsInError() method can be used to obtain the offending members, GetColumnError() can be used to obtain the error description, while the ClearErrors() method removes each error listing for the row. The RowError property allows you to configure a textual description of the error for a given row.
IsNull()	Gets a value indicating whether the specified column contains a null value.
ItemArray	Gets or sets all of the values for this row using an array of objects.
RowState	Used to pinpoint the current state of the DataRow using values of the RowState enumeration.
Table	Use this property to obtain a reference to the DataTable containing this DataRow.

Table 13-6. Values of the DataRowState Enumeration

DATAROWSTATE ENUMERATION VALUE	MEANING IN LIFE
Deleted	The row was deleted using the Delete method of the DataRow.
Detached	The row has been created but is not part of any DataRowCollection. A DataRow is in this state immediately after it has been created and before it is added to a collection, or if it has been removed from a collection.
Modified	The row has been modified, and AcceptChanges() has not been called.
New	The row has been added to a DataRowCollection, and AcceptChanges() has not been called.
Unchanged	The row has not changed since AcceptChanges() was last called.

To illustrate the various states a DataRow may have, the following class documents the changes to the RowState property as a new DataRow is created, inserted in, and removed from a DataTable:

```
public class DRState
{
    public static void Main()
    {
        // Build a single-column DataTable.
        DataTable myTable = new DataTable("Employees");
        DataColumn colID = new DataColumn("EmpID",                .
                            Type.GetType("System.Int32"));
        myTable.Columns.Add(colID);

        // The DataRow.
        DataRow myRow;

        // Create a new (detached) DataRow.
        myRow = myTable.NewRow();
        Console.WriteLine(myRow.RowState.ToString());

        // Now add it to table.
        myTable.Rows.Add(myRow);
        Console.WriteLine(myRow.RowState.ToString());

        // Trigger an 'accept.
        myTable.AcceptChanges();
        Console.WriteLinemyRow.RowState.ToString());

        // Modify it.
        myRow["EmpID"] = 100;
        Console.WriteLine(myRow.RowState.ToString());

        // Now delete it.
        myRow.Delete();
        Console.WriteLine(myRow.RowState.ToString());
        myRow.AcceptChanges();
    }
}
```

The output should be clear (Figure 13-5).

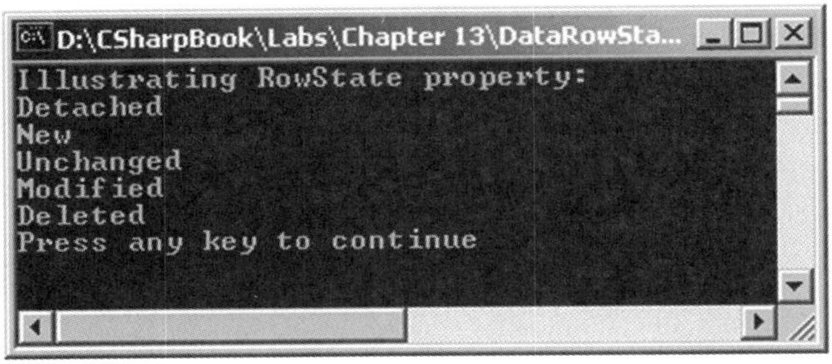

Figure 13-5. Changes in row states

As you can see, the ADO.NET DataRow is smart enough to remember its current state of affairs. Given this, the owning DataTable is able to identify which rows have been modified. This is a key feature of the DataSet, given that when it comes time to send updated information to the data store, only the modified values are submitted. Clearly this behavior helps optimize trips between the layers of your system.

The ItemArray Property

Another helpful member of the DataRow is the ItemArray property. This method returns a complete snapshot of the current row as an array of System.Object types. Also, you can insert a new row using the ItemArray property, rather than listing each DataColumn explicitly. Assume the current table now has two DataColumns (EmpID and FirstName). The following logic adds some new rows by assigning an array of objects to the ItemArray property and then promptly prints the results (see Figure 13-6):

```
// Declare the array variable.
object [] myVals = new object[2];
DataRow dr;

// Create some new rows and add to DataRowCollection.
for(int i = 0; i < 5; i++)
{
    myVals[0] = i;
    myVals[1]= "Name " + i;
    dr = myTable.NewRow();
    dr.ItemArray = myVals;
    myTable.Rows.Add(dr);
}
```

```
// Now print each value.
foreach(DataRow r in myTable.Rows)
{
    foreach(DataColumn c in myTable.Columns)
    {
        Console.WriteLine(r[c]);
    }
}
```

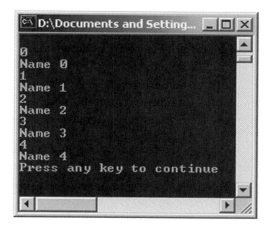

Figure 13-6. Using the ItemArray property

SOURCE CODE   *The DataRowState is included under the Chapter 13 subdirectory.*

Details of the DataTable

The DataTable is an in-memory representation of a tabular block of data. While you can manually compose a DataTable programmatically, you will more commonly obtain a DataTable dynamically using a DataSet and the types defined in the System.Data.OleDb or System.Data.SqlClient namespaces. Table 13-7 describes some core properties of the DataTable.

To help visualize the key components of a DataTable, consider Figure 13-7. Be aware that this is *not* a traditional class hierarchy that illustrates the is-a relations between these types (e.g., the DataRow *does not* derive from DataRowCollection). Rather, this diagram points out the logical has-a relationships between the DataTable's core items (e.g., the DataRowCollection has a number of DataRow types).

Table 13-7. Properties of the DataTable

DATATABLE PROPERTY	MEANING IN LIFE
CaseSensitive	Indicates whether string comparisons in the table are case sensitive (or not). The default value is false.
ChildRelations	Returns the collection of child relations (DataRelationCollection) for this DataTable (if any).
Columns	Returns the collection of columns that belong to this table.
Constraints	Gets the collection of constraints maintained by the table (ConstraintCollection).
DataSet	Gets the DataSet that contains this table (if any).
DefaultView	Gets a customized view of the table that may include a filtered view or a cursor position.
MinimumCapacity	Gets or sets the initial number of rows in this table. (The default is 25.)
ParentRelations	Gets the collection of parent relations for this DataTable.
PrimaryKey	Gets or sets an array of columns that function as primary keys for the data table.
Rows	Returns the collection of rows that belong to this table.
TableName	Gets or sets the name of the table. This same property may also be specified as a constructor parameter.

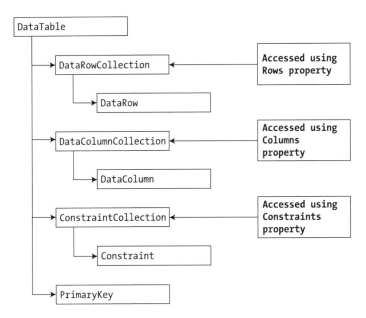

Figure 13-7. Collections of the DataTable

Building a Complete DataTable

Now that you have been exposed to the basics, let's see a complete example of creating and manipulating an in-memory data table. Assume you are interested in building a DataTable representing the current inventory in a database named Cars. The Inventory table will contain four columns: CarID, Make, Color, and PetName. Also, the CarID column will function as the table's primary key (PK) and support autoincrementation. The PetName column will allow null values. (Sadly, not everyone loves their automobiles as much as we might!) Figure 13-8 shows the overall schema.

CarID (PK)	Make	Color	PetName
0	BMW	Green	Chucky
1	Yugo	White	Tiny
2	Jeep	Tan	(null)
3	Caravan	Pink	Pain Inducer

Figure 13-8. The Inventory DataTable

The process begins by creating a new DataTable type. When you do so, you specify the friendly name of the table as a constructor parameter. This friendly name can be used to reference this table from the containing DataSet, as shown here:

```
// Create a new DataTable.
DataTable inventoryTable = new DataTable("Inventory");
```

The next step is to programmatically insert each column using the Add() method of the DataColumnCollection (accessed using the DataTable.Columns property). The following logic adds the CarID, Make, Color, and PetName columns to the current DataTable (recall that the underlying data type of each column is set using the DataType property):

```
// DataColumn var.
DataColumn myDataColumn;

// Create CarID column and add to table.
myDataColumn = new DataColumn();
myDataColumn.DataType = Type.GetType("System.Int32");
myDataColumn.ColumnName = "CarID";
myDataColumn.ReadOnly = true;
myDataColumn.AllowDBNull = false;
myDataColumn.Unique = true;
```

```
// Set the autoincrement behavior.
myDataColumn.AutoIncrement = true;
myDataColumn.AutoIncrementSeed = 1000;
myDataColumn.AutoIncrementStep = 10;
inventoryTable.Columns.Add(myDataColumn);

// Create Make column and add to table.
myDataColumn = new DataColumn();
myDataColumn.DataType = Type.GetType("System.String");
myDataColumn.ColumnName = "Make";
inventoryTable.Columns.Add(myDataColumn);

// Create Color column and add to table.
myDataColumn = new DataColumn();
myDataColumn.DataType = Type.GetType("System.String");
myDataColumn.ColumnName = "Color";
inventoryTable.Columns.Add(myDataColumn);

// Create PetName column and add to table.
myDataColumn = new DataColumn();
myDataColumn.DataType = Type.GetType("System.String");
myDataColumn.ColumnName = "PetName";
myDataColumn.AllowDBNull = true;
inventoryTable.Columns.Add(myDataColumn);
```

Before you add the rows, take the time to set the table's primary key. To do so, set the DataTable.PrimaryKey property to whichever column necessary. Because more than a single column can function as a table's primary key, be aware that the PrimaryKey property requires an array of DataColumn types. For the Inventory table, assume the CarID column is the only aspect of the primary key, as shown here:

```
// Make the ID column the primary key column.
DataColumn[] PK = new DataColumn[1];
PK[0] = inventoryTable.Columns["CarID"];
inventoryTable.PrimaryKey = PK;
```

Last but not least, you need to add valid data to the table. Assuming you have an appropriate ArrayList maintaining Car types, you can fill the table as shown here:

```
// Iterate over the array list to make rows (remember, the ID is
// autoincremented).
foreach(Car c in arTheCars)
```

```
{
    DataRow newRow;
    newRow = inventoryTable.NewRow();
    newRow["Make"] = c.make;
    newRow["Color"] = c.color;
    newRow["PetName"] = c.petName;
    inventoryTable.Rows.Add(newRow);
}
```

To display your new local in-memory table, assume you have a Windows Forms application with a main Form displaying a DataGrid. As you saw in Chapter 11, the DataSource property is used to bind a DataTable to the GUI. The output is shown in Figure 13-9.

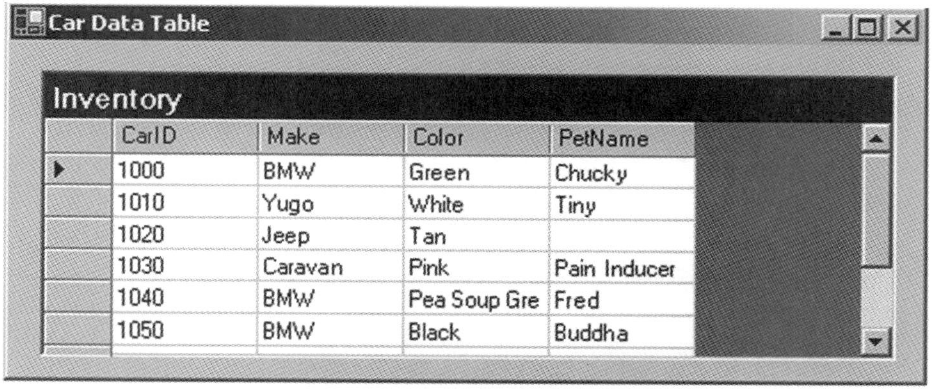

Figure 13-9. Binding the DataTable to a DataGrid

Here, you added rows by specifying the string name of the column to modify. However, you may also specify the numerical index of the column, which can be very helpful when you need to iterate over each column. Thus, the previous code could be updated as shown here (and still achieve the same end result):

```
foreach(Car c in arTheCars)
{
    // Specify columns by index.
    DataRow newRow;
    newRow = inventoryTable.NewRow();
    newRow[1] = c.make;
    newRow[2] = c.color;
    newRow[3] = c.petName;
    inventoryTable.Rows.Add(newRow);
}
```

Manipulating a DataTable: Deleting Rows

What if you wish to remove a row from a data table? One approach is to call the Delete() method of the DataRowCollection type. Simply specify the index (or DataRow) representing the row to remove. Assume you update your GUI as shown in Figure 13-10.

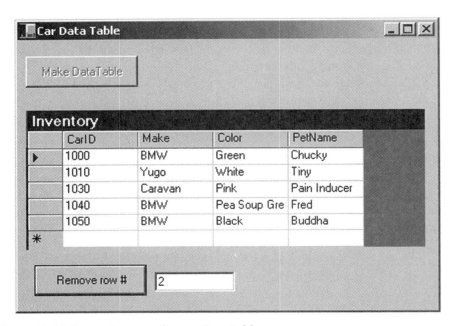

Figure 13-10. Removing rows from a DataTable

If you look at the previous screen shot, you will notice that you specified the second row in the DataTable, and therefore CarID 1020 has been blown away. The following logic behind the new Button's Click event handler removes the specified row from your in-memory DataTable:

```
// Remove this row from the DataRowCollection.
protected void btnRemoveRow_Click (object sender, System.EventArgs e)
{
    try
    {
        inventoryTable.Rows[(int.Parse(txtRemove.Text))].Delete();
        inventoryTable.AcceptChanges();
    }
    catch(Exception ex)
```

```
    {
        MessageBox.Show(ex.Message);
    }
}
```

The Delete() method might have been better named MarkedAsDeletable() given that the row is typically not removed until the DataTable.AcceptChanges() method has been called. In effect, the Delete() method simply sets a flag that says "I am ready to die when my table tells me." Also understand that if a row has been marked for deletion, a DataTable may reject those changes before calling AcceptChanges(), as shown here:

```
// Mark a row as deleted, but reject the changes.
protected void btnRemoveRow_Click (object sender, System.EventArgs e)
{
    inventoryTable.Rows[txtRemove.Text.ToInt32()].Delete();

    // Do more work. . .

    inventoryTable.RejectChanges();     // Restore RowState.
}
```

Manipulating a DataTable: Applying Filters and Sort Orders

You may wish to see a small subset of a DataTable's data, as specified by some sort of filtering criteria. For example, what if you wish to only see a certain make of automobile from the in-memory Inventory table? The Select() method of the DataTable class provides this very functionality. Update your GUI once again, this time allowing users to specify a string that represents the make of the automobile they are interested in viewing (Figure 13-11).

The Select() method has been overloaded a number of times to provide different selection semantics. At its most basic level, the parameter sent to Select() is a string that contains some conditional operation. To begin, observe the following logic for the Click event handler of your new Button:

```
protected void btnGetMakes_Click (object sender, System.EventArgs e)
{
    // Build a filter based on user input.
    string filterStr = "Make='" + txtMake.Text + "'";

    // Find all rows matching the filter.
    DataRow[] makes = inventoryTable.Select(filterStr);
```

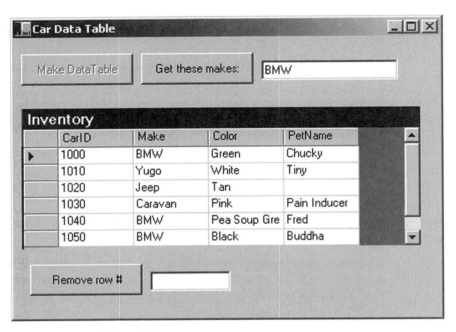

Figure 13-11. Specifying a filter

```
// Show what we got!
if(makes.Length = = 0)
    MessageBox.Show("Sorry, no cars...", "Selection error!");
else
{
    string strMake = null;
    for(int i = 0; i < makes.Length; i++)
    {
        DataRow temp = makes[i];
        strMake += temp["PetName"].ToString() + "\n";

    }
    MessageBox.Show(strMake, txtMake.Text + " type(s):");
}
}
```

Here, you first build a simple filter criteria based on the value in the associated TextBox. If you specify BMW, your filter is Make = 'BMW'. When you send this filter to the Select() method, you get back an array of DataRow types, which represent each row that matches the filter criteria (Figure 13-12).

Figure 13-12. Filtered data

A filter string can be composed of any number of relational operators. For example, what if you wanted to find all cars with an ID greater than 1030? You could write the following (see Figure 13-13 for output):

```
// Now show the pet names of all cars with ID greater than 1030.
DataRow[] properIDs;
string newFilterStr = "ID > '1030'";
properIDs = inventoryTable.Select(newFilterStr);
string strIDs = null;

for(int i = 0; i < properIDs.Length; i++)
{
    DataRow temp = properIDs[i];
    strIDs += temp["PetName"].ToString()
            + " is ID " + temp["ID"] + "\n";
}
MessageBox.Show(strIDs, "Pet names of cars where ID > 1030");
```

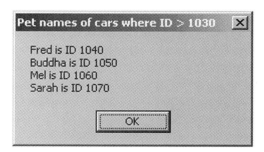

Figure 13-13. Specifying a range of data

Filtering logic is modeled after standard SQL syntax. To prove the point, assume you wish to obtain the results of the previous Select() command alphabetically based on pet name. In terms of SQL, this translates into a sort based on the PetName column. Luckily the Select() method has been overloaded to send in a sort criterion, as shown here:

```
makes = inventoryTable.Select(filterStr, "PetName");
```

This returns something like what is shown in Figure 13-14.

Figure 13-14. Ordered data

If you want the results in descending order, call Select(), as shown here:

```
// Return results in descending order.
makes = inventoryTable.Select(filterStr, "PetName DESC");
```

In general, the sort string contains the column name followed by "ASC" (ascending, which is the default) or "DESC" (descending). If need be, multiple columns can be separated by commas.

Manipulating a DataTable: Updating Rows

The final aspect of the DataTable you should be aware of is the process of updating an exiting row with new values. One approach is to first obtain the row(s) that match a given filter criterion using the Select() method. Once you have the DataRow(s) in question, modify them accordingly. For example, assume you have a new Button that (when clicked) searches the DataTable for all rows where Make is equal to BMW. Once you identify these items, you change the Make from 'BMW' to 'Colt':

```
// Find the rows you want to edit with a filter.
protected void btnChange_Click (object sender, System.EventArgs e)
{
    // Build a filter.
    string filterStr = "Make='BMW'";
    string strMake = null;
```

```
    // Find all rows matching the filter.
    DataRow[] makes = inventoryTable.Select(filterStr);

    // Change all Beemers to Colts!
    for(int i = 0; i < makes.Length; i++)
    {
        DataRow temp = makes[i];
        strMake += temp["Make"] = "Colt";
        makes[i] = temp;
    }
}
```

The DataRow class also provides the BeginEdit(), EndEdit(), and CancelEdit() methods, which allow you to edit the content of a row while temporarily suspending any associated validation rules. In the previous logic, each row was validated with each assignment. (Also, if you capture any events from the DataRow, they fire with each modification.) When you call BeginEdit() on a given DataRow, the row is placed in edit mode. At this point you can make your changes as necessary and call either EndEdit() to commit these changes or CancelEdit() to roll back the changes to the original version. For example:

```
// Assume you have obtained a row to edit.
// Now place this row in edit mode'.
rowToUpdate.BeginEdit();

// Send the row to a helper function, which returns a Boolean.
if( ChangeValuesForThisRow( rowToUpdate) )
{
    rowToUpdate.EndEdit();    // OK!
}
else
{
    rowToUpdate.CancelEdit();  // Forget it.
}
```

Although you are free to manually call these methods on a given DataRow, these members are automatically called when you edit a DataGrid widget that has been bound to a DataTable. For example, when you select a row to edit from a DataGrid, that row is automatically placed in edit mode. When you shift focus to a new row, EndEdit() is called automatically. To test this behavior, assume you have manually updated each car to be of a given Make using the DataGrid (Figure 13-15).

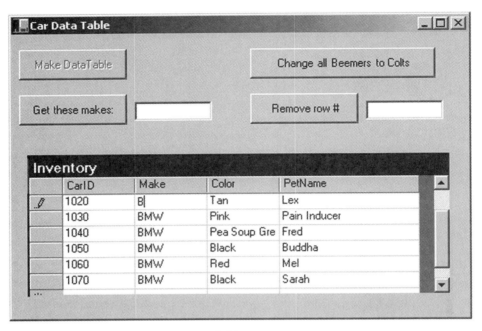

Figure 13-15. Editing rows in a DataGrid

If you now request all BMWs, the message box correctly returns *all* rows, as the underlying DataTable associated to the DataGrid has been automatically updated (Figure 13-16).

Figure 13-16. The Inventory DataTable

Understanding the DataView Type

In database nomenclature, a *view object* is a stylized representation of a table. For example, using Microsoft SQL Server, you could create a view for your current

Inventory table that returns a new table only containing automobiles of a given color. In ADO.NET, the DataView type allows you to programmatically extract a subset of data from the DataTable.

One great advantage of holding multiple views of the same table is that you can bind these views to various GUI widgets (such as the DataGrid). For example, one DataGrid might be bound to a DataView showing all autos in the Inventory, while another may be configured to display only green automobiles. On a related note, the DataTable type provides the DefaultView property that returns the default DataView for the table.

Here is an example. Your goal is to update the user interface of the current Windows Forms application to support two additional DataGrid types. One of these grids only shows the rows from the Inventory that match the filter Make='Colt'. The other grid only shows red automobiles (i.e., Color='Red'). Figure 13-17 shows the GUI update.

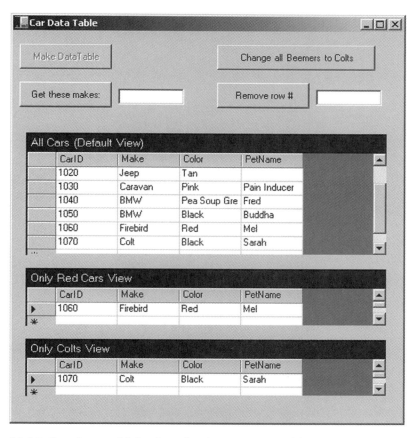

Figure 13-17. Creating multiple views for the Inventory table

To begin, you need to create two member variables of type DataView:

```
public class mainForm : System.Windows.Forms.Form
{
    // Views of the DataTable.
    DataView redCarsView;          // I only show red cars.
    DataView coltsView;            // I only show Colts.
...
}
```

Next, assume you have a new helper function named CreateViews(), which is called directly after the DataTable has been fully constructed, as shown here:

```
protected void btnMakeDataTable_Click (object sender, System.EventArgs e)
{
    // Make the data table.
    MakeTable();

    // Make views.
    CreateViews();
    ...
}
```

Here is the implementation of this new helper function. Notice that the constructor of each DataView has been passed the DataTable that will be used to build the custom set of data rows:

```
private void CreateViews()
{
    // Set the table that is used to construct these views.
    redCarsView = new DataView(inventoryTable);
    coltsView = new DataView(inventoryTable);

    // Now configure the views using a filter.
    redCarsView.RowFilter = "Color = 'red'";
    coltsView.RowFilter = "Make = 'colt'";

    // Bind to grids.
    RedCarViewGrid.DataSource = redCarsView;
    ColtsViewGrid.DataSource = coltsView;
}
```

As you can see, the DataView class supports a property named RowFilter, which contains the string representing the filtering criteria used to extract matching rows. Once you have your view established, set the grid's DataSource property accordingly. That's it! Because DataGrids are smart enough to detect changes to their underlying data source, if you click the Make Beemers Colts button, the ColtsViewGrid is updated automatically.

In addition to the RowFilter property, Table 13-8 describes some additional members of the DataView class.

Table 13-8. Members of the DataView Type

DATAVIEW MEMBER	MEANING IN LIFE
AddNew()	Adds a new row to the DataView.
AllowDelete AllowEdit AllowNew	Configure whether the DataView allows deleting, inserting, or updating of its rows.
Delete()	Deletes a row at the specified index.
RowFilter	Gets or sets the expression used to filter which rows are viewed in the DataView.
Sort	Gets or sets the sort column or columns and sort order for the table.
Table	Gets or sets the source DataTable.

SOURCE CODE *The complete CarDataTable project is included under the Chapter 13 subdirectory.*

Understanding the Role of the DataSet

You have been examining how to build a DataTable to represent a single table of data held in memory. Although DataTables can be used as stand-alone entities, they are more typically contained in a DataSet. In fact, most data access types supplied by ADO.NET only return a populated DataSet, not an individual DataTable.

Simply put, a DataSet is an in-memory representation of any number of tables (which may be just a single DataTable) as well as any (optional) relationships between these tables and any (optional) constraints. To gain a better understanding of the relationship among these core types, consider the logical hierarchy shown in Figure 13-18.

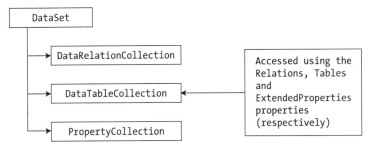

Figure 13-18. Collections of the DataSet

The Tables property of the DataSet allows you to access the DataTableCollection that contains the individual DataTables. Another important collection used by the DataSet is the DataRelationCollection. Given that a DataSet is a disconnected version of a database schema, it can programmatically represent the parent/child relationships between its tables.

For example, a relation can be created between two tables to model a foreign key constraint using the DataRelation type. This object can then be added to the DataRelationCollection through the Relations property. At this point, you can navigate between the connected tables as you search for data. You will see how this is done a bit later in the chapter.

The ExtendedProperties property provides access to the PropertyCollection type, which allows you to associate any extra information to the DataSet as name/value pairs. This information can literally be anything at all, even if it has no bearing on the data itself. For example, you can associate your company's name to a DataSet, which can then function as in-memory metadata, as shown here:

```
// Make a DataSet and add some metadata.
DataSet ds = new DataSet("MyDataSet");
ds.ExtendedProperties.Add("CompanyName", "Intertech, Inc");

// Print out the metadata.
Console.WriteLine(ds.ExtendedProperties["CompanyName"].ToString());
```

Other examples of extended properties might include an internal password that must be supplied to access the contents of the DataSet, a number representing a data refresh rate, and so forth. Be aware that the DataTable itself also supports the ExtendedProperties property.

Members of the DataSet

Before exploring too many other programmatic details, take a look at the public interface of the DataSet. The properties defined by the DataSet are centered on providing access to the internal collections, producing XML data representations and providing detailed error information. Table 13-9 describes some core properties of interest.

Table 13-9. Properties of the Mighty DataSet

DATASET PROPERTY	MEANING IN LIFE
CaseSensitive	Indicates whether string comparisons in DataTable objects are case-sensitive (or not).
DataSetName	Gets or sets the name of this DataSet. Typically this value is established as a constructor parameter.
DefaultViewManager	Establishes a custom view of the data in the DataSet.
EnforceConstraints	Gets or sets a value indicating whether constraint rules are followed when attempting any update operation.
HasErrors	Gets a value indicating whether there are errors in any of the rows in any of the tables of this DataSet.
Relations	Get the collection of relations that link tables and allow navigation from parent tables to child tables.
Tables	Provides access to the collection of tables maintained by the DataSet.

The methods of the DataSet mimic some of the functionality provided by the aforementioned properties. In addition to interacting with XML streams, other methods exist to allow you to copy the contents of your DataSet, as well as establish the beginning and ending points of a batch of updates. Table 13-10 describes some core methods.

Now that you have a better understanding of the role of the DataSet (and some idea what you can do with one), let's run through some specifics. Once this discussion of the ADO.NET DataSet is complete, the remainder of this chapter will focus on how to obtain DataSet types from external sources (such as a relational database) using the types defined by the System.Data.SqlClient and System.Data.OleDb namespaces.

Building an In-Memory DataSet

To illustrate the use of a DataSet, create a new Windows Forms application that maintains a single DataSet, containing three DataTable objects named Inventory,

Table 13-10. Methods of the Mighty DataSet

DATASET METHOD	MEANING IN LIFE
AcceptChanges()	Commits all the changes made to this DataSet since it was loaded or the last time AcceptChanges() was called.
Clear()	Completely clears the DataSet data by removing every row in each table.
Clone()	Clones the structure of the DataSet, including all DataTables, as well as all relations and any constraints.
Copy()	Copies both the structure and data for this DataSet.
GetChanges()	Returns a copy of the DataSet containing all changes made to it since it was last loaded or since AcceptChanges() was called.
GetChildRelations()	Returns the collection of child relations that belong to a specified table.
GetParentRelations()	Gets the collection of parent relations that belong to a specified table.
HasChanges()	Overloaded. Gets a value indicating whether the DataSet has changes, including new, deleted, or modified rows.
Merge()	Overloaded. Merges this DataSet with a specified DataSet.
ReadXml() ReadXmlSchema()	Allow you to read XML data from a valid stream (file based, memory based, or network based) to the DataSet.
RejectChanges()	Rolls back all the changes made to this DataSet since it was created or the last time DataSet.AcceptChanges was called.
WriteXml() WriteXmlSchema()	Allow you to write the contents of a DataSet to a valid stream.

Customers, and Orders. The columns for each table will be minimal but complete, with one column marking the primary key for each table. Most importantly, you can model the parent/child relationships between the tables using the DataRelation type. Your goal is to build the database shown in Figure 13-19 in memory.

Here, the Inventory table is the parent table to the Orders table, which maintains a foreign key (CarID) column. Also, the Customers table is the parent table to the Orders table. (Again note the foreign key, CustID.) As you will soon see, when you add DataRelation types to your DataSet, they may be used to navigate between the tables to obtain and manipulate the related data.

To begin, assume you have added a set of member variables to your main Form, representing the individual DataTables and containing DataSet, as shown here:

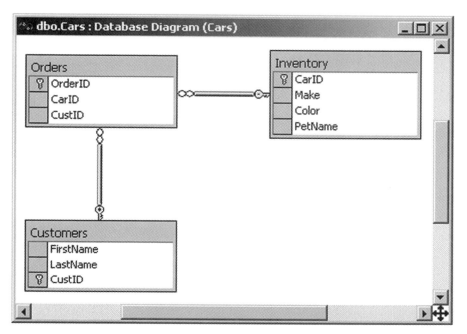

Figure 13-19. The In-Memory Automobile database

```
public class mainForm : System.Windows.Forms.Form
{
    // Inventory DataTable.
    private DataTable inventoryTable = new DataTable("Inventory");

    // Customers DataTable.
    private DataTable customersTable = new DataTable("Customers");

    // Orders DataTable.
    private DataTable ordersTable = new DataTable("Orders");

    // Our DataSet!
    private DataSet carsDataSet = new DataSet("CarDataSet");
...
}
```

Now, to keep things as OO as possible, build some (very) simple wrapper classes to represent a Car and Customer in the system. Note that the Customer class maintains a field that identifies the car a customer is interested in buying, as shown here:

```
public class Car
{
    // Make public for easy access.
    public string petName, make, color;
    public Car(string petName, string make, string color)
    {
        this.petName = petName;
        this.color = color;
        this.make = make;
    }
}

public class Customer
{
    public Customer(string fName, string lName, int currentOrder)
    {
        this.firstName= fName;
        this.lastName = lName;
        this.currCarOrder = currentOrder;
    }
    public string firstName, lastName;
    public int currCarOrder;
}
```

The main Form maintains two ArrayList types that hold a set of cars and customers, which are populated with some sample data in the scope of the Form's constructor. Next, the constructor calls a number of private helper functions to build the tables and their relationships. Finally, this method binds the Inventory and Customer DataTables to their corresponding DataGrid widgets. Notice that the following code binds a given DataTable in the DataSet using the SetDataBinding() method:

```
// Your list of Cars and Customers.
private ArrayList arTheCars, arTheCustomers;

public mainForm()
{
    // Fill the car array list with some cars.
    arTheCars = new ArrayList();
    arTheCars.Add(new Car("Chucky", "BMW", "Green"));
    . . .
```

```
    // Fill the other array list with some customers.
    arTheCustomers = new ArrayList();
    arTheCustomers.Add(new Customer("Dave", "Brenner", 1020));
    . . .


    // Make data tables (using the same techniques seen previously).
    MakeInventoryTable();
    MakeCustomerTable();
    MakeOrderTable();
    // Add relation (seen in just a moment).
    BuildTableRelationship();

    // Bind to grids (Param1 = DataSet, Param2 = name of table in DataSet).
    CarDataGrid.SetDataBinding(carsDataSet, "Inventory");
    CustomerDataGrid.SetDataBinding(carsDataSet, "Customers");
}
```

Each DataTables is constructed using the techniques examined earlier in this chapter. To keep focused on the DataSet logic, I will not repeat every detail of the table-building logic here. However, be aware that each table is assigned a primary key that is autoincremented. Here is some partial table-building logic (check out same code for complete details):

```
private void MakeOrderTable()
{
. . .
    // Add table to the DataSet.
    carsDataSet.Tables.Add(customersTable);

    // Create OrderID, CustID, CarID columns and add to table. . .
    // Make the ID column the primary key column. . .
    // Add some orders.
    for(int i = 0; i < arTheCustomers.Count; i++)
    {
        DataRow newRow;
        newRow = ordersTable.NewRow();
        Customer c = (Customer)arTheCustomers[i];
        newRow["CustID"] = i;
        newRow["CarID"] = c.currCarOrder;
        carsDataSet.Tables["Orders"].Rows.Add(newRow);
    }
}
```

The MakeInventoryTable() and MakeCustomerTable() helper functions behave almost identically.

Expressing Relations Using the DataRelation Type

The really interesting work happens in the BuildTableRelationship() helper function. Once a DataSet has been populated with a number of tables, you can *optionally* choose to programmatically model their parent/child relationships. Be aware that this is not mandatory. You can have a DataSet that does little else than hold a collection of DataTables in memory (even a single DataTable). However, when you do establish the interplay between your DataTables, you can navigate between them on the fly and collect any sort of information you may be interested in obtaining, all while disconnected from the data source.

The System.Data.DataRelation type is an OO wrapper around a table-to-table relationship. When you create a new DataRelation type, specify a friendly name, followed by the parent table (for example, Inventory) and the related child table (Orders). For a relationship to be established, each table must have an identically named column (CarID) of the same data type (Int32 in this case). In this light, a DataRelation is basically bound by the same rules as a relational database. Here is the complete implementation of the BuildTableRelationship() helper function:

```
private void BuildTableRelationship()
{
    // Create a DR obj.
    DataRelation dr = new DataRelation("CustomerOrder",
        carsDataSet.Tables["Customers"].Columns["CustID"],     // Parent.
        carsDataSet.Tables["Orders"].Columns["CustID"]);       // Child.

    // Add to the DataSet.
    carsDataSet.Relations.Add(dr);

    // Create another DR obj.
    dr = new DataRelation("InventoryOrder",
        carsDataSet.Tables["Inventory"].Columns["CarID"],      // Parent.
        carsDataSet.Tables["Orders"].Columns["CarID"]);        // Child.

    // Add to the DataSet.
    carsDataSet.Relations.Add(dr);
}
```

As you can see, a given DataRelation is held in the DataRelationCollection maintained by the DataSet. The DataRelation type offers a number of properties that allow you to obtain a reference to the child and/or parent table that is participating in the relationship, specify the name of the relationship, and so on. (See Table 13-11.)

Table 13-11. Properties of the DataRelation Type

DATARELATION PROPERTY	MEANING IN LIFE
ChildColumns ChildKeyConstraint ChildTable	Obtain information about the child table in this relationship as well as the table itself.
DataSet	Gets the DataSet to which the relations' collection belongs.
ParentColumns ParentKeyConstraint ParentTable	Obtain information about the parent table in this relationship as well as the table itself.
RelationName	Gets or sets the name used to look up this relation in the parent data set's DataRelationCollection.

Navigating Between Related Tables

To illustrate how a DataRelation allows you to move between related tables, extend your GUI to include a new Button type and a related TextBox. The end user is able to enter the ID of a customer and obtain all the information about that customer's order, which is placed in a simple message box (Figure 13-20).

Figure 13-20. Navigating data relations

The Button's Click event handler is as shown here (error checking removed for clarity):

```
protected void btnGetInfo_Click (object sender, System.EventArgs e)
{
    string strInfo = "";
    DataRow drCust = null;
    DataRow[] drsOrder = null;

    // Get the specified CustID from the TextBox.
    int theCust = int.Parse(this.txtCustID.Text);

    // Now based on CustID, get the correct row in Customers table.
    drCust = carsDataSet.Tables["Customers"].Rows[theCust];
    strInfo += "Cust #" + drCust["CustID"].ToString() + "\n";

    // Navigate from customer table to order table.
    drsOrder =   drCust.GetChildRows(carsDataSet.Relations["CustomerOrder"]);

    // Get customer name.
    foreach(DataRow r in drsOrder)
        strInfo += "Order Number: " + r["OrderID"] + "\n";

    // Now navigate from order table to inventory table.
    DataRow[] drsInv =
        drsOrder[0].GetParentRows(carsDataSet.Relations["InventoryOrder"]);

    // Get Car info.
    foreach(DataRow r in drsInv)
    {
        strInfo += "Make: " + r["Make"] + "\n";
        strInfo += "Color: " + r["Color"] + "\n";
        strInfo += "Pet Name: " + r["PetName"] + "\n";
    }
    MessageBox.Show(strInfo, "Info based on cust ID");
}
```

As you can see, the key to moving between data tables is to use a handful of methods defined by the DataRow type. Let's break this code down step by step. First, you obtain the correct customer ID from the text box and use it to grab the correct row in the Customers table (using the Rows property, of course), as shown here:

```
// Get the specified CustID from the TextBox.
int theCust = int.Parse(this.txtCustID.Text);
```

```
// Now based on CustID, get the correct row in Customers table.
DataRow drCust = null;
drCust = carsDataSet.Tables["Customers"].Rows[theCust];
strInfo += "Cust #" + drCust["CustID"].ToString() + "\n";
```

Next, you navigate from the Customers table to the Orders table, using the CustomerOrder data relation. Notice that the DataRow.GetChildRows() method allows you to grab rows from your child table, and once you do, you can read information out of the table, as shown here:

```
// Navigate from customer table to order table.
DataRow[] drsOrder = null;
drsOrder =   drCust.GetChildRows(carsDataSet.Relations["CustomerOrder"]);


// Get customer name.
foreach(DataRow r in drsOrder)
strInfo += "Order Number: " + r["OrderID"] + "\n";
```

Your final step is to navigate from the Orders table to its parent table (Inventory), using the GetParentRows() method. At this point, you can read information from the Inventory table using the Make, PetName, and Color columns, as shown here:

```
// Now navigate from order table to inventory table.
DataRow[] drsInv =
    drsOrder[0].GetParentRows(carsDataSet.Relations["InventoryOrder"]);

foreach(DataRow r in drsInv)
{
    strInfo += "Make: " + r["Make"] + "\n";
    strInfo += "Color: " + r["Color"] + "\n";
    strInfo += "Pet Name: " + r["PetName"] + "\n";
}
```

As a final example of navigating relations programmatically, the following code prints out the values in the Orders table that is obtained indirectly using the InventoryOrders relationship:

```
protected void btnGetChildRels_Click (object sender, System.EventArgs e)
{
    // Ask the CarsDataSet for the child relations of the inv. table.
    DataRelationCollection relCol;
    DataRow[] arrRows;
```

```
string info = "";
relCol = carsDataSet.Tables["inventory"].ChildRelations;

info += "\tRelation is called: " + relCol[0].RelationName + "\n\n";
// Now loop over each relation and print out info.
foreach(DataRelation dr in relCol)
{
    foreach(DataRow r in inventoryTable.Rows)
    {
        arrRows = r.GetChildRows(dr);

        // Print out the value of each column in the row.
        for (int i = 0; i < arrRows.Length; i++)
        {
            foreach(DataColumn dc in arrRows[i].Table.Columns )
            {
                info += "\t" + arrRows[i][dc];
            }
            info += "\n";
        }
    }
    MessageBox.Show(info,
            "Data in Orders Table obtained by child relations");
}
}
```

Figure 13-21 shows the output.

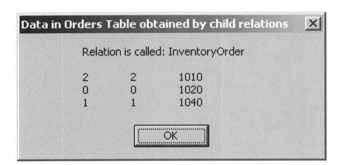

Figure 13-21. Navigating parent/child relations

Hopefully this last example has you convinced of the usefulness of the DataSet type. Given that a DataSet is completely disconnected from the underlying data source, you can work with an in-memory copy of data and navigate around each table to make any necessary updates, deletes, or inserts. Once this is done, you can submit your changes to the data store for processing. Of course you don't yet know how to get connected! There is one final item of interest regarding the DataSet before addressing this issue.

Reading and Writing XML-Based DataSets

A major design goal of ADO.NET was to apply a liberal use of XML infrastructure. Using the DataSet type, you can write an XML representation of the contents of your tables, relations, and other schematic details to a given stream (such as a file). To do so, simply call the WriteXml() method, as shown here:

```
protected void btnToXML_Click (object sender, System.EventArgs e)
{
    // Write your entire DataSet to a file in the app directory.
    carsDataSet.WriteXml("cars.xml");
    MessageBox.Show("Wrote CarDataSet to XML file in app directory");
    btnReadXML.Enabled = true;
}
```

If you now open your new file in the Visual Studio.NET IDE (Figure 13-22), you will see that the entire DataSet has been transformed to XML. (If you are not comfortable with XML syntax, don't sweat it. The DataSet understands XML just fine.)

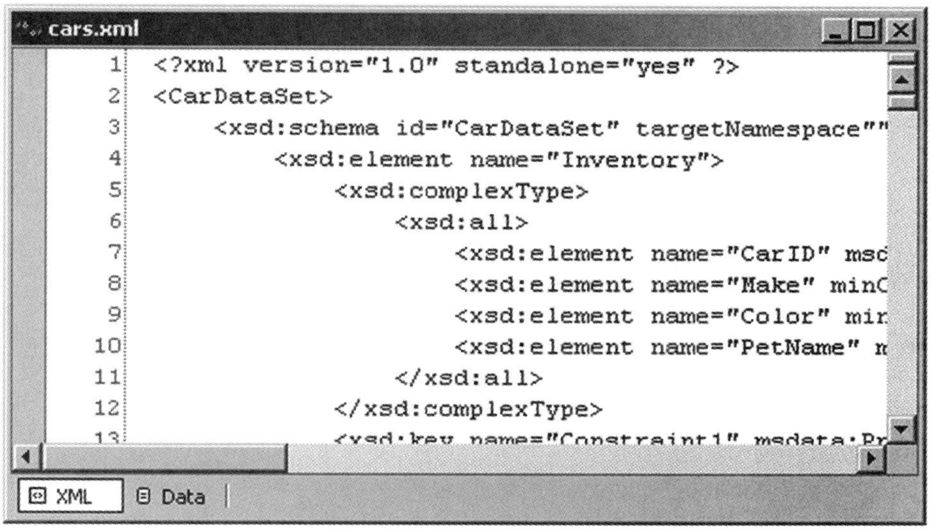

Figure 13-22. The DataSet as XML

To test the ReadXml() method of the DataSet, perform a little experiment. The CarDataSet application has a Button that will clear out the current DataSet completely (including all tables and relations). After the in-memory representation has been gutted, instruct the DataSet to read in the cars.xml file, which as you would guess restores the entire DataSet, as shown here:

```
protected void btnReadXML_Click (object sender, System.EventArgs e)
{
    // Kill current DataSet.
    carsDataSet.Clear();
    carsDataSet.Dispose();
    MessageBox.Show("Just cleared data set...");
    carsDataSet = new DataSet("CarDataSet");

    carsDataSet.ReadXml( "cars.xml" );

    MessageBox.Show("Reconstructed data set from XML file...");
    btnReadXML.Enabled = false;

    // Bind to grids.
    CarDataGrid.SetDataBinding(carsDataSet, "Inventory");
    CustomerDataGrid.SetDataBinding(carsDataSet, "Customers");
}
```

Be aware that under the hood, these XML-centric methods are using types defined in the System.Xml.dll assembly (specifically the XmlReader and XmlWriter classes). Therefore, in addition to setting a reference to this binary, you also need to make explicit reference to its types, as shown here:

```
// Need this namespace to call ReadXml() or WriteXml()!
using System.Xml;
```

Figure 13-23 shows your final product.

SOURCE CODE   *The CarDataSet application is included under the Chapter 13 subdirectory.*

Building a Simple Test Database

Now that you understand how to create and manipulate a DataSet in memory, you can get down to the business of making a data connection and seeing how to obtain a populated DataSet. In keeping with the automotive theme used

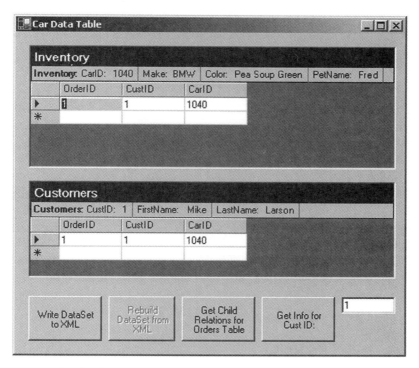

Figure 13-23. The final in-memory DataSet application

throughout this text, I have included two versions of a sample Cars database (available for download at www.apress.com) that models the Inventory, Orders, and Customers tables examined during the chapter.

The first version is a SQL script that builds the tables (including their relationships) and is intended for users of SQL Server 7.0 (and greater). To create the Cars database, begin by opening the Query Analyzer utility that ships with SQL Server. Next, connect to your machine and open the cars.sql file. Before you run the script, be sure that the path listed in the SQL file points to *your installation* of MS SQL Server. Thus, be sure you edit the following DDL (in bold) as necessary:

```
CREATE DATABASE [Cars]  ON (NAME = N'Cars_Data', FILENAME
=N' D:\MSSQL7\Data \Cars_Data.MDF' ,
SIZE = 2, FILEGROWTH = 10%)

LOG ON (NAME = N'Cars_Log', FILENAME
= N' D:\MSSQL7\Data\Cars_Log.LDF' ,
SIZE = 1, FILEGROWTH = 10%)
GO
```

Now run your script. Once you do, open up the SQL Server Enterprise Manager (Figure 13-24). You should see the Cars database with all three interrelated tables (with some sample data to boot).

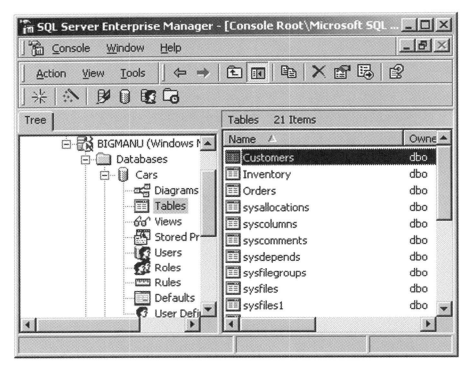

Figure 13-24. The SQL Server Cars database

The second version of the Cars database is for users of MS Access. Under the Access DB folder you will find the cars.mdb file, which contains the same information and underlying structure as the SQL Server version. During the remainder of this chapter, I will assume that you are connecting to the SQL Server Cars database rather than the Access equivalent. In just a bit, however, you will see how to configure an ADO.NET connection string to hook into an *.mdb file.

ADO.NET Managed Providers

If you are coming to ADO.NET from a classic ADO background, you can assume that a managed provider is the .NET equivalent of an OLE DB provider. In other words, the managed provider is your gateway between a raw data store and a populated DataSet.

As mentioned earlier in this chapter, ADO.NET ships with two canned managed providers. The first of these is the OleDb managed provider, which is composed of the types defined in the System.Data.OleDb namespace. The OleDb provider allows you to access data located in any data store that supports the OLE DB protocol. Thus, like with classic ADO, you may use the ADO.NET managed provider to access SQL Server, Oracle, or MS Access databases. Because the types in the System.Data.OleDb namespace must communicate with unmanaged code (e.g., the OLE DB providers), you need to be aware that a number of .NET to COM translations occur behind the scenes, which can affect performance.

The other managed provider (the SQL provider) offers direct access to MS SQL Server data stores, and *only* SQL Server data stores (version 7.0 and greater). The System.Data.SqlClient namespace contains the types used by the SQL provider and provides the same functionality as the OleDb provider. In fact, for the most part, both namespaces have similarly named items. The key difference is that the SQL provider does not use the OLE DB or classic ADO protocols and thus offers numerous performance benefits.

Recall that the System.Data.Common namespace defines a number of abstract types that provide a common interface for each managed provider. First, each defines an implementation of the IDbConnection interface, which is used to configure and open a session with the data store. Objects that implement the IDbCommand interface are used to issue SQL queries against the database. Next is IDataReader, which allows you to read data using a forward-only, read-only cursor. Last but not least are types that implement IDbDataAdapter, which are responsible for populating a DataSet on behalf of the interested client.

For the most part you will not need to interact with the System.Data.Common namespace directly. However, to use either provider requires that you specify the proper using directive, as shown here:

```
// Going to access an OLE DB compliant data source.
using System.Data;
using System.Data.OleDb;

// Going to access SQL Server (7.0 or greater).
using System.Data;
using System.Data.SqlClient;
```

Working with the OleDb Managed Provider

Once you are comfortable with one managed provider, you can easily manipulate other providers. Begin by examining how to connect using the OleDb managed provider. When you need to connect to any data source other than MS SQL Server, you will use the types defined in System.Data.OleDb. Table 13-12 provides a walkthrough of the core types.

Table 13-12. Types of the System.Data.OleDb Namespace

SYSTEM.DATA.OLEDB TYPE	MEANING IN LIFE
OleDbCommand	Represents a SQL query command to be made to a data source.
OleDbConnection	Represents an open connection to a data source.
OleDbDataAdapter	Represents a set of data commands and a database connection are used to fill the DataSet and update the data source.
OleDbDataReader	Provides a way of reading a forward-only stream of data records from a data source.
OleDbErrorCollection OleDbError OleDbException	OleDbErrorCollection maintains a collection of warnings or errors returned by the data source, each of which is represented by an OleDbError type. When an error is encountered, an exception of type OleDbException is thrown.
OleDbParameterCollection OleDbParameter	Much like classic ADO, the OleDbParameterCollection collection holds onto the parameters sent to a stored procedure in the database. Each parameter is of type OleDbParameter.

Establishing a Connection Using the OleDbConnection Type

The first step to take when working with the OleDb managed provider is to establish a session with the data source using the OleDbConnection type. Much like the classic ADO Connection object, OleDbConnection types are provided with a formatted connection string, containing a number of name/value pairs. This information is used to identify the name of the machine you wish to connect to, required security settings, the name of the database on that machine, and, most importantly, the name of the OLE DB provider. (See online help for a full description of each name/value pair.)

The connection string may be set using the OleDbConnection. ConnectionString property or as a constructor argument. Assume you wish to connect to the Cars database on a machine named BIGMANU using the SQL OLE DB provider. The following logic does the trick:

```
// Build a connection string.
OleDbConnection cn = new OleDbConnection();
```

```
cn.ConnectionString = "Provider=SQLOLEDB.1;" +          // Which provider?
                      "Integrated Security=SSPI;" +
                      "Persist Security Info=False;" +   // Persist security?
                      "Initial Catalog=Cars;" +          // Name of database.
                      "Data Source=BIGMANU;";            // Name of machine.
```

As you can infer from the preceding code comments, the Initial Catalog name refers to the database you are attempting to establish a session with (Pubs, Northwind, Cars, and so on). The Data Source name identifies the name of the machine that maintains the database. The final point of interest is the Provider segment, which specifies the name of the OLE DB provider that will be used to access the data store. Table 13-13 describes some possible values.

Table 13-13. Core OLE DB providers

PROVIDER SEGMENT VALUE	MEANING IN LIFE
Microsoft.JET.OLEDB.4.0	You want to use the Jet OLE DB provider to connect to an Access database.
MSDAORA	You want to use the OLE DB provider for Oracle.
SQLOLEDB	You want to use the OLE DB provider for MS SQL Server.

Once you have configured the connection string, the next step is to open a session with the data source, do some work, and release your connection to the data source, as shown here:

```
// Build a connection string (can specify User ID and Password if needed).
OleDbConnection cn = new OleDbConnection();
cn.ConnectionString =   "Provider=SQLOLEDB.1;" +          // Which provider?
                        "Integrated Security=SSPI;" +
                        "Persist Security Info=False;" +   // Persist security?
                        "Initial Catalog=Cars;" +          // Name of database.
                        "Data Source=BIGMANU;";            // Name of machine.
cn.Open();
    // Do some interesting work here.
cn.Close();
```

In addition to the ConnectionString, Open(), and Close() members, the OleDbConnection class provides a number of members that let you configure attritional settings regarding your connection, such as timeout settings and transactional information. Table 13-14 gives a partial rundown.

Table 13-14. Members of the OleDbConnection Type

OLEDBCONNECTION MEMBER	MEANING IN LIFE
BeginTransaction() CommitTransaction() RollbackTransaction()	Used to programmatically commit, abort, or roll back a current transaction.
Close()	Closes the connection to the data source. This is the preferred method.
ConnectionString	Gets or sets the string used to open a session with a data store.
ConnectionTimeout	Gets or sets the time to wait while establishing a connection before terminating the attempt and generating an error. The default value is 15 seconds.
Database	Gets or sets the name of the current database or the database to be used once a connection is open.
DataSource	Gets or sets the name of the database to connect to.
Open()	Opens a database connection with the current property settings.
Provider	Gets or sets the name of the provider.
State	Gets the current state of the connection.

Building a SQL Command

The OleDbCommand class is an OO representation of a SQL query, which is manipulated using the CommandText property. Many types in the ADO.NET namespace require an OleDbCommand as a method parameter to send the request to the data source. In addition to holding the raw SQL query, the OleDbCommand type defines other members that allow you to configure various characteristics of the query (Table 13-15).

Working with the OleDbCommand type is very simple, and like with the OleDbConnection object, there are numerous ways to achieve the same end result. As an example, note the following (semantically identical) ways to configure a SQL query using an active OleDbConnection object. In each case, assume you already have an OleDbConnection named cn:

```
// Specify a SQL command (take one).
string strSQL1 = "Select Make from Inventory where Color='Red'";
OleDbCommand myCommand1 = new OleDbCommand(strSQL1, cn);
```

```
// Specify SQL command (take two).
string strSQL2 = "Select Make from Inventory where Color='Red'";
OleDbCommand myCommand2 = new OleDbCommand();
myCommand.Connection = cn;
myCommand.CommandText = strSQL2;
```

Table 13-15. Members of the OleDbCommand Type

OLEDBCOMMAND MEMBER	MEANING IN LIFE
Cancel()	Cancels the execution of a command.
CommandText	Gets or sets the SQL command text or the provider-specific syntax to run against the data source.
CommandTimeout	Gets or sets the time to wait while executing the command before terminating the attempt and generating an error. The default is 30 seconds.
CommandType	Gets or sets how the CommandText property is interpreted.
Connection	Gets or sets the OleDbConnection used by this instance of the OleDbCommand.
ExecuteReader()	Returns an instance of an OleDbDataReader.
Parameters	Gets the collection of OleDbParameterCollection.
Prepare()	Creates a prepared (or compiled) version of the command on the data source.

Working with the OleDbDataReader

Once you have established the active connection and SQL command, the next step is to submit the query to the data source. There are a number of ways to do so. The OleDbDataReader type is the simplest, fastest, but least flexible way to obtain information from a data store. This class represents a read-only, forward-only stream of data returned one record at a time as a result of a SQL command.

The OleDbDataReader is useful when you need to iterate over large amounts of data very quickly and have no need to work an in-memory DataSet representation. For example, if you request 20,000 records from a table to store in a text file, it would be rather memory intensive to hold this information in a DataSet. A better approach would be to create a data reader that spins over each record as rapidly as possible. Be aware however, that DataReaders (unlike DataSets) maintain a connection to their data source until you explicitly close the session.

To illustrate, the following class issues a simple SQL query against the Cars database, using the ExecuteReader() method of the OleDbCommand type. Using the Read() method of the returned OleDbDataReader, we dump each member to the standard IO stream:

```
public class OleDbDR
{
    static void Main(string[] args)
    {
        // Step 1: Make a connection.
        OleDbConnection cn = new OleDbConnection();
        cn.ConnectionString = "Provider=SQLOLEDB.1;" +
            "Integrated Security=SSPI;" +
            "Persist Security Info=False;" +
            "Initial Catalog=Cars;" +
            "Data Source=BIGMANU;";
        cn.Open();

        // Step 2: Create a SQL command.
        string strSQL = "SELECT Make FROM Inventory WHERE Color='Red'";
        OleDbCommand myCommand = new OleDbCommand(strSQL, cn);

        // Step 3: Obtain a data reader ala ExecuteReader().
        OleDbDataReader myDataReader;
        myDataReader = myCommand.ExecuteReader();

        // Step 4: Loop over the results.
        while (myDataReader.Read())
        {
            Console.WriteLine("Red car: " +
                myDataReader["Make"].ToString());
        }

        myDataReader.Close();
        cn.Close();
    }
}
```

The result is the listing of all red automobiles in the Cars database (Figure 13-25).

Recall that DataReaders are forward-only, read-only streams of data. Therefore, there is no way to navigate around the contents of the OleDbDataReader. All you can do is read each record and use it in your application:

```
// Get the value in the 'Make' column.
Console.WriteLine("Red car: {0}", myDataReader["Make"].ToString());
```

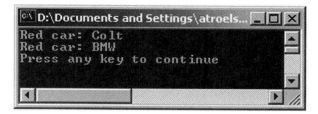

Figure 13-25. The OleDbDataReader in action

When you are finished using the DataReader, make sure to terminate the session using the appropriately named method, Close(). In addition to the Read() and Close() methods, there are a number of other methods that allow you to obtain a value from a specified column in a given format (e.g., GetBoolean(), GetByte(), and so forth). Also, the FieldCount property returns the number of columns in the current record, and so forth.

SOURCE CODE   *The OleDbDataReader application is included under the Chapter 13 subdirectory.*

Connecting to an Access Database

Now that you know how to pull data from SQL Server, let's take a moment to see how to obtain data from an Access database. To illustrate, let's modify the previous OleDbDataReader application to read from the cars.mdb file.

Much like classic ADO, the process of connecting to an Access database using ADO.NET requires little more than retrofitting your construction string. First, set the Provider segment to the JET engine, rather than SQLOLEDB. Beyond this adjustment, set the data source segment to point to the path of your *.mdb file, as shown here:

```
// Be sure to update the data source segment if necessary!
OleDbConnection cn = new OleDbConnection();
cn.ConnectionString = "Provider=Microsoft.JET.OLEDB.4.0;" +
                      @"data source = D:\Chapter 13\Access DB\cars.mdb";
 cn.Open();
```

Once the connection has been made, you can read and manipulate the contents of your data table. The only other point to be aware of is that, given that the use of the JET engine requires OLEDB, you must use the types defined in the System.Data.OleDb namespace (e.g., the OleDb managed provider). Remember, the SQL provider only allows you to access MS SQL Server data stores!

Executing a Stored Procedure

When you are constructing a distributed application, one of the design choices you face is where to store the business logic. One approach is to build reusable binary code libraries, which can be managed by a surrogate process such as the Windows 2000 Component Services manager. Another approach is to place the system's business logic on the data layer in the form of stored procedures. Yet another approach is to supply a blend of each technique.

A stored procedure is a named block of SQL code stored at the database. Stored procedures can be constructed to return a set of rows (or native data types) to the calling component and may take any number of optional parameters. The end result is a unit of work that behaves like a typical function, with the obvious differences of being located on a data store rather than a binary business object.

Let's add a simple stored procedure to the existing Cars database called GetPetName, which takes an input parameter of type integer. (If you ran the supplied SQL script, this stored proc is already defined.) This is the numerical ID of the car for which you are interested in obtaining the pet name, which is returned as an output parameter of type char. Here is the syntax:

```
CREATE PROCEDURE GetPetName
    @carID int,
    @petName char(20) output
AS
SELECT @petName = PetName from Inventory where CarID = @carID
```

Now that you have a stored procedure in place, let's see the code necessary to execute it. Begin as always by creating a new OleDbConnection, configure your connection string, and open the session. Next, create a new OleDbCommand type, making sure to specify the name of the stored procedure and setting the CommandType property accordingly, as shown here:

```
// Open connection to data store.
OleDbConnection cn = new OleDbConnection();
cn.ConnectionString = "Provider=SQLOLEDB.1;" + "Integrated Security=SSPI;" +
                      "Persist Security Info=False;" + "Initial Catalog=Cars;" +
                      "Data Source=BIGMANU;";
cn.Open();


// Make a command object for the stored proc.
OleDbCommand myCommand = new OleDbCommand("GetPetName", cn);
myCommand.CommandType = CommandType.StoredProcedure;
```

The CommandType property of the OleDbCommand class can be set using any of the values specified in the related CommandType enumeration (Table 13-16).

Table 13-16. Values of the CommandType Enumeration

COMMANDTYPE ENUMERATION VALUE	MEANING IN LIFE
StoredProcedure	Used to configure an OleDbCommand that triggers a stored procedure.
TableDirect	The OleDbCommand represents a table name whose columns are all returned.
Text	The OleDbCommand type contains a standard SQL text command. This is the default value.

When you issue basic SQL queries (e.g., "SELECT * FROM Inventory") to the data source, the default CommandType.Text setting is appropriate. However, to issue a command to hit a stored procedure, specify CommandType. StoredProcedure.

Specifying Parameters Using the OleDbParameter Type

The next task is to establish the parameters used for the call. The OleDbParameter type is an OO wrapper around a particular parameter passed to (or received from) the stored procedure. This class maintains a number of properties that allow you to configure the name, size, and data type of the parameter, as well as its direction of travel. Table 13-17 describes some key properties of the OleDbParameter type.

Given that you have one input and one output parameter, you can configure your types as so. Note that you then add these items to the OleDbCommand type's ParametersCollection (which is, of course, accessed via the Parameters property):

```
// Create the parameters for the call.
OleDbParameter theParam = new OleDbParameter();

// Input.
theParam.ParameterName = "@carID";
theParam.DbType = OleDbType.Integer;
theParam.Direction = ParameterDirection.Input;
theParam.Value = 1;                          // Car ID = 1.
myCommand.Parameters.Add(theParam);
```

```
// Output.
theParam = new OleDbParameter();
theParam.ParameterName = "@petName";
theParam.DbType = OleDbType.Char;
theParam.Size = 20;
theParam.Direction = ParameterDirection.Output;
myCommand.Parameters.Add(theParam);
```

The final step is to execute the command using OleDbCommand.ExecuteNonQuery(). Notice that the Value property of the OleDbParameter type is accessed to obtain the returned pet name, as shown here:

```
// Execute the stored procedure!
myCommand.ExecuteNonQuery();
```

```
// Display the result.
Console.WriteLine("Stored Proc Info:");
Console.WriteLine("Car ID: " + myCommand.Parameters["@carID"].Value);
Console.WriteLine("PetName: " + myCommand.Parameters["@petName"].Value);
```

Table 13-17. Members of the OleDbParameter Type

OLEDBPARAMETER PROPERTY	MEANING IN LIFE
DataType	Establishes the type of the parameter, in terms of .NET.
DbType	Gets or sets the native data type from the data source, using the OleDbType enumeration.
Direction	Gets or sets whether the parameter is input only, output only, bidirectional, or a return value parameter.
IsNullable	Gets or sets whether the parameter accepts null values.
ParameterName	Gets or sets the name of the OleDbParameter.
Precision	Gets or sets the maximum number of digits used to represent the Value.
Scale	Gets or sets the number of decimal places to which Value is resolved.
Size	Gets or sets the maximum parameter size of the data.
Value	Gets or sets the value of the parameter.

Figure 13-26 shows the output.

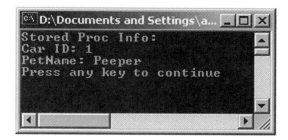

Figure 13-26. Triggering the stored procedure

SOURCE CODE   *The OleDbStoredProc project is included under the Chapter 13 subdirectory.*

The Role of the OleDbDataAdapter Type

At this point you should understand how to connect to a data source using the OleDbConnection type, issue a command (using the OleDbCommand and OleDbParameter types), and work with the OleDbDataReader. This is just fine when you want to iterate over a batch of data very quickly or trigger a stored procedure. However, the most flexible way to obtain a complete DataSet from the data store is through the use of the OleDbDataAdapter.

In a nutshell, this type pulls information from a data store and populates a DataTable in a DataSet using the OleDbDataAdapter.Fill() method, which has been overloaded a number of times. Here are a few possibilities (FYI, the integer return type holds the number of records returned):

```
// Fills the data set with records from a given source table.
public int Fill(DataSet yourDS, string tableName);

// Fills the data set with the records located between
// the given bounds from a given source table.
public int Fill(DataSet yourDS, string tableName,
                int startRecord, int maxRecord);
```

Before you can call this method, you need a valid OleDbDataAdapter object reference. The constructor has also been overloaded a number of times, but in general you need to supply the connection information and the SQL SELECT statement used to fill the DataTable.

The OleDbDataAdapter type not only is the entity that fills the tables of a DataSet on your behalf, but also is in charge of maintaining a set of core SQL statements used to push updates back to the data store. Table 13-18 describes some core members of the OleDbDataAdapter type.

Table 13-18. Core Members of the OleDbDataAdapter

OLEDBDATAADAPTER MEMBER	MEANING IN LIFE
DeleteCommand InsertCommand SelectCommand UpdateCommand	Used to establish SQL commands that will be issued to the data store when the Update() method is called. Each of these properties is set using an OleDbCommand type.
Fill()	Fills a given table in the DataSet with some number of records.
GetFillParameters()	Returns all parameters used when performing the select command.
Update()	Calls the respective INSERT, UPDATE, or DELETE statements for each inserted, updated, or deleted row for a given table in the DataSet.

The key properties of the OleDbDataAdapter (as well as the SqlDataAdapter) are DeleteCommand, InsertCommand, SelectCommand, and UpdateCommand. A data adapter understands how to submit changes on behalf of a given command. For example, when you call Update(), the data adapter uses the SQL commands stored in each of these properties automatically. As you will see, the amount of code required to configure these properties is a bit on the verbose side. Before you check these properties out firsthand, let's begin by learning how to use a data adapter to fill a DataSet programmatically.

Filling a DataSet Using the OleDbDataAdapter Type

The following code populates a DataSet (containing a single table) using an OleDbDataAdapter:

```
public class MyOleDbDataAdapter
{
    // Step 1: Open a connection to Cars db.
    OleDbConnection cn = new OleDbConnection();
    cn.ConnectionString = "Provider=SQLOLEDB.1;" +
                    "Integrated Security=SSPI;" +
                    "Persist Security Info=False;" +
                    "Initial Catalog=Cars;" +
                    "Data Source=BIGMANU;";
    cn.Open();
```

```
// Step 2: Create data adapter using the following SELECT.
string sqlSELECT = "SELECT * FROM Inventory";
OleDbDataAdapter dAdapt = new OleDbDataAdapter(sqlSELECT, cn);

// Step 3: Create and fill the DataSet, close connection.
DataSet myDS = new DataSet("CarsDataSet");
try
{
    dAdapt.Fill(myDS, "Inventory");
}
catch(Exception ex)
{
    Console.WriteLine(ex.Message);
}
finally
{
    cn.Close();
}

// Private helper function.
PrintTable(myDS);
return 0;
}
```

Notice that unlike your work during the first half of this chapter, you did *not* manually direct a DataTable type and add it to the DataSet. Rather, you specified the Inventory table as the second parameter to the Fill() method. Internally, Fill() builds the DataTable given the name of the table in the data store using the SELECT command. In this iteration, the connection between the given SQL SELECT statement and the OleDbDataAdapter was established as a constructor parameter:

```
// Create a SELECT command as string type.
string sqlSELECT = "SELECT * FROM Inventory";
OleDbDataAdapter dAdapt = new OleDbDataAdapter(sqlSELECT, cn);
```

As a more OO-aware alternative, you can use the OleDbCommand type to hold onto the SELECT statement. To associate the OleDbCommand to the OleDbDataAdapter, use the SelectCommand property, as shown here:

```
// Create a SELECT command object.
OleDbCommand selectCmd = new OleDbCommand("SELECT * FROM Inventory", cn);
```

```
// Make a data adapter and associate commands.
OleDbDataAdapter dAdapt = new OleDbDataAdapter();
dAdapt.SelectCommand = selectCmd;
```

Notice that in this case, you attach the active OleDbConnection as a parameter to the OleDbCommand. Figure 13-27 shows the end result.

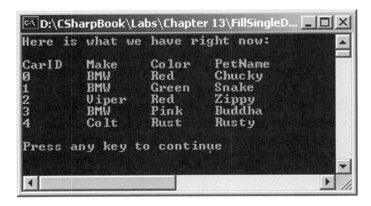

Figure 13-27. The OleDbDataAdapter in action

The PrintTable() method is little more than some formatting razzle-dazzle:

```
public static void PrintTable(DataSet ds)
{
    // Get Inventory table from DataSet.
    Console.WriteLine("Here is what we have right now:\n");
    DataTable invTable = ds.Tables["Inventory"];

    // Print the Column names.
    for(int curCol= 0; curCol< invTable.Columns.Count; curCol++)
    {
        Console.Write(invTable.Columns[curCol].ColumnName.Trim() + "\t");
    }
    Console.WriteLine();

    // Print each cell.
    for(int curRow = 0; curRow < invTable.Rows.Count; curRow++)
    {
        for(int curCol= 0; curCol< invTable.Columns.Count; curCol++)
        {
            Console.Write(invTable.Rows[curRow][curCol].ToString().Trim()
                    + "\t");
        }
```

```
        Console.WriteLine();
    }
}
```

SOURCE CODE   *The FillSingleDSWithAdapter project is under the Chapter 13 subdirectory.*

Working with the SQL Managed Provider

Before you see the details of inserting, updating, and removing records using a data adapter, I would like to introduce the SQL managed provider. As you recall, the OleDb provider allows you to access any OLE DB compliant data store, but is less optimized than the SQL provider.

When you know that the data source you need to manipulate is MS SQL Server, you will find performance gains if you use the System.Data.SqlClient namespace directly. Collectively, these classes constitute the functionality of the SQL managed provider, which should look very familiar given your work with the OleDb provider (Table 13-19).

Table 13-19. Core Types of the System.Data.SqlClient Namespace

SYSTEM.DATA.SQLCLIENT TYPE	MEANING IN LIFE
SqlCommand	Represents a Transact-SQL query to execute at a SQL Server data source.
SqlConnection	Represents an open connection to a SQL Server data source.
SqlDataAdapter	Represents a set of data commands and a database connection used to fill the DataSet and update the SQL Server data source.
SqlDataReader	Provides a way of reading a forward-only stream of data records from a SQL Server data source.
SqlErrors SqlError SqlException	SqlErrors maintains a collection of warnings or errors returned by SQL Server, each of which is represented by a SQLError type. When an error is encountered, an exception of type SQLException is thrown.
SqlParameterCollection SqlParameter	SqlParametersCollection holds onto the parameters sent to a stored procedure held in the database. Each parameter is of type SQLParameter.

Given that working with these types is almost identical to working with the OleDb managed provider, you should already know what to do with these types, as they have the same public interface. To help you get comfortable with this new set of types, the remainder of the examples use the SQL managed provider.

The `System.Data.SqlTypes` Namespace

On a quick related note, when you use the SQL managed provider, you also have the luxury of using a number of managed types that represent native SQL server data types. Table 13-20 gives a quick rundown.

Table 13-20. Types of the System.Data.SqlTypes Namespace

SYSTEM.DATA.SQLTYPES WRAPPER	NATIVE SQL SERVER
SqlBinary	binary, varbinary, timestamp, image
SqlInt64	bigint
SqlBit	bit
SqlDateTime	datetime, smalldatetime
SqlNumeric	decimal
SqlDouble	float
SqlInt32	int
SqlMoney	money, smallmoney
SqlString	nchar, ntext, nvarchar, sysname, text, varchar, char
SqlNumeric	numeric
SqlSingle	real
SqlInt16	smallint
System.Object	sql_variant
SqlByte	tinyint
SqlGuid	uniqueidentifier

Inserting New Records Using the `SqlDataAdapter`

Now that you have flipped from the OleDb provider to the realm of the SQL provider, you can return to the task of understanding the role of data adapters. Let's examine how to insert new records in a given table using the SqlDataAdapter (which would be nearly identical to using the OleDbDataAdapter). As always, begin by creating an active connection, as shown here:

```
public class MySqlDataAdapter
{
    public static void Main()
```

```
        {
              // Step 1: Create a connection and adapter (with select command).
              SqlConnection cn = new
                    SqlConnection("server=(local);uid=sa;pwd=;database=Cars");

              SqlDataAdapter dAdapt = new
                    SqlDataAdapter("Select * from Inventory", cn);

              // Step 2: Kill record you inserted.
              cn.Open();
              SqlCommand killCmd = new
                    SqlCommand("Delete from Inventory where CarID = '1111'", cn);
              killCmd.ExecuteNonQuery();
              cn.Close();
        }
}
```

You can see that the connection string has cleaned up quite a bit. In particular, notice that you do not need to define a Provider segment (as the SQL types only talk to a SQL server!). Next, create a new SqlDataAdapter and specify the value of the SelectCommand property as a constructor parameter (just like with the OleDbDataAdapter).

The second step is really more of a good housekeeping chore. Here, you create a new SqlCommand type that will destroy the record you are about to enter (to avoid a primary key violation). The next step is a bit more involved. Your goal is to create a new SQL statement that will function as the SqlDataAdapter's InsertCommand. First, create the new SqlCommand and specify a standard SQL insert, followed by SqlParameter types describing each column in the Inventory table, as shown here:

```
public static void Main()
{
    ...
    // Step 3: Build the insert Command!
    dAdapt.InsertCommand = new SqlCommand("INSERT INTO Inventory" +
        "(CarID, Make, Color, PetName) VALUES" +
        "(@CarID, @Make, @Color, @PetName)", cn)";

    // Step 4: Build parameters for each column in Inventory table.
    SqlParameter workParam = null;
```

```
    // CarID.
    workParam = dAdapt.InsertCommand.Parameters.Add(new
        SqlParameter("@CarID", SqlDbType.Int));
    workParam.SourceColumn = "CarID";
    workParam.SourceVersion = DataRowVersion.Current;

    // Make.
    workParam = dAdapt.InsertCommand.Parameters.Add(new
        SqlParameter("@Make", SqlDbType.VarChar));
    workParam.SourceColumn = "Make";
    workParam.SourceVersion = DataRowVersion.Current;

    // Color.
    workParam = dAdapt.InsertCommand.Parameters.Add(new
        SqlParameter("@Color", SqlDbType.VarChar));
    workParam.SourceColumn = "Color";
    workParam.SourceVersion = DataRowVersion.Current;
// PetName.
    workParam = dAdapt.InsertCommand.Parameters.Add(new
        SqlParameter("@PetName", SqlDbType.VarChar));
    workParam.SourceColumn = "PetName";
    workParam.SourceVersion = DataRowVersion.Current;
}
```

Now that you have formatted each of the parameters, the final step is to fill the DataSet and add your new row (note that the PrintTable() helper function has carried over to this example):

```
public static void Main()
{
    ...
    // Step 5: Fill data set.
    DataSet myDS = new DataSet();
    dAdapt.Fill(myDS, "Inventory");
    PrintTable(myDS);

    // Step 6: Add new row.
    DataRow newRow = myDS.Tables["Inventory"].NewRow();
    newRow["CarID"] = 1111;
    newRow["Make"] = "SlugBug";
    newRow["Color"] = "Pink";
    newRow["PetName"] = "Cranky";
    myDS.Tables["Inventory"].Rows.Add(newRow);
```

```
// Step 7: Send back to database and reprint.
try
{
    dAdapt.Update(myDS, "Inventory");
    myDS.Dispose();
    myDS = new DataSet();
    dAdapt.Fill(myDS, "Inventory");
    PrintTable(myDS);
}
catch(Exception e){ Console.Write(e.ToString()); }
}
```

When you run the application, you see the output shown in Figure 13-28.

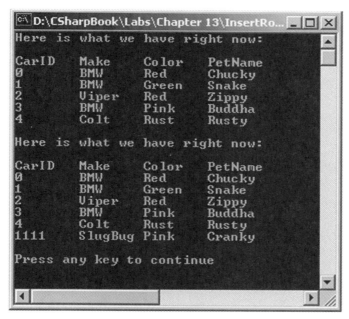

Figure 13-28. The InsertCommand Property in action

SOURCE CODE   *The InsertRowsWithSqlAdapter project can be found under the Chapter 13 subdirectory.*

Updating Existing Records Using the SqlDataAdapter

Now that you can insert new rows, look at how you can update existing rows. Again, start the process by obtaining a connection (using the SqlConnection type) and creating a new SqlDataAdapter. Next set the value of the

UpdateCommand property, using the same general approach as when setting the value of the InsertCommand. Here is the relevant code in Main():

```
public static void Main()
{
    // Step 1: Create a connection and adapter (same as previous code)
    . . .

    // Step 2: Establish the UpdateCommand.
    dAdapt.UpdateCommand = new SqlCommand
        ("UPDATE Inventory SET Make = @Make, Color = " +
        "@Color, PetName = @PetName " +
        "WHERE CarID = @CarID" , cn);

    // Step 3: Build parameters for each column in Inventory table.
    // Same as before, but now you are populating the ParameterCollection
    // of the UpdateCommand.  For example:
    SqlParameter workParam = null;
    workParam = dAdapt.UpdateCommand.Parameters.Add(new
        SqlParameter("@CarID", SqlDbType.Int));
    workParam.SourceColumn = "CarID";
    workParam.SourceVersion = DataRowVersion.Current;

    // Do the same for PetName, Make, and Color params.

    // Step 4: Fill data set.
    DataSet myDS = new DataSet();
    dAdapt.Fill(myDS, "Inventory");
    PrintTable(myDS);

    // Step 5: Change columns in second row to 'FooFoo'.
    DataRow changeRow = myDS.Tables["Inventory"].Rows[1];
    changeRow["Make"] = "FooFoo";
    changeRow["Color"] = "FooFoo";
    changeRow["PetName"] = "FooFoo";

    // Step 6: Send back to database and reprint.
    try
    {
        dAdapt.Update(myDS, "Inventory");
        myDS.Dispose();
        myDS = new DataSet();
        dAdapt.Fill(myDS, "Inventory");
        PrintTable(myDS);
    }
```

```
        catch(Exception e)
        { Console.Write(e.ToString()); }
}
```

Figure 13-29 shows the output.

```
D:\CSharpBook\Labs\Chapter 13\Upd...  _ □ ×
Here  is  what  we  have  right  now:

CarID     Make        Color       PetName
0         BMW         Red         Chucky
1         FooFoo      Green       Snake
2         Saab        Red         Zippy
3         BMW         Pink        Buddha
4         Colt        Rust        Rusty

Here  is  what  we  have  right  now:

CarID     Make        Color       PetName
0         BMW         Red         Chucky
1         FooFoo      FooFoo      FooFoo
2         Saab        Red         Zippy
3         BMW         Pink        Buddha
4         Colt        Rust        Rusty

Press  any  key  to  continue
```

Figure 13-29. Updating existing rows

SOURCE CODE   *The UpdateRowsWithSqlAdapter project is found under the Chapter 13 subdirectory.*

Autogenerated SQL Commands

At this point you can use the data adapter types (OleDbDataAdapter and SqlDataAdapter) to select, delete, insert, and update records from a given data source. Although the general process is not rocket science, it is a bit of a bother to build up all the parameter types and configure the InsertCommand, UpdateCommand, and DeleteCommand properties by hand. As you would expect, some help is available.

One approach is to use the SqlCommandBuilder type. If you have a DataTable composed from a single table (not from multiple joined tables), the SqlCommandBuilder automatically sets the InsertCommand, UpdateCommand, and DeleteCommand properties based on the initial SelectCommand! In addition to the no-join restriction, the single table must have been assigned a primary key, and this column must be specified in the initial SELECT statement. The benefit is that you have no need to build all those SqlParameter types by hand.

To illustrate, assume you have a new Windows Forms example, which allows the user to edit the values in a DataGrid. When finished, the user may submit changes back to the database using a Button type. First, assume the following constructor logic:

```
public class mainForm : System.Windows.Forms.Form
{
    private SqlConnection cn = new
        SqlConnection("server=(local);uid=sa;pwd=;database=Cars");

    private SqlDataAdapter dAdapt;

    private SqlCommandBuilder invBuilder;
    private DataSet myDS = new DataSet();

    private System.Windows.Forms.DataGrid dataGrid1;
    private System.Windows.Forms.Button btnUpdateData;
    private System.ComponentModel.Container components;

    public mainForm()
    {
        InitializeComponent();

        // Create the initial SELECT SQL statement.
        dAdapt = new SqlDataAdapter("Select * from Inventory", cn);

        // Autogenerate the INSERT, UPDATE,
        // and DELETE statements.
        invBuilder = new SqlCommandBuilder(dAdapt);

        // Fill and bind.
        dAdapt.Fill(myDS, "Inventory");
        dataGrid1.DataSource = myDS.Tables["Inventory"].DefaultView;
    }
    . . .
}
```

Beyond closing the connection upon exiting, that's it! At this point the SqlDataAdapter has all the information it needs to submit changes back to the data store. Now assume that you have the following logic behind the Button's Click event:

```
private void btnUpdateData_Click(object sender, System.EventArgs e)
{
    try
    {
        dataGrid1.Refresh();
        dAdapt.Update(myDS, "Inventory");
    }
    catch(Exception ex)
    {
        MessageBox.Show(ex.ToString());
    }
}
```

As usual, you call Update() and specify the DataSet and table to update. If you take this out for a test run, you see something like Figure 13-30 (be sure you exit out of edit more on the DataTable before you submit your results!).

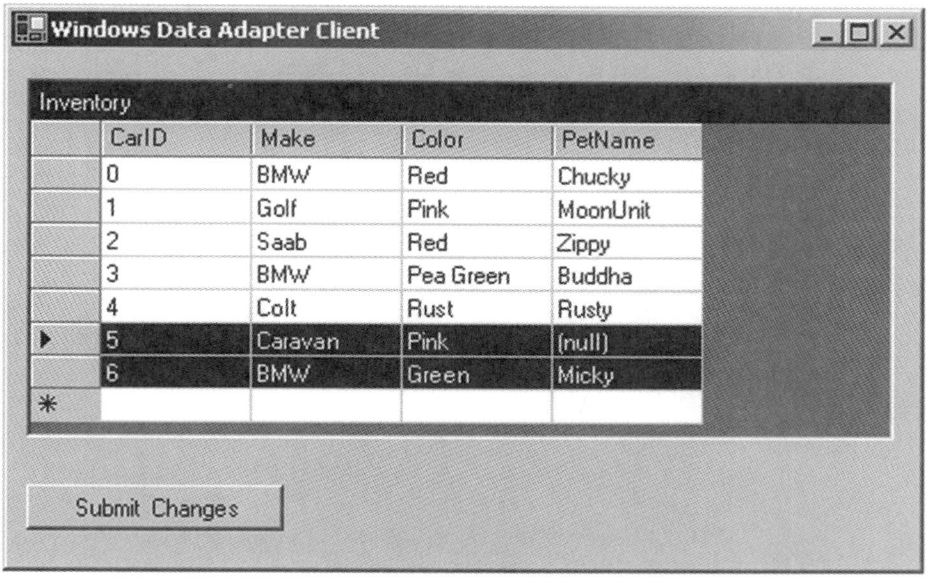

Windows Data Adapter Client

Inventory

	CarID	Make	Color	PetName
	0	BMW	Red	Chucky
	1	Golf	Pink	MoonUnit
	2	Saab	Red	Zippy
	3	BMW	Pea Green	Buddha
	4	Colt	Rust	Rusty
▶	5	Caravan	Pink	(null)
	6	BMW	Green	Micky
*				

Submit Changes

Figure 13-30. Extending the DataSet with new DataRows

Excellent! I am sure you agree that autogenerated commands are far simpler than working with the raw parameters. Like all things, of course, there are trade-offs. Specifically, if you have a DataTable composed from a joint operation, you cannot use this technique. Also, as you have seen, when you work with parameters in the raw, you have a much finer level of granularity.

SOURCE CODE   *The WinFormSqlAdapter project is included under the Chapter 13 subdirectory.*

Filling a Multitabled DataSet (and Adding DataRelations)

To wrap things up, let's come full circle and build a final Windows Forms example that mimics the application you created during the first half of this chapter. The GUI is simple enough. In Figure 13-31 you can see three DataGrid types that hold the data retrieved from the Inventory, Orders, and Customers tables of the Cars database. In addition, the single Button pushes any and all changes back to the data store:

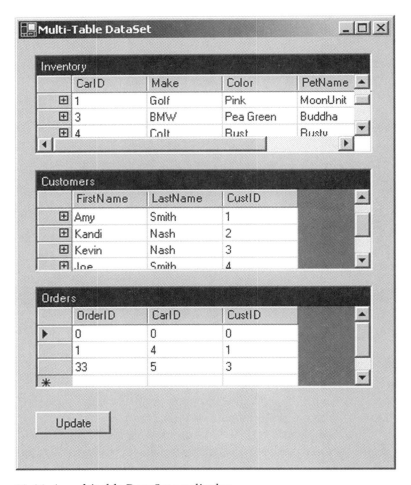

Figure 13-31. A multitable DataSet on display

To keep things even simpler, we will use autogenerated commands for each of the three SqlDataAdapters (one for each table). First, here is the Form's state data:

```
public class mainForm : System.Windows.Forms.Form
{
    private System.Windows.Forms.DataGrid custGrid;
    private System.Windows.Forms.DataGrid inventoryGrid;
    private System.Windows.Forms.Button btnUpdate;
    private System.Windows.Forms.DataGrid OrdersGrid;
    private System.ComponentModel.Container components;

    // Here is the connection.
    private SqlConnection cn = new
            SqlConnection("server=(local);uid=sa;pwd=;database=Cars");

    // Our data adapters (for each table).
    private SqlDataAdapter invTableAdapter;
    private SqlDataAdapter custTableAdapter;
    private SqlDataAdapter ordersTableAdapter;

    // Command builders (for each table).
    private SqlCommandBuilder invBuilder = new SqlCommandBuilder();
    private SqlCommandBuilder orderBuilder = new SqlCommandBuilder();
    private SqlCommandBuilder custBuilder = new SqlCommandBuilder();

    // The dataset.
    DataSet carsDS = new DataSet();
. . .
}
```

The Form's constructor does the grunge work of creating your data-centric member variables and filling the DataSet. Also note that there is a call to a private helper function, BuildTableRelationship(), as shown here:

```
public mainForm()
{
    InitializeComponent();

    // Create adapters.
    invTableAdapter = new SqlDataAdapter("Select * from Inventory", cn);
    custTableAdapter = new SqlDataAdapter("Select * from Customers", cn);
    ordersTableAdapter = new SqlDataAdapter("Select * from Orders", cn);
```

```
    // Autogenerate commands.
    invBuilder = new SqlCommandBuilder(invTableAdapter);
    orderBuilder = new SqlCommandBuilder(ordersTableAdapter);
    custBuilder = new SqlCommandBuilder(custTableAdapter);

    // Add tables to DS.
    invTableAdapter.Fill(carsDS, "Inventory");
    custTableAdapter.Fill(carsDS, "Customers");
    ordersTableAdapter.Fill(carsDS, "Orders");

    // Build relations between tables.
    BuildTableRelationship();
}
```

The BuildTableRelationship() helper function does just what you would
expect. Recall that the Cars database expresses a number of parent/child relationships. The code looks identical to the logic seen earlier in this chapter, as
shown here:

```
private void BuildTableRelationship()
{
    // Create a DR obj.
    DataRelation dr = new DataRelation("CustomerOrder",
        carsDS.Tables["Customers"].Columns["CustID"],
        carsDS.Tables["Orders"].Columns["CustID"]);

    // Add relation to the DataSet.
    carsDS.Relations.Add(dr);

    // Create another DR obj.
    dr = new DataRelation("InventoryOrder",
        carsDS.Tables["Inventory"].Columns["CarID"],
        carsDS.Tables["Orders"].Columns["CarID"]);
    // Add relation to the DataSet.
    carsDS.Relations.Add(dr);

    // Fill the grids!
    inventoryGrid.SetDataBinding(carsDS, "Inventory");
    custGrid.SetDataBinding(carsDS, "Customers");
    OrdersGrid.SetDataBinding(carsDS, "Orders");
}
```

Now that the DataSet has been filled and disconnected from the data source, you can manipulate each table locally. To do so, simply insert, update, or delete values from any of the three DataGrids. When you are ready to submit the data back for processing, click the Form's Update Button. The code behind the Click event should be clear at this point, as shown here:

```
private void btnUpdate_Click(object sender, System.EventArgs e)
{
    try
    {
        invTableAdapter.Update(carsDS, "Inventory");
        custTableAdapter.Update(carsDS, "Customers");
        ordersTableAdapter.Update(carsDS, "Orders");
    }
    catch(Exception ex)
    {
        MessageBox.Show(ex.Message);
    }
}
```

Once you update, you can find each table in the Cars database correctly altered.

At this point you should feel comfortable working with both the OleDb and SQL managed providers and understand how to manipulate and update the resulting DataSet. Obviously there are many other additional facets of ADO.NET, such as transactional programming, security issues, and so forth. I assume you will keep exploring as you see fit.

One other aspect of ADO.NET you have not investigated are the numerous VS.NET data Wizards. Suffice it to say, when you drag a Data widget (from the Toolbox Window) onto a design time template, you can launch a number of wizards that create connection strings for SqlConnection and OleDbConnection types; automatically build the SELECT, INSERT, DELETE, and UPDATE command for a given data adapter; and so forth. After your hard work in this chapter, learning how to interact with these tools should be a cakewalk.

SOURCE CODE   *The MultiTableDataSet project is included under the Chapter 13 subdirectory.*

Summary

ADO.NET is a new data access technology developed with the disconnected *n*-tier application firmly in mind. The System.Data namespace contains most of the core types you need to programmatically interact with rows, columns, tables, and views. As you have seen, the System.Data.SqlClient and System.Data.OleDb namespaces define the types you need to establish an active connection.

The centerpiece of ADO.NET is the DataSet. This type represents an in-memory representation of any number of tables and any number of optional interrelationships, constraints, and expressions. The beauty of establishing relations on your local tables is that you are able to programmatically navigate between them while disconnected from the remote data store.

Finally, this chapter examined the role of the data adapter (OleDbDataAdapter and SqlDataAdapter). Using this type (and the related SelectCommand, InsertCommand, UpdateCommand, and DeleteCommand properties), the adapter can resolve changes in the DataSet with the original data store. While there is more to the ADO.NET namespaces than I had time to cover in this single chapter, you should now have a strong foundation on which to build.

Index

A

Access database, connecting to using
ADO.NET, 447

ACID rules for transactions, 336

<Activated> element, 142–143

Activation (COM+ settings), 294–295

Activator.CreateInstance method, 142–143

Activator.GetObject method, 133, 190–191, 350

Active Directory, integration with MSMQ,
360–361

ActiveX, 20

ActiveXMessageFormatter, 376, 384

AddCallback method, 212

ADO (Active Data Objects), 20, 396

ADO.NET

    as a managed library, 396

    the big picture, 396–397

    building a database, 438–440

    building a DataTable, 413–422

    vs. classic ADO, 396

    connecting to an Access database, 447

    data access with, 395–468

    DataColumn type, 399–406

    DataRelation type, 432–437

    DataRow type, 407–411

    DataTable details, 411–412

    DataView type, 422–425

    for disconnected systems, 395

    managed providers, 397, 440–451, 455–461

    need for, 395–397

    for n-tier applications, 395

    OleDb managed provider, 440, 441–451

    role of the DataSet, 425–432

    XML-based DataSets, 437–438

ADO.NET DataSets, vs. disconnected
recordsets, 396

ADO.NET namespaces, 30–31, 397–398

Age of enlightenment, 19–21

Aggregation, object pooling and, 331

Agile objects, 96, 102–104, 108–109

    calling from two contexts, 104

    creating, 98

    executing within caller's context, 104

App.config file, 40–41

AppDomain class (CLR), 93

Application, layering, 2–3

Application configuration file, 39–41, 57–58

Application domains, 92–104

    assembly running in, 95

    benefits of, 92–93

    channel sink chain in, 117

    containing many contexts, 95

    defined, 92

    programming with, 93–95

    static members in caller's, 107

<Application> element, 132, 134

Application Export Wizard (COM+), 347

Application proxy, creating, 346

Application recycling and pooling (COM+),
351–353

Application root references, 78

Application server

    defined, 15

    duplicating, 5

    load balancing, 5

ApplicationActivationAttribute constructor, 306–307

ApplicationIDAttribute, 307

ApplicationNameAttribute, 307

Arrays, returning from a Web service, 259–268

ASAP (As Soon As Possible) deactivation, 322–327

    vs. Dispose method, 325–327

    with object pooling and JIT activaction, 332–333

ASP (Active Server Pages), 20–21

ASP.NET

    code-behind option, 249–251

    hosting remotable objects in, 167–172

    IIS and Web service relationship to, 248–249

    including WSDL contract definitions, 267

    session object, 268–269

    Web services, 237, 248–249

ASP.NET Web service project template in VS .NET, 252

ASP.NET-hosted services, debugging, 171

Assemblies, 32

    applying strong names to, 45–52

    build and revision numbers of, 55–56

    building and configuring, 33–54

    building and deploying bug-free, 56

    built by Soapsuds tool, 194

    copying into client application directory, 52

    creating strong-named interop, 391

    deploying, 176–186

    digitally signing, 46

    distributing to clients, 112–113, 130

    flavors of, 32

    GUID generation for, 285–287

    installing in the GAC, 50–52

    registering for COM interop, 278–279

running in an application domain, 95

    setting version information for, 54–56

    tracking two different versions of, 192

Assembly binding, 68–69

    defined, 38

    failure of, 66

    forcing logging of all, 68

Assembly Binding Log, viewing, 66–68

Assembly Binding Log Viewer tool, 67

Assembly binding process, summary of, 68

Assembly binding process diagram, 69

Assembly ID (TLBID), 286, 303

Assembly Linker tool (al.exe), 62

Assembly manifest, 32, 36–39, 50

Assembly metadata-COM+ catalog-COM+ context relationship, 297

Assembly names

    as part of type names, 196

    on client and server, 176–177, 182

    issue of, 192, 196–197

    within square brackets, 196–197

Assembly reference, 36

Assembly Registration Tool (regasm.exe), 278–279

Assembly request details, 38

Assembly types, consuming, 35–36

AssemblyDelaySign attribute, 53

<AssemblyIdentity> element, 57

AssemblyKeyFile attribute, 53, 300

AssemblyVersion attribute, 54

Asymmetric cryptography and strong names, 45–47

AsyncAdd method, 219, 221, 223–224

AsyncCallback delegate, 210–214, 217–219, 227, 233

AsyncDelegate property, 212

Asynchronous calls, 201–228

    message queuing for, 360

    using call context with, 233–235

    using delegates, 206–214, 259

    to a Web service, 258–259

Asynchronous message reading, 374–375

Asynchronous remoting, summarized, 227–228

AsyncResult class, 212

ATM terminal, 4

Attribute class (CLR), 70–71

Attributes, 68–72, 75, 293

AttributeUsage attribute, 71

AutoCompleteAttribute, 324, 344

AutoDual enum value (ClassInterfaceType), 283–284, 287, 312

Autogenerated commands vs. raw parameters, 463

Autogenerated SQL commands, 461–464

Autoincremented columns, 404–405

Autoincrementing fields, 404–405

Automatic GUID generation, turning off, 303

Automatic transactions (COM+), 292, 335–345

B

BeginInvoke method (delegate), 206–213, 219, 233

    object parameter, 213

    providing a callback, 210

BeginInvoke signature, 208

Binary compatibility, explained, 285

BinaryFormatter vs. XmlSerializer, 260

Binary formatters, 86, 170–171, 260, 376, 382–384

BinaryMessageFormatter, 376, 382–384

BinaryOperatorDelegate, 208

<BindingRedirect> element, 57

BindToMoniker method, 386

Breaking compatibility, explained, 285

Browser-based user interface, issues of, 18

B2B scenarios, Web services for, 239

BuildTableRelationship helper function, 432, 465–466

Business application logic, 2, 4

C

C# code

    delegates in, 203–204

    destructors in, 80

C++ code

    destructors in, 80

    function pointers in, 201–202

    garbage collection in, 78

C++ COM development, 19

Call context, 228–236

    defined, 229

    vs. thread local storage, 229–230

    using with asynchronous calls, 233–235

    using with Remoting, 230–232

Call context headers, 235–236

Callback interface, passing to server, 217

Callback method, 233–234

    executing on a delegate's thread, 212

    retrieving asynchronous results from, 213

Callbacks (*see also* Remote callbacks)

    defined, 210

    executing synchronously vs. asynchronously, 226

CallContext class, 229, 231, 235–236

CallContextData type, 232

CallContext.GetData method, 231

CallContext.GetHeaders method, 236

Calling thread, synchronizing, 209–210

CancelEdit (DataRow), 421

CCW (COM Callable Wrapper), 273, 277

    restrictions of, 278

    tasks of, 277

Centralized computing, 13–14

CGI (Common Gateway Interface), 20

Channel configuration for remoting, 135–138

<Channel> element, 132, 136

Channel port, client opening, 226

Channel sink chain, 116–117

Channel sinks, defined, 116

Channel templates, 135, 136–138

<Channels> element, 132, 135–136

Channels/channel objects, 109, 114–117

    defined, 114

    formatter object, 110, 114

    pluggable, 114

    registering, 115–116

Chatty (fine-grained) interface, 6–8

Chunky (course-grained) interface, 3, 6–8

CIL (Common Intermediate Language), 32–33

Circular references, 77

Class

    registering as a well-known object, 121

    saving as XML to a file, 260–261

Class ID (CLSID), 286–287, 303

Class library assembly, creating, 34

Class Library project, 177–180

Classic ADO, vs. ADO.NET, 396

ClassInterfaceAttribute, 280, 282–283, 312, 315

ClassInterfaceType.AutoDual setting, 283–284, 287, 312

ClassInterfaceType.None setting, 315

Client

    building for client-activated objects, 142–143

    building for interface assemblies, 189–192

    building for a serviced component, 303–304

    building using metadata assembly, 181–183

    building for WKO, 123–127

    configuring for remoting, 133–135

    deploying assemblies to, 130

    exposing a .NET class to COM client, 280–283

    interacting with managed providers, 397

    late-bound, 287

    opening channel ports for, 226

    periodic pinging of, 144

    running Soapsuds on, 193–194

    sharing pooled objects, 329

    that are also servers, 154–155

    using interface assemblies for metadata, 186–192

Client application domain, channel sink chain in, 117

Client application output (MathClient), 125, 155

Client assembly (MathClient), 36–39, 49–50

<Client> element, 134, 143

Client for IIS hosted service, building, 169–170

Client manifest (MathClient), 50

Client remoting channel, registering, 154

Client target build directory, 37

Client-activated objects, 138–159, 355
    building the client, 142–143
    building the server, 140–142
    default lease values for, 146–147
    interface assemblies and, 192
    metadata assembly with, 184–186
    vs. SingleCall objects, 139
    Soapsuds and, 197
    unique GUID-based URI for, 142
    vs. well-known objects, 110–11

ClientCallbackSink object, creating, 225–226

ClientCallbackSink.ResultCallback method, 226

Client/server architecture
    n-tier, 15–16
    three-tier, 15–16
    two-tier, 14–15

Client-side sponsor, 153–156
    complications of, 156
    responding to renewal requests, 155

CLR attributes, 69–71

CLR (common language runtime), 30

CLR types, conversion to XML Schema types, 242

CLS (Common Language Specification), 29–30

CLS-compliant publicly exposed items, 29

CLSID (class ID), 286–287, 303

Code libraries (DLLs), 3, 32, 133

<CodeBase> element, 64–66

Code-behind (ASP.NET option), 249–251, 254

Collections
    of DataTables, 395, 412
    of DataSets, 426

Column XML representation, configuring, 406

ColumnMapping property, 406

Columns
    autoincremented, 404–405
    indexed numerically, 415
    in relational databases, 400

COM (Component Object Model), 19
    complaints about, 22
    location transparency, 92
    vs. .NET, 23–24
    .NET completely replacing, 18

COM development in Visual Basic, 21

COM interop, 273–288
    need for, 273
    registering an assembly for, 278–279
    writing managed code for, 279–280

COM marshaling, 396

COM object lifetime, managing, 274

COM servers, registering for use, 278

COM Service Control Manager (SCuM), 38

COM solution to type interoperability, 28

COM versioning, managed code and, 285–288

COM versioning rules, 285

COM+ Application Export Wizard, 347

COM+ catalog
    defined, 290
    populating, 296–298

COM+ catalog-COM+ context-assembly metadata relationship, 297

COM+ catalog-COM+ context-COM+ relationship, 291

COM+ (Component Services), 17, 22, 276, 289–356
  activated and deactivated objects, 319
  application settings, 294
  as unmanaged code, 276
  ASAP deactivation, 322–327
  automatic transactions, 292
  component settings, 294–295
  configuration settings, 292–295
  declarative attributes, 292–293
  displaying component methods, 310–317
  exposing objects to clients using DCOM, 346–348
  interaction with .NET, 317–319
  interface and method settings, 295
  JIT activation, 292, 319–328
  lazy registration, 297–298
  loosely coupled events, 292
  object construction, 334–335
  object pooling, 292
  overview of, 289–295
  queued components, 292, 384–391
  role-based security, 291
  server activation, 306–310
  SOAP services, 354–355
  survey of, 291–292
  transaction services, 335–345
  tree view, 293
  use of COM interop .NET services, 273
COM+ context, 290–291, 304–306, 317–318
COM+ library-activated application, .NET and, 318–319
COM+ 1.5
  application recycling and pooling, 351–353
  new features of, 351–355
CommandType enumeration values, 449

CommandType property (OleDbCommand class), 448–449
Common namespace, 398, 441
Compatible context, 96
Complex types, returning from a Web service, 259–268
Component, defined, 294
Component interoperability (.NET vs. COM), 23
Component methods, displaying, 310–317
Component server activation, 306–310
Component Services. *See* COM+ (Component Services)
Component status view usage statistics, 305–306
Component-based programming, 19
Computer Management tool
  confirming sent messages, 368
  message body in, 364
Computer resources, relative quantity of, 9
Concurrency (COM+ component settings), 295
<Configuration> element, 130
Configured object, defined, 291
Connect method (RemotingServices class), 126
Connecting to an Access database using ADO.NET, 447
Connection, establishing with OleDbConnection, 442–444
ConnectionString property (OleDbConnection), 442
Console class (in System namespace), 30–31
Constraints, in relational database theory, 400
Construct method (ServicedComponent class), 335
ConstructionEnabledAttribute, 335

Constructor, calling as a well-known object, 139

Consuming assembly types, 35–36

Consuming serviced components, 346–351

Consuming standard COM interfaces, 274

Consuming Web services, 255–258

Context, 95–104, 290–291, 304–306, 317–318

Context agile objects, 96, 102–104, 108–109

    calling from two contexts, 104

    creating, 98

    executing within caller's context, 104

Context bound, explained, 109

Context bound objects

    creating, 98

    defined, 96, 290

Context done bit, 322, 324

Context example, 96–99

Context happy bit, 322, 324

Context information, retrieving, 100–101

Context object, 100

Context properties, discovering at runtime, 101

ContextBoundObject class, 96–97

ContextUtil class, 304–306, 322, 340, 344–345

Cookies, to manage session state, 269

Coordinating DTC

    defined, 336

    diagrammed, 337

Course-grained interface, 7

CreateCustomerService method, 192

CreateInstance method, 142–143

CreateViews helper function, 424

CTS (Common Type System), 28, 30, 242, 270

CTS type fidelity, 270

Culture information, for spoken languages, 45

Current executing context, referencing, 100

Current lease time, 146–147

Custom attributes, 71–72

Custom callback interface, 227

Custom delegates

    defining, 204

    passing to server, 217

    remote callbacks with, 219–223

Custom interfaces, 277, 315–317

Custom types (*see also* Type)

    returning from a Web service, 259–268

    sending in messages, 376–384

    Soapsuds and, 196–197

Customer class/object, 6–8, 113–114, 177, 180, 183

Customer data operations, 106–107

Customer project descriptions, 177, 186

CustomerClient console application, 181–191

CustomerFactory class, 191

CustomerServer console application, 178–179, 188

CustomerService type, 177, 180

    attempting to run locally, 182

    how Soapsuds defines, 194–195

D

Data access with ADO.NET, 395–468

Data adapters, 396, 452, 456

Data logic, 4

Data namespace (ADO.NET), 397–398, 400

Data source logic (business applications), 2, 4

Data structure of a type, 263

Data types, in relational database theory, 400

Database, building, 438–440

Database connection, as a scarce resource, 16

Database layer, distributed, 3

Database manipulation, 395–468

DataColumn type (ADO.NET), 399–406

    adding to a DataTable, 403

    building, 401–403

    configuring as a primary key, 403–404

    select properties of, 401–402, 406

DataColumnCollection.Add method, 413

DataColumn.ColumnMapping property, 406

DataGrid

    binding a DataTable to, 415

    editing rows in, 422

DataRelation type (ADO.NET), 426, 432–437

    adding to a DataSet, 464–467

    properties of, 433

DataRelationCollection, 426

DataRow members, 408

DataRow type (ADO.NET), 407–411, 434, 463

DataRow.BeginEdit method, 421

DataRow.CancelEdit method, 421

DataRow.EndEdit method, 421

DataRow.GetChildRows method, 435

DataRow.GetParentRows method, 435

DataRow.ItemArray property, 410–411

DataRow.RowState property, 407–410

DataSet (ADO.NET data type), 396

    as XML, 437

    building in-memory, 427–432

    collections of, 426

    defined, 425

    extending with new DataRows, 463

    filling multitabled, 464–467

    filling using OleDbDataAdapter type, 452–455

    getting from the data store, 451

    members of, 427

    methods of, 428

    populated through a managed provider, 397

    properties of, 427

    reading and writing XML-based, 437–438

    role of, 425–432

DataSet application, in-memory, 439

DataTable (ADO.NET data type)

    adding a DataColumn to, 403

    applying filters and sort orders, 417–420

    binding, 415, 430–431

    building, 413–422

    collections of, 412

    deleting rows in, 416–417

    details of, 411–412

    manipulating, 416–422

    properties of, 412

    updating rows in, 420–422

DataTable.AcceptChanges method, 417

DataTableCollection, accessing, 426

DataTable.DefaultView property, 423

DataTable.NewRow method, 407

DataTable.PrimaryKey property, 414

DataTable.Select method, 417, 420

DataView type (ADO.NET), 422–425

DataView type members, 425

DataView.RowFilter property, 425

DCOM (Distributed COM), 20–21, 92

    complaints about, 22

    reference counting, 144

    type library, 176

    using to expose objects, 346–348

DDE (Dynamic Data Exchange), 19

Dead queue, 389–390

Dead-letter messages (system queue), 369

Declarative attributes
> explained, 292–293
> vs. .NET attributes, 293

Default constructor for a class, 140, 197

Default constructor to connect to remote type, 197

Default context, explained, 95

Default interface
> changing, 315–317
> defined, 279

Default interface name, 279

Default lease, 145–147

Default lease settings, 147

Default lease values for client-activated objects, 146–147

Default versioning policy, 56

DefaultView property (DataTable), 423

Delayed signing, 52–53

Delegates, 201–206
> asynchronous, 259
> custom, 204, 217, 219–223
> dissecting, 205–206
> instantiating and passing to a server, 222
> marshaled by value, 223
> power of, 215
> public and private, 220
> for remote asynchronous calls, 214–227
> signature of, 205
> using for local asynchronous calls, 206–214

Dependent client (MSMQ), 362–363

<DependentAssembly> element, 57

Description services, 240

Deserialization, defined, 84

Deterministic finalization (reference counting), 76

Digital signature, 46

Digitally signing an assembly, 46

Direct paths, referencing message queues with, 369

Dirty read, explained, 353

DisableCommit (ContextUtil), 345

Disco files
> role of, 242–243
> static or dynamic, 242

Disconnected n-tier application, 467

Disconnected Recordsets vs. ADO.NET DataSets, 396

Disconnected systems, ADO.NET for, 395

Discovery services, 240

DisplayContextInfo method, 101–103

Disposable objects, 82–83

Dispose (bool) method, 327–328

Dispose method
> vs. ASAP deactivation, 325–327
> on a configured object, 326
> overriding, 327–328
> within finally of a try block, 83

DisposingSponsor class, 158–159

Distinct physical components, explained, 1

Distributed applications
> and Component Services, 290
> how to design, 6
> how not to design, 5
> storing the business logic, 448

Distributed computing, Microsoft and, 18–24

Distributed design, five principles of, 3–11

Distributed programming
> defined, 1
> evolution of, 1–25
> with .NET remoting, 119–173
> overview of, 1–12
> short history of, 13–18

Distributed transactions, 273

Distributing sparingly, 3–4

DLLs (code libraries), 3, 32, 133

DNA (Distributed interNet Architecture), 22

DoClientCallback method, 221, 224

Document style (WSDL), 246

Domain mode (MSMQ), 360, 362

Domains. *See* Application domains

Done bit, 324

    defined, 322

    setting, 340, 342–343

Doomed bit

    defined, 339

    setting, 340, 342–343

DTC (Distributed Transaction Coordinator), 336–337

    statistics view, 337

    stopping and starting, 336

Dumb terminal, defined, 13

Duplicating application servers, 5

Dynamic discovery, enabling on a Web site, 243

Dynamic discovery files, 242

Dynamic proxy generation, 112–113

E

E-commerce applications, 4–6, 358

E-commerce message queuing, 358

EnableCommit (ContextUtil), 345

Encoded style (SOAP), 246

EndInvoke method (delegate), 206–209, 212, 234

EndInvoke signature, 208

Endpoint (of application within network), 115

Enterprise Manager (SQL Server), 440

Enterprise Services, 289

EnterpriseServices namespace, 299, 331

Error messages, 163

Event log

    with objects created at application startup, 332

    showing COM+ executed methods, 321–322

EventLog class, 163

Exception handling (messages), 375

Exception handling (queued components), 388–391

ExceptionClass attribute, 390

ExecuteNonQuery method (OleDbcommand), 450

ExecuteReader method (OleDbCommand), 445

Executing context, referencing, 100

EXE files, 32

Expired object, invoking a method on, 148

ExtendedProperties property, 426

F

Fields, enabling autoincrementing, 404–405

Filter string, 419

Filtering logic, 419

Filters (DataTable), 417–420

Finalize method, 79–80

Fine-grained interface, 7

Firewalls, 369, 396

Flexibility issue, 270

ForceLog registry entry, setting, 68

Foreign key constraint, 426

Formatter objects, 110, 114–117

Freachable queue, 79

Fully qualified names, 31, 196–197

Function pointers, 201–203

G

GAC (Global Assembly Cache), 44, 46
    installing an assembly in, 50–52
    publisher policy file in, 63
Gacutil.exe utility, 51
Garbage collection, 75–84, 144
    in C++, 78
    internals of, 78–79
    in perspective, 84
    reasons to use, 77–78
    vs. reference counting, 76–78
    in Visual Basic, 78
GetChildRows method, 435
GetCustomAttributes method, 73–74
GetData method, 229–231
GetHeaders method (CallContext class), 236
GetInfo method, 300–301, 305, 324
GetLifetimeService method, 145–146
GetObject method, 133, 190–191, 350
GetParentRows method, 435
Greedy client problem, 144, 319
GUID generation, automatic, 285–286
GuidAttribute constructor, 286–287, 307, 314
GUIDs (globally unique identifiers), 285
    applying manually, 286–287
    late-bound clients and, 287
    trouble with, 301–303
    turning off automatic generation of, 303

H

Happy bit, 322, 324, 340, 342–343
Header class, 235
Horizontal scaling (scaling out), 12
Hosting remotable objects in a Windows
    service, 159–167
HTML, 17, 20–21, 240–241
HTML vs. XML, 241

HTTP, 17, 240
HTTP channel, 114–115, 122, 125, 170
HTTP channel remoting, metadata
    deployment, 200
HTTP channel template, 137–138
HTTP request, 20
HTTP for SOAP transport, 247
HTTPClientChannel constructor, 170–171
HttpContext, 269

I

IAsyncResult interface, 208–209
IAsyncResult.AsyncState property, 213, 225
IAsyncResult.AsyncWaitHandle property, 210
IAsyncResult.IsComplete property, 209, 375
IClientCallback interface, 224–225
IContextProperty interface, 100
ICustomer interface, 187, 190, 196–197
ICustomerService interface, 190–191
ID attribute (XML), 261–262
IDataReader interface, 441
IDbCommand interface, 441
IDbDataAdapter interface, 441
Identity (COM+ application settings), 294
IDispatch interface, 281, 287, 280
IDisposable interface, 81–83, 156–158
IE (Internet Explorer), 20
IGetInfo interface, defining, 315
IID (interface ID), 286–287
IIS client, building, 169–170
IIS (Internet Information Server), 20, 167
    binary formatter in, 170–171
    hosting and Web services, 171–172
IIS virtual directory, creating, 168–169
IIS-to-ASP.NET-to-Web service
    relationship, 248–249
IL (Common Intermediate Language), 32–33

ILDasm tool, 36–37, 48

ILease interface, 145–146

ILease.Register method, 152–154

ILogicalThreadAffinitive interface, 230

IMessage object, 116

IMessageFormatter interface, 376

Independent client (MSMQ), 362–363

Infinite leases, setting, 151

Initial lease time, 146

InitializeLifetimeService method, 149–151

In-memory database, 429

In-memory DataSet application, 427–432, 439

InsertCommand property (SqlDataAdapter), 458–459

InstallUtil (installutil.exe), 164

Instance fields, 108

Interface assemblies

    building the client, 189–192

    building the server, 187–189

    and client-activated objects, 192

    deploying, 186–192

    vs. metadata assembly, 186

Interface ID (IID), 286–287

InterfaceQueuing attribute, 388

Interfaces

    changing the default, 315–317

    chunky vs. chatty, 6–8

    consuming, 274

    generating automatically, 283–284

    implementing explicitly, 280–283

    programming to, 10–11

    provided by CCW, 277

    remote callbacks using, 223–227

Intermediate language, 32–33

Interop assembly

    building, 275–276

    building with tlbimp.exe, 276

building with VS .NET, 275–276

creating strong-named, 391

defined, 275

Interop assembly wrapper, 275

Interoperability, type and, 28–30

Inventory DataTable, 413, 422–423

Invoke method (of delegate), 206–207

IObjectControl interface, 320–322

IPCs (Interprocess Communication channels), 91

IPlaybackControl interface, 389–391

IPlaybackControl.FinalServerRetry method, 390

IQueuableLogger interface, 387–389

ISAPI extension, 20, 167, 248

ISAPI (Internet Service API), 167

ISerializable interface, 87–89, 230

ISimpleMath interface, 228, 232, 280–282

Isolation levels (transaction), 353

IsOutofContext method, 98

ISponsor interface, 151–152

ISponsor.Renewal method, 151–152

IsTransparentProxy method, 98

ItemArray property (DataRow), 410–411

J

Java bytecode, 33

Java solution to type interoperability, 28

JET engine (OLEDB), 447

JIT activation (COM+), 273, 292, 319–328

    with ASAP deactivation, 332–333

    and object pooling, 329, 332–333

    and stateless objects, 319–320

    summarized, 328

JIT Activation services (COM+), 296

JIT (Just-In-Time) compiler, 33

JustInTimeActivation attribute, 296

K

Key pair (public/private), 46

    generating, 47–49

    in a safe and private place, 48–49

L

Language independence (.NET vs. COM), 23

Language interoperability, type and, 28

Layering an application, 2–3

Lazy registration (COM+), 297–298

Lease information for a type, 145

Lease settings, 145

    after method invocations, 148

    custom values for, 149

    infinite, 151

Lease times, types of, 146–147

Lease-based lifetime for Singleton objects, 151

Lease-based object lifetime, 84, 144–159

LeaseManagerPollTime attribute, 156

Leases, defined, 144

Leasing Distributed Garbage Collector, 111, 144

Least common denominator set of primitive types, 28

Library activation, using with listeners, 351

Library-activated COM+ application, .NET and, 318–319

<Lifetime> element, 149, 156

Lifetime encapsulation (reference counting), 76

Lifetime of an object, 145–150

Lifetime settings, 156

Listener thread, establishing, 115

ListenerHelper object (queued components), 385–387

Listeners

    implementing, 348–349

    using library activation with, 351

Literal style (WSDL), 246

Load balancing application servers, 5

Load-balanced scenarios, stateful objects in, 10

Local asynchronous calls, using delegates, 206–214

Local copy of related tables, 396

Localizing related concerns, 4–6

Location transparency, 130

    COM, 92

    .NET vs. COM, 23

Logger.IQueuableLogger interface, 387–389

Logical process, explained, 92

Logical thread spanning physical threads, 233

Logical threads, 230, 233, 235

Loosely coupled events (COM+), 292

M

Machine configuration file error message, 59

Machine versioning policy, setting, 60

Machine.config file, 58-59, 136–137

Machine-scoped binding policies, etting, 60

Machine-wide version policies, setting, 58

Managed client

    building, 303–304

    implementing, 350

Managed code, 30, 273
  building serviced components in,
    295–335
  calling into unmanaged code, 275
  and COM versioning, 285–288
  to unmanaged interop, 274–276
  versioning options, 287–288
  writing for COM interop, 279–280
  writing queued components in,
    384–391
Managed providers (ADO.NET), 440–451,
  455–461
  clients interacting with, 397
  DataSets populated through, 397
Managed types, GUID generation for,
  285–287
Manifests (assembly), 32, 36–39, 50
MappingType enumeration values, 406
Marshal by reference (MBR), 105–107,
  109, 223
Marshal by value (MBV), 105, 108, 113, 223
  class, 231
  in Web services, 259
Marshal.BindToMoniker method, 386
MarshalByRefObject, 106, 120, 145–146,
  154, 221, 225
Marshaled objects, explained, 105–109, 114
Marshaling
  and context agility, 108–109
  of data between managed and
    unmanaged code, 274, 277
Marshal.ReleaseComObject method, 386
MathLibrary assembly, 39
  with Copy Local property, 51
  machine versioning policy, 60
  referencing, 36
  strong-named version of, 49–50
  viewing in the GAC, 50

MathLibrary manifest, public key in, 48
MathLibrary publisher policy file, in the
  GAC, 63
MathLibrary version, in client's manifest,
  55–56
MathLibrary.dll file, 33, 35
MemberInfo parameter, type instance in, 75
Message body, viewing, 364
Message class, 368
Message formatters, 376–384
  choosing, 384
  types of, 370, 376
Message object, 368–369
Message queues
  creating and managing, 363–367
  polling, 372–373
  referencing with direct paths, 369
Message queuing (.NET), 357–392. *See also*
  Messages; MSMQ
  architecture, 359
  for asynchronous calls, 360
  building the receiver, 370–375
  building the sender, 365–369
  overview of, 357–360
  vs. Remoting or Web services, 360
  subcomponents, 361–362
MessageQueue class, 365–366, 372–375
MessageQueue.BeginReceive method, 372,
  374–375
MessageQueue.EndReceive method,
  374–375
MessageQueueException, 373
MessageQueue.Receive method, 372–373
MessageQueue.Send method, 367–368
Message.Body property, 378, 380
Message.BodyStream property, 380
Messaging namespace, 357, 365, 376

Messages, 110
 confirming sent, 368
 deserializing, 378
 exception handling, 375
 reading asynchronously, 374–375
 sending, 367
 sending custom types in, 376–384
 serializing, 377–382
Metadata, 32, 72
 distributing, 113
 generating automatically with Soapsuds, 193
 generating for specific types only, 198
 Soapsuds type vs. Web service, 264
 using interface assemblies for, 186–192
Metadata assemblies
 building the client, 181–183
 building the server, 177–180
 with client-activated objects, 184–186
 deploying, 176–186
 vs. interface assemblies, 186
Metadata assembly name, and implementation name, 176–177, 182
Metadata deployment, 175–200
Method call
 on an expired object, 148
 on a well-known object, 114
Methods (component)
 displaying, 310–317
 displaying the easy way, 312–314
 displaying the right way, 315–317
 event log showing executed, 321–322
MFC (Microsoft Foundation Classes), 30
Microsoft, and distributed computing, 18–24
MMC snap-ins, 58, 61
Mscorcfg.msc, 58–61
Mscorlib assembly, 38

MSMQ (Microsoft Message Queuing), 357–392. *See also* Message queuing (.NET)
 Active Directory integration with, 360–361
 creating and managing message queues, 363–367
 dependent client, 362–363
 domain mode, 360, 362
 HTTP Support, 361
 independent client, 362–363
 installation options, 360–363
 installing and configuring, 360–363
 iterations, 360
 local storage, 362
 private queues, 362
 public queues, 362
 serializing messages, 377–382
 triggers, 361
 workgroup mode, 360, 362
MSMQ 3.0, 360
MTS (Microsoft Transaction Server), 22, 289
Multitable DataSet, filling, 464–467

N

Namespaces, 30–31, 397–398
Name/value pairs, 442
.NET
 as an evolution, 23
 building Web services in, 248–255
 vs. COM, 23–24
 completely replacing COM, 18
 consuming Web services in, 255–258
 interaction with COM+, 317–319
 leveraging COM+ runtime, 273
 three Cs of, 28–30
.NET assemblies. *See* Assemblies
.NET class, exposing to COM clients, 280–283

.NET Framework channel templates, 136

.NET Framework configuration tool
(mscorcfg.msc), 58–61

.NET infrastructure, 27–33

.NET Leasing Distributed Garbage
Collector, 111, 144

.NET message queuing. *See* Message
queuing (.NET)

.NET object lifetime, managing, 277

.NET Remoting. *See* Remoting

.NET Remoting architecture, high-level
view of, 110

.NET Remoting framework, 109–117

.NET Services Installation tool
(regsvcs.exe), 296–298, 300, 307

New keyword, 126–127, 190–191, 195

NewRow method (DataTable), 407

NewVersion attribute, 57

NonSerialized attribute, 382

N-tier application
ADO.NET for, 395
disconnected, 467

N-tier architecture, benefits of, 15–16

O

Object lifetime, 145–150
configuring, 149–150
leased-based, 84
managing COM, 274
managing .NET, 277

Object pooling, 292, 319, 329–333
advantages of, 329–330
enabling, 331–333
with JIT activation and ASAP
deactivation, 332–333
requirements of, 330–331

ObjectPoolingAttribute, 331

Objects
activated and deactivated, 319
allocated at application startup, 329
ASAP deactivation of, 322–327
client-activated, 138–159
client-activated vs. SingleCall, 139
construction in COM+, 334–335
destroying stateful, 144
disposable, 82–83
exposing with DCOM, 346–348
exposing with .NET Remoting, 348–351
implementing well-known, 119–138
invoking methods on expired, 148
JIT activation and, 319–320
managing resource-intensive, 156–159
with many small methods, 6
marshaling, 105–109
method calls on well-known, 114
passed by value, 84
pointers, 105
returning from a Web service, 259–268
serialized using SOAP formatter, 87
serializing into a file, 86
stateful vs. stateless, 8–10, 228
worker objects, 341–343

ObjRef (CLR object), 113–114, 176, 187, 223

Obsolete attribute, 70

OldVersion attribute, 57

OLE DB core providers, 443

OLE (Object Linking and Embedding), 19

OLE Transactions, 336

OLEDB JET engine, 447

OleDb managed provider (ADO.NET), 397,
440, 441–451

OleDb Namespace (ADO.NET), 398, 442

OleDb Namespace types, 442

OleDbCommand class, 444–445

CommandType property, 448–449

OleDbConnection parameter, 454

ParametersCollection, 449

SelectCommand property, 453–454

OleDbcommand.ExecuteNonQuery method, 450

OleDbCommand.ExecuteReader method, 445

OleDbConnection type, 442–444

as a parameter to OleDbCommand, 454

type members, 444

OleDbConnection.ConnectionString property, 442

OleDbDataAdapter type, 451–455

in action, 454

core members, 452

Fill method, 451

OleDbDataAdapter object reference, 451

OleDbDataReader type, 445–447

OleDbParameter type, 449–451

OleDbParameter type members, 450

OLTP applications, 21–22

OLTP (Online Transaction Processing), 21

OneWayAttribute, 216–217, 226

OnMessageArrival callback function, 374–375

OnStart and OnStop methods, 162

OnTimer function, 373

Ordered data, 420

Out parameter, 216

Out-of-band data, passing security token as, 229

P

Parallel processing, 5

ParametersCollection (OleDbCommand class), 449

Participating DTCs, defined, 336

PC dominance, era of, 19

Performance, scalability related to, 11–12

Phantom inserts problem, 353

Physical threads, 230

call context information over, 235

logical thread spanning, 233

Pinging of clients, periodic, 144

Platform interoperability, type and, 28

Player object (queued components), 385–388

Pluggable objects, 114

Policy precedence, 64

Polling a message queue, 372–373

Pooling applications (COM+ 1.5), 352–353

Pooling objects. *See* Object pooling

Port numbers, 122, 154

Presentation logic (business) 2, 4

Primary interop assembly, explained, 275

Primary key

configuring a DataColumn as, 403–404

setting for a table, 414

Primary thread, keeping alive, 122

PrimaryKey property (DataTable), 414

Primitive types, least common denominator set of, 28

PrintTable helper function, 454, 458

Private assembly, 32

building, 33–44

probing and, 43–44

use of the term, 54

Private delegate, 220

Private key, 52

Private message queues (MSMQ), 362–367

Probing

defined, 39

private assemblies and, 43–44

process of, 42–43

Process isolation, 91

Processes, 91–92

Process-to-application domain-to-context relationship, 96

PropertyCollection type, 426

Proxies, 109, 111–114, 346. *See also* Web service proxy

    representing remote objects, 105, 125–127

    use of, 176

    use of WSDL, 244

Proxy generation

    dynamic, 112–113

    and ObjRef, 113–114

Proxy wrapper, 195

Public delegate, 220

Public instance fields, 108

Public interface, 228

Public key file, 52

Public key token, 46–47, 52

Public keys, 46–48, 52–53

Public message queues, 362, 367

Public static fields, 107

Publicly exposed items, CLS-compliant, 29

Public/private key pair, 46

    generating, 47–49

    in a safe and private place, 48–49

Publisher policy, 56

    configuring, 61–64

    forcing off, 63–64

Publisher policy assembly, building, 61–63

Publisher policy file in the GAC, 63

Q

QFE (Quick Fix Engineering), 56

Query Analyzer utility (SQL Server), 439

Queued component architecture, 385–387

Queued components (COM+), 292, 384–391

    COM+- generated queues, 389

    exception handling, 388–391

    explained, 385

    implementing, 387–388

    interface for, 295, 387

    writing in managed code, 384–391

Queues (message). *See* Message queues

R

RAD (rapid application development), 14

Raw parameters vs. autogenerated commands, 463

RCW (Runtime Callable Wrapper), 273–274

    generating code for, 275

    tasks of, 274

RDMS (relational database management system), 14

Reachable objects, explained, 78

Read committed isolation level, 353

Read uncommitted isolation level, 353

ReadXml method, 438

Real proxy, defined, 111

Receivers (message queuing), 359, 370–375

Recorder object (queued components), 385–387

Recordsets, vs. ADO.NET DataSets, 396

Recycling applications (COM+ 1.5), 351–352

Ref parameter, 216

Reference counting, 144

    advantages of, 76

    disadvantages of, 77

    vs. garbage collection, 76–78

Referenced assembly, moving out of application directory, 39

Reflection, 72–75, 85

Regasm.exe (Assembly Registration Tool), 278–279

Register method (ILease), 152–154

RegisterActivatedClientType method, 142

RegisterActivatedServiceType method, 140

Registering an assembly for COM interop, 278–279

Registering channels, 115–116

Registering a class as a well-known object, 121

RegisterWellKnownClientType method, 126

RegisterWellKnownServiceType method, 122, 128

RegistrationHelper class, 297

Registry items, removing orphaned, 301–303

Regsvcs.exe (.NET Services Installation tool), 296–298, 300, 307

Regular assembly, use of the term, 54

Regular private assembly, use of the term, 54

Related tables, 426, 432

   local copy of, 396

   navigating between, 433–437

Relational database theory, 400

Relations property, 426

ReleaseComObject method, 386

Remotable objects, hosting in ASP.NET, 167–172

Remote asynchronous calls, delegates for, 214–227

Remote callbacks, 217–227

   with AsyncCallback, 217–219

   with custom delegates, 219–223

   implementing using interfaces, 223–227

   techniques for establishing, 217

Remote object

   calling asynchronously, 201–228

   proxy representing, 125–127

stateful or stateless, 228

Remote server, verifying, 193

Remote type assembly, distributing to client, 112–113

Remote type metadata, distributing, 113

Remoting, 91–118, 175–236

   channel configuration for, 135–138, 154

   configuring the client for, 133–135

   configuring the server for, 131–133

   distributed programming with, 119–173

   explained, 91–92

   exposing objects with, 348–351

   vs. message queuing, 360

   transparency with, 215

   using call context with, 230–232

   vs. Web services, 172, 270–271

Remoting architecture, high-level view of, 110

Remoting configuration, 130–138, 141, 143, 154

Remoting design and infrastructure, 109

Remoting details, 107–108

<Remoting> element, 130, 134

Remoting framework, 109–117

Remoting hosts, building, 159–172

Remoting issues, 130

Remoting namespace, 133

RemotingConfiguration class, 126, 132–133, 140, 142, 163

RemotingConfiguration.Configure method, 132–133, 163

RemotingServices class, 98, 126

RemotingServices.Connect method, 126

Renewal method (ISponsor), 151–152

Renewal-on-call lease time, 146–147

Repeatable read isolation level, 353

Resource management, 75–84

Resource usage thresholds, 330

Resource-intensive objects, managing, 156–159

Resources, 75–84

    relative quantity of, 9

    scarce, 16, 81

ResultCallback method, 225

Retry queues, 388

Role-based security (COM+), 291

Root object, 339–344

Row states, changes in, 410

Row updates (DataTable), 420–422

RowFilter property (DataView), 425

Rows

    deleting in a DataTable, 416–417

    editing in a DataGrid, 422

    updating using SqlDataAdapter, 461

RowState property (DataRow), 407–410

RPC style (SOAP), 246

Running process, VS .NET attaching to, 165–167

<Runtime> element, 130

S

Safe mode, with publisher policy off, 63

Satellite assembly, defined, 45

Scalability, 11–12

Scale, defined, 11

Scaling, types of, 11–12

Scaling out, 12

Scaling up, 11

Scarce resources, 16, 81

Schema (table), 399

SCP (serviced component proxy), 318

Security (COM+)

    application settings, 294

    component settings, 295

    interfaces and methods, 295

Security token, passing as out-of-band data, 229

Select method (DataTable), 417, 420

Semantic Web, 238

Senders (message queuing), 365–369

Serializable attribute, 8, 69, 71, 85–87, 105, 230–231, 382

Serializable isolation level, 353

Serialization, 84–89

    .NET Remoting vs. Web services, 270

    and objects passed by value, 84

Serialization namespace, 259, 381

SerializationInfo object, 88

Serializing MSMQ messages, 377–382

Server

    building for client-activated objects, 140–142

    building for interface assemblies, 187–189

    building for metadata assembly, 177–180

    building for WKOs, 119–123

    configuring for remoting, 131–133

    responding to renewal requests, 155

    running Soapsuds on, 198

Server activation (COM+), 306–310

Server application domain, channel sink chain in, 117

Server Explorer (VS .NET), 364–365

Server output (MathServer), 126

    after configuring lease settings, 149

    after InitializeLifetimeService, 150

    after SingleCall activation, 129

    after Singleton activation, 129

<Service> element, 132, 142

ServiceBase.Run method, 162

Serviced class, creating, 299–317

Serviced components
building in managed code, 295–335
consuming, 346–351
defined, 289
implementing, 299–301
ServicedComponent class, 299–300, 320, 325, 327, 335, 387
ServicedComponent hierarchy, 300
ServiceProcessInstaller object, 164–165
ServiceProcessInstaller Properties window, 165
Services, debugging ASP.NET-hosted, 171
Services MMC snap-in, 164
Session cookies, 269
Session object (ASP.NET), 268–269
SetAbort method, 340–341, 344–345
SetComplete method, 340–341
SetData method, 229–230
SetDataBinding method, 430–431
SetHeaders method (CallContext class), 235
SGML, 17
Shared assembly, 32, 44–54
Shared name, 44, 53–54
Shopping cart application, 4–6
ShowLeaseInfo method, 146
Signatures (of methods), 205
SimpleContext application, 99
SimpleMath class, 33, 35, 73, 126
SimpleMath.cs file, 34
SimpleMathResult class, 222
SingleCall vs. client-activated object, 139
SingleCall mode, 122
defined, 110
vs. Singleton mode, 127–129
SingleCall object, 139–140, 189, 355
Singleton mode, 122
defined, 110

vs. SingleCall mode, 127–129
Singleton object, 127, 151, 162
Singleton object lease-based lifetime, 151
SOAP, 240
formatting styles, 246
renamed XML Protocol by W3C, 247
role of, 244–247
SOAP body, 244
SOAP envelope, 244
SOAP formatter
and network bandwidth, 170
serialization using, 86–87
SOAP header, 244
SOAP message, layout of, 244
SOAP services, 345, 355
SoapFormatter, 115, 260
Soapsuds tool (soapsuds.exe), 193–199
assembly built by, 194
and client-activated objects, 197
and exposed custom types, 196–197
running on the client, 193–194
running on the server, 198
when to avoid using, 200
Soapsuds type metadata vs. Web service metadata, 264
Soapsuds-generated code, 194–195
Solution Explorer (Visual Studio .NET), 253, 255
Sort orders (DataTable), 417–420
Sponsorship, explained, 157
SponsorshipTimeout attribute, 156
Sponsors/Sponsor objects, 157
building and registering, 151–153
client-side, 153–156
SQL commands, 3
autogenerated, 461–464
building, 444–445

SQL managed provider (ADO.NET), 397, 441, 455–461

SQL Server

database in, 440

Enterprise Manager, 440

Query Analyzer utility, 439

SQL (Structured Query Language), 3

SqlClient namespace (ADO.NET), 398, 455

SqlClient namespace core types, 455

SqlCommandBuilder type, 461

SqlDataAdapter

InsertCommand property, 458–459

inserting new records using, 456–459

UpdateCommand property, 460

updating records using, 459–461

SqlTypes namespace (ADO.NET), 398, 456

SqlTypes namespace types, 456

StackBuilder, defined, 110

Stateful objects

destroying, 144

in load-balanced scenarios, 10

remote, 228

vs. stateless objects, 8–10

Stateless objects

defined, 8–9

JIT activation and, 319–320

pooling, 330

remote, 228

vs. stateful objects, 8–10

Static discovery files, 242

Static fields, 107

Static methods, 107–108

Stored procedure

defined, 448

executing, 448–451

specifying parameters to, 449

triggering, 451

Stream object (System.IO), 380

Strong name, 44, 53–54

applying to an assembly, 45–52, 54, 275, 391

and asymmetric cryptography, 45–47

need for, 44

Strong Name utility (sn.exe), 47, 52–53

Strong-named interop assembly, 275, 391

Strong-named private assembly, 54

Synchronization, 96–99

SynchronizationAttribute, 96–97

Synchronous method calls, 201

System registry, 278, 301-302

System.Data namespace (ADO.NET), 397–400

System.Data namespace types, 398–399

System.Data.Common namespace, 398, 441

System.Data.DataRelation type, 432

System.Data.dll, 398–399

System.Data.OleDb namespace, 398, 442

System.Data.OleDb namespace types, 442

System.Data.SqlClient namespace, 398, 455

System.Data.SqlClient namespace core types, 455

System.Data.SqlTypes namespace, 398, 456

System.Data.SqlTypes namespace types, 456

System.Diagnostics.EventLog class, 163

System.EnterpriseServices namespace, 299, 331

System.IO.Stream object, 380

System.Messaging namespace, 357, 365, 376

System.Object methods, 108

System.Object version running locally, 265

System.Runtime.Remoting namespace, 133

System.Threading namespace, 127

System.Threading.Timer class, 372

System.Type class, 72

System.Web.HttpContext, 269

System.Web.Services.WebServices class, 268

System.Xml.Serialization namespace, 259, 381

System.Xml.XmlTextReader, 380

T

Table parent/child relations, navigating, 436

Table schema, 399

Tables

    local copy of related, 396

    navigating between related, 433–437

    relations between, 426, 432

TCP channel

    vs. HTTP channel, 114–115, 170

    remoting metadata deployment, 200

TCP/IP network protocol, 17, 115

Terminal (ATM), 4

Thin client, defined, 13

Thread affinity, object pooling and, 331

Thread local storage, vs. call context, 229–230

Thread safety, reference counting and, 77

Thread synchronization, 127

Threading namespace, 127

Threads

    logical spanning physical, 233

    physical or logical, 230, 235

Three-tier client/server architecture, 15–16

Timer class, 372–373

TimerCallback delegate, 373

TimeSpan class, 150

TLBID (assembly ID), 286, 303

Tlbimp.exe (Type Library Importer), 276, 391

ToString method, 264–265

Trace messages, 120, 163

Transaction isolation levels, configurable, 353–354

Transaction lifetime, 339–340

Transaction voting, 339–341

TransactionAttribute, 338

TransactionOption enumerator, 338

Transactions

    ACID rules for, 336

    automatic, 292, 335–345

    determining the outcome of, 339–345

    distributed, 273

    enabling, 338

    voting on the outcome of, 339–341

    with worker objects, 341–343

Transparency, with .NET Remoting, 215

Transparent proxy

    defined, 111

    wrapper around, 195

Triggers (MSMQ), 361

Two-phase commit, defined, 336

Two-tier client/server architecture, 14–15

Type (*see also* Custom types)

    the bane of interoperability, 28–30

    data structure of, 263

    importance of, 28

    lease information for, 145

    Web service returning generic, 265–268

Type class, 72–73

Type libraries

    building, 176

    DCOM, 176

Type Library Importer (tlbimp.exe), 276, 391

Type metadata deployment issues, summary of, 200

Type name
    fully qualified, 196–197
    matching on server and client,
       176–177, 182
Type object, 72–73
Type system, 28
Typeof operator, 378

U

UDDI, 240, 242–243
UDDI repository, 242
Unique GUID-based URI, 142
Unmanaged code (COM components), 273
Unmanaged to managed interop, 276–288
UpdateCommand property
    (SqlDataAdapter), 460
Updating records using SqlDataAdapter,
    459–461
Updating rows (DataTable), 420–422
URL
    parts of, 123
    specifying, 198
User interface, issues of browser-based, 18
Using keyword, 31, 83
UUID attribute, 287
Uuidgen.exe tool, 287

V

Version information for an assembly,
    setting, 54–56
Versioning
    defined, 54
    .NET, 54–68
    .NET vs. COM, 23
Versioning options (managed code), 287–288
Vertical scaling (scaling up), 11

View object, defined, 422
Visual Basic, 19, 21, 30, 78
Visual Basic 4, 21
Visual Basic garbage collection, 78
Visual Studio .NET (VS .NET)
    Add Installer, 164
    attaching to a running process, 165–167
    building Web services with, 251–256
    data wizards, 467
    Server Explorer, 364–365
    Solution Explorer, 253, 255
    using to build an interop assembly,
       275–276
    Windows Service project template, 160
Visual Studio (VS)
    Add Web Reference feature, 255
    Copy Local property, 51

W

WaitHandle object, 210
Web
    discussed, 237
    vision of queriable, 238
Web appliance, defined, 13
Web architecture, 17–18
Web browsers, 17
Web reference, setting, 255–256
Web servers, 17
Web service clients, 238, 268
Web service metadata vs. Soapsuds
    metadata, 264
Web service project files, 253–254
Web service proxy, 255
    building in VS .NET, 256
    configuring to hold cookies, 269
    using, 257–258

Web services, 237–271
    application of, 238
    as inherently stateless, 268
    as platform agnostic, 239
    B2B scenarios, 239
    building in .NET, 248–255
    building with VS .NET, 251–255
    calling asynchronously, 258–259
    composition of, 239–247
    consuming in .NET, 255–258
    correlating data from various sites, 239
    critical infrastructure services, 240
    enabling session management, 268
    for heterogeneous environments, 238
    IIS hosting and, 171–172
    marshaling by value in, 259
    vs. message queuing, 360
    need for, 238–239
    vs. .NET remoting, 172, 270–271
    overview of, 237–247
    relationship to IIS and ASP.NET,
        248–249
    returning custom types from, 259–268
    returning generic types from, 265–268
    supported protocols, 239–240
    testing, 250
    use of the term, 237
    use of XML, 241
    WSDL for, 243–244, 246
    XmlSerializer in, 262–265
    Yellow Pages for, 242
Web.config file, 168–170, 355
WebMethodAttribute, 249, 268
WebServices class, 268
<Wellknown> element, 132, 134
Well-known object (WKO)
    building a client for, 123–127
    building a server for, 119–123
    vs. client-activated objects, 110–111
    implementing, 119–138
    method call on, 114
    nondefault constructor as, 139
    registering a class as, 121
Windows event log, 163
Windows service
    building, 161–164
    debugging, 165–167
    hosting of remotable objects, 159–167
    installing, 164–165
    Name property, 161
    starting in the IDE, 165
Windows Service project template (VS
    .NET), 160
Wire format services, 240
WKO. *See* Well-known object
Worker objects
    defined, 341
    transactions with, 341–343
    using, 343–345
Workgroup mode (MSMQ), 360, 362
Working together in parallel, explained, 2
Workload, distributing, 2
Wrapped proxy, 195, 198–199
Wrapper for an interop assembly, 275
Write once run anywhere (Java), 28
WriteToConsole method, 216–217
WriteXml method, 406, 437
WSDL contract
    data structure of a type, 263
    definitions, 267
WSDL document, 243–244
    formatting, 246
    for a Web service, 246

WSDL query string, 193

    role of, 243–244

    for a Web service, 243–244

    and W3C, 247

WSDL variations, 246

WSDL (Web Service Description Language), 193, 240, 246

Wsdl.exe tool, 255

W3C (World Wide Web Consortium), 247

X

XML, 58, 239

    vs. HTML, 241

    role of, 240–242

XML elements, custom, 261–262

XML Protocol (W3C SOAP standard), 247

XML schema, 240

XML Schema type fidelity, 270

XML Schema types, conversion to CTS types, 242

XML Web services, 237–271

XML-based DataSets, reading and writing, 437–438

XmlInclude attribute, 267

XmlMessageFormatter, 370–371, 376, 377–382

XmlSerializer class, 260–262

    vs. BinaryFormatter and SoapFormatter, 260

    in Web services, 262–265

XmlTextReader, 380

Y

Yellow Pages for Web services, 242

Apress Titles

ISBN	PRICE	AUTHOR	TITLE
1-893115-73-9	$34.95	Abbott	Voice Enabling Web Applications: VoiceXML and Beyond
1-893115-01-1	$39.95	Appleman	Dan Appleman's Win32 API Puzzle Book and Tutorial for Visual Basic Programmers
1-893115-23-2	$29.95	Appleman	How Computer Programming Works
1-893115-97-6	$39.95	Appleman	Moving to VB .NET: Strategies, Concepts, and Code
1-59059-023-6	$39.95	Baker	Adobe Acrobat 5: The Professional User's Guide
1-59059-039-2	$49.95	Barnaby	Distributed .NET Programming
1-893115-09-7	$29.95	Baum	Dave Baum's Definitive Guide to LEGO MINDSTORMS
1-893115-84-4	$29.95	Baum, Gasperi, Hempel, and Villa	Extreme MINDSTORMS: An Advanced Guide to LEGO MINDSTORMS
1-893115-82-8	$59.95	Ben-Gan/Moreau	Advanced Transact-SQL for SQL Server 2000
1-893115-91-7	$39.95	Birmingham/Perry	Software Development on a Leash
1-893115-48-8	$29.95	Bischof	The .NET Languages: A Quick Translation Guide
1-893115-67-4	$49.95	Borge	Managing Enterprise Systems with the Windows Script Host
1-893115-28-3	$44.95	Challa/Laksberg	Essential Guide to Managed Extensions for C++
1-893115-39-9	$44.95	Chand	A Programmer's Guide to ADO.NET in C#
1-893115-44-5	$29.95	Cook	Robot Building for Beginners
1-893115-99-2	$39.95	Cornell/Morrison	Programming VB .NET: A Guide for Experienced Programmers
1-893115-72-0	$39.95	Curtin	Developing Trust: Online Privacy and Security
1-59059-008-2	$29.95	Duncan	The Career Programmer: Guerilla Tactics for an Imperfect World
1-893115-71-2	$39.95	Ferguson	Mobile .NET
1-893115-90-9	$49.95	Finsel	The Handbook for Reluctant Database Administrators
1-59059-024-4	$49.95	Fraser	Real World ASP.NET: Building a Content Management System
1-893115-42-9	$44.95	Foo/Lee	XML Programming Using the Microsoft XML Parser
1-893115-55-0	$34.95	Frenz	Visual Basic and Visual Basic .NET for Scientists and Engineers
1-893115-85-2	$34.95	Gilmore	A Programmer's Introduction to PHP 4.0
1-893115-36-4	$34.95	Goodwill	Apache Jakarta-Tomcat
1-893115-17-8	$59.95	Gross	A Programmer's Introduction to Windows DNA
1-893115-62-3	$39.95	Gunnerson	A Programmer's Introduction to C#, Second Edition
1-59059-009-0	$49.95	Harris/Macdonald	Moving to ASP.NET: Web Development with VB .NET
1-893115-30-5	$49.95	Harkins/Reid	SQL: Access to SQL Server
1-893115-10-0	$34.95	Holub	Taming Java Threads
1-893115-04-6	$34.95	Hyman/Vaddadi	Mike and Phani's Essential C++ Techniques
1-893115-96-8	$59.95	Jorelid	J2EE FrontEnd Technologies: A Programmer's Guide to Servlets, JavaServer Pages, and Enterprise JavaBeans
1-893115-49-6	$39.95	Kilburn	Palm Programming in Basic
1-893115-50-X	$34.95	Knudsen	Wireless Java: Developing with Java 2, Micro Edition
1-893115-79-8	$49.95	Kofler	Definitive Guide to Excel VBA
1-893115-57-7	$39.95	Kofler	MySQL
1-893115-87-9	$39.95	Kurata	Doing Web Development: Client-Side Techniques
1-893115-75-5	$44.95	Kurniawan	Internet Programming with VB

ISBN	PRICE	AUTHOR	TITLE
1-893115-38-0	$24.95	Lafler	Power AOL: A Survival Guide
1-893115-46-1	$36.95	Lathrop	Linux in Small Business: A Practical User's Guide
1-893115-19-4	$49.95	Macdonald	Serious ADO: Universal Data Access with Visual Basic
1-893115-06-2	$39.95	Marquis/Smith	A Visual Basic 6.0 Programmer's Toolkit
1-893115-22-4	$27.95	McCarter	David McCarter's VB Tips and Techniques
1-59059-021-X	$34.95	Moore	Karl Moore's Visual Basic .NET: The Tutorials
1-893115-76-3	$49.95	Morrison	C++ For VB Programmers
1-59059-003-1	$39.95	Nakhimovsky/Meyers	XML Programming: Web Applications and Web Services with JSP and ASP
1-893115-80-1	$39.95	Newmarch	A Programmer's Guide to Jini Technology
1-893115-58-5	$49.95	Oellermann	Architecting Web Services
1-59059-020-1	$44.95	Patzer	JSP Examples and Best Practices
1-893115-81-X	$39.95	Pike	SQL Server: Common Problems, Tested Solutions
1-59059-017-1	$34.95	Rainwater	Herding Cats: A Primer for Programmers Who Lead Programmers
1-59059-025-2	$49.95	Rammer	Advanced .NET Remoting
1-893115-20-8	$34.95	Rischpater	Wireless Web Development
1-893115-93-3	$34.95	Rischpater	Wireless Web Development with PHP and WAP
1-893115-89-5	$59.95	Shemitz	Kylix: The Professional Developer's Guide and Reference
1-893115-40-2	$39.95	Sill	The qmail Handbook
1-893115-24-0	$49.95	Sinclair	From Access to SQL Server
1-893115-94-1	$29.95	Spolsky	User Interface Design for Programmers
1-893115-53-4	$44.95	Sweeney	Visual Basic for Testers
1-59059-002-3	$44.95	Symmonds	Internationalization and Localization Using Microsoft .NET
1-59059-010-4	$54.95	Thomsen	Database Programming with C#
1-893115-29-1	$44.95	Thomsen	Database Programming with Visual Basic .NET
1-893115-65-8	$39.95	Tiffany	Pocket PC Database Development with eMbedded Visual Basic
1-893115-59-3	$59.95	Troelsen	C# and the .NET Platform
1-59059-011-2	$59.95	Troelsen	COM and .NET Interoperability
1-893115-26-7	$59.95	Troelsen	Visual Basic .NET and the .NET Platform
1-893115-54-2	$49.95	Trueblood/Lovett	Data Mining and Statistical Analysis Using SQL
1-893115-68-2	$54.95	Vaughn	ADO.NET and ADO Examples and Best Practices for VB Programmers, Second Edition
1-59059-012-0	$49.95	Vaughn/Blackburn	ADO.NET Examples and Best Practices for C# Programmers
1-893115-83-6	$44.95	Wells	Code Centric: T-SQL Programming with Stored Procedures and Triggers
1-893115-95-X	$49.95	Welschenbach	Cryptography in C and C++
1-893115-05-4	$39.95	Williamson	Writing Cross-Browser Dynamic HTML
1-893115-78-X	$49.95	Zukowski	Definitive Guide to Swing for Java 2, Second Edition
1-893115-92-5	$49.95	Zukowski	Java Collections
1-893115-98-4	$54.95	Zukowski	Learn Java with JBuilder 6

Available at bookstores nationwide or from Springer Verlag New York, Inc. at 1-800-777-4643; fax 1-212-533-3503. Contact us for more information at sales@apress.com.

Apress Titles Publishing SOON!

ISBN	AUTHOR	TITLE
1-59059-022-8	Alapati	Expert Oracle 9i Database Administration
1-59059-041-4	Bock	CIL Programming: Under the Hood of .NET
1-59059-053-8	Bock/Stromquist/ Fischer/Smith	.NET Security
1-59059-019-8	Cagle	SVG Programming: The Graphical Web
1-59059-015-5	Clark	An Introduction to Object Oriented Programming with Visual Basic .NET
1-59059-000-7	Cornell	Programming C#
1-59059-014-7	Drol	Object-Oriented Macromedia Flash MX
1-59059-033-3	Fraser	Managed C++ and .NET Development
1-59059-038-4	Gibbons	Java Development to .NET Development
1-59059-030-9	Habibi/Camerlengo/ Patterson	Java 1.4 and the Sun Certified Developer Exam
1-59059-006-6	Hetland	Instant Python with Ten Instant Projects
1-59059-044-9	MacDonald	.NET User Interfaces with VB .NET: Windows Forms and Custom Controls
1-59059-001-5	McMahon	A Programmer's Introduction to ASP.NET WebForms in Visual Basic .NET
1-893115-74-7	Millar	Enterprise Development: A Programmer's Handbook
1-893115-27-5	Morrill	Tuning and Customizing a Linux System
1-59059-028-7	Rischpater	Wireless Web Development, Second Edition
1-59059-026-0	Smith	Writing Add-Ins for .NET
1-893115-43-7	Stephenson	Standard VB: An Enterprise Developer's Reference for VB 6 and VB .NET
1-59059-035-X	Symmonds	GDI+ Programming in C# and VB .NET
1-59059-032-5	Thomsen	Database Programming with Visual Basic .NET, Second Edition
1-59059-007-4	Thomsen	Building Web Services with VB .NET
1-59059-027-9	Torkelson/Petersen/ Torkelson	Programming the Web with Visual Basic .NET
1-59059-018-X	Tregar	Writing Perl Modules for CPAN
1-59059-004-X	Valiaveedu	SQL Server 2000 and Business Intelligence in an XML/.NET World

Available at bookstores nationwide or from Springer Verlag New York, Inc. at 1-800-777-4643; fax 1-212-533-3503. Contact us for more information at sales@apress.com.

books for professionals by professionals™

apress™

About Apress

Apress, located in Berkeley, CA, is a fast-growing, innovative publishing company devoted to meeting the needs of existing and potential programming professionals. Simply put, the "A" in Apress stands for *"The Author's Press™"* and its books have *"The Expert's Voice™."* Apress' unique approach to publishing grew out of conversations between its founders Gary Cornell and Dan Appleman, authors of numerous best-selling, highly regarded books for programming professionals. In 1998 they set out to create a publishing company that emphasized quality above all else. Gary and Dan's vision has resulted in the publication of over 50 titles by leading software professionals, all of which have *The Expert's Voice™*.

Do You Have What It Takes to Write for Apress?

Apress is rapidly expanding its publishing program. If you can write and refuse to compromise on the quality of your work, if you believe in doing more than rehashing existing documentation, and if you're looking for opportunities and rewards that go far beyond those offered by traditional publishing houses, we want to hear from you!

Consider these innovations that we offer all of our authors:

* **Top royalties with *no* hidden switch statements**
  Authors typically only receive half of their normal royalty rate on foreign sales. In contrast, Apress' royalty rate remains the same for both foreign and domestic sales.

* **A mechanism for authors to obtain equity in Apress**
  Unlike the software industry, where stock options are essential to motivate and retain software professionals, the publishing industry has adhered to an outdated compensation model based on royalties alone. In the spirit of most software companies, Apress reserves a significant portion of its equity for authors.

* **Serious treatment of the technical review process**
  Each Apress book has a technical reviewing team whose remuneration depends in part on the success of the book since they too receive royalties.

Moreover, through a partnership with Springer-Verlag, New York, Inc., one of the world's major publishing houses, Apress has significant venture capital behind it. Thus, we have the resources to produce the highest quality books *and* market them aggressively.

If you fit the model of the Apress author who can write a book that gives the "professional what he or she needs to know™," then please contact one of our Editorial Directors, Gary Cornell (gary_cornell@apress.com), Dan Appleman (dan_appleman@apress.com), Peter Blackburn (peter_blackburn@apress.com), Jason Gilmore (jason_gilmore@apress.com), Karen Watterson (karen_watterson@apress.com), or John Zukowski (john_zukowski@apress.com) for more information.